PAPYRUS

Papyrus

THE INVENTION OF BOOKS
IN THE ANCIENT WORLD

Irene Vallejo

Translated from the Spanish by Charlotte Whittle

ALFRED A. KNOPF   NEW YORK   2022

Library of Congress Cataloging-in-Publication Data
Names: Vallejo Moreu, Irene, author. | Whittle, Charlotte, translator.
Title: Papyrus : the invention of books in the ancient world / Irene Vallejo ;
    translated from the Spanish by Charlotte Whittle.
Other titles: Infinito en un junco. English
Description: First edition. | New York : Alfred A. Knopf, 2022. |
    Includes bibliographical references and index.
Identifiers: LCCN 2022001667 | ISBN 9780593318898 (hardcover) |
    ISBN 9780593318904 (ebook)
Subjects: LCSH: Books—History—To 400.
Classification: LCC Z5 .V3413 2022 | DDC 002.09—dc23/eng/20220520
LC record available at https://lccn.loc.gov/2022001667

Book Design by Maria Carella

Jacket image: Papyrus reed (*Cyperus papyrus*). Photo 12 / Universal Images Group /
Getty Images
Jacket design by Jenny Carrow

Manufactured in the United States of America
First American Edition

For my mother, a soft and steady hand

They look like drawings,
But there are voices inside the letters.
Every page is an infinite box of voices.

—Mia Couto, Sands of the Emperor Trilogy

The inert signs of an alphabet become living meanings in the mind . . .
Literacy, like all learned activities, appears to alter our brain
organization.

—Siri Hustvedt, *Living, Thinking, Looking*

It pleases me to think how astonished old Homer, whoever he was,
would be to find his epics on the shelf of such an unimaginable being as
myself,
in the middle of an unrumored continent.

—Marilynne Robinson, *When I Was a Child I Read Books*

Reading is always a passage, a journey,
a departure where we discover ourselves. Reading,
even though it is typically a sedentary act,
returns us to our nomadic state.

—Antonio Basanta, *Leer contra la nada*
(Reading Against Nothingness)

Above all, the book is a repository of time. A prodigious trap with
which human intelligence and sensitivity overcame that ephemeral,
fleeting condition that led the experience of life into the oblivion of
nothingness.

—Emilio Lledó, *Los libros y la libertad*
(Books and Freedom)

CONTENTS

Prologue   *xiii*

PART ONE
GREECE IMAGINES THE FUTURE

The City of Pleasures and Books   *3*
Alexander: The World Is Never Enough   *7*
The Macedonian Friend   *12*
Balancing at the Edge of the Abyss: The Library and
    the Musaeum of Alexandria   *19*
A Story of Fire and Passageways   *43*
Books and Skin   *55*
A Detective's Task   *66*
Homer: Enigma and Twilight   *68*
The Lost World of Orality: A Tapestry of Echoes   *73*
The Alphabet: A Peaceful Revolution   *92*
Voices from the Mist, Uncertain Times   *101*
Learning to Read the Shadows   *110*
The Triumph of Unruly Words   *115*
The First Book   *117*
Traveling Bookstores   *121*
The Religion of Culture   *126*
A Man with a Prodigious Memory and a Group
    of Avant-Garde Girls   *129*
Women, Weavers of Stories   *144*

The Other Tells Me My Story   *158*

The Drama of Laughter: Our Debt to Rubbish Dumps   *172*

A Passionate Affair with Words   *181*

Poison and Fragility   *195*

The Three Destructions of the Library of Alexandria   *201*

Lifeboats and Black Butterflies   *216*

How We Began to Be Strange   *228*

PART TWO
THE ROADS TO ROME

A City with a Bad Reputation   *235*

The Literature of Defeat   *241*

The Invisible Threshold of Slavery   *252*

In the Beginning Were the Trees   *258*

Poor Writers, Rich Readers   *260*

A Young Family   *272*

Bookselling: A Risky Business   *280*

The Birth and Triumph of Books with Pages   *297*

Public Libraries in Palaces of Water   *311*

Two Men from Hispania: The First Fan
      and the Aging Writer   *319*

Herculaneum: Preservation Amid Destruction   *324*

Ovid Clashes with Censorship   *328*

Sweet Inertia   *332*

Journey to the Center of Books and How to Name Them   *335*

What Is a Classic?   *342*

Canon: The History of a Reed   *351*

Shards of Women's Voices   *362*

What Was Believed Eternal Turned Out to Be Fleeting   *367*

Dare to Remember   376

Epilogue: Forgotten Men, Anonymous Women   381

Acknowledgments   387

Notes   389

Bibliography   411

Index   421

Mysterious bands of men on horseback travel the roads of Greece. The country folk watch them with suspicion from their plots of land, or the doors to their huts. They know from experience that only those who represent danger travel: soldiers, mercenaries, and slave traders. They frown and grumble until the men disappear over the horizon. Country folk do not look kindly upon armed strangers.

The horsemen ride on, paying the villagers no heed. For months, they have climbed mountains, traversed ravines, crossed valleys, forded rivers, and sailed from island to island. Their muscles have hardened and their endurance increased since they were sent on this peculiar mission. To achieve their task, they must venture into violent realms in a world that is almost continually at war. These are hunters in search of a special kind of prey. Prey that is silent, cunning, and vanishes without a trace.

If these menacing envoys were to sit down in a tavern in some port or other to drink wine, eat seared octopus, talk, and make merry with strangers (something they never do, out of caution), they could tell great tales of their travels. They have entered lands racked with plague. They have crossed regions scorched by fire. They have seen the warm ashes of destruction and the brutality of rebels and mercenaries at war. Since maps of extensive territories do not yet exist, they have strayed and wandered directionless for days on end, beneath the fury of sun and storms. They've been forced to drink foul waters that have caused them horrendous diarrhea. Whenever it rains, their carts and mules get stuck in the morass; they have pulled amid cries and curses until they collapsed to their knees, their faces pressed to the earth. When night falls on them, far from shelter, only their capes shield them from scorpions. They have known the maddening torment of lice and the constant threat of the bandits roaming the roads. Often as they ride through vast, desolate terrain, they shudder to imagine these outlaws lying in wait, holding their breath, lurking at a bend in the road, ready to fall upon them, murder them in cold blood, plunder their bags, and leave their warm corpses among the bushes.

It makes sense for them to be wary. The king of Egypt has entrusted great sums of money to them before sending them to carry out his orders across the sea. In those times, only a few decades after the death of Alexander, it was highly dangerous, almost suicidal, to travel with a large fortune. And though thieves' daggers, contagious diseases, and shipwrecks threaten to cause such an expensive mission to fail, the pharaoh insists on sending his agents out from the country of the Nile, crossing borders and traversing great distances in all directions. The king thirsts after his prey with impatient desire, while his secret hunters scour the Earth, facing unknown perils.

The country folk who spied from their doorways, or the mercenaries and bandits, would have widened their eyes and dropped their jaws in amazement had they known what the foreign horsemen pursued.

Books. They were searching for books.

It was the best kept secret of the Egyptian court. The Lord of the Two Lands, one of the most powerful men of his time, would sacrifice lives (the lives of others, of course—that's always the way with kings) to obtain all the books in the world for his Great Library in Alexandria. He was chasing the dream of an absolute, perfect library, a collection that would gather together every single work by every single author since the beginning of time.

I am always afraid to write the first lines, to enter inside a new book. When I have explored all the libraries, when my notebooks are bursting with fevered jottings, when I can no longer think of any reasonable excuses, or even nonsensical ones to keep waiting, I still put it off a few days, during which I understand what cowardice really means. I simply don't feel like I can. Everything should be there—tone, sense of humor, poetry, rhythm, promises. I should be able to glimpse the still unwritten chapters, struggling to be born, where the seeds of the first chosen words have been sown. But how is it done? Right now, I feel heavy with doubts. With every book, I go back to the beginning, and my heart races as if it were the very first time. To write is to try to find out what we would write if we wrote, says Marguerite Duras, moving from the infinitive to the conditional and then to the subjunctive as if she could feel the ground splitting beneath her feet.

It isn't so different, in the end, from any of the things we start doing without knowing how to do them: speaking another language, driving, being a mother. Living.

After all the agonies of doubt, after exhausting every possible delay and excuse, one hot July afternoon, I face the void of the blank page. I've decided to open with the image of some enigmatic hunters stalking their prey. I identify with them. I appreciate their patience, their stoicism, the time they have taken, their steadiness, the adrenaline of the search. For years I have worked as an academic, consulting sources, keeping records, trying to get to know the historical material. But when it comes down to it, I'm so amazed by the true and recorded history I discover that it seeps into my dreams and acquires, without my volition, the shape of a story. I'm tempted to step into the skin of those who traveled the roads of an ancient, violent, tumultuous Europe in pursuit of books. What if I start by telling the story of their journey? It might work, but how can I keep the skeleton of facts distinct beneath the muscle and blood of imagination?

The initial idea seems to me as fantastical as the journey in search of King Solomon's mines or the Lost Ark, but historical documents show that in the megalomaniacal minds of the kings of Egypt, it was truly possible. It might have been the last and only time—there, in the third century BC—that the dream of gathering all the books in the world, without exception, in a universal library, could become a reality. Today it seems like the plot of a fascinating, abstract story by Borges—or perhaps his great erotic fantasy.

In the era of the great Alexandrian project, there was no such thing as an international book trade. Books could be bought in cities with a long-standing cultural life, but not in the young Alexandria. Sources tell us that the kings used the immense advantages of absolute power to enrich their collection. What they could not purchase, they seized. If throats had to be slit or harvests laid waste to get hold of a coveted book, they ordered that it be done, telling themselves that their country's splendor was more important than minor scruples.

Of course, deception was part of the repertory of things they were willing to do to meet their goals. Ptolemy III coveted the official versions of the works of Aeschylus, Sophocles, and Euripides, preserved in the archives of Athens since their earliest performances at theater festivals. The pharaoh's ambassadors asked to borrow the valuable scrolls to have them copied by their meticulous scribes. The Athenian authorities demanded the exorbitant security deposit of fifteen talents of silver, an equivalent today of millions of dollars. The Egyptians paid up, gave extravagant thanks, solemnly swore to return the loan before—shall we say—twelve moons had passed, threatened themselves with gruesome curses if the books weren't returned in perfect condition, and proceeded to pocket them, forfeiting the deposit. The Athenian rulers were forced to tolerate the outrage. The proud capital in the times of Pericles was now reduced to a provincial city in a kingdom that could no longer compete with the power of Egypt, which dominated the grain trade, the oil of the time.

Alexandria was the country's main port and its dynamic new center of operations. An economic force on such a scale has always been able to cheerfully abuse its power. All boats that docked in the city of the Library, no matter their point of origin, were subject to immediate search. Customs officials requisitioned any written document found on board, had it copied on new papyrus, returned the copies, and kept the originals. These books seized on boarding ended up on the shelves of the Library with a brief note describing their provenance ("books from ships").

When you are on top of the world, no favor is too much to ask. It was said that Ptolemy II sent messengers to the kings and rulers of every country on Earth. In a sealed letter, he would ask them to take the trouble of sending him simply everything they had for his collection: all the work of the poets and prose writers of their kingdom, the orators and philosophers, the doctors and seers, the historians, and everyone else.

Furthermore—and this was my way into the story—the kings sent agents out to the dangerous roads and seas of the world, with a full purse and orders to buy the largest possible quantity of books and to find the most ancient copies, wherever they happened to be. Such an appetite for books and the prices they could command attracted swindlers and forgers. They proffered scrolls of valuable counterfeit texts, aged the papyrus, merged several works into one to increase its length, and came up with all kinds of other skillful manipulations. One wise man with a sense of humor had a marvelous time writing fraudulent works, fake originals calculated to tempt the ambition of the Ptolemies. The titles were amusing and today could make for best sellers—for instance, "What Thucydides Left Unsaid." Replace "Thucydides" with "Kafka" or "Joyce" and just imagine the excitement the forger would cause when he appeared at the Library with the writer's phony memories and guilty secrets under his arm.

Despite prudent suspicions of fraud, the Library's buyers were afraid to miss out on a potentially priceless book and risk incurring the pharaoh's wrath. The king inspected the scrolls in his collection at regular intervals, with the same pride with which he inspected military parades. He would ask the librarian, Demetrius of Phalerum, how many books now made up the collection. And Demetrius would update him on the number: "There are now more than twenty dozen thousand, oh King; and I endeavor to add what we need to reach five hundred thousand." The hunger for books that was unleashed in Alexandria was beginning to sow the seeds of a fervent passion.

I was born in a country and an era when a book is an easy object to obtain. In my house, there are books everywhere you look. In periods of intense work, when I request dozens of them from the various libraries that tolerate my raids, I usually leave them stacked in towers on chairs or even on the floor. I also leave them open and facing down like gable roofs in search of a house to shelter. Now, to prevent my two-year-old son from creasing the pages, I make stacks just above the couch, and when I sit down to relax, I feel their corners touching the back of my neck. When I total up the price of the books versus the average rent in the city where I live, my books turn out to be costly tenants. But all of them, from the large books of photography to the old glued pocket-sized paperbacks that always spring shut like clams, make the house a more welcoming place.

The story of the efforts, journeys, and hardships undergone to fill the shelves of the Library of Alexandria may seem appealingly exotic. These are strange events, adventures like the fabled voyages to the Indies in search of spices. Books are so common here and now, so devoid of the aura of technological novelty, that prophets of their doom abound. Every so often I read with dismay articles predicting the extinction of books, which say that they will be replaced by electronic devices and defeated by the endless choices of leisure activities on offer. The most ominous of these claims is that we are on the verge of the end of an era, a true apocalypse of shuttered bookstores and abandoned libraries. They seem to suggest that books will soon be displayed in glass cases at museums of anthropology, near the collections of prehistoric arrow tips. With these images engraved on my imagination, I scan my endless rows of books and vinyl records, wondering if this old world of which I'm so fond is about to disappear.

But are we sure?

The book has withstood the test of history, has proved it can go the distance. Each time we awake from the dream of our revolutions or the nightmare of our catastrophes, the book is still there. In the words of Umberto Eco, the book belongs to the same category as the spoon, the hammer, the wheel, or a pair of scissors. Once invented, these things cannot be surpassed.

Of course, technology is dazzling and has the power to dethrone old monarchies. But all of us yearn for the things we've lost—photographs, archives, old jobs, memories—due to the speed with which they age and become obsolete. First it was songs on cassettes, movies recorded on VHS. We devote a frustrating amount of effort to collecting the things technology is determined to put out of style. When optical discs first appeared, they told us we'd finally solved our storage problems forever, but then they came back to tempt us with new discs in a smaller format, which invariably required new devices. The irony is that we can still read a manuscript patiently copied over ten centuries ago, but we can no longer watch a video or see the contents of a disc recorded just in the last few years, unless we keep all our successive computers and recording equipment in rooms full of junk in our homes, like a museum of obsolescence.

Let's not forget that the book has been our ally for centuries in a war that is absent from history textbooks. The struggle to preserve our most valuable creations: words, which are scarcely a puff of air; the stories we tell to give meaning to chaos and to survive it; the true, false, always provisional knowledge we scratch across the hard rock of our ignorance.

That's why I decided to dive into this research. In the beginning there were questions, swarms of questions: When did books first appear? What is the secret history of efforts to reproduce or destroy them? What was lost along the way, and what was saved? Why have some of them become classics? How much has succumbed to the jaws of time, the talons of fire, the poison of water? Which books have been burnt in rage, and which have been copied with greatest passion? Are they one and the same?

This account is an attempt to continue the adventure of those book hunters. I would like somehow, to be their unlikely travel companion, on the scent of lost manuscripts, unknown stories, and voices in danger of being silenced. Perhaps those groups of explorers were just henchmen employed in the service of kings possessed by a megalomaniacal obsession. Maybe they didn't understand the momentousness of their task, which to them seemed absurd, and under the open skies at night, as the fire's embers sputtered out, they grumbled that they'd had enough of risking their lives for the dream of a madman. Surely they would have preferred to be sent on a mission with better chances of promotion, like quashing a rebellion in the Nubian Desert or inspecting cargo boats on the Nile. But I suspect that as they searched for traces of every book as if they were pieces of scattered treasure, without knowing it, they were laying the foundations of our world.

Part One

GREECE IMAGINES
THE FUTURE

1

The young and bored merchant's wife sleeps alone. It's been ten months since her husband set sail for Egypt from the Mediterranean island of Cos, and not a single letter has arrived from the country of the Nile since then. She is seventeen years old, hasn't yet given birth, and can't bear the monotony of her cloistered life in the gynaeceum, waiting for something to happen, staying inside to avoid wagging tongues. There isn't much to do. It seemed amusing at first to tyrannize the female slaves, but this isn't enough to fill her days, so it makes her happy to receive visits from other women. It doesn't matter who comes to the door, she desperately needs distraction to lighten the leaden hours as they drag on.

A slave announces the arrival of the elderly Gyllis. The merchant's wife is guaranteed to be entertained for a while: her old wet nurse Gyllis is a foulmouthed woman who curses with flair.

"Mother Gyllis! It's months since you've been to my house."

"You know how far away I live, my child, and these days I am weaker than a fly."

"Come now," says the merchant's wife. "You're still strong enough for the occasional frolic."

"Go ahead and mock me," Gyllis answers. "I leave that to the youngsters."

With a wicked smile and a crafty prelude, the old woman eventually reveals what she has come to say. A strong and handsome young man, who has twice won the Olympic wrestling prize, has set his sights on the merchant's wife, is aflame with desire, and wishes to be her lover.

"Now do not be angry, and hear what he has to say. The thorn of passion has dug deep into his flesh. Allow yourself to find joy with him. Or are you going to stay here, keeping that chair warm?" Gyllis asks, tempting the young woman. "You will be withered before you know it, all your youth and beauty snuffed out by ashes."

"Hush, hush . . ."

"And what is your husband up to in Egypt? He writes you no letters, he has forgotten you. By now he must have wet his lips on another cup."

To conquer the girl's last shred of resistance, Gyllis describes with her silver tongue all that Egypt, and especially Alexandria, has to offer a distant, ungrateful husband: fabulous riches, the delights of a constantly warm and sensual climate, gymnasiums, spectacles, troupes of philosophers, books, gold, wine, youths, and as many alluring women as there are stars in the sky.

I have loosely translated the opening of a short Greek play, written in the third century BC, that conveys a strong flavor of the daily life of the period. No doubt minor works such as this were not performed, except perhaps at some kind of dramatic reading. Humorous and sometimes picaresque, they open windows onto a forbidden world of mistreated slaves and cruel masters, procuresses, mothers driven to their wits' end by their teenage children, and sex-starved women. Gyllis is one of the earliest *celestinas* in literary history, a professional go-between who knows the secrets of her trade and takes aim at her victims' weakest defenses: the universal fear of growing old. Yet despite her cruel talent, this time Gyllis fails. The conversation ends with the girl calling Gyllis affectionate names. The merchant's wife remains faithful to her absent husband, or perhaps would prefer not to run the terrible risk of adultery. Have you gone soft in the head? she asks Gyllis, while also consoling her with a sip of wine.

Along with its humor and fresh style, the play conveys an illuminating picture of how ordinary people viewed Alexandria in its heyday: the city of pleasures and books; the capital of sex and language.

2

The legend of Alexandria grew and grew. Two centuries after the play about Gyllis and the young woman she tempts was written, Alexandria was the scene of one of the greatest erotic myths of all time: the love story of Cleopatra and Mark Antony.

By that time, Rome had become the center of the greatest Mediterranean empire, but when Mark Antony set foot in Alexandria for the first time, the city he left behind was still a labyrinth of dark, winding, and muddy streets. He found himself transported to an intoxicating place whose palaces, temples, wide avenues, and monuments radiated grandeur. The Romans felt sure of their military power and were convinced that the future was theirs, but they couldn't possibly compete with the seduction of such a golden past and such decadent luxury. Through a combination of excitement, pride, and tactical calculations, this powerful general and the last queen of Egypt formed a political and sexual alliance that scandalized traditional Romans. To their even greater displeasure, it was said that Mark Antony was going to transfer the capital of the empire to Alexandria. Had the couple won the battle for control of the Roman Empire, perhaps today's tourists would flock to Egypt to have their picture taken in the Eternal City, with its coliseum and its forums.

Much like her city, Cleopatra embodies that unique fusion of culture and sensuality. Plutarch writes that Cleopatra was in fact no great beauty. People didn't stop in their tracks to stare at her in the street. What she had in abundance was magnetism and intelligence and a silver tongue. The timbre of her voice had such sweetness that it transfixed everyone who heard it. And her speech, he continues, could adapt to any language she chose, like a many-stringed instrument. She could converse with Ethiopians, Hebrews, Arabs, Syrians, Medes, and Parthians without the aid of an interpreter. Astute and well-informed, she won several rounds in the struggle for power both within and beyond her country, though in the end she lost the decisive battle. Her problem is that she has been spoken of only from the point of view of her enemies.

Books play an important role in this tempestuous story, too. When Mark Antony believed he was on the cusp of ruling the world, he wanted to dazzle Cleopatra with an extraordinary gift. He was well aware that gold, jewels, and banquets would fail to light the spark of amazement in his lover's eyes, since she was accustomed to squandering them daily. On one occasion, in the haze of an alcoholic dawn, she performed the provocative and ostentatious gesture of dissolving a fabulously oversized pearl in vinegar and drinking it. So Mark Antony chose a gift that Cleopatra could not possibly scorn with a bored expression: he laid two hundred thousand volumes for the Great Library at her feet. In Alexandria, books served as fuel for passion.

Two authors who died in the twentieth century have become our guides to the city's hidden corners, adding layers of patina to the myth of Alexandria. Constantine Cavafy was a bureaucrat of Greek origin who toiled without promotion in an obscure position at the Irrigation Service of the British-run Egyptian Ministry of Public Works. By night he dove into a universe of pleasure, full of cosmopolitan characters and international iniquity. He knew the labyrinth of Alexandria's brothels like the back of his hand. They provided the only refuge for his homosexuality, "forbidden and strictly condemned by all," as he himself wrote. Cavafy was a passionate reader of the classics and a poet who kept his work almost secret.

In what today are his best-known poems, real and fictitious characters from Ithaca, Troy, Athens, and Byzantium are brought back to life. Other, apparently more personal, poems delve, sometimes with irony, sometimes with sorrow, into the poet's own experience of maturity: nostalgia for his youth, his initiation into pleasure, and anguish at the passage of time. Yet categorizing them by subject matter is a superficial exercise. Cavafy was as thrilled by the past he read and imagined as he was by his own memories. As he slunk around Alexandria, he saw the pulse of the absent city beating beneath the real one that had replaced it. Although the Great Library had disappeared, its echoes, whispers, and murmurs kept trembling in the atmosphere. For Cavafy, this great fellowship of ghosts made the cold streets, where the lonely and tormented living would wander, easier to inhabit.

The characters in The Alexandria Quartet—Justine, Darley, and especially Balthazar, who claims to have met him—often remember Cavafy as "the old poet of the city." These four novels by Lawrence Durrell, an Englishman suffocated by his country's austerity and climate, also broaden the erotic and literary resonances of the Alexandrian myth. Durrell got to know the city during the turbulent years of the Second World War, when Egypt was occupied by British troops and was a hotbed of espionage, conspiracies, and, as always, pleasures. No one has described more accurately the colors and physical sensations that Alexandria awakened. The oppressive silence and the vast summer sky. The scorching days. The dazzling blue of the sea, the breakwaters, the yellow shoreline. Inland, Lake Mariout, sometimes as hazy as a mirage. Between the waters of the port and those of the lake are endless streets teeming with beggars and flies circling in clouds of dust. Palm trees, luxury hotels, hashish, and dissipation. The parched air charged with electricity. Lemon and violet sunsets. Five languages, five races, a dozen religions, five fleets reflected in the oily water. In Alexandria, writes Durrell, the flesh awakens, pressing upon prison bars.

The Second World War devastated the city. In the final novel of the Quartet, Clea describes a landscape of melancholy. Tanks run aground on the beaches like dinosaur skeletons, great cannons like fallen trees from a petrified forest, stray Bedouins wandering among the land mines. The city, which was always perverse, now has the air of a huge public urinal, she concludes. After 1952, Lawrence Durrell never returned to Alexandria. The age-old Jewish and Greek communities fled in the wake of the Suez Crisis, the end of an era in the Middle East. Returning travelers tell me the cosmopolitan, sensual city has migrated into the memory of books.

ALEXANDER

The World Is Never Enough

3

There is no single Alexandria. A series of cities by that name traces the route of Alexander the Great from Turkey to the Indus River. Different languages have distorted the original sound, though sometimes the distant melody can still be discerned. Alexandretta, Iskenderun in Turkish. Alexandria Carmania, currently Kerman, in Iran. Alexandria Margiana, now Merv, in Turkmenistan. Alexandria Eschate, which could be translated as "Alexandria at the End of the Earth," today Khujand in Tajikistan. Alexandria Bucephalos, the city founded in memory of the horse that accompanied Alexander from childhood, afterward called Jalalpur, in Pakistan. The war in Afghanistan has made us familiar with other ancient Alexandrias: Bagram, Herat, Kandahar.

Plutarch tells that Alexander founded seventy cities. He wanted to mark the fact that he had been there, the way children paint their names on walls or on the doors of public restrooms. ("I was here." "I won a battle here.") The atlas of his campaigns forms an enormous wall where the conqueror left a record of himself again and again.

Alexander's driving force, the reason for the boundless energy that could launch him on a twenty-five-thousand-kilometer conquering expedition, was his thirst for fame and admiration. He harbored a profound belief in the legends of heroes; what's more, he lived and competed among them. He was obsessed with the character Achilles, the most feared and powerful warrior in Greek mythology. He had singled him out as a boy, when his teacher, Aristotle, taught him the Homeric poems; Alexander dreamed of following in Achilles's footsteps. He felt the same reverence for Achilles that boys today feel for their sports heroes. It's said that Alexander always slept with his copy of *The Iliad* and a dagger under his pillow. The picture elicits a smile. We think of a little boy who has drifted off with his trading card album open, dreaming of winning a championship amid the fervent howls of his fans.

Except that Alexander made his wildest dreams of success come true. The list of his conquests, achieved in only eight years—Anatolia, Persia, Egypt, central Asia, India—catapulted him to the summit of military exploits. Compared to him, Achilles, who gave his life in the ten-year siege of just one city, seems like an unremarkable novice.

The Egyptian Alexandria was born—we would expect no less—from a literary dream, a Homeric whisper. As he slumbered, Alexander sensed a grey-haired old man approaching. Drawing to his side, the mysterious stranger recited some lines from *The Odyssey* that mention an island called Pharos, off the coast of Egypt, surrounded by the sonorous swell of waves. The island existed and could be found near the floodplain where the Nile delta meets the waters of the Mediterranean. Alexander, according to the logic of the times, believed his vision to be an omen and founded the city he had envisaged on that spot.

He was struck by the beauty of the place. There, the desert of sand touched the desert of water, two lonely, immense, everchanging landscapes sculpted by wind. Alexander himself traced the future city's outline in flour in the form of an almost perfect rectangle, showing where the main square should be placed, which gods should have their temples, and where the perimeter of the wall would run. In time, the tiny island of Pharos would be connected to the delta by a long causeway and would house one of the seven wonders of the world.

Once the construction had begun, Alexander continued on his journey, leaving behind a small population of Greeks, Jews, and shepherds who for a long time had lived in nearby villages. The native Egyptians, in keeping with the colonial logic of every era, were incorporated as citizens of a lower status.

Alexander would not see the city again. Less than a decade later, his corpse would return. But in the year 331 BC, when he founded Alexandria, he was twenty-four years old and he felt invincible.

4

He was young and ruthless. On his way to Egypt, he had defeated the army of the Persian King of Kings twice in a row. He had seized control of Turkey and Syria, declaring them freed from Persian oppression. He conquered the strip of Palestine and Phoenicia; each city surrendered without resistance, except for two: Tyre and Gaza. When they fell after seven months of siege, their liberator dealt them a brutal punishment. The last survivors were crucified along the coast: a row of two thousand bodies nearing their deaths at the sea's shore. The women and children were sold into slavery.

Alexander ordered the governor of the brutalized Gaza to be tied to a cart and dragged to his death, just like Hector's body in *The Iliad*. He must have liked to think he was living out his own epic poem, and from time to time he would imitate some gesture, some symbol, some legendary act of cruelty.

On other occasions, it seemed to him more heroic to be generous to the defeated. When he captured the family of Darius, the Persian king, he treated the women with respect and refrained from taking them hostage. He ordered that they continue to reside undisturbed in their own quarters and be allowed to keep their dresses and jewels. He also let them bury their dead who had fallen in battle.

When Alexander entered Darius's pavilion, his eyes were met with gold, silver, and alabaster. He could smell myrrh and other fragrant aromas and saw rooms adorned with carpets, tables, and dressers. This was a kind of abundance he had never known at the provincial court of his native Macedonia. He remarked to his friends, "It seems that this is what being a king is all about." They presented him with a treasure chest, the rarest and most beautiful item among Darius's possessions. "What could be so valuable as to be kept in here?" he asked his men. Each one made his suggestions: money, jewels, essences, spices, the spoils of war. Alexander shook his head and, after a brief silence, ordered that his *Iliad*, from which he was never parted, be placed inside.

5

He never lost a battle. He always faced the hardships of the campaigns like the other men, with no special treatment. Only six years after succeeding his father as king of Macedonia, at the age of twenty-five, he had defeated the greatest army of the age and taken possession of the treasures of the Persian Empire. It wasn't enough for him. He went on until he reached the Caspian Sea, crossed what is now Afghanistan, Turkmenistan, and Uzbekistan, made his way over the snowy mountain passes of the Hindu Kush, and braved shifting desert sands all the way to the Oxus River, now known as the Amu Darya. He kept on through places where no Greek had ever set foot, such as Samarkand and the Punjab. He was no longer accomplishing brilliant victories, but squandering his energy on an exhausting guerrilla war.

There is a word in Greek that describes his obsession: *póthos*. It is the desire for something absent, something that lies beyond reach, a desire that causes suffering since it is impossible to fulfill. It gives a name to the sinking feeling of unrequited love and also to the anguish of grief, to the unbearable yearning for a person no longer there. Alexander found no relief from his thirst to persevere in his quest to escape mediocrity and boredom. He was not yet thirty when he began to fear that the world might not be big enough for him. What would he do if one day he ran out of territories to conquer?

Aristotle had taught him that the end of the Earth could be found on the other side of the mountains of the Hindu Kush, and Alexander wanted to explore the last frontier. The idea of seeing the end of the Earth held a magnetic attraction. Would he find the Great Outer Sea of which his teacher had spoken? Or would the waters cascade over a bottomless abyss? Or would the end be invisible, a thick fog fading into white?

But Alexander's men, sick and ill-humored beneath the rains of the monsoon season, refused to go any deeper into India. They had heard tales of a huge unknown kingdom beyond the Ganges. The world gave no sign of ending.

A veteran soldier spoke on behalf of them all: under the command of their young king, they had traveled thousands of kilometers, massacring at least 750,000 Asians along the way. They had been forced to bury their best friends, fallen in combat. They had endured famine, glacial cold, thirst, and desert crossings. Many had died of unknown diseases, like dogs by the wayside, or had been horrifically maimed. The few who'd survived could no longer muster the strength they'd had in their youth. Now, their horses limped along on painful hooves and the supply wagons were mired in roads turned to mud by the monsoon. Even the buckles on their belts were rusty, their provisions rotting from the humidity. The holes in their boots had been there for years. They wanted to go home, caress their wives and hug the children who would scarcely remember them. They longed for the land of their birth. If Alexander decided to continue his expedition, he should no longer count on his Macedonians.

Alexander flew into a rage and, like Achilles early in *The Iliad*, withdrew to his tent uttering threats. A psychological struggle began. At first the soldiers kept quiet, but then they grew bold enough to jeer at their king for losing his temper. They had given him the best years of their lives and would not allow themselves to be humiliated.

The tension lasted two days. Then the formidable army turned around and headed for home. Alexander did lose one battle, after all.

THE MACEDONIAN FRIEND

6

Ptolemy was an expedition partner and confidant to Alexander. By origin, he was not remotely connected to Egypt. Born into a noble but undistinguished family in Macedonia, he never imagined that he might one day be pharaoh of the rich country of the Nile, where he set foot for the first time at almost forty, knowing nothing of its language, customs, or complex bureaucracy. But Alexander's conquests and their enormous consequences were one of those historical surprises that can't possibly be predicted before they happen.

Though the Macedonians were proud, they were aware that the rest of the world considered their country backward, tribal, and insignificant. On the scale of Greek independent states, of course, they were many steps below the Athenians and Spartans in pedigree. They kept their traditional monarchy while most city-states of the Hellas had experimented with more sophisticated forms of government and, to make matters worse, they spoke a dialect difficult for others to understand. When one of their kings wished to compete in the Olympic Games, he was granted permission only after careful scrutiny. In other words, they were allowed into the Greek club begrudgingly. For the rest of the world, they simply didn't exist. Back then, the East was the epicenter of civilization, well illuminated by its history; the West was the dark and savage territory where the

barbarians lived. In the atlas of geographic perceptions and prejudice, Macedonia lay on the outskirts of the civilized world. Probably
few Egyptians could have found the homeland of their next king on
a map.

Alexander put an end to this scorn. He was such a powerful
figure that all Greeks adopted him as their own. In fact, they have
turned him into a national symbol. When Greece spent centuries
under Ottoman rule, the Greeks spun legends in which the great
hero Alexander came back to life to free his land from foreign
oppression.

Napoleon's ascent from provincial Corsican to fully fledged
Frenchman also occurred as he conquered Europe: victory is a passport to which no one can object.

Ptolemy was always close to Alexander. Shield bearer to the
prince in the Macedonian court, he accompanied him in his meteoric
campaign of conquests as part of the exclusive Companion cavalry
and was one of his trusted personal bodyguards. After the mutiny
in the Ganges, he suffered the hardships of the return, which went
beyond even the worst predictions: the soldiers suffered the combined aggressions of malaria, dysentery, tigers, serpents, and poison-
ous insects. The rebel villages of the region were attacking an army
exhausted from marching in the humid tropical heat. In the winter
of their return, only a quarter of the soldiers who had reached India
remained.

After so much triumph, suffering, and death, the spring of
324 BC was bittersweet. Ptolemy and the remaining troops were
enjoying a brief rest in the city of Susa, in the southeast of present-day
Iran, when the unpredictable Alexander decided to throw a grandiose party, which, to everyone's great surprise, included simultaneous
weddings for him and his officials. In these spectacular festivities,
which lasted five days, he married eighty generals and relatives to
women—or, more likely, girls—belonging to the Persian aristocracy.
To his own inventory of wives (his Macedonian customs allowed for
polygamy) he added the oldest daughter of Darius III and another
woman from a powerful Eastern clan. In a theatrical and highly calculated gesture, he opened the ceremonies to his troops. Ten thousand soldiers received a royal dowry for marrying Eastern women. It

was an effort to favor mixed marriages carried out on a scale never before attempted. The idea of a mixed-race empire was galloping through Alexander's mind.

Ptolemy played his part in the mass weddings of Susa. His bride was the daughter of a rich Iranian satrap, a provincial governor. Like most of the officials, he might have preferred to be given a medal for his services and five days of straightforward revelry. In general, Alexander's men hadn't even the slightest desire to fraternize with the Persians they'd massacred on the battlefield not long before, much less associate with them by marriage. In the new empire, new tensions between nationalism and cultural fusion were being forged that would soon explode.

Alexander didn't have time to impose his vision. He died of a raging fever at the beginning of the following summer in Babylon, at the age of thirty-two.

7

As he dictates his memoir in Alexandria, an elderly Ptolemy with the face of Anthony Hopkins confesses to his scribe the secret that plagues and torments him: Alexander did not die of natural causes. He himself and other officials poisoned him. The film—*Alexander*, directed by Oliver Stone in 2004—turns Ptolemy into a shadowy figure, a Greek Macbeth, a loyal warrior who carries out Alexander's orders and later becomes his assassin. At the end of the movie, the character rips off his mask, uncovering a darkened face. Could it have happened this way? Or should we assume that Stone is taking the liberty of slipping in a wink, as he did in *JFK*, to conspiracy theories and popular fascination with assassinated leaders?

Alexander's Macedonian officials were undoubtedly nervous and resentful in the year 323 BC. By that time, most of the soldiers in his army were from Iran or India. Alexander was allowing barbarians into the regiments of the elite and even conferring nobility upon some of them. Obsessed with the Homeric exaltation of courage, he sought to recruit the best, regardless of ethnic origin. His oldest comrades in arms found this policy detestable and offensive. But was it reason enough to break the deep bonds of loyalty and run the enormous risk that assassinating their king implied?

We will never know for sure if Alexander was assassinated or if it was an infection—malaria, or a simple flu—that finished off an exhausted body, gravely wounded in battle in nine different places and subjected to almost superhuman overexertion. At the time, his sudden death became a weapon that the king's successors used shamelessly in their fight for power, accusing one another of the supposed assassination. The rumor of poisoning spread like wildfire: it was the most shocking and dramatic version of events. Amid a tangle of propaganda, accusations, and ambitions of succession, historians cannot solve the enigma; they can only evaluate what is likely and unlikely in each hypothesis.

The figure of Ptolemy, a loyal friend or perhaps a traitor, remains trapped in a realm of shadows.

8

Two hobbits, Frodo and Sam, have arrived at the sinister location of Cirith Ungol's staircase in the western mountains of Mordor. To overcome their fear, they speak of their unexpected life of adventures. All this happens near the abrupt ending of *The Two Towers*, the second part of J. R. R. Tolkien's Lord of the Rings. Samwise, whose main pleasures in the world are a delicious meal and a great story, remarks, "Still, I wonder if we shall ever be put into songs or tales. We're in one, of course, but I mean: put into words, you know, told by the fireside, or read out of a great big book with red and black letters, years and years afterwards. And people will say: 'Let's hear about Frodo and the Ring!' And they'll say: 'Oh yes, that's one of my favorite stories.'"

This was Alexander's dream: to have his own legend, to be recorded in books and persist in memory. And he achieved this. His brief life is a myth in both East and West; the Koran and the Bible each speak of him. In Alexandria, in the centuries after his death, a fantastic tale was woven of his journeys and adventures, written in

Greek and later translated into Latin, Syriac, and dozens of other languages. We know it as *The Alexander Romance*, and it has reached our times with a series of variations and omissions. Some scholars believe that aside from certain religious texts, this outlandish and far-fetched work was the most widely read book in the premodern world.

In the second century AD, the Romans added "Magnum"— "the Great"—to his name. But the followers of Zoroaster would call him "Alexander the Terrible" instead. They never forgave him for setting fire to the palace of Persepolis, where the king's library was reduced to ash. It was there that the Avesta, the sacred book of the Zoroastrians, was burned, among other works, and the faithful were forced to rewrite the work from memory.

Alexander's ambiguities and shades of grey are already reflected in the writings of historians of the ancient world, who offer a gallery of varied portraits. Arrian is captivated, Curtius Rufus discovers patches of darkness, and Plutarch can't resist an exciting anecdote, whether it be shadowy or luminous. All of them fantasize. They allow Alexander's biography to slip into the terrain of fiction, giving in to their writerly instincts for sniffing out a great story. A traveler and geographer of the Roman era quipped that those who write about Alexander always prefer the marvelous over the truth.

The vision of contemporary historians depends on the degree of their idealism and the era in which they write. Early in the twentieth century, heroes were still bathed in glory; since the Second World War, the Holocaust, the atomic bomb, and decolonization, we have become much more skeptical. Some authors now put Alexander on the analyst's couch and diagnose him with megalomania, cruelty, and indifference toward his victims. Some have compared him to Adolf Hitler. The debate continues, acquiring the nuances of new sensibilities.

I am surprised and fascinated by the fact that popular culture hasn't abandoned him like a fossil from another era. I have come across Alexander fans in the least expected places, people who can do a quick sketch on a napkin of the troops' movements in his great battles. The music of his name continues to reverberate. Caetano Veloso dedicates the song "Alexandre" to him on his album *Livro*, while the

British band Iron Maiden named one of their most legendary songs "Alexander the Great." This heavy metal song whips up an almost sacred fervor: the band from Leyton never plays it live, and rumor has it among their followers that it will be heard only at their final concert. People keep naming their sons Alexander—or Iskandar, the Arabic version of his name—in the warrior's memory, almost all over the world. Each year his effigy is reproduced on millions of products the real Alexander wouldn't know what to make of: T-shirts, ties, cell phone cases, video games.

Alexander, who lived in pursuit of immortality, has come to embody the very legend of which he dreamed. But if anyone were to ask me—as Tolkien wrote—my favorite story to tell by the fireside, I wouldn't choose his victories or his quests, but the extraordinary adventure of the Library of Alexandria.

9

"The king is dead," a Babylonian scribe wrote on his astrological tablet. By sheer coincidence, the document has reached us almost intact. It was June 10 of the year 323 BC, and there was no need to read the constellations to guess that dangerous times were afoot. Alexander left behind two vulnerable heirs: a half brother whom everyone considered a halfwit and an unborn son in the womb of Roxana, one of his three wives. Pondering the omens on that afternoon, the Babylonian scribe, well schooled in history and the workings of the monarchy, might have reflected on how the chaos of succession can unleash a chain of cruel and confusing wars. That was what many feared at the time, and that is exactly what came to pass.

The bloodshed soon began. Roxana murdered Alexander's other two widows to ensure that her son would have no competitors. The most powerful Macedonian generals declared war on one another. As the years went by, they would methodically slaughter every member of the royal family: the idiot half brother, Alexander's mother, his wife Roxana, and their son, who never reached the age of two. Meanwhile, the empire was crumbling. Seleucus, one of Alexander's officials, sold off the conquered territories in India to a native commander for the incredible price of five hundred war elephants, which he used to keep fighting his Macedonian rivals. Armies of mercenaries offered themselves for decades to the highest bidder. After years of combat, ferocity, vengeance, and many lost lives, three warlords remained: Seleucus in Asia, Antigonus in Macedonia, and Ptolemy in Egypt. Of all of them, Ptolemy was the only one spared a violent death.

Ptolemy settled in Egypt, where he would spend the rest of his life. For decades he fought his old companions with blood and fire to hold on to the throne. And during moments of respite from the civil wars, he tried to get to know and to understand the immense country he was governing. Everything there was awe-inspiring: the pyramids, the ibis, the sandstorms, the ripples in the dunes, the galloping of the camels, the strange gods with animal heads, the eunuchs, the wigs and the shaved heads, the throngs of people on feast days, the sacred cats whose killing was deemed a crime, the hieroglyphics, the palace rituals, the prodigious scale of the temples, the immense power of the priests, the dark and muddy Nile dragging itself through its delta and out to sea, the crocodiles, the plains where abundant crops were nourished by the bones of the dead, the beer, the hippopotamuses, the desert where nothing remains beyond the ravages of time, the embalming, the mummies, life transformed into ritual, the love of the past, the cult of death.

Ptolemy must have felt disoriented, confused, and alone. He didn't speak the Egyptian language, was awkward at ceremonies, and suspected the courtiers of laughing at him. But he had learned from Alexander to act boldly. If you can't understand the symbols, invent others. If Egypt challenges you with its fabulous antiquity, move the capital to Alexandria, the only city without a past, and turn it into the beating heart of the entire Mediterranean. If your subjects are mistrustful of anything new, bring the boldest instances of thought and science to converge on their territory.

Ptolemy channeled great riches into building the Library and Musaeum of Alexandria.

BALANCING AT
THE EDGE OF THE ABYSS

The Library and Musaeum of Alexandria

10

Although we cannot be certain, I like to imagine that the idea of creating a universal library was born in the mind of Alexander. The plan has the scale of his ambition; it bears the mark of his thirst for totality. "The Earth," Alexander proclaimed in one of the first decrees he issued, "I consider mine." Bringing together all existing books is another—symbolic, intellectual, peaceful—way of possessing the world.

The book collector's passion is similar to that of the traveler. Every library is a journey, every book a passport that never expires. As Alexander traversed Africa and Asia, he was never without his copy of *The Iliad*, to which historians say he would turn in search of advice and to feed his desire for transcendence. Like a compass, reading opened up paths into the unknown.

In a chaotic world, acquiring books is a balancing act on the edge of the abyss. This is the conclusion Walter Benjamin draws in his marvelous essay "Unpacking My Library." "To renew the old world— that is the collector's deepest desire when he is driven to acquire new things," writes Benjamin. The Library of Alexandria was a magical encyclopedia that gathered together the knowledge and fictions of antiquity to prevent them from being scattered and lost. But it was also conceived as a new space from which to set out toward the future.

Earlier libraries were private and specialized in subjects of use to their owners. Even those belonging to schools or broad professional groups were simply a tool in the service of their particular needs. The Library of Alexandria's closest predecessor, the library of Ashurbanipal in Nineveh, in the north of what is now Iraq, was destined for the king's use. The Library of Alexandria, varied and comprehensive, contained books on every single subject, written in every corner of the known world. Its doors were open to all those with a thirst for knowledge, to scholars of every nationality, and to anyone with literary aspirations to show. It was the first library of its kind and the one that came closest to possessing every book in existence.

Furthermore, it came close to the hybrid ideal of empire of which Alexander dreamed. The young king who married three foreign women and had semi-barbarian children was planning, according to the historian Diodorus, to transplant the population of Europe to Asia and vice versa, to build a community of friendship and family between continents. His sudden death prevented him from carrying out this project of mass immigration and deportation, a peculiar combination of violence and humanitarian zeal.

The Library opened up to the whole wide world. It included the most important works of other languages, translated into Greek. One Byzantine treatise writer said of the period, "From every village they recruited wise men, those who spoke their own language, but also knew Greek to perfection; each group was given its respective texts, and each text was then translated." This was the birthplace of the well-known Greek version of the Jewish Torah known as the Septuagint. The translation of the Iranian texts attributed to Zoroaster, of more than two million lines, was still remembered centuries later as an extraordinary endeavor. An Egyptian priest named Manetho composed for the Library a list of pharaonic dynasties and their exploits from mythical times up to Alexander's conquest. To write this compendium of Egyptian history in Greek, he searched for, consulted, and excerpted from original documents preserved in dozens of temples. Berossus, another bilingual priest, and expert in cuneiform literature, translated the Babylonian traditions into Greek. The Library even had a treatise on India based on local sources, written by a Greek ambassador to the court of Pataliputra, near the shores of the Ganges. Never before had anyone embarked on a translation project of such magnitude.

The Library made the best part of Alexander's dream come true: his universalism, his passion for knowledge, his unprecedented desire for fusion. On the shelves of Alexandria, borders were dissolved, and the words of the Greeks, the Jews, the Egyptians, the

Iranians, and the Indians finally coexisted in peace. This mental territory was perhaps the only space that proved welcoming to all of them.

11

Even Borges was bewitched by the idea of possessing all the books in existence. His story "The Library of Babel" takes us into a prodigious library, a labyrinth encompassing all dreams and words. Yet we soon find that this is a disturbing place. In it, we see our fantasies tainted with nightmare, transformed into an oracle of our own contemporary fears.

According to Borges, the universe (which others call the Library) is a kind of monstrous beehive that has existed since the beginning of time. It is made up of endless, identical hexagonal galleries connected by spiral staircases. In each hexagon we find lamps, shelves, and books. To the left and right of the landing are two cubicles—one is for sleeping while standing up, and the other is a urinal. These are the bare necessities: light, reading, latrines. The corridors are peopled with strange public servants whom the narrator, who is one of them, describes as imperfect librarians. Each is in charge of a certain number of galleries in this infinite geometric circuit.

The books in the Library contain all possible combinations of twenty-two letters and two punctuation marks—in other words, all that can be imagined or expressed in every language, whether remembered or forgotten. And so, the narrator tells us, somewhere on one of the shelves, the chronicle of your death can be found. And the story of the future, in meticulous detail. And the autobiographies of the archangels. And the true catalog of the Library, in addition to thousands and thousands of fake ones. The inhabitants of the beehive have the same limitations as we do: they speak only a couple of languages and their lives are brief. The statistical possibilities of anyone finding the book they're looking for, in the immensity of these tunnels, or even a book they understand, are thus extremely remote.

And this is the great paradox. Seekers of books, mystics, destructive fanatics, suicidal librarians, pilgrims, worshippers of idols, and madmen roam through the hexagons of the beehive. But nobody reads. Amid the overwhelming excess of random pages, the pleasure of reading is obliterated. All energy is consumed in the search and in the attempt to decipher.

We could understand this simply as an ironic tale woven from myths both biblical and bibliophile, poured into an architecture inspired by the prisons of Piranesi and the endless stairs of Escher. But today, the Library of Babel fascinates readers as a prophetic allegory of the virtual world, the boundlessness of the internet, that gigantic network of information and texts, filtered through the algorithms of search engines, where we get lost like ghosts in a labyrinth.

In a surprising anachronism, Borges foretold what the world today would be like. The story intuits an aspect of contemporary life: the electronic network, what we now call the web, replicates the workings of libraries. The internet began with the dream of a global conversation. Itineraries, avenues, aerial routes would have to be made for words to travel. Each text needed a reference—a link—thanks to which a reader would be able to find it from any computer, anywhere in the world. Timothy John Berners-Lee, the scientist responsible for the ideas that structure the web, found inspiration in the orderly, flexible space of public libraries. Imitating its mechanisms, to each virtual document he assigned an address that was unique and allowed access from another computer. This universal localizer, also known as the URL, is the exact equivalent of a library catalog number. Berners-Lee then devised the protocol of hypertext transferral, better known by the initials "http," which works like the request cards we fill out to ask a librarian to find the book we want to read. The internet emerged—multiplied, vast and ethereal—from libraries.

I imagine the experience of walking into the Library of Alexandria might have resembled the way I felt the first time I used the internet: the surprise, the dizziness immense spaces can sometimes cause. I think of a traveler disembarking at the port of Alexandria, quickening his pace toward the fortress of books, someone like me in their appetite for reading, overcome, almost blinded by the thrilling possibilities of abundance they start to glimpse from the Library's entrance. Each of us in our different era would think the same: in no other place has so much information been gathered together, so much potential knowledge, so many stories through which to experience the fear and delight of being alive.

12

Let us go back. The Library doesn't yet exist. Ptolemy's bravado about the great Greek capital in Egypt came up against a squalid reality. Two decades after its foundation, Alexandria was still a small city in the process of being built, populated by soldiers and sailors, a small clutch of bureaucrats attempting to rein in chaos, and the peculiar collection of shrewd businessmen, criminals, adventurers, and smooth-talking hustlers who always seek opportunity in an unexplored land. The straight streets, planned by a Greek architect, were filthy and reeked of excrement. Slaves' backs were crisscrossed with scars from the lashings they endured. The atmosphere was like that of a western, thrumming with violence, grit, and depredation. The lethal east wind known as the "khamsin," which centuries later bedeviled the troops of Napoleon and Rommel, whipped the city when spring arrived. In the distance, the khamsin storms were like bloodstains in the faraway sky. Later, darkness would blot out the light and the sand would begin its invasion, raising up suffocating, blinding walls of dust that would seep into homes, cause throats and noses to shrivel, and get into eyes, driving people to desperation, misdeeds, and madness. After hours of this oppressive whirlwind there was a ragged wail, and the walls of sand would slump into the sea.

Ptolemy decided to settle in this spot with all of his court, and to tempt the best scientists and writers of his time to this barren land at the edge of oblivion.

The frenzied work began. He had a canal constructed, connecting the Nile to Lake Mariout and the sea. He designed a magnificent port. And he ordered a palace to be built by the sea, protected by a dam, an enormous fortress to serve as a barricade in case of siege; a small, forbidden city to be accessed by very few: the home of an unexpected king in an unlikely city.

He spent a great deal of money to build his dreams. Ptolemy hadn't received the largest share of Alexander's empire, but it was undoubtedly the most fruitful. Egypt was synonymous with wealth. Fabulous harvests of grain grew on the fertile shores of the Nile, goods that could dominate the markets of the time. Besides which, Egypt exported the most widely used writing material of the period: papyrus.

The papyrus reed's roots sink into the waters of the Nile. The stem is as thick as an arm and can reach between three and six meters in height. With its flexible fibers, people of modest means would make cords, mats, sandals, and baskets. Ancient stories recall them: the basket in which the baby Moses was abandoned by his mother on the shores of the Nile was made of papyrus coated with pitch and asphalt. In the third millennium BC, Egyptians discovered that these reeds could be used to make sheets for writing, and by the first millennium, the discovery had reached the people of the Near East. For centuries, the Jews, the Greeks, and later the Romans wrote their texts on papyrus scrolls. As Mediterranean societies became literate and more complex, they needed more and more papyrus, and prices rose according to the feverish demand. Outside Egypt the plant was scarce, and like the coltan used in our smartphones, it became a strategic product. A powerful market came into being, distributing papyrus on commercial routes through Africa, Asia, and Europe. The kings of Egypt developed a monopoly over its manufacture and trade; experts in the Egyptian language believe that "papyrus" and "pharaoh" share the same root.

Let's imagine a morning shift at the pharaoh's workshops. A group of the king's workers arrive at the riverbank to cut reeds one morning. The rustle of their steps wakes the sleeping birds, who take flight from the reedbed. They work in the fresh air of morning, and at noon they deposit great armfuls of reeds in the workshop. With precise movements, they peel off the bark and cut the triangular stem into thin strips around thirty to forty centimeters long. They place the first layer of vertical strips on a flat board, then another layer of horizontal fibers at a right angle to the first. With a wooden mallet, they pound the superimposed layers in such a way that the secreted sap acts as a natural glue. They flatten the surface of the reeds, burnishing them with pumice stone or shells. Finally, they glue the papyrus sheets together at the edges, one after another, with a paste made from flour and water, until they form a long strip that can be rolled up for storage. Usually, some twenty sheets are joined together and the seams carefully buffed until a flat surface is achieved that will not catch on the scribe's pen. The merchants do not sell individual sheets but scrolls; whoever should need to write a letter or a brief document must cut off a piece of the length they require. The scrolls are between thirteen and thirty centimeters high, and their length usually varies between 3.2 and 3.6 meters. But the length is as variable as the number of pages in our modern-day books: the longest scroll from the British Museum's Egyptian collection, the Great Harris Papyrus, was originally 42 meters.

The papyrus scroll represented an extraordinary amount of progress. After centuries of searching for the right format, of humans writing on stone, mud, wood, or metal, language had finally found its home in organic matter. The first book in history was born when words—as ethereal as air—found refuge in the pith of an aquatic plant. Compared to its inert and rigid ancestors, the book was a light, flexible object from the beginning, ready for journeys and adventure.

Papyrus scrolls bearing long texts traced by hand with pen and ink: these were the books that began to arrive at the nascent Library of Alexandria.

13

Alexander's generals remained under his spell even after his death. They began to imitate his gestures, his clothing, the hat he wore, the way he tilted his head. They continued to hold banquets the way he liked them and reproduced his image on the coins they made. One of the Companions let his wavy hair grow out and wore it loose so as to look like him. Eumenes, a battlefield commander, claimed that Alexander came to speak to him in his dreams. Ptolemy started a rumor that he was Alexander's half brother on his father's side. On one occasion, several rival heirs agreed to gather in a tent presided over by the dead ruler's empty throne and scepter; as they debated, they felt as if their absent king was still guiding them from the beyond.

While Alexander's followers longed for him and worshipped his ghost, they were also busy breaking up the far-reaching empire he left them, wiping out his close relatives one after another, and betraying the loyalties that had united them. This is the kind of devotion Oscar Wilde must have had in mind when he wrote in *The Ballad of Reading Gaol*, "Yet each man kills the thing he loves."

In the fight for Alexander's memory, Ptolemy forged ahead with ingenuity. One of his most brilliant moves was to take possession of the young king's corpse. He had understood better than anyone the priceless symbolic value of putting his mortal remains on display.

In the autumn of 322 BC, a procession left from Babylon to Macedonia to bury Alexander in the country of his birth. They carried the body, embalmed in honey and spices, inside a golden coffin, in a funeral carriage that contemporary sources describe as a touchingly kitsch display of canopies, purple drapes, tassels, golden sculptures, embroidery, and crowns. Ptolemy had become a friend of the official in charge of the cortege. With the help of this accomplice, he diverted the route toward Damascus, intercepted the procession with a great army, and seized the casket. General Perdiccas, who had prepared the royal tomb in Macedonia, gnashed his teeth when he learned of the theft and launched an attack on Egypt, but was put to death by his own officers after a disastrous campaign. Ptolemy triumphed. He moved the corpse to Alexandria and put it on display in a mausoleum open to the public, which, like Lenin's tomb in Moscow's Red Square, became a necrophilic tourist attraction. There, Alexander was visited by the first Roman emperor, Augustus, who laid a garland upon the glass cover of the sarcophagus and asked to touch the body. Gossiping tongues would claim that when the emperor kissed the corpse, he accidentally broke its nose—kissing a mummy entails a certain amount of risk. The sarcophagus was destroyed in one of the great popular rebellions that shook Alexandria. Despite rumors about its location, archaeologists have found no trace of the tomb. Some believe the corpse may have met an end worthy of the cosmopolitan Alexander: cut into pieces and made into thousands of amulets, distributed across the wide world he once conquered.

It is said that when Augustus paid homage to Alexander in his mausoleum, he was asked if he would like to see the sepulcrum of the Ptolemies. "I have come to see a king, not to see dead bodies," he answered. His words sum up the drama of the Diadochi, Alexander's successors: everyone thought they were a gang of mediocre stand-ins, a dull postscript to the legend. They lacked the legitimacy of charisma, and only through their relationship to the dead king could they inspire authentic respect. That's why they masqueraded as Alexander in every possible way, wishing to be taken for him, like meticulous modern-day Elvis impersonators.

In the context of this game of resemblances and comparisons, King Ptolemy wanted Aristotle to teach his sons, just as he had Alexander. But the philosopher had died in 322 BC, only a few months after his famous student. Somewhat disappointed at having to lower his standard, Ptolemy sent his messengers to the Lyceum, Aristotle's school in Athens, to offer the most brilliant scholars of the day generously paid work in Alexandria. Two of them accepted the offer; one would educate the princes while the other would organize the Great Library.

The new chief of book acquisition and management was Demetrius of Phalerum. He invented the hitherto nonexistent position of librarian. His youth as a student at the Lyceum had prepared him for the intellectual tasks and responsibility that lay ahead, and he later spent a decade in the maelstrom of politics. In Athens, he had seen the first library organized according to a rational system—the collection belonged to Aristotle himself, who was known as "the Reader." Aristotle, in more than two hundred treatises, sought to describe the structure of the world and parceled it out into categories: physics, biology, astronomy, logic, ethics, aesthetics, rhetoric, politics, metaphysics. There, among the shelves of his teacher and his calm classifications, Demetrius must have understood that owning books is a balancing act performed on a tightrope. An effort to unite the disparate pieces of the universe until they formed a whole that made sense. A harmonious architecture in face of chaos. A sculpture made of sand. A sanctuary where we safeguard all that we fear we may forget. A memory of the world. A dam holding back the tsunami of time.

Demetrius brought to Egypt the Aristotelian model of thought, which in those days was on the cutting edge of Western science. It was said that Aristotle had taught the Alexandrians how to organize a library. The claim can't be taken literally, since the philosopher had never been to the land of the Nile. His influence arrived by indirect paths, via one of his excellent students, who had disembarked in the young city fleeing political turmoil. Yet despite his good intentions, Demetrius succumbed to intrigue at Ptolemy's court. He became embroiled in a conspiracy, fell out of favor, and was arrested. But his passage through Alexandria left an enduring legacy. Thanks to him, a watchful ghost moved into the Library: Aristotle, the lover of books.

14

Every now and then, Demetrius was obliged to send Ptolemy a report on how his task was progressing, which would begin like this: "To the great King, from Demetrius. In obedience to your order to add those books which are missing to the Library's collection, to complete it, and to adequately restore those mistreated by the vagaries of fortune, I have put great care into my task and now share with you an account of my work."

And it was no easy task. It was hardly possible to obtain Greek books without traversing great distances; in the country's temples, palaces, and mansions, the scrolls were abundant, but these were in Egyptian, and Ptolemy refused to stoop so low as to learn the language of his subjects. Cleopatra, according to contemporaries an astonishing polyglot, and the last in the line of the Ptolemies, was the only member of the dynasty able to speak and read the pharaonic tongue.

Demetrius sent agents, saddled with supplies and armed to the hilt, to Anatolia, the islands of the Aegean Sea, and Greece, to hunt down works in Greek. In those days, as I have mentioned, customs officers received instructions to search every ship that dropped anchor in the port of Alexandria and seize any text they found on board. Recently purchased or confiscated scrolls were taken to storehouses, where Demetrius's assistants would identify each one, taking an inventory. These books were papyrus tubes without a cover or spine, and without the blurbs and endorsements that today describe the acclaim, importance, and mastery of the work in question. It was difficult to identify a book's contents at first glance, and if someone owned more than a dozen books and sought to consult them often it was a truly bothersome task. For a library, this problem posed a great challenge that was only imperfectly solved. Before books were piled onto the shelves, a small sign, liable to fall off, was placed at the end of each scroll, detailing the author, the work, and the origin of the copy.

It is said that on one of the king's visits to the Library, Demetrius proposed to incorporate the books of the Torah into his collection in a careful edition. "What is preventing you?" asked the king, who had given him carte blanche. "We need a translation, since they are written in Hebrew."

Few people knew Hebrew, even in Jerusalem, where most of the population spoke Aramaic, the language in which Jesus would preach centuries later. The Jews in Alexandria, a powerful community that occupied a whole neighborhood of the city, began to translate their scriptures into Greek in a slow, fragmentary way, since the faith's most orthodox members were opposed to innovation. The matter was hotly debated in the synagogues of the time, just like the celebration of the Catholic mass in the vernacular rather than Latin centuries later. So if the person in charge of the Library wanted a complete and precise version of the Torah, he would have to commission it.

According to tradition, Demetrius asked permission to write to Eleazar, the high priest of Jerusalem. He asked him in the name of Ptolemy to send learned men to Alexandria who were experts in Hebrew law and could translate it. Eleazar replied with pleasure to the letter and the gifts that accompanied it. After a month-long journey across the Sinai's blistering sands, seventy-two learned Jews, six from each tribe, the crème de la crème of rabbinic doctrine, arrived in Egypt to stay at a mansion near the beach on the island of Faro, "immersed in a profound peace." Demetrius visited them often with his staff to check on how their task was progressing. It is said that they finished the translation of the Pentateuch in seventy-two days on that calm retreat and later returned to their city. The Greek Bible is known as the Septuagint, in recollection of this story.

Aristeas, who recounts these events, swears he was there in person. Today we know that his letter is a fiction, but that real information is couched among the branches of this tale. The world was changing and Alexandria was its mirror. The Greek language was becoming the new lingua franca. It wasn't, of course, the language of Euripides and Plato, but a more accessible version known as Koiné, a contact variety akin to the faltering international English often used to communicate in hotels and airports. The Macedonian kings had decided to impose Greek on the whole empire as a symbol of political domination and cultural supremacy, forcing their neighbors to take the trouble to learn it if they wished to make themselves understood. Nevertheless, some of Alexander and Aristotle's universalism made its way into their proud, chauvinist heads. They knew that to govern their new subjects they needed to understand them. The economic and intellectual efforts made to translate their books can be explained through this lens, especially their religious texts, which are maps of the soul. The Library of Alexandria wasn't only born to give shelter to the past and its legacy. It was also the outpost of a society we could consider globalized, much like our own.

15

That proto-globalization was known as Hellenism. Customs, beliefs, and common ways of life took root in the territory conquered by Alexander from Anatolia to the Punjab. Greek architecture was imitated in places as remote as Libya and the island of Java. The Greek language was used to communicate with Asians and Africans. Plutarch claims that Homer was read in Babylon and that children in Persia, Susa, and Gedrosia—a region that today covers Pakistan, Afghanistan, and Iran—would sing the tragedies of Sophocles and Euripides. By way of trade and intermarriage, a large section of the world came to experience a remarkable degree of cultural assimilation. From Europe to India, the landscape was dotted with cities bearing easily recognized features—wide streets laid out on a grid plan, agoras or public plazas, theaters, gymnasiums, inscriptions in Greek, and temples with decorated façades. Those were the distinctive marks of that version of imperialism, just like the Coca-Cola, McDonald's, glowing advertisements, shopping centers, Hollywood movies, and Apple products of today's homogenized world.

Just like in our times, there were strong currents of discontent. In conquered areas, many subjects resisted being colonized by the invaders. But there were also curmudgeonly Greeks who hearkened back to a time of aristocratic independence and failed to adjust to the new cosmopolitanism. They sighed for the lost purity of the past. Suddenly, lowlife foreigners were cropping up at every turn. In a world of broadened horizons, immigration was expanding and free workers began to resent the competition of Eastern slaves. Fear of the other, of those who were different, was on the rise. A grammarian by the name of Apion grumbled that the Jews occupied the best neighborhood in Alexandria, next to the royal palace, and Hecataeus, a Greek who visited Egypt in the time of Ptolemy, lamented the xenophobia of the Jews. Conflict between different communities sometimes led to bloodshed. The historian Diodorus tells that an angry mob of Egyptians lynched a foreigner for killing a cat, an animal they held to be sacred.

These changes induced anxiety. Many Greeks, who for centuries had lived in small cities run by their own citizens, saw themselves suddenly incorporated into large kingdoms. A sense of uprootedness began to spread, a feeling of displacement, of being lost in a universe that was too large, governed by distant, inaccessible powers. Individualism developed; loneliness became more acute.

Hellenic civilization—anguished, frivolous, dramatic, convulsive, and reeling from rapid change—began to harbor contradictory impulses. To quote Dickens, "It was the best of times, it was the worst of times." Skepticism and superstition blossomed at the same time; curiosity and prejudice; tolerance and intolerance. Some began to consider themselves citizens of the world, while in others, nationalism took greater hold. Ideas reverberated and traveled beyond borders, intermingling easily. Eclecticism reigned. Stoic thought, a dominant current throughout Hellenism and the period of the Roman Empire, taught that suffering could be avoided through serenity, the absence of desire, and inner strength. The Buddhists of the East could identify with this program for self-improvement.

Among the Greeks, the failure of the ideals of the past unleashed an intense wave of nostalgia and, simultaneously, made parodying old heroic tales a new pastime. If Alexander had conquered the world while clinging to his copy of *The Iliad*, soon afterward, an anonymous poet ridiculed those legends in a comic epic, the *Batrachomyomachia*, which told of the battle between Physignathus, king of the frogs, and Psycharpax, king of the mice. Faith in the gods and myths was extinguished, leaving in its wake a combination of irreverence, bewilderment, and longing. Decades later, Apollonius of Rhodes, a nostalgic Alexandria librarian, paid homage to the ancient epic in his poem on the adventures of Jason and the Argonauts. Film buffs will detect the same tension in Clint Eastwood's revisionist western *Unforgiven*, and in Tarantino's ironic, iconoclastic glee as he explodes the genre in *Django Unchained*. Humor and melancholy coexisted in a way all too familiar in our times.

16

Ptolemy had achieved his aim. Until Rome superseded it, Alexandria was the seat of a civilization that permeated borders. Moreover, it was also the capital of economic power. The splendid Lighthouse, one of the Seven Wonders of the World, served the same symbolic function as the Twin Towers of the World Trade Center in New York.

To the south of Alexandria, immense, dark granaries broke up the horizon. Stored there were crops from the fertile floodplains lapped by the Nile. Thousands of sacks were carried to the docks along a network of canals. Egyptian ships set sail, overflowing with goods, for the principal port cities of the era, where their cargo was keenly awaited to cast out the ghost of hunger. The great urban centers of antiquity had grown beyond the capacity of the surrounding rural areas. Alexandria guaranteed bread, which was synonymous with stability and an indispensable condition of power. If the Egyptians decided to raise their prices or reduce the supply, a whole country might descend into violence and rebellion.

Though it was a young and powerful city, nostalgia lurked in the very foundations of Alexandria. The king longed for times gone by that he never knew, but that obsessed him—the golden age of Athens, the heady days of Pericles, the philosophers, the great historians, the theater, the Sophists, the speeches, the high concentration of extraordinary people in a small, proud capital that called itself "the school of Greece." For centuries, the Macedonians had heard tales of the splendor of Athens in their almost barbaric country, and the reports and rumors fascinated them. They invited the aging Euripides to spend his last years among them and also managed to draw Aristotle to their court. Those illustrious guests gave them hope. They tried to imitate the refinement of Athens, wishing to feel cultured, to rid themselves of their humiliating reputation for being less Greek than all the rest. As they gazed from the margins, their admiration only enlarged the myth.

I am reminded of a novel by Giorgio Bassani, *The Garden of the Finzi-Continis*. I have read and reread it many times and think it is one of my favorite books. The great mansion belonging to the wealthy Jews of Ferrara, with their garden, the tennis court, and the high walls surrounding it, represents a place that you long to enter, but where, once invited in, you feel like an insecure upstart. You do not belong to this world, no matter how in love with it you might be. They will let you in for just one magical summer, to enjoy long tennis matches, explore the garden, and fall into a web of desire, but the doors will be closed again. And that space will forever be bound to your melancholy. Nearly all of us, at some point in our lives, have spied into our own garden of the Finzi-Continis from the outside. For Ptolemy, this was Athens. With his memory wounded by the city beyond his reach, he founded the Musaeum of Alexandria.

For a Greek, a musaeum was a sacred enclosure honoring the Muses, the daughters of Mnemosyne, the goddesses of inspiration. Plato's Academy, and later the Lyceum of Aristotle, were located in groves consecrated to the Muses because the practice of thought and education could be understood as metaphorical, brilliant acts of devotion to the nine goddesses. Ptolemy's Musaeum went further: it was one of Hellenism's most ambitious institutions, an early version of the research centers, universities, and think tanks we know today. The greatest writers, poets, scientists, and philosophers of the era were invited to the Musaeum. Those chosen held their positions for life and were free of any material worry, so they could dedicate all their energy to thought and creation. Ptolemy assigned them a salary, free living quarters, and a place at a luxurious dining hall. Furthermore, he made them exempt from paying taxes, perhaps the best gift of all in those times of voracious royal coffers.

For centuries, the Musaeum brought together a dazzling constellation of names, just as Ptolemy had wished: Euclid, the mathematician who formulated the theorems of geometry; Strabo, the greatest physicist of the era; the astronomer Aristarchus; Eratosthenes, who calculated the Earth's circumference with astonishing precision; Herophilos, a pioneer of anatomy; Archimedes, the inventor of hydrostatics; Dionysius Thrax, who wrote the first Greek grammar; the poets Callimachus and Apollonius of Rhodes. Revolutionary theories were born in Alexandria, such as the heliocentric model of the solar system, which, when recovered in the sixteenth century, would bring about the Copernican shift and Galileo's prison sentence. The taboo against dissecting dead bodies—and also live prisoners, so say gossiping tongues—was broken, which allowed for progress in the field of medicine. New branches of knowledge were developed, such as trigonometry, grammar, and manuscript preservation. It was there that the study of philology spread its wings. Great engineering discoveries were made, like the Archimedes screw, which is still used in irrigation. And, seventeen centuries before Watt's measurement of horsepower, Hero of Alexandria published a description of a steam engine, even if it was only used to propel the movement of mechanical dolls and other toys. His work on automatons is considered an early precursor of robotics.

The Library occupied an essential place in that small city of scholars. Few times in history has such a conscious and deliberate effort been made to bring the most brilliant minds of an era together in one place. And never before had the greatest thinkers had access to so many books, to the memory of previous knowledge, to the whispers of the past, with which to learn the profession of thinking.

The Musaeum and Library were part of the palace enclosure, protected by the fortress walls. The lives of those earliest professional researchers unfolded in the isolation of this fortified space. Their routine consisted of lectures, classes, and public debates, but mostly of silent research. The director of the Library was also tutor to the king's children. At sundown, all of them dined together in a hall where sometimes Ptolemy himself would join the banquet to listen to their conversations, their dueling wits, their discoveries, and their affectations. Perhaps he believed he had managed to make his own Athens, his own walled garden.

Thanks to a satirical author from the period, we know the customs of the members of the Musaeum, quiet scholars relieved of all quotidian worries, shielded from the harshness of their times. "In the teeming land of Egypt," says the poet and humorist, "many scholars grow fat, scribbling out books and sparring with one another in the Muses' cage." Another poem brought a writer back from the underworld to advise the Musaeum's inhabitants not to feel so much mutual resentment. Indeed, sparring was a regular issue among these learned men leading their cloistered lives, removed from the hubbub of worldly affairs. Historical sources reveal that disagreements, jealousy, anger, rivalries, and slander were common among them. Nothing out of the ordinary in our present-day university departments, with their endless minor feuds.

17

These days, there is a furious competition to build the highest skyscraper in the world. Alexandria, in its own time, also entered the race: for centuries, the city's lighthouse was one of the tallest buildings in the world. This iconic tower was emblematic of royal vanity, like the Sydney Opera House or the Guggenheim Museum in Bilbao, which give shape to the wet dreams of modern rulers. And it also became the symbol of a golden age of science.

In the beginning, Pharos was a place; it was the name of the island in the Nile delta of which Alexander dreamed, and where he decided to found a city. Another small island called Fårö lies in the Baltic Sea, where Ingmar Bergman shot his film *Through a Glass Darkly*, among many others, and where he withdrew to lead the life of a hermit. But we no longer remember what the first place was called; the name of the lighthouse has overtaken that of the site where it stood, and the word survives in the languages of today due to their Greek inheritance, for example, as *faro* in Spanish, and *phare* in French.

Before its construction began, Ptolemy gave a Greek engineer the task of connecting the island of Pharos to the docks of Alexandria via a causeway that was more than a kilometer long, which divided the port into two separate harbors for merchant and military vessels. Amid the swarm of boats rose the great white tower. The Arabs who saw it still standing in medieval times describe a structure with three parts—cubic, octagonal, and cylindrical—connected by ramps. At the top, at a height of some one hundred and twenty meters, there was a mirror that reflected the sun by day and the blaze of a fire by night. In the silence of darkness, slaves traversed the ramps with loads of fuel for keeping the flames alive.

The lighthouse mirror is enveloped in legend. In those days, lenses were an advanced technology, objects of fascination that could transform one's gaze and the world. Among the scientists at the Musaeum, who were dedicated to uncovering all pathways to knowledge, there were also experts in optics; the great mirror would be made according to their specifications. Though we cannot know for sure if they achieved this, tales from Arab travelers many centuries later speak of lenses that made it possible to keep watch from the lighthouse for ships sailing toward Alexandria at a great distance. It was said that from the top of the lighthouse you could see the city of Constantinople reflected in the moon-shaped mirror. Based on these hazy recollections—part truth, part exaggeration—we might perhaps find in the lighthouse an ancestor of the telescope, an immense eye that could probe the distant sea and stars.

It was the last and most modern of the Seven Wonders of the Ancient World. It represented what Alexandria wished to be: the lighthouse city, the crossroads, the capital of a wider world, the luminous signal that guided and gave direction to every voyage. And although it was destroyed by a string of earthquakes from the tenth to the fourteenth centuries, it left its mark on every lighthouse that came after it, all of which have followed its architectural model.

But the Library, which in a certain sense was also a lighthouse, is a place no ancient author can help us imagine. In every source that refers to it, details about the space, the layout of its rooms and courtyards, its atmosphere, its nooks and crannies are as imprecise as if they were reflected in a mirror in the dark.

18

Reading is a ritual involving gestures, positions, objects, spaces, materials, movements, shades of light. To imagine how our ancestors read we need to know the web of circumstances, in every period, that surrounded the private routine of entering into a book.

Handling a scroll is nothing like opening a book with pages. When a scroll was opened, the eyes would meet with a row of columns of text, one after another, from left to right, on the inner side of the sheet of papyrus. As he went on, the reader would unfurl the scroll with his right hand to reveal the new text, while rolling up the previously read columns with his left. A deliberate, rhythmic, internalized movement; a slow dance. Once it had been read, the book was rolled up in reverse, from the end to the beginning; politeness demanded that it be rewound for the next reader, like a cassette. Pottery, sculptures, and relief carvings show men and women absorbed in reading, performing these gestures. They might be standing, or seated with the book in their lap. Both hands are occupied; the scroll cannot be unfurled with just one. Their positions, behavior, and gestures are different from ours, yet at the same time recall them: back slightly rounded, body hunched over the words, and for a moment the reader departs from his world and sets out on a journey, transported by the side-to-side flick of his pupils.

The Library of Alexandria welcomed many such stationary travelers, but we can't know for sure what setting or places it offered for reading. There are scarcely any descriptions, and those we do have are strangely vague. We can only guess what these silences might conceal. The most decisive information comes from Strabo, an author born in what is now Turkey, who arrived in Alexandria from Rome around the year 25 BC to work on an ambitious geographical treatise that was to complement his historical research. In his account of his time in the city, where he visited the lighthouse, the great causeway, the port, the streets laid out on a grid, the neighborhoods, Lake Mariout, and the canals of the Nile, he says the Musaeum forms part of the immense royal palace. As the centuries went by, the palace had gradually been expanded, each king adding new rooms and buildings, until according to Strabo the whole complex took up a third of the city. In that extensive fortress to which few people had access, Strabo observed a bustling microcosm. After carefully looking around, he wrote a description of the Musaeum and of Alexander's mausoleum and said not a single word about the Library.

The Musaeum, he explains, is made up of a *peripatos*, a covered gallery decorated with columns, an *exedra*, a semicircular outdoor area with seats, and a great hall where the scholars dine together. They live communally and have a priest who oversees the Musaeum, who was formerly appointed by the kings, but is now chosen by Augustus.

That is all.

Where was the Library? Perhaps we have searched in vain, and though it is right in front of us we do not see it because it doesn't conform to our expectations. Some experts suppose that Strabo does not mention the Library, where he undoubtedly worked, because it wasn't an independent building. Perhaps it was a set of open niches in the walls of the Musaeum's great gallery. The scrolls would be stacked there on shelves, within the researchers' reach. Documents and books less frequently used, the rarest and most valuable, would be stored in adjacent rooms.

This is the most plausible hypothesis on Greek libraries—that they were shelves rather than rooms. They did not have facilities for readers, who would have worked in an adjoining arcade, sunny but protected from the elements like the cloisters of a monastery. If everything happened as we imagine, readers at the Musaeum of Alexandria would choose a book and find a seat in the *exedra*. Or they might withdraw to their lodgings to read lying down. Or they might read while pacing slowly among the columns, under the blind gaze of the statues. And in this way, they would travel the roads of invention and the paths of memory.

19

In our times, however, some of the most fascinating examples of contemporary architecture are libraries, spaces open to experimentation and the play of light. Consider the much-admired Staatsbibliothek in Berlin, designed by Hans Scharoun and Edgar Wisniewski. Wim Wenders included a scene filmed there in *Wings of Desire.* The camera slides through the immense open reading room, pans up the stairs, and views the impressive vertical space from the overlapping mezzanines floating like box seats in a theater. People swarm beneath the light flooding in from above, among the parallel blocks of shelves, carrying stacks of books pressed to their waists. Or they sit, making a range of gestures of concentration (a chin resting on a hand, a fist supporting a cheek, a pen twirled between fingers like a propeller).

A group of angels enter the library unnoticed, dressed in that memorable 1980s look: dark oversized coats, turtlenecks, and in the case of Bruno Ganz, hair in a small ponytail. The angels cannot be seen by humans, so they can come close to them freely, sit by their side, or place a hand on their shoulder. Intrigued, the angels peer at the books the humans are reading. They touch a pen held by a student, contemplating the mystery of the words flowing from that small object. Next to some children, they copy the gesture of following lines of text with an index finger, unable to understand it. With curiosity and amazement, they observe all around them faces lost in thought and gazes absorbed in words. They long to understand what the living feel in those moments, why books capture their attention so profoundly.

Angels have the gift of being able to hear people's thoughts. Though no one is speaking, they pick up the constant murmur of whispered words as they pass. These are the silent syllables of reading, which create an intimate form of communication, a sonorous solitude that for the angels is surprising, miraculous, almost supernatural. The phrases people read echo inside their heads like a song sung a cappella, like an invocation.

The air at the Library of Alexandria would have been full of hushed murmurs, just like in this scene. In ancient times, when the eyes recognized the letters, the tongue would pronounce them, the body would sense the rhythm, and the foot would tap on the floor as if keeping time. Writing was heard. Few people imagined that they could read any other way.

Let's talk about you for a moment, the person reading these lines. Right now, with the book open in your hands, you are engaged in a mysterious, unsettling activity, though habit prevents you from being amazed. Think carefully. You are completely quiet, eyes moving over rows of letters made into meaning, that deliver ideas independent from the world now surrounding you. In other words, you have withdrawn to an inner chamber where absent voices speak, where there are ghosts only you can see (in this case, my phantom self), and where the pace of time's passage is the measure of your level of interest or boredom. You have created a parallel world like the illusion of cinema, a world that depends on you alone. At any moment, you can avert your gaze from these lines and return to the action and movement of the outside world. But in the meantime, you remain on the edge, in the place where you've chosen to be. There is an almost magical aura to the act of reading.

But it hasn't always been this way. From the early centuries of writing up to the Middle Ages, the norm was to read aloud for oneself or others, and writers uttered their phrases as they wrote them, listening to their musicality. Books were not a song sung in the mind as they are today, but rather a melody that sprang from the lips and was heard aloud. The reader became a performer, lending the book his vocal cords. A written text was understood as a basic score, which is why the words appeared one after another, in an unbroken chain, with no spaces or punctuation—they had to be pronounced to be understood. When a book was read, there were usually witnesses. Public readings were common, and well-loved stories were passed on by word of mouth. We shouldn't imagine the galleries of ancient libraries as silent, but as teeming with the voices and echoes of pages. Save for certain exceptions, ancient readers lacked the freedom you now enjoy to read the ideas and fantasies in written texts at will, to stand up and think, or to daydream whenever you like, to choose and to hide your choices, to interrupt or abandon your reading, to create your own universes. This individual freedom that is yours is a triumph of independent over tutelary thought and has been achieved little by little, over time.

Perhaps this is why the first people to read like you, in silence, in conversation with the author, were considered so remarkable. In the fourth century, Augustine was so intrigued to see Bishop Ambrose of Milan read in such a way that he made note of it in his *Confessions*. It was the first time someone had done anything like it in front of him. Clearly, it seemed out of the ordinary. As the bishop reads, he tells us, his eyes travel across the pages and his mind understands what they say, but his tongue stays quiet. Augustine realizes that despite his physical proximity, this reader is not beside him, but rather has escaped to another, freer, more fluid world of his choosing; he is traveling without moving, without revealing to anyone where he can be found. The spectacle was disconcerting and fascinated Augustine.

You are a special kind of reader. You come from a long line of innovators. This silent dialogue between you and me, free and secret, is an extraordinary invention.

20

On his death, Ptolemy had resolved the vagaries of his position for more than ten generations of successors. The dynasty that began with him would last nearly three hundred years, until the Romans annexed Egypt to their empire. All the kings in the family—fourteen in total—were called Ptolemy, and ancient authors don't always take pains to distinguish between them (or perhaps they lose track themselves). Reading these sources conjures the mirage of a single vampiric ruler who lives three centuries while the Hellenic world—hedonistic, nostalgic, subjugated—teeters and changes hands around him.

The golden age of the Library and the Musaeum corresponds to the rule of the first four Ptolemies. In the oases between battles and court conspiracies, all of them enjoyed the somewhat eccentric company of their own particular collection of scholars. They each had their intellectual passions: Ptolemy I wished to chronicle the great adventure he had experienced and wrote an account of Alexander's conquests; Ptolemy II took a keen interest in zoology; Ptolemy III, in literature; and Ptolemy IV was a dramatist in his free time. Later, this enthusiasm entered a gradual decline, and cracks began to show in the splendors of Alexandria. It is said that Ptolemy X suffered financial hardships, and to pay his soldiers' wages gave orders for Alexander's golden sarcophagus to be replaced with a cheaper coffin made of alabaster or rock crystal. He had the gold melted down to make coins to solve his predicament, but the Alexandrians never forgave him this sacrilegious act. Sometime later, for that handful of drachmas, he ended up in exile and was eventually murdered.

But the good times lasted decades, and cascades of books kept arriving in Alexandria. In fact, Ptolemy III founded a second library beyond the confines of the palace district, in the Serapeum, the temple built to honor Serapis, the god who became the protector of Alexandria. The Great Library was reserved for scholars, while its affiliate library was open to all. In the words of a professor of rhetoric who saw it soon before its destruction, the books at the Serapeum "put the entire city in a position to philosophize." It may have been the first public library truly open to rich and poor, elites and outcasts, free men and slaves.

The public library was supplied with copies from the main one. Thousands of scrolls from throughout the Hellenic world arrived at the Library and were studied, compared, and corrected by the scholars in residence, who carefully prepared definitive versions based on them. The duplicates of these authoritative editions fed the collection of the Library's public branch.

The temple to Serapis was a small acropolis perched on a narrow promontory with views of the city and the sea. You reached the top breathless after climbing a monumental staircase. A long, covered gallery surrounded the enclosure, and along this corridor in alcoves or in small rooms open to the public lay the books. The Great Library's offshoot, and most likely the main one too, did not have its own building; it was a tenant of the portico.

The Byzantine writer Tzetzes claims that the library at the Serapeum had 42,800 scrolls in its collection. It would be wonderful to know the real number of books held in both libraries. It's an enthralling question for historians and researchers. How many books might there have been in the world in those days? It's hard to believe the ancient authors, since the figures vary wildly from one to the next, just as government estimates of participants in protests differ from counter estimates made by their organizers. Here's a glimpse of the precise disparity in numbers. Of the Great Library, Epiphanius mentions the surprisingly exact figure of 54,800 scrolls; Aristaeus, 200,000; Tzetzes, 49,000; Aulus Gellius and Ammianus Marcellinus, 700,000.

There is one thing we know for sure: the unit of measurement for calculating the library's size was the scroll. It's an ambiguous system—there must have been many duplicate titles, and most works did not fit onto a single scroll but encompassed several. Moreover, the number of scrolls would have fluctuated, increasing with acquisitions and decreasing in cases of fire, accident, and loss.

Ancient libraries, when inventory methods hadn't yet been developed and technological support wasn't available, could not know exactly how many titles they possessed at a given time, and it may not have concerned them much. In my view, the figures that have reached us are mere projections of the fascination the Library of Alexandria evoked. Born as a dream—the desire to house all existing knowledge under one roof—in the end, it acquired the proportions of legend.

A STORY OF FIRE
AND PASSAGEWAYS

21

One of the strangest periods of my life took place in a city inhabited by millions of books. A city that, perhaps inspired by that odd community made of paper, is determined to exist in an invented past.

I remember my first morning in Oxford. With all my ID cards at the ready, proud to be taking up my research fellowship, I was planning to go straight to the Bodleian Library and dedicate a few hours of pleasure to my initial exploration. But I was intercepted in the entry hall, where a library employee, after hearing the reason for my visit, ushered me into a separate office as if my behavior were so suspicious and my intentions so shady that they must be discussed behind closed doors to avoid sullying the innocence of the scholars and tourists. A bald man behind a desk interrogated me without making eye contact. I answered all his questions, justified my presence, and showed him the papers he asked for with somewhat intimidating politeness. There was a long silence while he entered my information into his vast database, and then, hands still on his keyboard, in a startling swerve in time, he suddenly stepped into the Middle Ages and informed me pompously that the time had come for me to take the oath. He handed me a small stack of laminated cards that showed, each in a different language, the words I would have to say. I did so. I swore to obey the rules. Not to steal, damage, or deface a single book. Not to set fire to the library or help cause a blaze and watch with diabolical pleasure as the roaring flames engulfed its treasures, reducing them to ash. All these preliminaries seemed governed by the distorted logic of borders, just like on a flight to the United States when they hand you those bizarre immigration forms that ask if you're planning to assassinate the president.

In any case, the oath wasn't enough. I had to go through the metal detectors, offer my bags for inspection, and check my backpack before finally passing through the metal turnstile at the library's entrance. As I submitted to the rest of the inspection, I remembered medieval libraries, where books were chained to the shelves or desk to prevent their theft. I thought of the fantastic curses directed at book thieves throughout history, darkly imaginative texts to which I am inexplicably drawn, perhaps because devising a good curse isn't something just anyone can do. An as yet unwritten anthology ought to begin with the threatening words inscribed at the library of the San Pedro de las Puellas monastery in Barcelona, quoted in Alberto Manguel's *A History of Reading*: "For him that steals, or borrows and returns not, a book from its owner, let it change into a serpent in his hand and rend him. Let him be struck with palsy, and all his members blasted. Let him languish in pain crying aloud for mercy, and let there be no surcease to his agony till he sing in dissolution. Let bookworms gnaw at his entrails in token of the Worm that dieth not. And when at last he goes to his final punishment, let the flames of Hell consume him for ever."

That day I was given a card that, I later discovered, made me a second-class citizen in the Oxford world. It granted me entry to the libraries and colleges, but only to certain areas and at authorized times; it allowed me to consult books and journals, but not to borrow them; and permitted me to observe the extravagant rites of academic life, but not dare to take part in them. I soon learned that Lewis Carroll studied and taught at Oxford for twenty-six years. And then it occurred to me that there'd been a gigantic misunderstanding: *Alice's Adventures in Wonderland* is sheer literary realism. In fact, it describes my experience in those early weeks to a T. The tempting places I glimpsed through the keyhole, where I would have needed a magic potion to fulfil the entry requirements. My head crashing into the ceiling. Rooms so suffocating that I wanted to stick my arms out of the window and my foot up the chimney. Tunnels, signs, mad tea parties, conversations whose logic couldn't possibly be pinned down. And fossilized characters absorbed in rituals full of surprises.

I also discovered that in Oxford, relationships—of doctoral collaboration or plagiarism, of feudal, sexual, and other varieties, or even friendship—are seasonal, and their rhythms conform to the academic calendar. I had made the mistake of arriving in the middle of the term, when the students had already emerged from the phase of sizing one another up and had worked out how to meet all their basic needs. The Calvinist hall of residence where I stayed didn't help me get to know anyone either. Its rules were as inhospitable as the city itself, and its curfew hours like those of a convent. I remember how sad the communal kitchen felt at seven o'clock with its row of eight fridges. In one of them was a space labeled with my room number, like the catalog number on the spine of a book, and even the holes in the egg storage compartment were equally apportioned in pairs. Everything was organized so that each remained in their numbered area, without invading anyone else's territory or supplies. You went down for dinner, made your little contribution to the communal trash, and went back up to the carpeted room assigned to you.

I was so desperate to speak that I began begging for words. I made my first linguistic advances at the Sackler Library, where I spent most of my time camped out. I'd noticed the porter had a jovial, florid face—presumably from drinking—which made him seem approachable. I also accosted a guard at the Ashmolean Museum whose skeptical gaze drew me in. I asked them about the city's secrets, the libraries' hidden details, entreating them to explain the many mysteries surrounding me, of which they were the keepers. I heard fascinating stories this way.

I asked them to explain the surprising ritual that was followed to request a book: the librarians took note of your request and summoned you back to a specific reading room a day or two later, at a precise time, to deliver the material to you. If it was almost the weekend, the wait could be as long as three or four days. Where are the books? I asked. And that was when they told me about the two cities, one on top of the other.

Every day, they answered, the librarians at the Bodleian receive a thousand new publications. They have to make room for them, because the next day another merciless thousand arrive. Each year, the collection increases by about a hundred thousand books and two hundred thousand journals, or, to put it another way, over three kilometers of shelves. And the regulations do not allow a single page to be removed. At the beginning of the twentieth century, the library network's buildings were completely overflowing from this deluge of books. At that point, they told me, the construction began on underground storerooms and a network of tunnels with conveyor belts underneath the city. During the Cold War, when fallout shelters were in fashion, that underground labyrinth reached its full mythical splendor. But the avalanche of paper overflowed these underground rooms as well, and the pressure it exerted became a threat to the city's sewage system. So they began sending the books elsewhere, outside the city—to an abandoned mine and to warehouses in the vicinity. There are librarians whose job is to transport the books, they added, though they look more like crane operators in neon outfits.

Thanks to these conversations—the first friendly ones I had experienced—I began to feel reconciled with Oxford. Walking around alone, I thought I could hear the echo of the conveyor belts moving the books beneath my steps and keeping me company. I imagined them there in their damp and secret tunnels, like the creatures from *Fraggle Rock* in my childhood, or like characters from the film *Underground*. I relaxed. I let down my guard. I accepted that in Oxford, eccentricity had an objective purpose. I felt more comfortable, even free, in my role as awkward outsider. And, with patience, I also managed to meet other memorable misfits.

Each morning in the mist, when I ventured into the hazy streets, I felt the whole city was resting on a sea of books, like a magic carpet in midflight.

22

One morning of steady rain and watery shadows on the walls, my friend the museum guard explained that the Ashmolean, where she worked and where I would visit her, had been the first public museum in the modern sense of the word. I was happy to learn this. I'm always excited to be in places where something happened for the first time, in the territory of new beginnings.

It was a minor historical turning point that at the time passed almost unnoticed: in 1677, Elias Ashmole gave his cabinet of curiosities—ancient coins, stuffed exotic animals—to the University of Oxford. It would no longer be a private collection, a family treasure to be inherited by his children and grandchildren as a symbol of their privileged social position, but would belong to the students and to anyone else curious enough to want to visit it.

In those days, innovations, which in a decidedly conservative world did not have a good reputation, were usually disguised as recovered traditions. In an effort to revive ancient glories, the public collection donated by Ashmole, a nameless and unprecedented novelty, was called a museum. This was a way of drawing an imaginary line between Alexandria and Oxford. There was already a great library; they needed their musaeum. Believing themselves to be restoring the past, they had created something different, something that would become a triumph: a fusion of ancient ideas and contemporary curiosity. It was this concept of the museum as a place of exhibition that ended up becoming established in Europe, and not the Alexandrian model of a community of scholars.

In 1759, the British Museum was founded in London. And in France, the National Assembly seized the Louvre Palace from the monarchy along with all of the works of art inside it, to turn it into a museum which opened its doors in 1793. It was a new, radical symbol. The revolutionaries wished to do away with the idea that the past belonged to a single social class. Ancient things couldn't keep being a whim of the aristocracy; the French Revolution expropriated history from the elite. By the end of the nineteenth century, attending exhibitions of ancient knickknacks, paintings by old masters, manuscripts, and first editions of books had become a fashionable pastime among Europeans. And it crossed the ocean to the United States. In 1870, a group of businessmen founded the Metropolitan Museum in New York; MoMA would be the first private museum of modern art. A mining magnate named Solomon R. Guggenheim and his descendants would follow suit in an area that today has given rise to a wide-ranging tourist, commercial, and even real-estate business. Thanks to Elias Ashmole's unusual decision, the legacy of Alexandria has radiated outward into a powerful network. Museums have been described as "the cathedrals of the twenty-first century."

There is an alluring paradox hidden here: the fact that we can all love the past is profoundly revolutionary.

23

The most ancient libraries we know about, in the Near East—Mesopotamia, Syria, Asia Minor, and Persia—also issued curses against book thieves and destroyers.

"He who carries off this tablet . . . May Shamash carry off his eyes . . . May Nabu and Nisaba . . . render him deaf . . . He who steals it by theft or takes it by force or has it robbed by his slave, may Nabu . . . spread his life like water."

"He who breaks this tablet or puts it in water or rubs it until you cannot recognize it [and] cannot make it be understood, may Ashur, Sin, Shamash, Adad and Ishtar, Bel, Nergal, Ishtar of Nineveh, Ishtar of Arbela, Ishtar of Bit Kidmurri, the gods of heaven and earth and the gods of Assyria, may all these curse him with a curse that cannot be relieved, terrible and merciless, as long as he lives, may they let his name, his seed, be carried off from the land, may they put his flesh in a dog's mouth!"

We can intuit the importance these remote collections held for their owners by reading the hair-raising threats they make. In those days, the book trade didn't yet exist, and you could only obtain one by copying it out yourself (for which you would need a professional scribe) or by seizing them from others as part of the spoils of war (for which you would need to defeat your enemy in a dangerous battle).

Invented five thousand years ago, the books we are speaking of, in fact the ancestors of books and of the electronic tablets we use today, were tablets made of clay. There were no papyrus reeds on the riverbanks of Mesopotamia, and while other materials such as stone, wood, and animal skin were scarce, clay was abundant. The Sumerians began to write on the earth beneath their feet. They made a surface for writing by modeling small lumps of clay into flat rectangles about twenty centimeters long, similar to our seven-inch tablets. And they developed a system of writing based on stamping grooves into soft clay. While water could erase the letters written on the clay, fire—the executioner of so many books—baked the clay tablets just like a potter's kiln, making them more durable. Most of the tablets found by archaeologists were preserved precisely because they were burned in the flames of a fire. Books conceal incredible tales of survival. On rare occasions—the fires of Mesopotamia and Mycenae, the rubbish dumps of Egypt, the eruption of Vesuvius—destructive forces have saved them.

The world's earliest libraries were humble places, small storerooms with shelves attached to the walls and tablets placed on them upright, one next to another. In fact, scholars who specialize in the ancient Near East prefer to call them archives. In these places, bills, delivery notes, receipts, inventories, marriage contracts, divorce agreements, legal records, and codes were kept. A small portion of these tablets was also devoted to literature, especially poems and religious hymns. In the excavations of the palace at Hattusa, the Hittite capital in what is now Turkey, several examples of a curious literary genre have been discovered: prayers to combat sexual impotence.

In the library of Hattusa—and before that in Nippur, in the south of Mesopotamia—tablets have been found that catalog the collections. Each work was identified by its first line or a brief summary of its content, since it wasn't yet customary to give books a title. To prevent long texts from getting scattered, the number of tablets that formed them was specified. Sometimes the name of the author and other secondary information was included. The existence of these inventories shows that libraries were beginning to grow as early as the thirteenth century BC, and that readers couldn't take in their contents with a simple glance at the tablets on the shelf. Moreover, it reveals an immense theoretical step forward: the awareness of a unified collection as an achievement and an aspiration. A catalog isn't simply an appendix to a library, but rather its concept, its connective tissue, and its culmination.

The libraries of the Near East were never public. They belonged to elite schools for scribes that needed the texts as a model for teaching, or else they were the exclusive privilege of kings. The Syrian monarch Ashurbanipal, who lived during the seventh century BC, was the greatest book collector before Ptolemy. Ashurbanipal says on a tablet that he created the library at Nineveh for his own "royal contemplation and reading." He also boasted a talent unusual among monarchs of the period: he knew the art of writing, "which among the kings, my predecessors, none has learned." Archaeologists have unearthed around thirty thousand tablets from his library, of which only five thousand are literary in content. The usual mixture of archival documents, books on omens, religion, and magic has been found, alongside some of the most famous works of Near Eastern literature.

The library of the proud King Ashurbanipal, the closest precedent to the Library of Alexandria, was less universal in nature. It was a set of documents and texts used for public rituals and ceremonies. Even the literary works were there for practical reasons, because the king had to be familiar with the foundational myths of his people. All of the libraries in the Near East ceased to exist and were plunged into oblivion. The writings of those great empires were buried in the desert sands along with their destroyed cities, and what was left of their writing, once discovered, was indecipherable. They were so completely forgotten that when travelers found cuneiform inscriptions among the ruins of the Achaemenid cities, many believed they were just there to decorate the door and window frames. After centuries of silence, it was the passion of researchers that unearthed their remains and managed to decipher the forgotten languages of their tablets.

The books of Athens, Alexandria, and Rome, however, never fell completely silent. Throughout the centuries they have continued to speak in whispers, sustaining a dialogue about myths and legends, but also philosophy, science, and law. Somehow, perhaps without knowing it, we are all part of this conversation.

24

The Library of Alexandria also had Egyptian ancestors, but these are the most blurred in the family photograph. During the pharaonic period, there were private libraries and libraries in temples, but our knowledge of them is vague. Sources mention Houses of Books, archives where administrative documents were kept, and Houses of Life, storehouses sheltering thousand-year traditions, where sacred texts were copied, interpreted, and protected. The most specific details we have of an Egyptian library come from the Greek traveler Hecataeus of Abdera, who managed to get a guided tour of the Temple of Amon at Thebes. He describes his walk through the labyrinth of halls, courtyards, alleys, and rooms of the enclosure as an exotic experience. He claims to have seen the sacred library in a covered gallery, and on it the words "The Place of the Cure of the Soul." Beyond the beauty of this idea—the library as a clinic for the soul—we know hardly anything about Egyptian book collections.

Like cuneiform writing, hieroglyphics were forgotten for more than a millennium. How could this have happened? Why did the long-written past become a tangle of incomprehensible drawings? In fact, very few people in Egypt knew how to read and write (only members of the caste of scribes, the most powerful group in the country after the king and his family). To become a scribe, they had to learn hundreds, eventually thousands of ideograms and phonograms. It was a long process to which only the wealthiest had access in exclusive schools, something akin to MBA programs for senior executives in the modern world. From among the scribes educated there, the senior bureaucrats and priests of the kingdom were chosen who later intervened in the pharaohs' succession struggles and wielded their influence according to their criteria and convenience. I can't resist quoting an Egyptian text that despite being from the remote past is strangely familiar. In it, Dua-Khety, a rich man advanced in years, launches an unmistakable tirade at his son Pepi for loafing around at the school for scribes, where the tuition is costing his family an arm and a leg:

> You must turn your mind to books . . . I have seen a
> coppersmith at work at his furnace. His fingers are like the
> claws of a crocodile . . . The barber shaves until the end
> of the evening, and he must go about from street to street,
> seeking out someone to shave . . . The reed cutter must go
> to the delta, and by the time he has toiled more than his
> arms can stand, the gnats have stung him and the mosquitos
> have bitten him to death . . . See, there is no office free from
> supervisors except the scribe's. He is the supervisor. If you
> understand writing, then it will be better for you than the
> professions of which I have spoken. You must join the ranks
> of the esteemed.

We don't know if Pepi took his father's sermon to heart and grudgingly studied to make his way in the Egyptian social elite. If so, after a few hard years of practicing strokes and enduring the punishments meted out by teachers known for their strictness, Pepi would have earned the right to show off the distinguished tools of the scribe: brushes with bristles in a range of thicknesses, a slotted writing palette, bags of pigments, a tortoise shell for mixing them in, and a hardwood stand on which to rest the papyrus and have something to lean on, since it wasn't customary to use a table to write, but rather to sit down and lean on crossed legs for support.

We do, however, know the story of the last Egyptian scribes, who witnessed the shipwreck of their civilization. Beginning with the edict of Theodosius I in the year 380, Christianity became the compulsory state religion, and pagan cults were prohibited in the Roman Empire. All the temples of the ancient gods were shuttered, except for the Temple of Isis on the island of Philae, to the south of the first cataract of the Nile. There, a group of priests took refuge, men who were repositories of the secrets of their sophisticated writing system and who had been forbidden from sharing their knowledge. One of them, Esmet-Akhom, engraved on the walls of the temple the last hieroglyphic inscription ever written, which ends with the words "for all time and eternity." Some years later, the emperor Justinian I resorted to military force to close the temple where the priests of Isis were holding out, taking the rebels as prisoners. Egypt buried its old gods, with whom it had lived for thousands of years. And, along with its gods, its objects of worship, and the language itself. In just one generation, everything disappeared. It has taken fourteen centuries to rediscover the key to that language.

At the beginning of the nineteenth century, a thrilling race to decipher Egyptian hieroglyphics began. The best European Orientalists faced the challenge of recovering the lost language, keeping a suspicious watch on one another all the while. These were years of passion and suspense in the scientific world, and also of envy and thirst for glory. The competition's starting shot was fired forty-eight kilometers from Alexandria, in July 1799. The previous year, Napoleon, who dreamed of following in Alexander's footsteps, had taken his troops to the scorching Egyptian desert, with the wholesome intention of bothering his British enemies. The expedition was a fiasco, but it led the Europeans to fall in love with pharaonic antiquities. In the area surrounding the port of Al Rashid, which the French called Rosetta, a soldier came across a stone covered in strange inscriptions while working on the construction of a military fortress. When his spade hit a heavy chunk of dark basalt buried in the mud, the soldier must have muttered a string of curses. He had no idea that he was about to bring something extraordinary to light. This chunk of rock would come to be universally known as the Rosetta Stone.

This striking artifact is a fragment of an ancient Egyptian stele, on which King Ptolemy V ordered a priestly decree to be translated into three kinds of writing—hieroglyphic, demotic (the last phase of Egyptian writing), and Greek—somewhat like the publication of an autonomous law in present-day Spain, in the region's three official languages. A captain from the engineering corps working in Rosetta understood that this broken stele was a valuable discovery and had the 760-kilo stone moved to the Egyptian Institute in Cairo, which had recently been founded by the swarm of scholars traveling alongside the troops of the French expedition. They took impressions with ink, which would later be distributed among those drawn to the challenge. When Admiral Nelson expelled the Napoleonic army from Egypt, he took possession of the Rosetta Stone, inciting the rage of the French, and had it taken to the British Museum, where today it is the most visited piece on display.

It was 1802. The battle of the wits began.

Anyone trying to decipher an unknown language will find themselves chasing shadows amid a chaos of words. Without any background knowledge, if you don't even know the subject of the enigmatic phrases, it's an almost impossible task. But when there exists a translation of the mysterious text in a known language, the researcher is no longer lost: they have a map of the uncharted territory in their hands. Linguists suspected immediately that the Greek fragment on the Rosetta Stone would open the door to the lost language of ancient Egypt. The adventure of deciphering it awakened a new interest in cryptography, which in the nineteenth and early twentieth centuries would grip the imagination of Edgar Allan Poe in his story "The Gold-Bug," and Arthur Conan Doyle in "The Adventure of the Dancing Men."

In the early years of the nineteenth century, the Egyptian enigma resisted attempts at interpretation by linguists, who were disoriented by the defacement of the inscriptions. The beginning of the hieroglyphic inscription and the end of the Greek were missing, so it was almost impossible to establish a clear correspondence between the Egyptian text and its translation. But in the 1920s the pieces began to come together, and the names of the Macedonian kings provided the essential clue. In the hieroglyphic inscription, several characters were sculpted inside oval rings that experts called cartridges. The first step forward was to suppose that the cartridges housed the names of the pharaohs. The British polymath Thomas Young managed to decipher Ptolemy's name, and the French scholar Jean-François Champollion later read that of Cleopatra. Thanks to this first group of uncovered sounds, Champollion, an extraordinary polyglot, discovered similarities between the enigmatic Egyptian language and Coptic, which he spoke. Based on this discovery, during years of obsessive work comparing inscriptions and striving to translate them, he developed a dictionary of hieroglyphics and an Egyptian grammar. He died soon after, at the age of forty-one, his health destroyed by decades of hardship, cold, poverty, and long days of study.

Ptolemy's name was the key. After centuries of silence, Egyptian scrolls and monuments recovered their voices.

Today there is an initiative called the Rosetta Project that aims to protect human languages from extinction. The linguists, anthropologists, and IT experts responsible for this project, based in San Francisco, have designed a nickel disk onto which they have microscopically etched the same text translated into a thousand languages. Even if the last person to understand one of these thousand languages were to die, the parallel translations would allow the lost meanings and sounds to be saved. The disk is a universal, portable Rosetta Stone, an act of resistance in the face of words passing irrevocably into oblivion.

BOOKS AND SKIN

25

Before the invention of printing, every book was unique. For a duplicate to exist, someone had to go through the process of copying it out, letter by letter, word by word. There were few copies of most works, and the chance that a given text might be completely eradicated was a tangible threat. In the ancient world, the last existing copy of a book might be rotting away on a shelf at any moment, devoured by termites or destroyed by humidity. And while the water or the jaws of an insect were having their way, another voice was falling silent forever.

This small-scale act of destruction happened time and again. In those days, books were fragile. From the outset, they were all more likely to vanish than to endure. Their survival depended on chance, accident, their owners' appreciation, and the raw materials from which they were made. They were flimsy objects fashioned from materials that deteriorated, broke, or disintegrated. The invention of the book is the story of a battle against time to improve the palpable, practical characteristics—lifespan, cost, durability, weight—of the physical format of texts. Every step forward, no matter how negligible it might seem, meant greater hope for the life of words.

Stone, of course, is long-lasting. Ancient people engraved their phrases on it, just as we still do on the plaques, gravestones, and pedestals dotting our cities. But a book can only be made of stone in a metaphorical sense. The Rosetta Stone, at a weight of almost eight hundred kilograms, is a monument, not an object. A book must be portable; it must allow the person who reads and writes to interact with it closely; it must be carried by readers and fit in their baggage.

The closest ancestors of books were tablets. I have already spoken of the clay tablets of Mesopotamia, which reached as far as Israel, Turkey, Crete, and Greece and were used in some areas until the beginning of the Christian era. Tablets hardened like adobe bricks when dried in the sun. When the surface was moistened, it was possible to erase the lines and write something new. They were seldom fired in kilns like bricks, since in that case the clay couldn't be reused. To keep them safe from humidity, they were stored piled up on wooden shelves and also in wicker baskets and other vessels. They were cheap and lightweight, but brittle and easily broken.

Today, preserved tablets have been found from the size of a credit card or cell phone to the largest examples measuring thirty or thirty-five centimeters. Even if both sides were used, there was not enough room for extensive texts. This was a major inconvenience: when a single work was split between several pieces of clay, the possibility was greater that some of the tablets, and along with them parts of the story, would be lost.

In Europe, tablets were even more common and were made of wood, metal, or marble, coated in wax and resin. A sharp bone or metal implement was used to write on the waxed surface, and it had a tip in the shape of a spatula on the other end to make it easy to erase mistakes. These tablets were used for most letters in the ancient world and also for notes, drafts, and all ephemeral texts. Children used them to learn to write, just as we use those unforgettable lined notebooks in school today.

Rectangular tablets were a major discovery in terms of form. The rectangle is uniquely pleasurable to the gaze. It delineates a balanced, concrete, and contained space. Most windows, display cases, screens, photographs, and paintings are rectangular. Books, too, after a series of searches and experiments, have ended up being rectangular, almost without exception.

The papyrus scroll represented extraordinary progress in the history of the book. The Jews, Greeks, and Romans adopted it with such enthusiasm that in the end they all considered it a feature of their own culture. Compared with tablets, sheets of papyrus are a fine, light, flexible material, and a large quantity of text can be stored in a very small space when they are rolled up. A scroll of the usual dimensions could contain an entire Greek tragedy, a brief dialogue by Plato, or a Gospel. This meant a prodigious step forward in the effort to preserve the products of ancient thought and imagination. Papyrus scrolls relegated tablets to secondary status (for notes, drafts, and other texts with short-term uses). They were like sheets of paper rejected by the printer, the scraps we use to make lists of items we won't end up crossing off or give to children for them to draw on.

Papyrus had its disadvantages, though. In Egypt's dry climate, it remained flexible and white, but Europe's humidity darkened and made it fragile. If papyrus leaves are moistened and dried out several times, they start to disintegrate. In ancient times, the most valued scrolls were stored in ceramic vessels, wooden boxes, or bags made of animal skin for safekeeping. Moreover, only one side of the scroll could be used—the surface on which the fibers ran horizontally, parallel to the written lines. On the other side, the vertical threads impeded the pen's movement. The text was written on the inside of the scroll to protect it from light and friction.

Papyrus scrolls—light, beautiful, and portable—were delicate objects. They could be worn out by reading and frequent use. They could be destroyed by cold and rain. Since they were made from organic matter, they awakened the gluttony of insects, and they were easily engulfed by flames.

As I have already mentioned, scrolls were made only in Egypt. They were imported products whose trade relied on a booming commercial structure that continued to thrive, even under Muslim domination, until the twelfth century. The pharaohs and Egyptian kings who held the monopoly determined the price of the eight varieties of papyrus circulating in the market. And, much like countries exporting oil today, Egyptian rulers enacted methods of pressure or sabotage at whim.

This was what happened at the beginning of the second century BC, with unexpected consequences for the history of the book. King Ptolemy V was consumed with envy and seeking a way to hinder the progress of a rival library founded in the city of Pergamum in what is now Turkey. The library had been established by Eumenes II, a culturally Greek, Hellenistic king who imitated, a century later, the avarice and unscrupulous methods of the first Ptolemies when it came to obtaining books. He also began a hunt for intellectual luminaries and attracted a group of scholars who formed a community parallel to that of the Musaeum. From his capital, Eumenes attempted to eclipse Alexandria's cultural brilliance at a moment when Egyptian political power was in decline. Ptolemy, aware that the best times were now in the past, was enraged by the challenge. He would not tolerate these affronts to the Great Library, which represented the pride of his lineage. It's said that when he discovered that his librarian, Aristophanes of Byzantium, was planning to take up residence in Pergamum under the protection of Eumenes, he had him thrown into jail, accusing the first of treason and the second of theft.

In addition to imprisoning Aristophanes of Byzantium, Ptolemy launched a fierce counterattack on Eumenes. He halted the supply of papyrus to Eumenes's kingdom, to vanquish the enemy library by depriving it of the best writing material in existence. The measure might have been devastating, but much to the vengeful king's frustration, the embargo instigated a great step forward that would also immortalize the name of his enemy. Pergamum responded by perfecting the ancient Eastern technique of writing on animal skin, a practice that up to that point had been secondary and local. In memory of the city that made its use widespread, the improved product was called, in Latin, *pergamena,* which later became "parchment" in English. A few centuries later, this discovery would alter both the appearance and the future of books. Parchment was made from calfskin, sheepskin, and goatskin. Craftsmen would soak the skins in a bath of lime for several weeks before pulling them tautly over a wooden frame to dry. The stretching process aligned the skin's fibers, creating a smooth surface that was later scraped until the parchment was as white, beautiful, and thin as desired. The result of this long production process was soft, fine sheets that could be used for writing on both sides, and above all—and this was the key—were durable.

The Italian writer Vasco Pratolini said literary creation consisted of handwriting exercises on a person's skin. Though he didn't have parchment in mind, it's a perfect image. When this new material for writing triumphed, books were transformed into precisely that: bodies inhabited by words, thoughts tattooed onto skin.

26

Our skin is a huge blank page; the body, a book. Time passes, writing its history on faces, arms, bellies, sexual organs, legs. As soon as we arrive in the world, an "O" is stamped onto our stomach in the form of the navel. Then later, other letters slowly begin to appear. The lines on the palms of our hands. Freckles, like punctuation. The marks of erasure left by doctors when they open the flesh and then sew it up. As the years go by, scars, wrinkles, dark spots, and varicose veins like branches trace the syllables that tell the story of a whole life.

I return to *Requiem,* by the extraordinary poet Anna Akhmatova. In it, she describes the long lines of women in front of the prison in Leningrad. Akhmatova was intimately familiar with misfortune: her first husband was shot; the second died of exhaustion in the gulag; her only son was detained several times and spent ten years in prison. One day, when she saw herself in the mirror—her gaunt appearance, the grooves carved into her face by her affliction—she recalled the ancient Mesopotamian tablets: "Now I know how cuneiforms cut by suffering show / their harsh unyielding texts impressed on cheeks." I too have occasionally met people whose faces resemble clay inscribed with sorrow. And after reading Akhmatova's poem, I can no longer help it: Assyrian tablets remind me of the faces of those who have lived and suffered greatly.

But time isn't the only thing that writes on the skin. Some people tattoo phrases and pictures on it, decorating themselves like illuminated parchments. I have never done so myself, but I still understand the urge to leave a mark, to color the body, turning it into a text. I remember the joyful weeks when a friend from my youth decided to get her first tattoo. She lifted the gauze covering it in front of me. I stared at the still tender letters, the reddened flesh of her arm; when the muscle tensed, the words seemed to tremble with a movement all their own. I was fascinated by that phrase that could throb, sweat, and bleed—a book infused with life.

I've always been intrigued to know what people write on the book of their skin. I once met a tattoo artist, and we talked about his work. He told me that most people get tattoos wanting to remember a person or an event forever. The problem is that our "forevers" tend to be fleeting, and statistically, these are the kinds of tattoos people most regret. Other clients choose inspiring phrases, song lyrics, poems. Even when the texts are clichés, poor translations, or make little sense, having them stamped on the body makes people feel unique, special, beautiful, and full of life. I believe the tattoo is a remnant of magical thinking, a leftover trace of ancestral faith in the aura of words.

The living parchment is not just a metaphor—human skin can carry written messages. It can be read. In exceptional situations, bodies can serve as a hidden conduit for information. The historian Herodotus tells a marvelous story, based on true events, about tattoos, spies, and intrigue in ancient times. In an era of great political turbulence, a Greek ruler called Histiaeus decided to urge his son-in-law Aristagoras, the tyrannical leader of the Ionian city of Miletus, to incite a revolt against the Persian Empire. It was a highly dangerous conspiracy in which both would risk their lives. The roads were being watched, and Aristagoras's messengers were sure to be searched before arriving at Miletus, in what is now Turkey. Where could they carry and conceal the letter that would condemn them to torture and a slow death if it was discovered? The general had an ingenious idea: he shaved the head of his most loyal slave, tattooed the message onto his scalp, and waited for the hair to grow back. The tattooed words were as follows: "Histiaeus to Aristagoras: stir Ionia to revolt." When the new hair sprouted, covering the subversive command, Histiaeus sent the slave to Miletus. For the sake of safety, the slave was told nothing of the plot, but was instructed to shave off his hair when he arrived at Aristagoras's house and tell him to take a look at his bald head. The messenger traveled as stealthily as a Cold War spy, stayed calm as he was searched, reached his destination without the plot being discovered, and shaved his head. The plan went forward. He never learned—no one can read their own crown—what the incendiary words tattooed on his head conveyed.

Skin, that mysterious web woven by time, and words are at the center of the thriller *Memento,* directed by Christopher Nolan. The film's perplexed protagonist, Leonard, suffers from anterograde amnesia caused by head trauma and cannot store recent memories; his awareness of his own actions soon vanishes without a trace. Each morning he wakes with no memory of the previous day, the previous months, or any of the time that has passed since the tragic accident that damaged his brain. Despite his affliction, Leonard is determined to find the man who raped and killed his wife and to take his revenge. He has devised a system that allows him to move through a world that is constantly being erased and is littered with intrigue, manipulation, and traps: he has the essential information about himself tattooed on his hands, arms, and chest, and every day, he rediscovers his story there. With his identity under threat of being forgotten, only by reading his tattoos can he continue his search and fulfill his purpose. The truth of the story eludes us amid the tangle of lies perpetrated by others, including Leonard, whom in the end we suspect of the crime. The film is structured like a puzzle, fragmented like its protagonist's mind, and like the contemporary world. It is also, indirectly, a reflection on the nature of books: extensions of memory, the only witnesses—imperfect, ambiguous, but irreplaceable—of the times and places living memory cannot reach.

27

Several times a month, I entered the Medici Riccardi Palace through a back door on the Via de' Gori, just at the end of the crenellated wall around its garden. The façade was a shade of vanilla often seen in Florence. I needed to breathe in the simplicity of those houses and courtyards before facing the baroque onslaught and the suffocating cascade of gold that awaited me inside the Riccardiana Library. It was there that I held a truly valuable parchment manuscript in my hands for the first time.

During my long hours of study in the opulent reading room, I was able to carefully hatch a detailed plan to trap my prey. I didn't really need to consult any manuscripts for my research, but I wore my best expression of academic seriousness for the library staff. The goal of my visit was purely hedonistic: I wanted to brush against that book and caress it; I wanted to experience the sensual pleasure so sternly monitored by those guardians of the library's riches. It was electrifying to touch a work of art created for the pleasure of an aristocrat and his coterie of privileged friends; it was a delicious transgression for a poor girl like me who was doing a juggling act to be able to rent an apartment in Florence. I'll never forget those moments of almost erotic intimacy with a fourteenth-century Petrarch. I admit that as I went through the ritual for gaining access to those priceless manuscripts—handing my backpack over to the librarians, keeping only a piece of paper and a pencil, donning the cotton gloves, submitting to surveillance by the guardians of the treasure—I felt some satisfying stabs of guilt that my eccentric book fetish was causing everyone such a nuisance. Sometimes I imagined that one of the allegorical figures floating among the clouds and heraldic shields painted on the ceiling was about to pounce on me. The plump blond woman levitating on high was especially threatening; if I remember rightly, she was Wisdom, brandishing the spherical Earth.

I was able to enjoy the fruits of my imposture for almost an hour, and the notes I took—playing the role of diligent paleographer—described only my joyous sensory impressions. When I turned the pages, the parchment crackled. The way books whisper, I thought, is different in every era. I was dazzled by the beauty and neatness of the expert penmanship. I saw the tracks of time in those pages dotted with patches of yellow, like my grandfather's hands.

Perhaps that's when the urge to write this essay was born, in the warmth of that book by Petrarch that whispered like a softly flickering fire. I have held other parchment manuscripts in my hands since then, and I have learned to study them better, but memory always clings to that first encounter.

As I ran my fingers over the codex's pages, the idea came to my mind that this marvelous parchment once covered the back of an animal whose throat had later been slit. In just a few weeks, livestock could go from living in the pasture, stable, or sty to becoming a page in a Bible. In the most well-documented period, the Middle Ages, monasteries would buy cow, sheep, goat, or pig skins chosen while the animal was still alive so that its quality could be assessed. Just as in human beings, animal skins vary according to age and type. The skin of a suckling lamb is smoother than that of a six-year-old goat. Some cows have damaged hides because they like to rub up against trees or because insects bite and sting them mercilessly. All these factors, along with the artisan's skill, had a significant effect on the final product. To peel and remove the flesh from the parchment, the skin was pulled as tight as a drum and painstakingly scraped up and down with a knife with a curved blade. So tautly was it stretched that a cut too deep by the knife, a poorly healed hair follicle, or the tiny prick of an old insect bite could expand into a hole the size of a tennis ball. Scribes copying books applied their imaginations to disguising the imperfections of their raw materials, and their ingenuity sometimes made the manuscript even more beautiful. A gap in the parchment could become a window through which a miniature head might peep from the next page. I have also seen the curious case of an opening repaired by the nuns at a Swedish convent using lacework that weaves an exquisite lattice of thread between the letters.

As I held that delicate parchment in my hands, gloved so as not to damage it, I meditated on cruelty. Just as baby seals are bludgeoned to death in our times so we can bundle ourselves up in warm coats made of their skin, the most lavish medieval manuscripts also demanded a considerable dose of sadism. There were beautiful books made of the silkiest, brightest white skins, which were known as vellum and came from newborn animals or even aborted embryos. I imagine the animals' wails and the blood spilled over centuries so that the words of the past would be able to reach us. Behind the exquisite work of parchment and ink, wounded skin and blood—the barbarity lurking in civilization's blind spots—are hidden like a pair of rejected twins. We prefer to be unaware that progress and beauty involve pain and violence. In accordance with this peculiar human contradiction, many books have served to spread outpourings of wise words about love, goodness, and compassion across the world.

A long manuscript could occasion the death of an entire flock. In fact, there wouldn't be enough animals in the world today for the mass slaughter our publications would require. According to the historian Peter Watson's calculations, if we assume every skin was half a square meter in size, a book of a hundred and fifty pages would demand the sacrifice of ten or twelve animals. Other experts assign hundreds of skins to a single copy of the Gutenberg Bible. Producing parchment copies of a work, the only way to give it a chance of survival, implied an enormous expense that for most people was out of reach. No wonder that owning a book, even a common copy, was for a long time the exclusive privilege of noblemen and religious orders. In one thirteenth-century Bible, the scribe, overwhelmed by the scarcity of materials, noted in the margin, "Oh, that the heavens were made of parchment and the sea of ink."

28

I lived in Florence for a year. It was strange to go to work every morning shielding my laptop from elbow jabs in the crush of tourists. On my way, I dodged the photographic hysteria of hundreds of people posing with stiff smiles plastered across their faces. I saw constant lines—undulating human centipedes—in front of museums. People sitting in the street, eating prepackaged food. Guides herding their flocks, speaking loudly in every possible language. Sometimes the hordes made it hard to get through, like crowds of fans awaiting a pop star's arrival. Everyone brandished their cell phone. Shouting. They had to make way for the carts pulled by indifferent horses. The smell of sweat, horse manure, coffee, tomato sauce. Yes, it was strange going to work amid that throng of people taking selfies. When I approached the university building and saw the mural of Picasso's *Guernica* from afar, I sighed with the relief of someone emerging from a subway station at rush hour, a little the worse for wear.

Peace and seclusion are also possible in Florence, but you have to go looking for them, away from the beaten path: they have to be earned. I found them for the first time one bright December morning in the Convent of San Marco. A couple of silent visitors were loitering on the ground floor, but on the next level I found myself alone and in disbelief, as if I had just escaped from a ferocious stampede on the savanna. Lulled by the crystalline atmosphere, I visited the monks' cells one by one, where Fra Angelico painted his sweet Franciscan frescoes, a visual declaration of love for the poor, the innocent, the hopeful, the meek, and the simple. They say that precisely there, surrounded by that beautiful procession, Cosimo, the patriarch of the Medicis, would withdraw to do penance for the abuses he committed to multiply his fortune and extend his banking subsidiaries across Europe. The great businessman had reserved a double cell for himself; the powerful, as we know, need more comforts than the rest of the world, even when atoning for their sins. Between two cells, at the beginning of a wide corridor, I came upon an extraordinary corner of the convent. Experts believe this was the place that housed the first modern library. Here, the splendid books donated to the city by the humanist Niccolò Niccoli were housed, "to the common good, to the public service, to a place open to all, so that all eager for education might be able to harvest from it as from a fertile field the rich fruit of learning."

For his part, Cosimo financed the construction of a Renaissance library, designed by the architect Michelozzo, which replaced the dark rooms and chained books of the medieval world with a space emblematic of the new times: a room bathed in natural light, designed to facilitate study and conversation. Sources describe the originality of the library's architecture admiringly: an airy arcade held up by two rows of delicate columns, with windows on both sides, serene-looking stone, walls of an aquatic shade of green to inspire calm, shelves loaded with books, and sixty-four benches made of cypress wood, where friars and visitors could read, write, and copy out texts. An entrance that gave access from the outside made Niccolò's dream a reality: his collection of four hundred manuscripts was open to all book lovers from Florence and abroad. Founded in 1444, after the destruction of its Greek and Roman predecessors, it was the first public library on the continent.

I walked slowly through the long hall. The tables have disappeared, replaced by glass cases displaying priceless manuscripts. Now that it's a museum, no one comes to this bright, silent Renaissance haven to read anymore, but it still has the warm feel of a lived-in space. Perhaps ghosts have taken refuge here—everyone knows they are fearful creatures that prefer lonely places, since they are afraid of the terrifying hordes of the living.

A DETECTIVE'S TASK

29

Copying a text faithfully by hand is no easy endeavor. It demands a series of repetitive and exhausting operations. The copyist must read a chunk of text in the book he is using as a model, hold it in his memory, reproduce it in exquisite calligraphy, and then return to the original, setting his gaze at the exact point where he left off. To be a good scribe, you needed razor-sharp concentration. Even the most highly trained, attentive person might make mistakes (misreadings, lapses due to fatigue, mental translations, misinterpretations and mistaken corrections, substituted words, jumps in the text). In fact, the copyist's personality is portrayed in the mistakes he makes. Though the hand that copied the book is anonymous, through errors we have been able to discover where the scribe was born, his cultural background, his mental agility and tastes; even his psychology surfaces in his omissions and the words he changes.

It is an established fact that every copy plants errors in the text it reproduces. A copy of the copy will repeat the errors of its model and will always add new ones to its own harvest. Artisanal products are never identical. Mass production can only be done by machines. Hand-copied books varied as their numbers increased, like in a game of telephone, where you discover that as the story passes from mouth to mouth, it ends up different from the original.

The frenzied and passionate competition between royal collectors had turned Alexandria into the greatest repository of books ever known. In the Great Library, many duplicate works could be found, especially those of Homer. The scholars at the Musaeum had the chance to compare versions and notice alarming discrepancies among them. They observed that the process of successive copies was stealthily altering their literary content. In many passages, what the author was trying to say couldn't be understood, and in other places, lines varied according to the copy. When they realized the extent of the problem, they understood that over the centuries, just as rocks are eroded by the constant rush of waves, texts would be eroded by the silent force of human fallibility, and the stories would become more and more incomprehensible, until they no longer made any sense at all.

The guardians of the Library then embarked on a mission, almost detective in nature, to compare all of the versions of every work at their disposal and reconstruct the texts' original form. They searched for the fossils of lost words and layers of meaning beneath the confusion and misunderstanding in which they were cloaked. This effort gave rise to progress in research and study methods and served as training for a great generation of critics. Alexandrian philologists prepared painstakingly corrected editions of the literary works they considered most valuable. These ideal versions were made available to the public as originals for later copies and even for the book trade. The editions we read and translate today are fruit of the work of the word detectives at Alexandria.

In addition to restoring texts already in circulation, the Musaeum of Alexandria (sometimes known as the Birdcage of the Muses) also produced mountains of expertise, disquisitions, and treatises on literature. Their contemporaries respected their unprecedented labors, but at the same time liked to make fun of the scholars, who were comical despite themselves. The favored target of these jokes was Didymus, who published an extraordinary three or even four thousand monographs. Didymus worked tirelessly at the Library during the first century BC, writing commentaries and glossaries as the world around him was torn apart by the Roman civil wars. Didymus was known by two epithets: Bronze-Guts (Chalcenterus), since he must have had insides as hard as nails to be able to write his numerous and extensive literary commentaries; and the Book-Forgetter (Biblioláthas), since he once denounced a theory in public as absurd, only to then be shown an essay in which he himself had defended it. Didymus's protégé Apion inherited his teacher's indefatigable profession, and it's said that the emperor Tiberius called him the World's Drum. During the Hellenic period, the Alexandrian philologists—passionate, meticulous, learned, and sometimes pedantic and tedious—rapidly covered ground that, with its successes and excesses, we have also covered ourselves, and for the first time in history the bibliography on literature began to fill more books than the literature itself.

HOMER

Enigma and Twilight

30

The Great Library acquired everything, from epic poems to recipe books. Amid that ocean of letters, scholars had to decide to which authors and works they would dedicate their efforts. There was no question who the great protagonist of Greek literature was, and Alexandria became the Homeric capital.

Homer is enveloped in mystery. He is a name without a life story, or perhaps just the nickname of a blind poet—the name Homer can be translated as "he who does not see." The Greeks knew nothing certain about him and couldn't even agree when they tried to assign him a date. Herodotus believed he had lived in the ninth century BC ("four centuries before my era and no more"), while other authors imagined him as contemporary with the Trojan War, in the twelfth century BC. Homer was a vague, shapeless memory, the shadow of a voice to which the music of *The Iliad* and *The Odyssey* were attributed.

In that period, everyone knew *The Iliad* and *The Odyssey*. Those who knew how to read had learned by reading Homer at school, and others had heard the adventures of Achilles and Odysseus told aloud. From Anatolia to the gateway to India, in the expanded, hybrid Hellenic world, being Greek ceased to be a matter of birth or genetics and had much more to do with loving the Homeric poems. The culture of the Macedonian conquerors could be boiled down to a set of distinctive characteristics native populations were obliged to adopt if they wanted to rise in status: the language, the theater, the gymnasium (where the men exercised naked, a scandal to other peoples), the athletic games, the symposium (a refined way of getting together to drink), and Homer.

In a society that never had sacred books, *The Iliad* and *The Odyssey* were the closest thing to the Bible. Whether fascinated by Homer or enraged with him, without a priestly class keeping watch, Greek writers, artists, and philosophers felt free to explore, question, satirize, and expand the Homeric horizons. It's said that Aeschylus humbly stated that his tragedies were merely "crumbs from the great banquet of Homer." Plato dedicated long pages to attacking the poet's presumed wisdom, expelling him from his ideal republic. On one occasion, a wandering scholar by the name of Zoilus, who promoted his lectures by subversively declaring himself "the scourge of Homer," set foot in Alexandria, and King Ptolemy attended his show in person to "accuse him of patricide." No one could remain indifferent to the epics of Achilles and Odysseus. Papyruses unearthed in Egypt confirm that *The Iliad* was by far the most read Greek book of ancient times, and passages from the poems have been discovered in the sarcophagi of Greco-Egyptian mummies—people who took Homeric verses with them on their voyage to eternity.

The Homeric poems were more than entertainment for an audience bewitched by them; they contained the dreams and mythologies of ancient peoples. Since time immemorial, humans have told one another the historic events that generation after generation have left an imprint on their memory. But time and again, we obsessively turn them into legends. From our twenty-first-century perspective, the invention of heroic deeds may seem like a primitive impulse, one we have already overcome. But in fact this isn't the case: every civilization chooses its national stories, consecrating its heroes, taking pride in its legendary past. Perhaps the last country to forge its own mythic universe was the United States, which exported its fascination with the western to the contemporary globalized world. John Ford reflects on the mythification of history in *The Man Who Shot Liberty Valance*, where the owner of a newspaper, tearing up his investigative reporter's well-documented article, concludes, "This is the West, sir. When the legend becomes fact, print the legend." It doesn't matter that the period longed for was in fact an ignominious one (Native American genocide, the Civil War, the Gold Rush, violent cowboys wielding their power, cities of outlaws, the defense of firearms and slavery). Something similar could be said—and some Greeks were brave enough to say it—about the great foundational Hellenic event, the Trojan War. But just as the movies have taught us to fall in love with the magnificent, dusty landscapes of the American West, with borderlands, with the pioneer spirit and the drive to conquer the land, Homer thrilled the Greeks with his violent and vibrant tales of the battlefield, and of veteran soldiers returning from war.

Like the best westerns, Homer's work is more than just a nationalist tract. It's true that his poems represented the aristocratic world and failed to rebel against its injustices or call it into question, but they also knew how to capture the nuances of its stories. There, we can recognize a mentality and a range of conflicts not so distant from our own—or, to be precise, two mentalities, because *The Odyssey* is much more modern than *The Iliad*.

The Iliad tells the story of a hero obsessed with fame and honor. Achilles can choose between a long and peaceful but lackluster life if he stays in his country, or a glorious death if he sets out for Troy. And he decides to go to war, even though the prophecies warn him that he will not return. Achilles belongs to the great family of those who are blinded by an ideal—brave, committed, melancholic, unsatisfied, stubborn, and prone to taking themselves very seriously indeed. From his boyhood, Alexander dreamed of emulating him and sought inspiration in *The Iliad* in the years of his stunning military campaign.

In the cruel universe of war, the young die and parents survive their children. One night, the king of Troy ventures to the enemy camp alone to beg them to return his son's body so he can give him a burial. Achilles, the assassin, the killing machine, takes pity on the old man, and in response to this picture of sorrowful dignity remembers his own father, whom he will never see again. It's a moving moment in which the conqueror and the conquered weep together and share in some of life's certainties: the universality of grief and the strangely beautiful flashes of humanity that briefly illuminate the catastrophe of war. But though *The Iliad* doesn't tell us, we know that the truce will not last. The war will go on, Achilles will die in battle, Troy will be razed, his men's throats will be slit and their women shared out as slaves among the victors. The poem ends at the edge of an abyss.

Achilles is a traditional warrior who lives in a harsh and tragic world. The wandering Odysseus, on the other hand—a literary creature so modern that Joyce was seduced by him—delights in fantastical, unpredictable, amusing adventures that are sometimes erotic, sometimes ridiculous. *The Iliad* and *The Odyssey* explore life paths distant in nature, and their heroes face the tests and vagaries of existence with opposite temperaments. Homer makes it clear that Odysseus values life intensely, with its imperfections, its moments of ecstasy, its pleasures, its bittersweet flavor. He is the forefather of all fictional travelers, explorers, sailors, and pirates—able to face any situation, a deceiver, a seducer, a collector of experiences, and a great storyteller. While he longs for his home and his wife, he entertains himself at leisure along the way. *The Odyssey* is the first literary representation of homesickness, which coexists in the poem, without too much conflict, with an adventurous, seafaring spirit. When his boat runs aground on the island of Calypso, the nymph with the lovely braids, Odysseus stays with her for seven years.

In that little Mediterranean Eden, where violets bloom and soft waves lap the idyllic beaches, Odysseus revels in sex with a goddess, enjoying immortality and eternal youth by her side. But after several years of pleasure, all this happiness turns to despair. He grows weary of the monotony of that endless vacation and weeps at the water's edge as he remembers his loved ones. On the other hand, Odysseus has enough experience with deities to think twice before admitting to his powerful mistress that he is bored. Calypso will be the one to broach this thorny conversation. "So, Odysseus, you wish to go back to your hearth and homeland? If only you knew the many sorrows fate has in store for you, you would stay here with me and be immortal. I am not inferior to your wife in bearing nor in stature, for no woman can compete with the body and face of a goddess."

It's a tempting offer: to live forever as the lover of a sultry nymph and always be in his prime, free of aging, illness, hard luck, prostate problems, and senile dementia. Odysseus answers, "Do not be angered, Goddess. I know full well that Penelope isn't your equal, but I still want to go home, to see the day of my return. If any god should harm me on the wine-red sea, I'll bear it with a patient soul. I've suffered so much already amid the waves and at war." And after Odysseus has decided to depart—the poet says, with delightful ease—the sun set, night fell, and they went off together to frolic and bask in each other's love. Five days later, he set out from the island, pleased to be spreading his sails to the wind.

Unlike Achilles, the wise Odysseus does not fantasize about a unique and glorious destiny. He could have been a god, but he chooses to return to Ithaca, the rocky little island he calls home, to face his father's decrepitude, his son's growing pains, and Penelope's menopause. Seasoned by struggles, he prefers authentic sorrows to insincere happiness. The gift Calypso offers is too much like a mirage, an escape, a dream brought on by hallucinogens, a parallel world. The hero's decision expresses a new kind of wisdom, a far cry from the strict code of honor that drove Achilles. This wisdom whispers to us that despite being humble, imperfect, and fleeting, despite all its limitations and all its afflictions, human life is worth living, though youth will vanish, our flesh will droop, and we'll end up limping along.

A Tapestry of Echoes

31

The first word in Western literature is "anger" (in Greek, *mênis*). This is how the opening hexameter of *The Iliad* begins, plunging us without hesitation into sound and fury. With the rage of Achilles, a journey begins that takes us through the territories of Euripides and on to Shakespeare, Conrad, Faulkner, Lorca, and Rulfo.

Yet despite this, Homer is more of an end than a beginning. In fact, he is the tip of an iceberg almost completely submerged in oblivion. When we write his name along with those of the great authors of world literature, we are conflating two worlds that can't be compared. *The Iliad* and *The Odyssey* were born in a world completely different from ours, in a time before writing was widespread, when language was fleeting, made up of gestures, air, echoes. A period of "winged words," as Homer described them, words carried away on the wind that could be preserved only in memory.

Homer's two epic texts came from a period when it makes little sense to speak of authorship. In the oral tradition of the time, poems were recited in public, perpetuating a custom inherited from nomadic tribes, when the elderly would tell their ancestors' old stories, recounting their heroes' feats while gathered around the fire. In those days, poetry was socialized: it belonged to everyone and to no one. Each poet could freely use the myths and songs that belonged to tradition, updating them, shedding the parts he considered irrelevant, adopting nuances, characters, made-up adventures, and verses heard from his fellow storytellers. Behind each tale lay a galaxy of poets who would have had no understanding of the concept of copyright. Over the long centuries when this oral culture flourished, Greek folklore changed and expanded, layer by layer, generation by generation, never reaching a closed or definitive version.

Illiterate poets created hundreds of poems that have been lost forever. Some left a shadow of their memory in the work of ancient writers, and from their allusions—summaries and brief fragments—we also know some of their plots. In addition to the Epic Cycle relating the story of the Trojan War, there was at least one other about the city of Thebes, birthplace of the unfortunate Oedipus. One very ancient song that predates *The Iliad* and *The Odyssey* had an Ethiopian warrior called Memnon as its protagonist. If the conjectures about its age are right, this would mean, surprisingly, that the oldest known song of heroic deeds in Europe chronicled the exploits of a Black man.

In the oral tradition, the bards performed at great festivals and at the banquets of noblemen. When someone versed in the art of winged words performed his repertoire of stories in front of an audience, no matter how small, he was "publishing" his work. If we want to picture this method of telling and hearing stories—which isn't yet literature, since it isn't set down in letters or writing—there are two sources of information. *The Iliad* and *The Odyssey* offer a glimpse of the life, work, and travails of the *aoidos*, or Greek epic poets. Anthropologists have also studied cultures in which the oral epic persists to this day, coexisting with the printed word and new technologies of communication. Though they might seem like visitors from the past, traditional songs refuse to disappear, and in some corners of the world are used to tell the stories of new wars and dangerous lives in the present. Scholars of folk traditions recorded a song by a Cretan bard that tells the story of the 1941 attack on the island by German paratroopers. As he remembers his friends who fell in the Battle of Crete, the bard is so moved that his voice falters and trembles and he falls silent.

Imagine a scene from daily life in the small palace of a local lord in the tenth century BC. A banquet is being held, and the host has engaged the services of a roving singer to enliven the evening. The stranger lingers on the threshold where beggars are made to wait, until he is invited to sit in the hall where local grandees drink wine and feast on roast meat, drops of fat dribbling down their chins. They fix their gazes on him and he grows ashamed of his grubby and threadbare tunic. Quietly, he tunes his instrument—a cithara—preparing himself for the exertion of his performance.

He is a great storyteller and has practiced the art of weaving words together since he was a child. With a clear voice accompanied by the strum of the instrument, sitting alone like a folk singer with his guitar, he envelops his audience in the magic of an enthralling tale of battles and adventure. The guests at the banquet shake their heads, nod, tap their feet to the rhythm. They are soon bewitched. The tale draws them in, makes their eyes glisten, and before they know it, they begin to smile. This is something on which the ancient Greeks and modern witnesses of recitals in Slavic villages concur: epic songs captivate, entrance, and fascinate those who hear them.

The skillful bard doesn't just conjure the story's action, he also has a repertoire of tricks at his disposal. On arriving in the area, he has gathered information about his employer's ancestors and has learned their names and characteristics, so that he can introduce them into the plot to rub shoulders with legendary heroes. He always slips in an episode to casually glorify the people of his client's region. He lengthens the song or cuts it short depending on his listeners' mood and the atmosphere in the room. If those in the audience enjoy descriptions of opulence, he embellishes the warrior's armor, his horse's bridle, the princess's jewels—as the bard often says, he needn't pay for these riches from his own purse. He masters the art of pauses and suspense, always stopping the story at a precisely calculated moment so that he will be invited to continue the next day. Night after night the performance goes on, sometimes for a week or more, until the host's interest begins to wane. Then the traveling musician returns to the road, to his life of wandering, in search of another refuge.

In the age of winged words, literature was an ephemeral art. Every performance of those oral poems was unique and happened only once. Like a jazz musician who takes a popular tune and embarks on a passionate improvisation without a score, the bards played with spontaneous variations on the songs they'd learned. Even when they recited the same poem, telling the same tale featuring the same heroes, it was never identical to the last time. Thanks to an early and disciplined training, they learned to use the poems' lines as a living, malleable language. They knew the plots of hundreds of myths, mastered the patterns of traditional language, had an arsenal of flexible phrases and words to fill the verses, and used those strands to weave a song for every performance that was at once faithful and new. But there was no desire to claim authorship: poets loved the legacy of the past, and if the traditional version was beautiful, they saw no reason to be original. Individual expression belongs to the time of writing; in those days, the prestige of artistic originality had yet to flourish.

Of course, to master their craft, storytellers needed a prodigious memory. The ethnologist Mathias Murko, who forged the path later continued by Milman Parry and Albert Lord, established in the early twentieth century that some Bosnian Muslim singers mastered thirty or forty songs, some mastered a hundred, and some more than a hundred and forty. The cantos could last seven or eight hours—like the Greek poems, each was a different version of the same story—and it took several whole nights, until dawn, to perform every line of them. When Murko asked at what age they began to learn, one of these singers answered that they played the instrument while still in their parents' arms, and that they told the tales from the age of eight. There were also child prodigies, Mozarts of storytelling. One recalled frequenting bazaar cafés at the age of ten with his family, where he absorbed all of the songs; he couldn't sleep until he had repeated the stories he'd heard, and by the time he drifted off, they were engraved in his memory. Sometimes, the bards would travel for hours to listen to a fellow singer. It was enough to hear a song once—twice, if they were very drunk—to be able to perform it themselves. That was how these inherited poems survived.

Something similar probably happened in Greece. The epic poets preserved the memory of the past because from early childhood, they lived in a dual world—in reality and in legend. When they spoke in verse, they felt transported to the world of the past, which they knew only through the enchantment of poetry. Like books made of flesh and blood, alive and with beating hearts—in a time without writing and therefore without history—they prevented experiences, lives, and accumulated knowledge from being swallowed by the nothingness of oblivion.

32

In the second half of the eighth century BC, a new invention silently began to transform the world, inciting a peaceful revolution that would bring radical change to memory, language, creative expression, the way we organize thought, and our relationship to authority, knowledge, and the past. The changes were slow but momentous. After the alphabet, nothing was ever the same again.

The earliest readers and writers were trailblazers. The world of orality refused to disappear—even today, it hasn't entirely vanished—and at first, the written word was subject to a certain degree of stigma. Many Greeks preferred words to be sung. They did not take kindly to innovations and they groused and grumbled when faced with them. Unlike us, the people of the ancient world believed that novelty led more to decadence than to progress. Some of that reluctance has persisted. All great inventions—writing, printing, the internet—have had detractors who saw them as harbingers of the apocalypse. There must surely have been curmudgeons who decried the wheel as a tool of civilizational decline, preferring to lug rocks around on their backs until they died.

But it was hard to resist the promise of this new invention. All societies wish to endure and to be remembered. The act of writing lengthened the life of memory, prevented the past from fading away forever.

In the earliest days, poems were born in the spoken word and traveled by oral routes, but some bards learned the alphabet and began to transcribe them on sheets of papyrus (or to dictate them) as a passport to the future. Perhaps some of them became aware at the time of the startling implications of that boldness. Writing the poems down meant fixing the text forever in a single form. In books, words are made as solid as glass. Writers had to choose the most beautiful possible version of the songs to survive all others. Until that moment, the oral poem was a living organism that grew and changed, but writing would calcify it. Elevating only one version of the story meant sacrificing all others, but at the same time, it meant saving it from being destroyed and forgotten.

Thanks to this daring, almost reckless act, two indelible works have reached us that have shaped our vision of the world. The fifteen thousand lines of *The Iliad* and the twelve thousand of *The Odyssey* that we now read as if they were novels occupy a liminal space between orality and the new world. Their author, a poet who acquired fluency with recitation but had contact with written culture, wove several traditional cantos together into a coherent plot. Was this figure on the threshold between two worlds someone called Homer? We'll never know. Every scholar imagines their own Homer: an illiterate bard in ancient times; the person responsible for the definitive versions of *The Iliad* and *The Odyssey*; a poet who gave them their finishing touches; a diligent copyist who signed the texts with his name; an editor seduced by the outlandish invention of books—air in written form. It never ceases to fascinate me that an author so essential to our culture should be no more than a ghost.

With the scant information available, it's impossible to shed light on the mystery. Homer's shadow vanishes in the mists of time. And this makes *The Iliad* and *The Odyssey* all the more fascinating: these exceptional documents allow us to come close to a world of winged tales and words that were lost forever.

33

You, the reader of this book, lived for a few years in an oral world. From your earliest babbling as a baby until you learned to read, words only existed for you as the sound of a voice. All around, you saw the mute drawings of letters, but they meant nothing to you. The grown-ups who ran the world were the ones who read and wrote. You didn't know what they were doing, but it mattered little—it was enough that you could speak. The first stories you ever heard came in through the shells of your ears; your eyes didn't yet know how to listen. Then came school with its downstrokes, loops, letters, syllables. The same transition from oral to written culture that humanity underwent took place on a smaller scale inside you.

Every night, sitting on the edge of my bed, my mother read books to me. She was the rhapsodist and I her captivated audience. The place, time, gestures, and silences were always the same—it was our own private ritual. As her eyes sought the place she had left off reading, she went back a few sentences to pick up the thread of the story, and all the day's troubles and all the fears that might come in the night were carried away on the tale's soft breeze. The time we spent reading seemed to me a small, impermanent paradise. I have since learned that every paradise is like that: modest and fleeting.

Her voice. I listened to her voice as she helped me imagine the sounds of the story she told: the splash of water against the hull of a boat, the soft crunch of snow underfoot, the clash of two swords, an arrow whistling through the air, mysterious steps, wolves howling, whispers behind a door. We felt so close, my mother and I, together in two places at once, closer than ever but split between parallel dimensions—outside and in, a clock ticking in the bedroom for half an hour while years went by in the story, at once alone and surrounded by many people as we befriended and spied on the characters.

One by one, I lost my milk teeth during those years. My favorite thing to do while she told me stories was to wiggle a dangling tooth with my finger, feel it detach from its root, come looser and looser, and, when it finally fell out with a few salty strands of blood, gaze at it in the palm of my hand. My childhood was breaking apart, leaving gaps in my body and little white shards behind me. The time for listening to stories would soon be over, though I didn't yet know it.

And when we came to an especially thrilling episode—a chase, a nearby assassin, an imminent discovery, a sign of betrayal—my mother would cough and feign a sore throat. This was the agreed-upon signal for the first interruption. *I can't go on reading.* Then I had to beg in despair: *No, don't stop here, keep going just a bit longer. I'm tired. Please, please.* We would act out this little scene, and then she would continue. Of course, I knew she was tricking me, but I was always afraid. In the end, one of the interruptions would be for real, and she would close the book, give me a kiss, leave me alone in the dark, and give herself over to that secret life lived by grown-ups at night—those thrilling, mysterious, longed-for nights, that foreign, forbidden land. The closed book remained on the nightstand, stubborn and quiet, leaving me exiled from the camps of the Yukon or the shores of the Mississippi, or the Château d'If, or the Admiral Benbow Inn, the Mountain of Souls, the jungle of Misiones, Lake Maracaibo, Benya Krik's neighborhood in Odessa, Ventimiglia, Nevsky Prospeckt, the island of Barataria, Shelob's lair in the borderlands of Mordor, the moorland by Baskerville Hall, Nizhny Novgorod, the Castle of No Return, Sherwood Forest, Frankenstein's laboratory, Baron Cosimo's trees in Ombrosa, the Little Prince's planet, the château of Yvonne de Galais, Fagin's den, the island of Ithaca. And though I might open the book in the right place, saved by the bookmark, it was no use, since I would see only lines full of spiders' legs that refused to reveal to me even a paltry word. Without my mother's voice, I could not conjure the magic. To read was to cast a spell, to coax speech from the pages of books that in those days seemed to me like enormous paper anthills.

34

The cliché would have us believe that oral cultures are primitive, simple, and tribal. If today we measure a country's progress by its literacy rates, it's hardly surprising that we project our notion of backwardness onto that ancient society. But we know that's not how it was. At least, not necessarily. The Inca culture of Peru, for example, conquered and governed a powerful empire without the help of writing (except for a system of messages conveyed by knotted cords, or quipus) and still created its own art and architecture on a colossal scale that every year draws hordes of tourists to the Andean heights of Cuzco and Machu Picchu.

Of course, the absence of writing was a cultural disadvantage. The greater the complexity achieved by oral societies, the more constant and distressing the threat of its being forgotten became. Inhabitants of these societies needed to preserve their laws, beliefs, discoveries, and technical knowledge—their identity. If they failed to pass on their achievements, each generation would have to start again, laboriously, from scratch. But they could communicate only through a system of echoes, as light and fleeting as air. Their sole hope of surviving the ravages of time was found in the frail human memory, so they trained their memories to hold as much as they possibly could, becoming athletes of recollection and fighting the limits of their own minds.

In their effort to endure, denizens of the oral world realized that rhythmic language was easiest to remember, and on the wings of this discovery, poetry was born. During recitation, the melody helps the speaker repeat each line without alteration, since it is when the music is broken that the sequence falters. All of us were made to learn poems in school. Years later, after forgetting so many other things, we find we can still remember these poems with extraordinary clarity.

It's no coincidence that in Greek mythology, the Muses were daughters of the goddess Mnemosyne, the origin of the word "mnemonic" and the personification of remembering and evocation. At that time, as in all times, no one could create if they couldn't remember. Despite their radical differences, if the oral bard and the postmodern writer have anything in common, it's the way they see their work as one version out of many possible ones, an act of nostalgia, a translation, and a constant repurposing of the past.

Rhythm isn't just an ally of memory; it also sparks pleasure. Dance, music, and sex all play with repetition, tempo, and cadence. Language also has infinite rhythmic possibilities. Greek epic flows in hexameters, which create a singular acoustic rhythm through combinations of long and short syllables. Hebrew verse, on the other hand, is more prone to syntactic rhythms: "There is a time for everything, and a season for every activity under the heavens: a time to be born and a time to die, a time to plant and a time to uproot, a time to kill and a time to heal, a time to tear down and a time to build." We might say that these verses from Ecclesiastes sing. Indeed, Pete Seeger wrote a song based on them that became a hit in 1965, "Turn! Turn! Turn! (To Everything There Is a Season)." In poetry's early days, the joy of rhythm served the continuity of culture.

Along with the music of language, other strategies for the preservation of memory were discovered. Oral poems passed on their lessons through stories full of action rather than through reflection; abstract phrases belong to written language. No poet would ever have said anything as pedestrian as "lies undermine trust." Instead, they would have told the story of the mischievous shepherd boy who enjoyed alarming the villagers by crying wolf. In the preliterate world, there was always some kind of adventure afoot, and characters made mistakes and suffered in their fictional guises so that the community could learn a lesson. When experience took the form of a story—as a legend, tale, fable, example, joke, prediction, or memory—it gained new meaning and could be passed on. The fantasy world of orality imagined stories full of vitality and movement in which the living rubbed shoulders with the dead, humans with gods, and embodied beings with ghosts. There, the connection between heaven, Earth, and hell allowed for a path of eternal return. Traditional tales even humanized animals, rivers, trees, the moon, and the snow, as if all of nature wished to join in the joyful and dizzying narrative. Today, children's literature maintains this ancient pleasure in exuberant action and the gleeful coexistence of talking animals and children.

Like the lost poems of that era, *The Iliad* and *The Odyssey* were, in the words of Eric A. Havelock, oral encyclopedias for the Greeks that compiled their inherited wisdom. With enthralling and forceful rhythm, they told the myth of the Trojan War, followed by the Greek conquerors' difficult journey home. The plot, drama, and adventure seized the audience's attention. And within the story, camouflaged by the rushing river of action, brief lessons were couched one after the other in clusters of lines ready to be memorized. Whoever listened to the poems as they were recited learned about navigation, agriculture, methods of building boats or houses, rules for holding a meeting, making a group decision, arming oneself for battle, or preparing for a burial. They absorbed how a warrior should behave in battle, how to speak to a priest, how to announce a challenge or make up for an offense, how to behave in the home, what the gods expect from mortals, what the law dictates, customs, and the code of honor. In Homeric verse, the narrator isn't a rebellious, bohemian individual expressing his originality, but the collective voice of a tribe.

Among these inherited teachings, we find valuable doses of ancient wisdom, but also expressions of oppressive ideology. In the first canto of *The Odyssey*, Telemachus tells his mother, Penelope, to be quiet, without thinking twice: "Mother, go to your chamber, think of your work at the loom, and watch over your slaves and their chores. Speech is for men, and most of all for me. I am the master of this palace." When we read this episode today, we're taken aback by the curtness of this youth beginning to claim his manhood, who wants to take charge of the home, relegating his mother to toil at the spinning wheel. But the poet approves of this early assertion of male dominance in the mouth of Odysseus's young son and offers it to his audience as an example. As far as the Greeks were concerned, speech belonged to men: it was their prerogative alone. In *The Iliad*, Zeus himself scolds his wife, Hera, during a banquet for trying to coax his intentions out of him, humiliating her in public by coarsely telling her in solemn epic hexameters to "shut up." With their words and actions, Homer's characters constantly offered models of conduct in the home, where the head of the family was lord and master.

Later on in *The Iliad* is an example of classism, also associated with the burning question of who is entitled to the use of words. When Thersites, a man of the people—the only commoner to appear in the poem, described as the ugliest of all the Greeks who fought at Troy—dares to use his voice at the assembly of warriors, Odysseus beats him with a scepter and commands him to let his betters speak: in other words, the kings and generals. Despite this affront, the rebellious Thersites has enough pluck to make a radical speech criticizing King Agamemnon's ambition: "Son of Atreus, why do you complain again? Your tents are overflowing with wealth and women. It is not right for a captain to bring ruin upon his warriors." The poem describes how Odysseus wounds the lame and foulmouthed Thersites, while the soldiers who gather around and watch the scene applaud, cheer, and guffaw. ("Odysseus beat his back and shoulders with his staff. Thersites cowered and a tear rolled down his face. A bloody bruise from the golden staff appeared upon his back, and he sat down and was overcome with fear.")

While we enjoy the Homeric epic with its captivating power and moments of overwhelming beauty, we should be wary and remember that the poem is a product of a world governed by patriarchal aristocracy, which the author extols without ever questioning its values. The idea of telling a story in a free and transgressive way is foreign to an era when poets were guardians of tradition. It wasn't until the invention of books and writing that some authors—always in the minority—began to speak with the voice of the rebels, the disobedient, the humiliated and aggrieved, the silenced women, the ugly and the downtrodden. Those like Thersites.

35

It's a great paradox: we come from a lost world we can only glimpse when it disappears. Our image of orality comes from books. We gain our familiarity with winged words through their opposite, words fixed in writing and therefore made motionless. Once transcribed, these stories lost their fluidity, their flexibility, the freedom of improvisation, and, in many cases, their characteristic language forever. For this legacy to be saved, it had to be mortally wounded.

It is wounded yet remains fascinating. The wealth of imagination at the dawn of our culture has survived without fully fading into the mists of time. We hear its distant echoes in the transcription of mythologies, fables, sagas, folk songs, and traditional tales. Transformed, recast, reinterpreted, we find it in *The Iliad* and *The Odyssey*, the Greek tragedies, the Torah (and the Old Testament), *The Ramayana, The Edda,* and *The Thousand and One Nights.* And it's precisely these exiled stories—literary refugees in the foreign land of written texts—that make up the backbone of our culture.

When the Muse learned to write, in Havelock's words, extraordinary changes were set in motion. No longer subject to the economy of memory, new texts could begin to multiply and became infinitely varied. The storehouse of knowledge was no longer only acoustic but became a material archive that could therefore broaden its scope. Literature gained the freedom to expand in all directions; it no longer had to stake out a patch in the limited space of memory. And this freedom also permeated the stories' subjects and points of view. Unlike orality, which favored traditional forms and ideas that its audience could recognize, literacy could open unknown horizons, since the reader had time to absorb and meditate calmly on new ideas. Books have room for eccentric proposals, individual voices, and challenges to tradition.

When it left orality behind, language underwent architectural adjustments. Syntax developed new logical structures, and vocabulary became more abstract. In addition, literature found new paths beyond the discipline of verse. Like Molière's bourgeois gentleman, who one fine day realized he'd been speaking in prose for forty years unawares, the Greek authors found that their characters no longer had to hold their dialogues in hexameters.

Prose became the vehicle for an astonishing world of facts and theories. Innovative linguistic formulations provided more space for thought. This broadening of perspectives gave rise to history, philosophy, and science. To describe his intellectual labor, Aristotle chose the word *theoría* and the corresponding verb *theoreîn*, which in Greek refer to the act of looking at something. This choice is highly revealing: the job of thinking about the world exists thanks to books and reading—in other words, once we could see words and think slowly about them, instead of just hearing them in the torrent of uttered speech.

All of these transformations came about slowly. We tend to imagine that new inventions quickly sweep away old habits, but such processes aren't measured at the speed of light so much as the growth of stalactites. Little by little, like drops sliding down stone and leaving fine trickles of calcite behind them, the written word gave rise to new kinds of awareness and mindsets. The departure from orality in ancient Greece took place over a period that spanned from the eighth to the fourth century BC. Around this time, Aristotle compiled an extensive collection of books, inspired by the ambitious Library of Alexandria. Strictly speaking, he was the first European man of letters.

In fact, we should speak not of substitution but of a curious bond between orality and written language, a delicate interweaving. For example, ironically, children in Greek schools learned to read with *The Iliad* and *The Odyssey*. Homer's place in education was always central; just as in the times of the oral encyclopedia, he remained the indisputable master and teacher of all of Hellas. On the other hand, great storytellers and skilled speechmakers undoubtedly continued to dazzle the Greeks, as their inexhaustible passion for rhetoric shows. In general, the political leadership of city-states fell upon those with a gift for verbal eloquence. Contrary to the division in the medieval world between feudal lords with more brawn than brains and the lettered men who served as their scribes, such a distinction never existed among the Greeks, who worshipped effective oratory sprinkled with expressive wit in their political leaders. The comic stereotype of the ancient world always represents them as full of importunate prattle. Owing to their unbridled love of words and their passion for debate, the Romans who conquered Greece considered them unredeemed charlatans.

If we listen carefully, we can still hear the echo of winged words in tragic choruses, in Pindar's hymns, in the story-filled *Histories* Herodotus wrote, and in Plato's dialogues. At the same time, all of these works have a novel slant in their language and individual consciousness. As usual, there was neither a complete rupture nor absolute continuity. Even the most innovative literary work always contains fragments and traces of countless earlier texts.

The case of Socrates presents a striking blend of the old and the new. Socrates, a small-scale craftsman, spent his life lurking around gymnasiums, workshops, and the Athenian agora, striking up philosophical conversations with whoever wished to stop and talk. His taste for wandering chatter and his indifference to home, in addition to making his marriage to Xanthippe a miserable one, won him fame as an eccentric. A formidable conversationalist, he refused to write down his teachings. He accused books of getting in the way of the dialogue of ideas, since the written word couldn't respond to the reader's questions or objections. No doubt he felt closer to ancient bards who lived in the open air than to pallid writers with dark circles under their eyes. But despite this, the Muse of philosophy, who seduced Socrates and inspired his gleeful unemployment, was a daughter of the written word. In the world of traditions, a character such as him, with his humble origins and striking ugliness—he was short, with a protuberant belly and a flat nose—would never have had the right to speak in public and was more likely to suffer the same fate as Thersites. Yet in the enlightened Athens of the time, the aristocrats not only passed up the chance to beat him in public but showed him respect and footed the bill for his roaming philosophical activities.

Socrates wasn't the only great thinker who, at the crossroads of communication, refrained from writing. Just like him, Pythagoras,

Diogenes, the Buddha, and Jesus of Nazareth all opted for orality. Yet all of them knew how to read and write. In the Gospel of John, just before launching his famous challenge ("Let he who is without sin cast the first stone"), Jesus crouches down and writes in the sand with a finger. John doesn't reveal the content of the phrase—perhaps the wind swept away a maxim as memorable as the last, or perhaps it was simply a list of errands—but what's significant is that the whole scene can be read at all. The disciples took on the task at which their mentors had sneered, and thanks to the apostles' chronicles, a clear picture of their passage through the world exists. Although those teachers took the side of orality, books became the decisive vehicle for spreading their message. When memory was the only repository of words, dissident ideas had little chance of surviving beyond a small circle of followers.

It's important to add some nuance: in the new era of writing, orality lost its monopoly over words but did not disappear; in fact, it remains alive inside us all. Until the twentieth century, those who knew how to read were a minority in all societies, and today, hundreds of millions of the world's people remain illiterate. Anthropologists know that the voice of myths and songs never fully fell silent. In the interwar period, Harvard University researcher Milman Parry went to the Balkans to witness epic recitations in the style of Homer and try to untangle the Homeric enigma. To his amazement, the story of his scientific journey itself became a new saga in the ancient style. In 1933, an illiterate bard performed a song that elevated the philologist to the unexpected rank of mythic hero: "A grey falcon flew / From the beautiful land of America. / He flew over lands and cities / Until he came to the shore of the sea. / . . . / Our history will speak of him / And remember him for many ages." Another American researcher, Hiram Bingham, who a couple of decades later brought attention to the existence of Machu Picchu, would enter the popular imagination as a kind of Indiana Jones, wielding his famous whip. For a brief period, a handful of university professors obtained a place on the list of heroes in the world of epic.

Though it may seem paradoxical, orality owes some enormous triumphs to technological progress. In ancient times, the power of the human voice could only reach those who were physically present.

The radio and telephone did away with those limitations: now, the sound of both solemn speeches and daily chatter can reach everyone in the world. With the proliferation of cell phones and telecommunications service, our words travel from one end of the Earth to another, their wingspan wider than ever.

Film, which in the beginning was silent, keenly embraced the transition to sound. During the silent era, cinemas employed the curious figure of the film explainer, who belonged to the ancient tribe of the rhapsodes, troubadours, puppeteers, and storytellers. Their job was to act as a kind of host, reading the intertitles to the illiterate audience. In the early days, their presence had a calming effect, since people were often alarmed the first time they saw a film. It was a mystery to them how a road—or a factory, a train, a city, the world—could emerge from a screen made of a sheet. When moving pictures entered our lives, explainers helped make them seem less uncanny. They came equipped with gadgets such as horns, ratchets, and coconut shells to reproduce the sounds represented on-screen. They drew the audience's attention to characters with a pointer. They responded to exclamations and improvised stirring monologues based on the action. They interpreted and enlivened the silent plot. They prompted laughter. Their role was ultimately to fill the unsettling void left by the absence of voices. The most entertaining and eloquent explainers were announced by name in the programs since many viewers were drawn to the cinema by them and not by the films.

Heigo Kurosawa was a much-admired *benshi*, a narrator of silent films for audiences in Japan. He shot to stardom, and people came to listen to him in droves. He introduced his younger brother Akira, who in those days wanted to be a painter, to the film world in Tokyo. In around 1930, with the dizzying arrival of sound, the *benshi* lost their jobs, their fame was eclipsed, and they were forgotten. Heigo killed himself in 1933. Akira spent his life directing films like the ones he learned to love through his older brother's voice.

36

While I am engrossed in the last chapter, absorbed in the distant voices of ancient times, a wave of contemporary chatter reaches me. The unprecedented news has triggered a torrent of commentary; social networks are abuzz with irony and indignation. Amid a chorus of "Seriously?" and "It was about time," the controversy rises to a crescendo. Newspapers and radio stations consult the usual experts. Twitter keeps spewing the latest outrageous news: the Swedish Academy has awarded the Nobel Prize in Literature to Bob Dylan.

I watch, amused by the media circus composed both of those who find it calamitous and those who are in favor. Enthusiasts rejoice that elitism and literary snobbery have finally gone up in smoke. The indignant are not convinced by the faux edginess of the musty Nobel committee. They suspect that there is no intention here to demystify or expand the criteria that make one a writer, nor any defeat of the gatekeepers who demand a visa for entry into the hallowed terrain of literature. Instead they see simple opportunism and thirst for public impact. The most furious prefer to call it a trivialization and wonder, scandalized, what will be next. After the singer-songwriter's triumph, will the sanctum sanctorum of the academy be overrun by a pack of illegitimate children of language—film and television scriptwriters, comic authors, designers of video games and multimedia projects, Twitter epigrammists? Are these the literary tribes of the future?

I'm consumed by the book I'm writing and think of Homer. I think of the multitudes of itinerant bards hidden behind his name. They came first. They sang for the rich in their palaces and the poor in the village plazas. In those days, being a poet meant walking along dusty roads in worn-out sandals, an instrument slung over your shoulder, performing at nightfall, feeling the rhythm course through your body. Those wandering artists dressed in rags, sent by the Muses, those wise bohemians who explained the way of the world in song—half encyclopedists, half jesters—are the ancestors of writers. Their poetry came before prose, and their music before silent reading.

A Nobel Prize for oral culture. How ancient the future can sometimes be.

37

When I was a little girl, I believed that books had been written for me, that the only copy in the world was the one in my house. I was completely convinced of this: my parents, at that time generous, all-powerful giants, had in their free time made up the tales they told me. As I savored them in bed, huddled under the blanket pulled up to my chin, my favorite stories read in my mother's unmistakable voice clearly existed only so that I could hear them. And they fulfilled their only purpose when I demanded of the giant storyteller, "More!"

I may have grown up, but my relationship with books is still very self-centered. When a story takes hold of me, when its shower of words seeps through me and I reach an almost painful understanding of what it tells, I'm convinced in my own private way that the author has changed my life, and once again I believe that I, and especially I, am the reader for whom that book was searching.

I've never asked anyone else if they have a similar feeling. In my case, it all goes back to the realm of childhood, and the essential reason for this, I believe, is that my first contact with literature was hearing it read aloud. It was a crossroads where all of time flows together—the present of writing, the past of orality; a small theater with only one spectator; a faithful lover; a liberating prayer. If someone reads to you aloud, they want you to experience pleasure; it's an act of love and a truce in the midst of life's battles. While you listen as if in a dream, the book and the reader fuse into a single presence, a single voice. And just as your reader varies their tone for you, their subtle smiles, their silences and their gaze, the story also rightfully becomes yours alone. You'll never forget the person who told you a good story in the shadows of night.

A woman listens to her young lover read to her at their every tryst. I'm fascinated by these moments described in *The Reader* by Bernhard Schlink. It all begins with *The Odyssey*, which the young man translated in his Greek classes in high school. Read it to me, she says. You have such a beautiful voice. When he leans in to kiss her, she withdraws: First you have to read me something. From that day on, the ritual of their encounters always involves reading. For half an hour—before they shower, have sex, or anything else—in the intimacy of desire, the young man unspools stories while his lover, Hanna, listens with rapt attention, sometimes laughing, sometimes snorting with disdain, sometimes crying out in anger. Through all the months and books—Schiller, Goethe, Tolstoy, Dickens—this boy with a faltering voice learns the skills of a true storyteller. When summer comes and the days grow longer, they give over even more time to reading. One sweltering summer's day, when they have just finished a book, Hanna refuses to start another. It's the last time they meet. A few days later, the boy arrives at the usual time and rings the bell, but the house is empty. She has suddenly disappeared without any explanation—the end of their reading is the end of their story. For years, he can't see a book without thinking of sharing it with her.

Sometime later, while studying law at a German university, he chances upon the dark story of his former lover: she worked as a guard at a Nazi concentration camp. There, too, she made the imprisoned women read to her, night after night, before herding them onto the train that would carry them to Auschwitz and certain death. As he connects the dots thanks to particular clues, it dawns on him that Hanna is illiterate. He reconstructs the story of a young, uneducated woman from the country, accustomed to menial work, drunk on the power of her position at a women's camp near Krakow. Seen in this new light, Hanna's harshness, which sometimes verges on cruelty, is explained, as are her silences, her inexplicable reactions, her thirst to be read to aloud, her marginalization, her efforts to hide her real self, her isolation. The young student's erotic memories become tinged with horror, but despite this he decides to record *The Odyssey* on cassettes and send them to her in jail to relieve her loneliness. While Hanna serves her long sentence, he sends her recordings of Chekhov, Kafka, Max Frisch, Fontane. Trapped in a labyrinth of guilt, fear, memory, and love, the couple take shelter in their old refuge of reading aloud. Those years of shared tales revive the thousand and one nights when Scheherazade calmed the bloodlust of the murderous sultan with her stories. Survivors of the catastrophe of the Second World War, the wounds of Europe still fresh, the protagonist and Hanna return to the old stories in search of absolution, in search of a cure, and in search of peace.

THE ALPHABET

A Peaceful Revolution

38

In the twenty-first century, we take for granted that everyone learns to read and write as a child. It seems an accessible skill, within anyone's reach. It's hard to imagine there might be illiterate people like Hanna among us.

But they exist. (There were 670,000 in Spain in 2016, according to the National Statistics Institute.) I knew an illiterate person. I witnessed her impotence in daily situations like getting her bearings in the street, finding the right train platform, deciphering the electricity bill (though I wonder if any of us who know how to read really understand them), finding the right voting ballot, ordering at a restaurant. Only familiar places and routines allayed her anxiety in a world she couldn't navigate like other people. She dedicated an exhausting amount of effort to hiding her illiteracy ("I left my glasses at home, could you read this to me?"), and in the end, the need to pretend cut her off from normal relationships. I especially remember the sense of helplessness, the repertoire of white lies needed to ask strangers for help without feeling ashamed, without feeling like a perpetual minor. In *La Cérémonie*, the director Claude Chabrol captured the dark and troubling side of this silent exclusion, depicting the repressed violence of an illiterate protagonist whose name, ironically, is Sophie. The film is based on the Ruth Rendell mystery *A Judgment in Stone*, which describes an illiterate woman's desperate—and ultimately bloody—obsession with keeping her secret.

We read more than ever. We are surrounded by signs, posters, publicity, screens, documents. The streets overflow with words, from graffiti on the walls to glowing advertisements. They flicker across our smartphones and computer screens. Texts in a range of forms coexist with us in our homes like calm companion animals. There have never been so many of them. Our days are filled with constant flurries of letters and the pings that announce their arrival. We devote several hours of our workday and leisure time to tapping on various keyboards. When we have to fill out a form at a window, no one is ever thoughtful enough to ask if we know how to read. Even in the most commonplace situations we would be shut out if we couldn't write quickly.

The poet Ana María Moix once told me that one day in the seventies, she arranged to have lunch with the prodigious brood of writers of the Latin American Boom: Mario Vargas Llosa, Gabriel García Márquez, Alfredo Bryce Echenique, José Donoso, Jorge Edwards . . . They went to a restaurant in Barcelona where you had to write down your order and hand it to the waiter. They soon started drinking and talking and forgot all about the menu, pretending not to notice the waiters' attempts to get their attention. In the end, the *maître* had to interrupt, annoyed by such lively chatter and so little interest in food. He approached without recognizing them and asked irately, "Doesn't anyone here know how to write?"

Today, we take for granted that the vast majority of people around us can read and write. But behind this lies an epic journey that is centuries long. Just like with computers, writing was at first the exclusive preserve of a handful of experts. A series of simplifications has allowed billions of people to use these tools in their daily lives. This progression—which in the case of computers was achieved in just a few decades—took thousands of years in the history of writing. Rapid change wasn't a typical feature of ancient times.

Six thousand years ago, the first written symbols appeared in Mesopotamia, but the origins of this invention are enveloped in silence and mystery. Later, writing was independently born in Egypt, India, and China. According to the most recent theories, the art of writing had a practical origin: property lists. These hypotheses assert that our ancestors learned numbers ahead of letters. Writing was introduced to solve the problems of wealthy proprietors and palace administrators who needed to keep records, since it was difficult to do their accounting orally. The transcription of legends and stories would come later. Humans, then, are economic and symbolic beings.

We began with written inventories and only later developed written inventions (first came accounting, and then accounts).

The first things noted down were simple diagrams (an ox head, a tree, a jar of oil, a small man). With these sketches, ancient landowners took inventories of their flocks, their forests, their storehouses, and their slaves. At first, they pressed those shapes onto clay with small stamps; later they traced them with objects like quills. The drawings tended to be simple and standardized, so they could be learned and deciphered. The next step was to draw abstract ideas. On primitive Sumerian tablets, a cross described enmity, two parallel lines, friendship, a duck with an egg, fertility. I like to imagine our ancestors savoring the excitement of capturing their thoughts for the first time, when they discovered that love, hate, terror, discouragement, and hope could be put in writing.

They soon encountered a problem: too many drawings were needed to give an account of the outer and inner worlds—from fleas to clouds, toothache to fear of dying. The number of symbols increased without end, overloading the memory. The solution was one of humanity's greatest strokes of genius. It was simple, original, and had incalculable consequences: to stop drawing representations of things and ideas, which are infinite, and start drawing the sounds of words, which make up a limited range. Thus, through a series of simplifications, letters arrived. By combining letters, we have achieved the most perfect script for language, and the most enduring. But letters never left their past as simple diagrams behind. Our "D" at first represented a door, "M" the movement of water, "N" was a snake, and "O" an eye. Even today, our texts are landscapes where, unbeknownst to us, we paint the ocean's waves, where dangerous animals lie in wait and eyes gaze at us without blinking.

39

Primitive writing systems were genuine labyrinths of symbols. They combined figurative drawings—pictograms and ideograms—with phonetic signs, differentiating marks that helped resolve ambiguities. It took knowing up to a thousand symbols and all their complex combinations to master writing. This marvelously intricate knowledge lay within reach for only a select minority of scribes, who were members of a secret and privileged profession. Apprentices of noble origin had to undergo a ruthless training process. One Egyptian text reads, "A young man's ear is in his back; he only listens when beaten!" In schools for scribes, young men with their backs crisscrossed with scars were toughened by years of violent discipline. Slacking off was not tolerated, and poor students could even be punished with imprisonment. But if they could withstand the cruelty and monotony of their studies, they climbed to the very top of the religious hierarchy. Those who mastered the art of writing made up an aristocracy sometimes more powerful than that of illiterate courtiers or even the monarch himself. The result of this training system was that for centuries, writing only gave a voice to established power.

The invention of the alphabet broke down barriers and opened doors that allowed many people, and not just a conclave of initiates, to gain access to written thought. This revolution took shape among the Semitic peoples. With the complex Egyptian system as their point of departure, they devised an extraordinarily simple formula, retaining only the signs representing simple consonants, the basic architecture of words. The most ancient traces of the alphabet were found on a rocky wall covered in graffiti, near a barren highway in Wadi el-Hol ("Ravine of Terror"), between Abydos and Thebes in Upper Egypt. These simple inscriptions made by migrants, which date to the year 1850 BC, are related to the ancient alphabetic writing of the Sinai Peninsula and the Canaanite territory of Syria Palaestina. Around 1250 BC, the Phoenicians—Canaanites who lived in coastal cities like Byblos, Tyre, Sidon, Beirut, and Ashkelon, developed a system of twenty-two signs. The ancient writing systems that required specialist training only accessible to privileged minds and were a burdensome load on the memory were left behind. To an Egyptian scribe accustomed to using hundreds of signs, using fewer than thirty letters to represent all the words in the language would seem a coarse method. He would have sneered and raised his eyebrows at our uninspiring "E," derived from a beautiful Egyptian hieroglyph—a man lifting his arms—which bore the poetic meaning: "Your presence brings joy." Yet for astute Phoenician sailors, the matter was entirely different: simplified alphabetic writing freed merchants from the grip of the scribe. Thanks to the alphabet, anyone could keep their own records and run their own business.

The expansive benefits of this invention didn't just affect merchants. For many beyond the circles of government and far from the guardians of orthodoxy, writing gave access to traditional stories for the first time, allowing them to distance themselves from the bewitching power of orality and, most importantly, to begin to doubt them. This was how literature and the critical spirit were born. Certain individuals dared to leave a trace of their feelings, their skepticism, their own vision of life. Little by little, books became a vehicle for individual expression. In Israel, the voices of belligerent prophets, who weren't necessarily scribes or priests, burst forth in the Bible; in Greece, people who weren't aristocratic by birth became curious seekers of answers to explain the world around them. Though rebels and revolutionaries were no better off than before, their ideals now had a chance of surviving them and being spread. Thanks to the alphabet, a number of lost causes have found success over time. Even if most written texts kept bolstering the power of kings and lords, certain spaces opened up to rebellious voices. Traditions were no longer completely set in stone. New ideas shook up musty social structures.

Around 1000 BC, we find Phoenician script on the sarcophagus of Ahiram, the king of Byblos (present day Jubayl), which was a city famous for exporting papyrus and the source of the Greek word for book: *biblíon*. All later branches of alphabetic writing descend from this Phoenician system. The most important was the Aramaic system, which gave rise to the Hebrew, Arabic, and Indian families. The Greek alphabet was also derived from this same mold, as was the Latin alphabet, which took root in the lands stretching from Scandinavia to the Mediterranean, and the swaths of territory previously colonized by the West.

40

The Greeks adopted the Phoenician writing system completely freely; it was not imposed. They adapted the invention to their needs and, at the leisurely pace of a change that was desired, set their most beloved oral traditions down in writing, saving them from the fragility of memory. They enjoyed the same independence in their alphabetic life as in their period of orality. This was an exceptional case. Many oral cultures have ended with a sudden collision, surrounded or conquered by peoples who have enforced the use of their language and the written word. Anthropologists and ethnologists have found living witnesses of this shift toward writing in colonized countries, where the introduction of the alphabet alongside the trauma of invasion is shot through with a trail of violence.

The Nigerian author Chinua Achebe's novel *No Longer at Ease* considers this conflicted love of invading letters. After the landing of the Westerners and the first glimpses of the annihilation of the millenarian culture into which they were born, the characters in this story are fascinated by the discovery of writing. At the same time, they have a painful sense that in the hands of the colonizers, this magical tool would have the power to deprive them of their own past. The foreign civilization holds the spell to perpetuate itself. Meanwhile, the indigenous world begins to crumble:

> And the symbol of the white man's power was the
> written word, or better still, the printed word. Once before
> he went to England, Obi heard his father talk with deep
> feeling about the mystery of the written word to an illiterate
> kinsman: "Our women made black patterns on their bodies
> with the juice of the *uli* tree. It was beautiful, but it soon
> faded. If it lasted two market weeks it lasted a long time.
> But sometimes our elders spoke about *uli* that never faded,
> although no one had ever seen it. We see it today in the
> writing of the white man. If you go to the native court and
> look at the books which clerks wrote twenty years ago or
> more, they are still as they wrote them. They do not say
> one thing today and another tomorrow, or one thing this

year and another next year. Okoye in the book today cannot become Okonkwo tomorrow. In the Bible Pilate said: 'What is written is written.' It is *uli* that never fades."

41

We don't know his name, or where he lived, or for how long. I say "him" because I imagine him as a man. Greek women of the era did not have freedom of movement; the independence and initiative needed to do such a thing was forbidden to them.

He lived in the eighth century BC, twenty-nine centuries ago. He changed my world. As I write these lines, I am grateful to this forgotten stranger whose intelligence made an extraordinary breakthrough, though he was perhaps unaware of the significance of his discovery. I imagine him as a traveler, perhaps an islander. I'm sure he was a friend to weather-beaten, bronze-faced Phoenician merchants. He must have drunk with them in port taverns by night, inhaling the salty air that mingled with steam rising from a plate of cuttlefish on the table as he listened to seafaring tales. Boats tossed on stormy seas, waves towering like mountains, shipwrecks, strange coasts, mysterious women's voices piercing the night. But what fascinated him most of all was a seemingly humble, unheroic talent. How did these simple merchants write so quickly?

The Greeks had encountered writing at the height of Cretan civilization and the Mycenaean kingdoms, with their constellations of arcane signs, in service only of palace accounting. These were syllabic systems of great complexity and limited, elitist use. Periods of pillage and invasion, along with the poverty of recent centuries, had almost plunged those labyrinths of signs into oblivion. For him, for whom the art of writing was a symbol of power, the quick strokes made by Phoenician sailors were a revelation. It was amazing, dizzying. He wanted to know their secret. He decided to decipher the mysteries of the written word.

He found himself a lettered informant, or several, perhaps paying them from his own purse. The place where these meetings happened was probably an island (the most likely candidates are Thera, commonly known as Santorini, Melos, and Cyprus), or even the

Lebanese coast (for example, the port of El Mina, where Euboean merchants had constant contact with the Phoenicians). From his impromptu teachers, he learned to use the magical tool that allowed the stamp of infinite words to be captured with just twenty-two simple drawings. He could appreciate the boldness of this invention. At the same time, he discovered that Phoenician writing contained certain riddles: only the consonants of each syllable were written down, leaving the task of guessing the vowels to the reader. The Phoenicians had sacrificed precision for the sake of greater ease.

Drawing on the Phoenician model, he invented his own language for the Greeks, the first alphabet in history with no ambiguities, as precise as a musical score. He began his adaptation based on fifteen Phoenician consonantal signs, in the same order, and with similar names ("aleph," "bet," "gimel" . . . became "alpha," "beta," and "gamma" . . .). He took letters of no use in his language, the so-called weak consonants, and used them for five vowels, the bare minimum required. He innovated only where he could improve on the original. It was an immense achievement. Thanks to him, a new, improved alphabet spread through Europe, with all the advantages of the Phoenician discovery and an added stroke of progress: reading ceased to be based on conjecture, and it therefore became even more accessible. Imagine what it would be like to read this sentence without any vowels: mgn wht t wld b lk t rd ths sntnc wtht ny vwls. Think for a moment how hard it is to identify the word "idea" based only on the consonant "d," or "air" from only an "r."

We know nothing about this stranger; all that we have is the extraordinary tool he left us. His identity is a footprint erased by the waves, yet there's no doubt that he existed. Experts believe that the invention of the Greek alphabet wasn't an anonymous process in the hands of a nameless, faceless collective. It was a deliberate and individual act of intelligence that required immense auditory sophistication to identify the basic parts—consonants and vowels—that make up words. A single achievement carried out at a specific time, in a single place. There is no indication in the history of Greek writing of a gradual transition from a less to a more complete system. Nor is there any trace of intermediate forms, attempts made, vacillations or retreats. There was simply an anonymous wise man—we'll never know who—frequenting taverns till dawn, a friend to foreign sailors in some place lapped by the sea's waves who dared to forge the words of the future, giving shape to all the letters we use. And we still write today, essentially, just as the creator of this prodigious tool imagined.

42

Thanks to the alphabet, writing changed hands. In the age of the Mycenaean palaces, a limited group of experts and scribes kept royal accounting records on clay tablets. These monotonous inventories of wealth are the only written record of the period. In Greece in the eighth century BC, on the other hand, the new invention revealed a different view of the period. The first alphabetic remains of which we are aware appeared on ceramic vessels or on stone. The words the potters and carvers engraved no longer speak of sales and possessions—slaves, bronze, weapons, horses, oil, or livestock. They memorialize special moments in the lives of common people who participate in banquets, and who drink, dance, and celebrate their pleasures.

Around twenty inscriptions have survived, dating between 750 and 650 BC. The most ancient is the Dipylon Amphora, discovered in an ancient cemetery in Athens. The remotest example of alphabetic writing, though incomplete, is the sensual, evocative line "Whoever of these dancers now plays most delicately . . ." These simple words transport us to a symposium celebrated in a Greek home, with laughter, games, and a dance competition whose prize is the vase on which this inscription appears. In *The Odyssey,* Homer described festive competitions such as this, often held at banquets, which formed part of the Greek idea of the good life. Judging by the terms of the inscription, this kind of dance would have been acrobatic, vigorous, and erotically charged. We can thus imagine that the winner would be young and capable of great physical exertion, including the somersaults and leaps the danced required. He was so proud that he always kept his memento of that day and, many years later, asked to be buried with his trophy. After twenty-seven centuries of silence, the vase was found in his tomb, the verse inscribed on it preserving echoes of music and traces of beautiful steps made in dance.

The second-earliest inscription, made in around 720 BC, was also found in a tomb, this time on the island of Ischia, at the far western edge of the Greek world. It reads, "I am the cup of Nestor good for drinking. Whoever drinks from this cup, desire for beautifully crowned Aphrodite will seize him instantly." The inscription is an homage to *The Iliad*, written in hexameters. Nestor's Cup shows that even on a peripheral island, in a world of traders and seafarers, people had an impeccable knowledge of Homer. And it reveals that the magic of letters transformed simple objects of daily use like a ceramic cup or vase into valuable possessions their owners took with them to the grave. A new era was dawning. The alphabet took writing beyond the closed atmosphere of the palace storehouses and made it dance, drink, and give in to desire.

VOICES FROM THE MIST, UNCERTAIN TIMES

43

In the babbling infancy of writing, storytelling voices emerged from the mists of anonymity. Authors wanted to be remembered, to overcome death with the power of their tales. We know who they are. They tell us their names so we can save them from being forgotten. Sometimes they even step out from the wings of the story and speak in first person, a kind of audacity the invisible narrator of *The Iliad* and *The Odyssey* never allows himself.

The shift can be seen in Hesiod, who wrote his principal works around the turn of the century, that is, around 700 BC. His hexameters preserve the flavor of orality, but also contain a new ingredient: the seed of what today we call autofiction. In his abrupt, uninhibited style, Hesiod—author, narrator, and character—tells us in detail about his family, experiences, and way of life. It might be said that Hesiod is Europe's first individual narrator, a distant literary grandfather to Annie Ernaux and Emmanuel Carrère. He tells us his father emigrated from Asia Minor to Boeotia: "You would not say he was fleeing from abundance, joy, and wealth, but from poverty." With his usual acerbic humor, he rails against the filthy, godforsaken village called Ascra where they came to live, "a cursed place, cruel in winter, hard in summer, and never good."

He also describes how his poetic vocation was born. Hesiod was a young shepherd who spent his days alone in the mountains, sleeping on the ground with his father's livestock. Roaming through summertime meadows, he built himself an imaginary world made of verses, music, and words—a sublime inner world, but also a dangerous one. One day as he grazed his flock at the foot of Mount Helicon he had a vision. The nine Muses appeared to him, taught him a song, and breathed his gift into him like a sigh, placing a laurel shoot in his hands. As they took him under their wings, they uttered an unsettling phrase: "We know how to tell lies that sound like truths, and we know how to sing the truth, when we will." This is one of the most ancient reflections on fiction—that true lie—and perhaps also an intimate confession. I like to think that here, Hesiod, a child poet surrounded by silent meadows, manure, and bleating—just like Miguel Hernández centuries later—reveals his obsession with words: those he loves, and those that terrify him with their power and potential for misuse.

In *Works and Days*, the shepherd poet tells not of past feats but the epic of his present. He describes a different kind of heroism: the arduous struggle to survive in harsh conditions. He uses those solemn Homeric hexameters to speak of planting and pruning, of castrating hogs, of the cawing of cranes, of ears of wheat, of oak trees, of the grubby earth and the wine that warms cold nights in the countryside. He forges myths, animal fables, and maxims of coarse country wisdom. He rails against his brother Perses, with whom he has fought over their inheritance. He airs the thorny details of family feuds over property, with no concern that he might seem greedy; on the contrary, he is a proud worker who knows the value of land. He explains that his idle, shameless brother has filed a claim against him and, not content with this extreme act of malice, is attempting to bribe the judge. He then goes on to condemn the rapaciousness of minor landowners and the scheming that goes on at the courts. He uses splendidly scathing expressions, like "ham-guzzling judges." Furious and somber in the style of the prophets, he threatens divine punishment to the authorities who always favor the powerful and prey on poor peasants to fatten their purses. Hesiod does not sing of aristocratic ideals. He is a descendant of the ugly Thersites, who in *The Iliad* reproached Agamemnon, the king, for prospering on the backs of everyone else in a war that benefited him alone.

Many Greeks in Hesiod's time wanted collective life to have a fairer foundation and for there to be a more equitable distribution of wealth. *Works and Days* spoke to them of the value of patience and hard work, of respect for one's fellow men, and of thirst for justice. The time of the alphabet meant Hesiod's caustic protest could endure. Despite insulting the kings, or perhaps because it did, in the end the poem became an essential work and was studied in schools. Among the ridges and furrows of a small, disputed property in the wretched village of Ascra, northeast of Attica, the first generation of social poetry had its beginnings.

44

According to Eric A. Havelock, the alphabet began as an interloper lacking in social status. The elites continued to act and recite. The widespread use of writing took soft, slow, gradual steps forward. For the first few centuries, stories took shape on the blank page of the mind, becoming public only when they were read aloud. In a certain sense they were still conceived with oral communication in mind. The written stories were simply meant to protect them from being forgotten. The oldest texts served as musical scores for language, which only specialists—authors and performers—read and used. The music of words reached its audience through their ears and not through their eyes.

Prose was born around the sixth century BC, and with it, actual writers, who no longer constructed their works in the mysterious corridors of memory but sat down to trace letters on tablets or papyrus scrolls. Authors began writing their texts themselves or dictating them to a secretary. The few—if any—copies that were made barely circulated. There is therefore no trace of a book trade or industry in the archaic period.

But when it came into contact with the alphabet, orality itself was transformed. Once they were written down, words began to be anchored in their order, like musical notes on a staff. The melody of the phrases now stayed the same forever; the spontaneous torrent, the agile response and the freedom of spoken language disappeared. In the ancient Mycenaean era, itinerant *aoidos* sang heroic legends as they strummed their instruments, allowing themselves to be carried away by the spirit of inspiration. With the appearance of books they were replaced by rhapsodes who recited memorized texts that were always identical and performed without musical accompaniment, marking time with a stick on the floor.

In the times of Socrates, written texts were not yet a common tool and still awakened suspicion. They were considered a substitute for the spoken word, which was winged, weightless, sacred. Although the Athens of the fifth century BC now had an incipient book trade, it wouldn't be until a century later, in Aristotle's times, when the habit of reading would not be considered strange. For Socrates, books were an aid to memory and knowledge, but he believed true sages would do well not to trust them. This question inspired a Platonic dialogue titled *Phaedrus*, which takes place a few steps from the walls of Athens in the shade of a leafy plane tree on the shores of the Ilissus. There, in the heat of the siesta, with cicadas chirping in the background, a conversation unfolds about beauty that drifts mysteriously toward the ambiguous gift of writing.

Centuries ago, Socrates says to Phaedrus, Theuth, the Egyptian god who invented dice, chess, numbers, geometry, astronomy, and letters, visited the king of Egypt and offered him these inventions so he could show them to his subjects. I'll translate what Socrates said:

> The king, Thamus, asked what the use of writing was, and Theuth replied, This knowledge will make the Egyptians wiser; it is an elixir of memory and wisdom. Thamus then replied: O most ingenious Theuth, being the parent of writing, you attribute to it qualities which it does

not possess. This discovery of yours will create forgetfulness in the learners, because they will not use their memories; they will put their trust in books and not remember for themselves. It will not be wisdom but only a semblance of wisdom that writing will give to men; they will hear many things and not truly learn them; they will be tiresome company, believing themselves wise without being so.

Having heard this exotic Egyptian myth, Phaedrus says he agrees with his teacher. This is usually the way with Socrates's followers, who never dare to contradict him. In fact, in Plato's dialogues, the disciples endlessly repeat phrases like "That's very true, Socrates," "I concede to you, Socrates," "I see you are right once again, Socrates." Although his interlocutor has given in, the philosopher deals his last blow: "The written word seems to speak to you as if it were intelligent, but if you ask it something, because you wish to know more, it keeps telling you the same thing over and over. Books cannot defend themselves."

Socrates feared that, with writing, men would abandon the effort of thought itself. Knowledge, he suspected, would be entrusted to texts, and it would be enough to have them within reach without bothering to truly understand them. Thus, knowledge would no longer be our own, indelibly integrated into our minds, but merely an external appendix. It's a shrewd argument, one whose impact is still felt. Right now, we are immersed in a transformation as radical as the Greek adoption of the alphabet. The internet is changing the way we use memory and the very mechanics of our knowledge. An experiment conducted in 2011 by Betsy Sparrow, Jenny Liu, and D. M. Wegner measured the memory capacity of a handful of volunteers. Only half the participants knew that the information they were asked to remember was stored in a computer. Those who thought the information was recorded relaxed their effort to learn it. Scientists term this phenomenon of the relaxation of memory "the Google effect." We tend to remember better where information is kept than the information itself. Clearly, there is more knowledge available to us than ever, but almost all of it is stored somewhere other than in our minds. This raises unsettling questions: Beneath this deluge of information, where is the wisdom? Is our lazy memory becoming simply an address book for locating information, with no trace of the information itself? Are we fundamentally more ignorant than our ancient ancestors with their prodigious memories?

The great irony of the matter is that Plato explained the master's scorn for books in a book, thus preserving his criticisms of writing for us, his future readers.

45

Beyond certain limits, our only chance to expand our memory depends on technology. These transformations are at once dangerous and fascinating. The line separating our minds from the internet is becoming increasingly blurred. The idea has taken hold among us that knowing something can be found with Google is equal to knowledge itself. Whenever something is discussed in a group, there's always someone who confirms it with their smartphone. Diving into the screen like an aquatic bird, after a quick search they emerge with the fish in their beak to dispel any doubts about an actor's name or the perfect day to catch a bananafish.

Since his experiments in the eighties, Wegner believed that if we remember where to find important information, even without retaining the knowledge itself, we are broadening the limits of our mental territory. This is the foundation of his theory of transactive memory. According to Wegner, no one remembers everything. We store information in the minds of others whom we can ask, in books, and in the internet's gigantic cybermemory.

The alphabet was an even more revolutionary technology than the internet. It built that communal memory for the first time, within the reach of anyone. Neither wisdom nor literature fit completely into a single mind, but thanks to books, each of us finds the door open to all the knowledge and stories in existence. We can believe, like Socrates, that we have become a pack of conceited fools. Or we can believe that, thanks to written culture, we are part of the largest and most intelligent brain that has ever existed. Borges, who belongs to the group of the second persuasion, wrote, "Of all man's instruments, the most wondrous, no doubt, is the book. The other instruments are extensions of his body. The microscope, the telescope, are extensions of his sight; the telephone is the extension of his voice; then we have the plow and the sword, extensions of the arm. But the book is something else altogether: the book is an extension of memory and imagination."

46

That day on the outskirts of Athens, under the dazzling midday sun, Socrates said to Phaedrus that written words are dead and spectral signs, illegitimate children of the only living discourse—the oral one.

The poet Friedrich Hölderlin, born twenty-one centuries later, would have liked to travel through time to that peaceful meadow, that distant day: "In the shade of the plane trees, / the Illisus flowed among flowers, / . . . / where Socrates won hearts / and Aspasia wandered among the myrtles, / . . . / while the agora echoed noisily / and my Plato forged paradises."

It often happens that times that feel decadent to those who live through them become for others a world of nostalgia. Hölderlin believed himself to be an ancient Athenian transplanted to an inhospitable Germany. His true homeland was that golden century against which Socrates railed for destroying authentic wisdom.

When he was barely thirty, the German poet began to suffer from mental breakdowns. They say he was afflicted with angry outbursts, anxiety, and compulsive, uncontrollable talking. After he was diagnosed as incurably ill, his family had him admitted to an institution. In the summer of 1807, a woodworker named Ernst Zimmer, a passionate reader of Hölderlin's *Hyperion*, visited and decided to take him to live at his house by the Neckar River. The poet remained there until his death in 1843, in the constant care of his reader's family.

Though he hardly knew him, Zimmer made the decision to take in, feed, and care for the author of the novel he loved in his madness. For almost four decades, the silent words of a book forged a bond between strangers that was stronger than blood. Perhaps letters are merely dead and spectral signs, illegitimate children of the spoken word, but as readers, we know how to breathe life into them. I would love to tell this story to that old curmudgeon Socrates.

47

Fahrenheit 451 is the temperature at which books catch fire and burn, and the title Ray Bradbury gave his futuristic fantasy novel. Or perhaps not so futuristic.

The story takes place in a dark era, in a country where reading has been outlawed. Firemen no longer put out fires, instead burning the books that some rebellious citizens hide in their homes. The government has decreed that the people must be happy, but books are full of harmful ideas and solitary reading lends itself to melancholy. The population must be protected from writers, whose malevolent thoughts are considered catching.

Dissidents are persecuted. They take refuge in the forests surrounding the cities, by the roads, on the banks of polluted rivers, on abandoned railway tracks. They travel constantly, under the light of the stars, disguised as vagabonds. They have memorized entire books, storing them in their heads where no one can see them or suspect they exist. "It wasn't planned, at first. Each man had a book he wanted to remember, and did. Then, over a period of twenty years or so, we met each other, traveling, and got the loose network together and set out a plan . . . When the war's over, some day, some year, the books can be written again, the people will be called in, one by one, to recite what they know and we'll set it up in type until another Dark Age, when we might have to do the whole damn thing over again." These fugitives, who have seen what they love destroyed, must travel down a long road as they flee, always in fear, with no certainty except for the books stored behind their calm eyes.

Bradbury's novel seems like a dystopian fable, but that's not what it is. In fact, something very similar really happened. In the year 213 BC, while a group of Greeks attempted to gather all the books in existence at Alexandria, the Chinese emperor Shihuangdi commanded that all the books in his kingdom be burned. Only treatises on agriculture, medicine, and prophecy were exempt. He wanted history to begin with him. His goal was to abolish the past because his opponents evoked it in their longing for the emperors of earlier times. According to a document from the period, the plan was carried out mercilessly. ("Those who use Antiquity to vilify the present times will be executed along with their families. Those who hide books will be branded with a hot iron and condemned to forced labor.") Shihuangdi's malevolence led to the destruction of thousands and thousands of books—all of the writings of Confucianism, among others. The emperor's henchmen went from door to door, seizing books and burning them on a pyre. More than four hundred men of letters who resisted were buried alive.

In the year 191 BC, under a new dynasty, many of those lost words were rewritten. Exposing themselves to incredible risks, many writers had preserved whole works in their memories, in secret, sheltering them from war, persecution, and the men charged with burning books.

This wasn't the only time something like this happened. When Alexander occupied and set fire to the city of Persepolis, every single copy of the sacred book of Zoroastrianism was burned. The faithful could reconstruct it since they knew it word for word. At the same time Bradbury was imagining his dystopian fantasy, during the cruel years of Stalinism, eleven of Anna Akhmatova's friends were memorizing the poems in her heartrending *Requiem* as soon as she wrote them, so that they might be preserved should any harm come to their author. Writing and memory are not adversaries. In fact, throughout history, each one has saved the other: words protect the vulnerable past; memory protects persecuted books.

When glimmers of oral culture still endured in ancient times, when books were less common but were more often reread, it wasn't unusual for readers to learn whole works by memory. The rhapsodes are known to have recited the fifteen thousand lines of *The Iliad* and the twelve thousand of *The Odyssey* in various sessions, but ordinary people could also faithfully repeat long literary texts. In one of his books, Saint Augustine recalls his companion in studies Simplician, who could recite entire speeches by Cicero and all of Virgil's poems—in other words, thousands and thousands of lines—from back to front, in reverse order. As he read, he engraved the lines that moved him onto "the waxed tablets of his memory," so as to remember and recite them at will, as if consulting a book. A second-century Roman doctor by the name of Antyllus went even further, claiming that memorizing books was good for one's health. He had an amusing and outlandish theory on the subject. According to him, those who have never made the effort to memorize a story, some lines of poetry, or a dialogue have more trouble eliminating certain harmful fluids from the body, whereas those who can recite long texts from memory expel those destructive substances as they breathe.

Perhaps we, like Bradbury's fugitives, the Chinese men of letters in Shihuangdi's times, the Zoroastrians, or Anna Akhmatova's friends, keep certain pages that matter to us safe in our minds unawares. "I am Plato's *Republic*," says a character in *Fahrenheit 451*. "I am Marcus Aurelius." "Chapter One of Thoreau's *Walden* [lives] in Green River, Chapter Two in Willow Farm." "Why, there's one town in Maryland, only twenty-seven people, no bomb'll ever touch that town, is the complete essays of a man named Bertrand Russell. Pick up that town, almost, and flip the pages, so many pages to a person." One of the ragged rebels, with greasy hair and grime under his nails, jokes, "Don't judge a book by its cover."

In a certain sense, we as readers all carry our own private, clandestine libraries inside us, of the words that have made their mark on our lives.

LEARNING TO READ THE SHADOWS

48

Books had to create their own audience. And when they did, they transformed the Greek way of life.

The alphabet took root in a culture of war. Only the aristocratic youth were educated, becoming versed in military, athletic, and musical matters. As children, they were taught by tutors in the palace. When they reached adolescence, between the ages of thirteen and eighteen, they learned the art of war from their adult lovers—Greek pederasty had an educational function. Love between mature fighters and their chosen youths, always from a high rank, was socially accepted. The Greeks believed sexual tension increased both men's bravery: the veteran warrior wished to shine before his young favorite, and his beloved tried to perform at the level of the distinguished soldier who chose him. With women banished to the gynaeceum, Greek city-states were boys' clubs where men watched, emulated, and fell in love with each other in their shared obsession with the heroism of war. Between battles, they turned their attention to banquets, tournaments, and hunting. And on the battleground, they put their chivalric ideals into practice in the bloodiest of massacres. The historian Thucydides says the Greeks always went out armed, since they could feel safe neither in cities nor on the roads. He also says the Athenians were the first to start leaving their weapons at home and start behaving a little less coarsely.

At some point in the sixth century BC, education ceased to be only military and athletic. This didn't mean training for battle disappeared, since the inhabitants of ancient cities were constantly fighting with neighboring states and impaling on spears those who lived just beyond their borders. But little by little, the teaching of numbers and letters began to gain ground. Only in certain strongholds like Sparta were the thirteen obligatory years of military training and discipline maintained.

And then, something unexpected happened. Alphabet fever spread beyond the noble circles that considered education a privilege of theirs alone. Proud aristocrats were forced to abide a growing number of upstarts who, with insufferable nerve, set out to initiate their children into the secrets of writing and were willing to pay to make it happen. That was how school was born. Personal instruction from a trainer or lover was no longer enough to meet everyone's needs and became a minority practice. More and more youths—free, but without aristocratic names—demanded to be educated, and the pressure of their aspirations gave rise to the earliest spaces where learning occurred in groups.

To date this decisive occurrence, we must comb through ancient texts in search of clues. We catch a glimpse of one of the earliest schools in a text with a disturbingly modern feel to it that tells the story of a crime on the remote island of Astypalea. In *Description of Greece*, Pausanias provides an account of a mass murder that shocked the people of the Dodecanese Islands in the year 492 BC. The crime lived on in the islanders' memories into the second century AD, when this traveling writer heard the grim tale, which today sounds like a cross between *Bowling for Columbine* and the legend of Samson. Pausanias writes of a resentful young man with a history of violence who burst into a school to vent his rage by massacring a group of children: "They say that Cleomedes of Astypalea killed his adversary Iccus of Epidaurus in a boxing match. For his brutality, the Olympic judges withdrew his victory. Cleomedes flew into a rage and on his return to Astypalea, went to the school where there were sixty children, and with his bare arms, toppled the column that held up the roof. The school fell down upon their heads and crushed them all to death."

Beyond its dark ending, this story reveals to us that at the beginning of the fifth century BC, a small island in the Aegean Sea barely thirteen kilometers wide had a school where sixty pupils gathered to learn on a given day. Other testimonies seem to confirm this. The alphabet was permeating Greek life at the time, even in remote villages of the kind that emerge from the back room of history only when they are battered by natural disasters or become the scene of a horrific crime.

49

My mother tried to teach me to read, but I refused out of fear. At my school, there was a boy called Alvarito whose parents were teachers and had taught him at home. While the rest of us were stammering through basic syllables, he read with astonishing fluency and a perfection so effortless it was hard to stomach. Revenge came in the schoolyard at recess when the other kids bullied him. Fatso, Four Eyes, they cried. They stamped on his backpack. They hung his jacket from the fig tree's branches where he couldn't reach it because he wasn't a nimble climber. Alvarito had violated an unspoken rule: he was too smart. His parents had to find him another school.

That won't happen to me, I thought proudly. And anyway, I had no need to get ahead of my classmates. My mother read me stories every night. As long as I couldn't read, our little nighttime theater wasn't in danger. What I really wanted was to learn to write. I didn't realize the two were essential to each other.

The day finally comes when I have a pencil between my fingers. It isn't easy to hold and has to be tamed. I press it vigorously against the paper so it can't escape, but sometimes it rebels, and the graphite tip breaks on the notebook. Then I have to sharpen it again. I can see myself: I'm sitting at a round vanilla-colored table with some other kids. Leaning over my work, I draw stems, downstrokes, loops, curves. The tip of my tongue sticks out between my lips, following the movement of my hand across the page. Rows of "m's" joined up with their neighbors. Rows of "b's" with their little bellies. I don't like the crossbar on the "t"; it complicates things.

A while later, I'm improving: I can join my letters now. The "m" has a tail that reaches out to the "o." At first it all looks like a muddle, a tangle of messy lines. I keep going. I'm left-handed and rub my fist over my work, blurring it as I go. I leave a grey trail. I continue, my hand blackened. Then, one morning, to my surprise, I crack the secret to writing. It's magical. *Mom.* The stems and loops are singing in silence. I've captured reality in a mesh made of letters. But they're no longer just letters; it's she who suddenly appears on the page: her voice so pretty, the waves in her chestnut hair, her warm gaze, her smile that's always timid because she's ashamed of her crooked teeth. I've called her forth with my pencil. There she is: *Mom!* I've just written and understood my first word.

In every society where writing is used, learning to read is something of a rite of passage. Children know that understanding words brings them closer to adult status. It's always an exciting step toward being a grown-up. It seals an alliance, lets us split off from a part of childhood we've overcome. It's a joyous, euphoric experience. Our new power is put to the test at every turn. Who would have thought the whole world was adorned with chains of letters, like a great procession? Now you have to decipher what's out in the street: phar-ma-cy, bak-ery, ap-aaaaart-ment for rent. The syllables burst in the mouth like fireworks, sparks flying. At home, around the table, you're assaulted by messages from all sides. The flurries of questions begin: What does lowcalorie mean? And mineralwater? Bestbeforedate?

In medieval Jewish society, a solemn ceremony marked the moment when a child started learning to read, when books made him part of a collective memory and a shared past. During the feast of Pentecost, the teacher sat the child who was to be initiated on his lap. He showed him a board where the signs of the Hebrew alphabet were written, and then a passage from the Hebrew scriptures. The teacher read aloud and the student repeated. Then honey was spread on the board and the initiate licked it off, so that the words would seep symbolically into his body. Letters were also written on peeled hard-boiled eggs and on cakes. The alphabet became sweet and salty, was chewed and absorbed. It began to form part of the self.

How could the alphabet, which deciphers the world and reveals our thoughts, not be magical? The ancient Greeks also found it bewitching. In those times, the letters were used to represent, in addition to words, numbers and musical notes. Each of their seven vowels represented one of the seven planets and the seven angels that preside over them. They were used for spells and as amulets.

In those remote Greek schools—on dreary afternoons with drizzling rain, the same view through the windows day after day—children sang the letters in chorus: "There's alpha, beta, gamma, and delta, and epsilon, and zeta." The teacher would draw them, and then, taking the pupil's hand in his, make him trace the letter over the top. The children repeated the examples thousands of times over. They copied brief one-line maxims, or took dictation. Like us, they learned poems from memory and strings of unusual words. I remember one of those tiresome childhood enumerations: macerate, granulate, contriturate. Never again have I had any use for those grating verbs.

The teaching methods were arduous, unrelenting. The teacher, or tamer, recited and the pupils repeated after him. The learning process moved slowly (it wasn't unusual for children of ten or twelve to still be learning to write). As soon as they were able, they began to read, repeat, summarize, comment, and copy a selection of essential texts, nearly always the same. Mainly it was Homer, but also Hesiod and other indispensable works. The ancients, who viewed children as a kind of miniature adult lacking talents and tastes of their own, offered them the same books read by grown-ups. There was nothing resembling the literature for children or young adults we have today, nothing to make things easier for them. Childhood hadn't yet been invented; Freud hadn't yet appeared to attribute vital importance to our early years. The best thing that could therefore be done for a child was to plunge him headfirst into the adult world, ridding him of his youth as if it were dirt.

The alphabet may have been magic, but the pedagogy was often sadistic. Corporal punishment was inseparable from Greek children's school routine, just as it had been for Egyptian and Jewish scribes. In a short, humorous work by Herodas, the teacher roars, "Where is the hard leather, the ox's tail I use to whip the troublemakers? Give it to me before my temper explodes."

THE TRIUMPH OF UNRULY WORDS

50

Over the centuries of the alphabet's gradual expansion, the Greeks kept on singing poems, but no longer in the same way. Certain voices ventured to say what no ancient text had dared to before. Sadly, only shards of those verses remain. Not a single complete book of philosophy or poetry has been preserved from before the year 500 BC; whole poems or quotes included in prose works are an exception. But the small fragments that were salvaged still have the power to move us, despite being incomplete.

This period was the golden age of the lyric, when poems, which were brief compared to *The Iliad* and were written down to be sung, ceased to look back on the past like the traditional legends of old. Instead, they spoke of the flow of present times and clung to the feelings they experienced. Now. Here. Me.

For the first time, writing was allied with unruly, irreverent words, words that clash with the values of their era. This remarkable tendency begins with Archilochus, a mercenary soldier and lyric poet who was the illegitimate son of a Greek nobleman and a barbarian slave. During his brief life—from about 680 to 640 BC—he had no fortune or privilege and thus had to fend for himself, selling his services to fight in the wars of others. As he himself said, his spear gave him his daily hunk of bread and poured him the wine he drank. A mercenary in the borderlands between culture and barbarism, he knew the sordid reality behind the ideals of war.

According to the code of honor, a soldier had to stand his ground on the battlefield and never retreat or flee. Archilochus, in a skirmish with the Thracian army, was forced to choose between dying on the spot behind his large and heavy shield or tossing it aside and running for his life. In ancient Greece, to be called a *rhipsaspis*—"one who throws away his shield"—was a serious insult. It's said that when Spartan mothers bid their sons farewell before battle, they warned them to come home "with their shield or upon it." In other words, with their shield on their arm, having fought bravely, or lying on top of it as a corpse.

What did Archilochus decide? To take to his heels and proclaim as much in a poem: "That excellent shield / I grudgingly tossed in a bush / is now brandished by a Thracian. / But I saved my skin. I don't care a fig for that shield, / let it go. I'll buy another just as good." No Homeric warrior would ever have dared to admit such a thing, nor would he have had the necessary sense of humor to do so. But Archilochus relished presenting himself as an antihero, shamelessly poking fun at convention. Though he was brave—he couldn't otherwise have made a living at war for so many years—he had a lust for life, "which cannot be got back nor bought when the last breath passes your teeth." He knew that the soldier who flees in time is good for more battles and to write more poems. It's precisely because of his defiant candor that I view him not as a coward, but rather as a scathing realist.

The language of his verse is frank and unvarnished, even verging on brutality. With Archilochus, a decisive realism takes hold in Greek lyric, opening the doors to a new, insolent form of poetry. He makes no effort to hide his vengeful, impassioned, mocking nature and finds explicit words for his sexual desire: "If only I could touch Neobule's hand" . . . "Just to fall upon her flesh, ready for action, touching thigh to thigh and belly to belly." In one brief fragment he was bold enough to speak of oral sex: "She went at it, head bent down, like a Thracian or a Phrygian drinking beer through a straw."

Like Achilles, Archilochus died on the battlefield, but he insisted that for him, the promise of posthumous glory was merely another kind of bluster: "No man is honored by his countrymen once he's dead; we'd rather have the applause of the living while we live." Richard Jenkyns, a professor at Oxford, considers him "Europe's first pain in the neck." I think this epitaph would have made him laugh heartily.

THE FIRST BOOK

51

There are no archaeological remains of Europe's most ancient books. Papyrus is a fragile, perishable material and cannot survive in humid climates for more than two hundred years. All we can do today is scour Greek texts for the earliest mentions of real, physical books that someone saw and touched in a place whose name they cared to remember. This search brings me to the cusp of the sixth and fifth centuries BC. It's said that during that period, Heraclitus placed a copy of his work *On Nature* in the Temple of Artemis in Ephesus.

Ephesus was a city-state in Anatolia, the ancient Asia Minor, in what is now Turkey. What we know as philosophy today sprang up suddenly, with no visible cause, at the beginning of the sixth century BC, on that narrow coastal strip occupied by the Greeks at the edge of the Asian world. The earliest philosophers were children of the borderlands, of mixed blood, of the threshold. While continental Greece remained anchored in the past, the inhabitants of the hybrid periphery set about devising radical new ideas.

It's no coincidence that the birth of Greek philosophy coincided with the early days of books. Unlike oral communication—based on traditional tales, well-known and easy to remember—writing allowed for the creation of a complex language that readers could absorb and quietly meditate upon. And it's far easier for someone holding a book in their hands, who can pause, reread, and stop to think, to develop a critical spirit than it is for someone captivated by a rhapsode's performance.

Heraclitus was nicknamed "the Riddler" and, later, "the Obscure." The murkiness of life and its extraordinary contradictions seem to spill into and permeate his writings. His work marks the beginning of difficult literature, where the reader must make an effort to wrest meaning from the words. Heraclitus is the father of Proust, with his labyrinthine sentences full of twists and turns; of Faulkner, with his disorienting, often disjointed monologues; and of Joyce, who gives the impression in *Finnegans Wake* that he is writing in several languages—some of his own invention—all at once. This isn't to say they're related due to similar styles. In fact, we have only a handful of Heraclitus's brief, enigmatic, powerful maxims. What they actually have in common is their attitude to words: if the world is cryptic, then the appropriate language to represent it should be dense, mysterious, and difficult to decipher.

Heraclitus believed reality could be explained as permanent tension. He called it "war," or a struggle between opposites. Day and night, wakefulness and sleep, life and death: all these become each other and can only exist in opposition; they are fundamentally two sides of the same coin. "It is sickness that makes health good and pleasant; hunger, plenty; hard work, rest . . . the immortals mortal, the mortals immortal, living the death of others and the life of others while they fade."

By birth, Heraclitus was entitled to the rank of king of his city. He ceded the post, which since the arrival of democracy had been more of a priestly position, to his younger brother. Apparently, he considered magicians, preachers, and fortune-tellers mere "traffickers in mysteries." It's said that he refused to make any laws for the Ephesians, preferring to play with children at the temple. They also say that he became haughty and disdainful. He had no concern for honors or power but was obsessed with finding the *logos* of the universe, which meant "word" but also "meaning." In the opening of the Gospel of John—"In the beginning was the Word"—we hear the voice of Heraclitus.

For him, change was the key to everything. Nothing endures.

Everything is in flux. We will never bathe in the same river twice. This watery image of a constantly changing world, which made its mark on Plato, is now part of us. We have rewritten and reformulated it thousands of times. From Jorge Manrique, "Our lives are rivers that flow into the sea of death," to Zygmunt Bauman and his liquid modernity. Borges, fascinated by Heraclitus's river, dedicated a poem to him in which the philosopher discovers his identity is also in flux, feeling "with the astonishment of a sacred horror / That he is also a river and a leak."

I believe Heraclitus's enigmatic phrases capture the mystery and wonder that gave rise to philosophy, and I believe they capture the present moment, too. To write this chapter, I reread the few fragments of his terse reflections that survived long enough to reach us. They seemed to me to explain our seismic current reality as we hover on the threshold of violence, debating between extremes: globalization and borders; multiculturalism and fear of minorities; the urge to give shelter or to force people out in fury; thirst for freedom and the dream of building a walled-in fortress; appetite for change and nostalgia for the greatness of yesterday.

The tension of these contradictions can be almost unbearable and make us feel trapped. But according to Heraclitus's reasoning, a minor adjustment to the balance of the world's dynamic forces changes everything. So the hope for transformation is always justified, too.

52

There is someone who wants to be famous at any cost. He has never excelled at anything but rebels against the idea of being just another anonymous man. He secretly dreams of people recognizing him in the street, pointing and murmuring. An inner voice whispers that one day he will be a celebrity, like the Olympic champions or the actors who seduce their audiences and leave them in awe.

He's decided to do something great; he just needs to find out what.

One day, he finally hatches a plan. Incapable of any great feat, he can always go down in history for wreaking destruction. In his city stands one of the Seven Wonders of the World, visited by kings and travelers from far-off lands. Up on a rocky promontory, perched among the clouds, the Temple of Artemis looks out over all of Ephesus. It took 120 years to build. The entrance is a thick forest of columns, and inside the temple, which is bedecked with gold and silver, stands the sacred image of the goddess who fell from the sky, the precious sculptures of Polykleitos and Phidias, and other priceless treasures.

On the moonless night of July 21 in the year 356 BC, when the great Alexander had just been born in faraway Macedonia, he slips through the shadows and climbs the steps that lead to the Temple of Artemis. The night watchmen are sleeping. In the silence pierced only by snores, he takes a lamp, spills the oil, and sets fire to the cloths that adorn the interior. The flames lick the woven threads and rise to the roof. At first, the fire crawls slowly, but once it scorches the wooden beams, the blazing dance begins, as if the building had been dreaming for centuries of burning down.

He watches, mesmerized, as the flames leap and roar. Then he leaves the building coughing to see how it lights up the night. Outside, the guards catch him with little trouble. They throw him into a dungeon in chains, where he spends a few happy hours alone, breathing in the smell of smoke. When tortured, he confesses: he planned to set fire to the world's most beautiful building so he could be known all over the world. Historians tell that in every city in Asia Minor, it was forbidden to reveal his name on pain of death. But he was not erased from history. He appears in every encyclopedia. The writer Marcel Schwob included his biography in a chapter of *Imaginary Lives*. Sartre dedicated a short story to him. He lends his name to the psychological disorder of those who commit the most barbaric, gratuitous acts for the sake of a few minutes on television or a most-viewed video on YouTube. Exhibitionism at any cost is not just a contemporary phenomenon.

His cursed name was Herostratus. In his memory, the pathological desire for notoriety has come to be known as Herostratus syndrome.

The fire he caused in order to launch himself to fame reduced that scroll of papyrus—the offering Heraclitus had made to the goddess—to ash. As it happens, the philosopher believed that fire annihilates the universe in a cyclical way and prophesied a final cosmic conflagration in his work. I don't know about the universe, but books—which burn well in all their forms—have a sorrowful history of destruction among the flames.

TRAVELING BOOKSTORES

53

How many books were there in the golden age of ancient Greece? What percentage of the population could read them? We have only shreds of information preserved by chance, blades of grass that float along on the breeze but don't allow us to calculate the size of the meadow from which they came. And most of them refer to an exceptional place, the city of Athens. The rest remains in shadow.

Seeking traces of this invisible literacy, we turn to images of readers represented in ceramic paintings. From 490 BC on, there are red-figure urns and vases decorated with scenes of children learning to read and write at school, or people sitting in chairs, reading a papyrus unfurled in their laps. Often the artist traces enlarged letters or words on the scrolls he draws, in such great detail that they can be read—verses by Homer or Sappho. In almost all cases, the book contains poetry. There is also a mythology textbook. What's most striking is that the usual protagonists of these small scenes are women, but, paradoxically, in the school scenes girls never appear. This contradiction leaves us with an unsolved mystery. Perhaps these women readers belonged to noble families and were educated at home, or perhaps it was simply more of a motif than a daily reality. We'll never know.

A gravestone dating from between 430 and 420 BC shows a young man sculpted in profile, absorbed in the words on a papyrus unrolled across his knees, head tilted slightly to one side, his ankles crossed, in exactly the position in which I am writing now. Beneath the carving that gives the chair its shape, we see an eroded lump of stone that looks like a dog sheltering underneath it. The carving depicts the calm of hours spent among books. That deceased Athenian was so enamored of reading that he took it with him to his grave.

At the cusp of the fifth and fourth centuries BC, some characters begin to appear who had until then been unknown: booksellers. It's in this period that the new word *bybliopólai* ("sellers of books") first features in texts by Athenian comic poets. According to them, stands selling literary scrolls would be set up in the agora, among the others offering garlic, vegetables, incense, and perfume. For a drachma, Socrates says in one of Plato's dialogues, anyone could buy a philosophical treatise at the market. It's surprising that books were readily available so soon, and in the case of difficult philosophical works, even more so. Judging by their low price, they must have been small or secondhand.

We know little about the prices of books. The cost of papyrus scrolls suggests that the standard fluctuated between two and four drachmas per copy—the equivalent of somewhere between one and six days' work. The high figures mentioned for rare editions—Lucian of Samosata speaks of a book that cost around seven hundred and fifty drachmas—are no indication of the normal prices of ordinary books. For the prosperous classes, even on the more modest rungs, books were a relatively accessible product.

At the end of the fifth century BC, the age-old tradition of mocking bookworms began, whose archetype would later be Don Quixote. Aristophanes, slyly welcoming intertextuality, makes fun of writers who "squeeze their works out of other books." Another author of comedies used a private library as a setting for one of his scenes. In it, a teacher proudly shows the famous hero Heracles his shelves stuffed with books by Homer, Hesiod, the tragedians, and the historians: "Take any book you like and read it; take your time, look at the titles." Heracles, who in Greek comedies is always depicted as a glutton, chooses a recipe book. We know that in those days, instruction manuals on a wide range of subjects circulated to satisfy readers' curiosity, and among them, the manual par excellence, was a recipe book by a fashionable Sicilian chef.

Athenian booksellers also had overseas customers, and thus the exportation of books began. The rest of the Greek world sought out literature created in Athens, especially librettos of tragedies, the great spectacle of the period. Attic theater captivated even those who loathed Athenian imperialism, as is the case with the powerful film industry of the United States. Xenophon, writing in the first half of the fourth century BC, tells that on the dangerous coast of Salmydessus in today's Turkey, he found a shoreline scattered with the debris of shipwrecks. Among the wreckage were "beds, small boxes, many books, and other things merchants usually transport in wooden boxes."

There must have been a certain amount of organization to stock the market with books, and people who ran the workshops where they were copied. But we have no clues to tell us how they worked or what the breadth of their reach was, so we are forced to enter the shaky terrain of conjecture. Surely the workshops would copy books with the permission of authors, who wished for a wider readership than their own circle of friends. But they also reproduced texts without consulting their creators. There was no such thing as copyright in ancient times.

One disciple of Plato's had copies made of his master's work and set out for Sicily to sell them. He was shrewd enough to guess that there would be a market for the Socratic dialogues there. His contemporaries give the impression that his sales initiative earned him an abysmal reputation in Athens, not for stealing his master's intellectual property, but rather for getting involved in business at all. This was considered thoroughly plebeian and improper for a man from a good family, especially one who belonged to Plato's circle.

The Platonic Academy undoubtedly had a library of its own, but the collection at the Lyceum of Aristotle must have surpassed all its predecessors by far. Strabo says that Aristotle was, "as far as we know, the first to collect books." It's said that Aristotle bought all the scrolls owned by another philosopher for the immense sum of three talents (eighteen thousand drachmas). I imagine him amassing essential texts for years, spanning the entire spectrum of the arts and sciences of the era, as his money gradually trickled away. Without reading constantly, he would never have been able to write what he wrote.

A small corner of Europe was beginning to be consumed by book fever.

54

Aristotle speaks of tragedians who wrote more for readers than for theater audiences. He adds that their books enjoy "wide circulation." What might a wide circulation have meant in those early days?

Another statement attributed to Aristotle reveals a world we haven't yet glimpsed. According to him, booksellers hauled great mountains of books around in carts. Perhaps he is referring to peddlers who took to the open road, clattering from village to village, loaded with literature.

In fact, as Jorge Carrión points out, bookstores with fixed locations are a modern anomaly in a mainly nomadic and poetic tradition. It was travelers who fed the Library of Alexandria with manuscripts; merchants of paper and ink who rolled ideas down the Silk Road as if they were wheels; roving salesmen of used books—among other goods—who set up at inns and fairs as recently as yesterday, having traveled great distances laden with chests, cumbersome boxes, and portable market stands. Today, depending on the geography, mobile libraries on buses or "biblioburros"—book donkeys—keep the old custom of globe-trotting books alive.

Parnassus on Wheels by Christopher Morley describes that nomadic existence. In the United States of the 1920s, Mr. Mifflin travels through rural America in a strange carriage that looks like a tram, pulled by a white horse. When he lifts the vehicle's side panels, the long wagon turns out to be a book stand with shelf after shelf stuffed with books. Inside, there is no lack of comfort or convenience: an oil stove, a folding table, a pallet to sleep on, a wicker chair, and geraniums on the little window ledges.

For years, Mifflin had worked as a teacher, "plugging away in a country school . . . on a starvation salary." His poor health leads him to move to the country. He builds his cart with his own hands, names it Parnassus on Wheels, and buys a large number of books in a secondhand store in Baltimore. Though he has no lack of cunning and a salesman's gift of the gab, Mifflin considers himself a roving preacher, called upon to spread the gospel of good books. He drags his cart from farm to farm, along dusty roads shared by wooden wagons and the earliest mass-produced automobiles. When he arrives at the home of some country folk, he jumps down from his driver's seat, crosses the yard full of hens scratching in the dirt, and does his best to convince a woman peeling potatoes of the importance of reading. He attempts to convert farmers to his zealous creed: "When you sell a man a book you don't sell him just twelve ounces of paper and ink and glue—you sell him a whole new life. Love and friendship and humor and ships at sea by night—there's all heaven and earth in a book, a real book I mean. Jiminy! If I were the baker or the butcher or the broom huckster, people would run to the gate when I came by—just waiting for my stuff. And here I go loaded with everlasting salvation—yes, ma'am, salvation for their little, stunted minds—and it's hard to make 'em see it."

These people with weathered skin and frostbitten hands have never had the chance to buy a work of literature, much less to have anyone explain its importance to them. Mifflin discovers that the deeper into the countryside he goes, the fewer books are to be seen and the worse those he does find are. With his singular eloquence, he proclaims that it would take an army of booksellers like him, willing to visit workers in person, tell their children stories, speak to the teachers in their tiny schools, and put pressure on the editors of agricultural magazines until books circulate through the country's veins and the holy grail reaches the remote farms of Maine.

If this was the situation in the United States in the early twentieth century, how must it have been for those merchants Aristotle mentions, among the sun-drenched olive groves, when books were young and everything was happening for the first time?

55

Alexander had unleashed the dizzying terrors of global-ization. Until then, most Greeks had been citizens of small states encompassing little more than one settlement and its surroundings. All of these minor countries were proud of their politics and cul-ture, fiercely independent, and often entangled in skirmishes with neighbors in the name of freedom. When the cities of Greece were annexed under new monarchies, their inhabitants found them-selves orphaned en masse. Proud communities floundered when they ceased to be independent centers and became part of a vast imperial periphery. Those who'd been citizens became subjects overnight. They continued to fight, preoccupied with alliances, treaties, negotiations, and declarations of war, but after the states lost their independence, the battles were no longer as fierce. New state power structures—incipient, authoritarian, and enmeshed in dynastic struggles—provided no anchor. Adrift, the Greeks sought other ways of mooring themselves. They embraced Eastern beliefs, imported rituals, philosophies that offered salvation. Some took ref-uge in a newly created religion: the religion of art and culture.

Faced with the eclipse of civic life, certain people decided to turn their attention to learning. They wished to educate themselves in the hope of holding on to their freedom and independence in a conquered world, to develop all their talents as far as possible, to achieve the best version of themselves, to sculpt their inner selves like a statue, to make their own lives into a work of art. This was the aesthetic of existence that so impressed Michel Foucault when he studied the Greeks for his *History of Sexuality*. In his final inter-view, Foucault spoke of his fascination with this ancient idea: "What strikes me is the fact that in our society, art has become something which is related only to objects and not to individuals, or to life. That art is something which is specialized or which is done by experts who are artists. But couldn't everyone's life become a work of art? Why should the lamp or the house be an art object, but not our life?"

Though the idea wasn't new, in the Hellenic era it became a refuge for those disoriented and bereft of their freedoms. In this period, *paideia*—Greek for "learning"—becomes for some the only task worth devoting oneself to in life. The meaning of the word *paideia* is enriched over time, and when Romans such as Varro or Cicero translate it into Latin, they choose the term *humanitas*. This is the dawning of European humanism and its later outgrowths. The echoes of this constellation of words have still not faded. The word "encyclopedia" incorporates the ancient *paideia* and descends from the expression *en kyklos paideia*, which can still be heard today in the global polyglot experiment of Wikipedia.

It is sometimes forgotten that this ancient faith in culture was born as a religious creed, with a mystical dimension and the promise of salvation. The faithful believed that in the afterlife, the souls of the chosen ones would live in meadows watered by cool springs, with theaters for the poets, dance troupes, concerts, and conversations around tables at never-ending banquets—in this case, with a copious flow of wine. For the most fraudulent philosophers, it would be heaven: no one would get annoyed with them there or tell them to stop their prattle.

This is why so many funeral monuments—epitaphs, carvings, or statues—commemorate the cultural knowledge of the deceased. The dead bid farewell to earthly existence with the airs of men of letters, orators, philosophers, art lovers, or musicians. But these tombs do not belong to intellectuals, teachers, or artists, as was first believed. We now know that in fact, in most cases, they were traders, doctors, or functionaries. But there was only one thing they wished to be remembered for: being initiated into the labors of intelligence and the wonders of art—the forms of wisdom protected by the Muses.

"The only worthwhile thing is education," writes one follower of this cult in the second century. "All other riches are trivial and human and are not worth the effort to seek them. Noble titles belong to our ancestors. Wealth is a gift of fate, who gives it and takes it away. Glory is fickle. Beauty is fleeting. Health, inconstant. Physical strength falls prey to illness and old age. Instruction is the only thing we have that is immortal and divine. Because only intelligence is rejuvenated by years and time, which steals away all things, but adds wisdom to age. Not even war, which sweeps and drags away all in its midst like a torrent, can take away what you know."

Old beliefs had come tumbling down, but in their place, immortality was within anyone's reach through culture, words, and books. Let's not forget that the Musaeum of Alexandria, to which the Great Library belonged, was a temple where a priest enacted the rituals of the Muses. It's touching to imagine those Greeks who dreamed of brandishing their scrolls when they called at the gates of paradise.

56

During the third to the first centuries BC, the literary landscape was transformed, and books found shelter on new horizons. Egyptian papyruses reveal that, though not universal, literacy was widespread even beyond the ruling class. Needless to say, the wealthy were the first to go to school and the last to leave. Nevertheless, at least in European Greece, free children had more chance than ever before of receiving an elementary education—the school laws of Miletus and Teos make this clear. The laws of Teos clarify that basic education was directed at boys and girls equally, and this also seems to have been the case elsewhere. Furthermore, in a great many cities of the Aegean and Asia Minor, educational offerings for the daughters of wealthy families blossomed. Finally, cracks are beginning to open through which we can glimpse the entry of girls into the classroom as students and the earliest generations of female readers.

The possibility of education was spreading across vast swaths of territory. A long list could be made of intellectuals born in insignificant cities with distant, sonorous names such as Kotyaion, Eucarpia, Rhodiapolis, Amaseia, or Seleucia. Libraries weren't just founded in capital cities, like the Library of Alexandria and its rival in Pergamum. More modest cultural institutions also emerged on the fringes. A second-century BC inscription found on the small island of Cos records the donations made by several private patrons to a local library.

Far and wide, across the lands in Africa and Asia invaded by the Macedonians, theaters, gymnasiums, and books expressed a Greek identity. For those who were native to these areas, mastering the language of their rulers by reading Thucydides and Plato helped them ascend to prestigious positions. Of course, the conquerors were convinced they were civilizing the barbarians and imposed their culture upon them. In a place as remote as Ai-Khanoum in Afghanistan, Greek texts are still preserved engraved on stone, undoubtedly reaching that faraway region through increasingly mobile books.

It's striking that the writers of this immense geographic expanse all read and referenced the same authors, starting with Homer all the way up to Aristotle and Menander. Learning to read and write from these books was the only thing a Greek born in what is now Iran and another born in Egypt, both so far from home, had in common.

The care and preservation of this literature could not be left to chance. This was the task that occupied the scholars who filled the fantastic labyrinth of books built at Alexandria.

A MAN WITH A PRODIGIOUS MEMORY AND A GROUP OF AVANT-GARDE GIRLS

57

Once upon a time, in the Great Library, there was a man with a prodigious memory. Day after day, he spent his time reading the scrolls in order, shelf by shelf. And the words his gaze caressed were engraved in his mind, transforming it little by little into a magical archive of all the books in existence.

His name was Aristophanes of Byzantium. His father was a mercenary commander and had trained his son for his daring and perilous line of work. But Aristophanes preferred motionless travel and was fond of the multiple lives one could imagine living while reading. On his brow, behind locks of grey hair like lichen, parallel furrows suggested the lines of an indecipherable text. One might have said that this thin and hoary man, always silent but haunted inside by infinite whispering ghosts, increasingly resembled the books he was always devouring.

One day, a poetry competition was held in Alexandria. The king selected six distinguished figures as literary judges. When one more judge was needed to make an odd number, someone slipped in Aristophanes's name. The seven judges heard the poets recite, but while the rest applauded, Aristophanes stayed silent, a neutral expression on his face. He let the others deliberate, not intervening in the discussion. Only at the end did he ask permission to speak, after which he proclaimed all the entrants in the competition to be frauds except for one. He rose, went into the Library's arcades, and based purely on memory, removed a mountain of scrolls from different shelves. Hidden there, word for word, were the poems those cheating writers had plundered. The word thieves could not fool Aristophanes, for whom each line was as unmistakable as a face. He remembered its place on the shelves just as others know the position of every star in the sky.

Legend tells that the king of Egypt named that reader with the extraordinary memory director of the Library.

This anecdote, recounted by Vitruvius, reveals that plagiarism and scandal are as old as literary contests themselves. The story of Aristophanes of Byzantium also reveals the expansion of the Great Library, which, a century after its creation, could be encompassed only by a memory of fabulous proportions. The time for lists and catalogs had arrived.

In fact, as the essayist Philipp Blom explains, every collector needs an inventory. The things they strive to gather might be scattered again one day, perhaps sold or plundered, leaving no trace of the passion and expertise that galvanized their previous owner. It's painful for even the most modest collectors of stamps, books, or records to imagine that in the future, those items chosen one by one and for highly personal reasons will return to the tangle and disarray of the thrift store. Only in its catalog can the collection survive its own wreckage; this is the proof that it existed as a whole, as a painstaking plan, and as a work of art.

In the catalog, the power of numbers is on full display. As I have mentioned before, according to sources, every now and then King Ptolemy would inspect the Library's shelves and ask the person in charge, "How many books do we have now?" The figure on the librarian's lips encapsulated the success or failure of Ptolemy's grand plan. The scene bears a certain resemblance to an episode involving Don Juan Tenorio, whom we might consider the literary archetype of an insatiable collector. In the opera *Don Giovanni*, Mozart and his librettist Da Ponte included the famous "Catalog Aria," where Don Giovanni's servant Leporello offers an inventory of his master's conquests: "This is a list / of the beauties my master has loved, / a list which I have compiled. / Observe, read along with me. / In Italy, six hundred and forty; / in Germany, two hundred and thirty-one; / a hundred in France; in Turkey ninety-one; / in Spain already one thousand and three." Like Don Juan, the Ptolemies needed servant-accountants to confirm that the sum of their achievements was on the increase, that they had the right to feel more and more important and powerful. In the same way, social networks today are the Leporellos of our virtual world and feed the narcissism and the drive to collect that dwells in each of us, keeping track of all the friends, followers, and likes that make up our own conquests.

The Library of Alexandria, which tried to touch infinity, also had an extensive catalog. We know it took up at least 120 scrolls, five times as many as Homer's *Iliad*. This fact alone retains a glimmer of the magnificent lost collection. And it proves that by this point, the flood of books had broken the levees of human memory. The sum of all knowledge, poetry, and written tales would never again dwell in a single mind, as it is said they did in the mind of Aristophanes.

58

The person responsible for the great catalog, in the third century BC, was Callimachus, a poet born in what is now Libya and the first literary cartographer. In the galleries, colonnades, inner rooms, and corridors of the Library of Alexandria, with its shelves full to the point of overflowing, one could already get lost. A map of the territory was needed, an order, a compass.

Callimachus is considered the father of librarians. I picture him filling out the first catalog cards in history—which would have been tablets—and inventing some remote ancestor of catalog numbers.

Perhaps he knew the secrets of Babylonian and Syrian libraries and was inspired by their organizational methods, but he went much further than any of his predecessors. He drew up an atlas of all the writers and all their works. He resolved problems of authenticity and false attributions. He located untitled scrolls in need of identification. When two authors had the same name, he investigated the identity of each, to differentiate them. In some cases, names and nicknames were confused. For example, the true but now forgotten name of Plato was Aristocles. Today we only know him by what seems to have been his gymnasium nickname, Plato, meaning "broad back" in Greek. The philosopher must have been very proud of his wrestling skills on the sand.

In short, the new geographer of books had to confront infinite conundrums with patience and a love of meticulous detail. For each author, Callimachus wrote a brief biography, researched the details that distinguished them—father's name, place of birth, nickname—and made a complete list of their works in alphabetical order. The title of each book was followed by a quote from the text's first line—if it was preserved—for ease of identification.

The idea of using the alphabet to order and archive texts was a great contribution made by the Alexandrian scholars. In our daily lives, we have accepted it as something so common, useful, and obvious that it doesn't even seem like an invention. But just like umbrellas, shoelaces, and book covers, it's a tool that someone came up with in a moment of inspiration preceded by a long quest. Some researchers believe that this simple stroke of genius might be precisely what Aristotle taught the librarians of Alexandria. It's an appealing hypothesis, though impossible to prove. In any case, the system came into being thanks to the intellectuals at the Musaeum. We're still following their example, with a different alphabet.

Callimachus's catalog, known as *The Pínakes*, "The Tables," has not been preserved, but enough references and allusions appear in texts from the following centuries to give us a rough idea of what it was like. Lists that were surely copied from *The Pínakes* have also reached us. For instance, the titles of seventy-three plays by Aeschylus and over a hundred by Sophocles, in alphabetical order. These enumerations are a genuine inventory of losses—today we can read only seven complete tragedies by each.

In one of his most consequential decisions, Callimachus organized the literature by genre, instituting forever the classification of books into the two main territories of verse and prose. Then he partitioned each of these literary countries into provinces: epic, lyric, tragedy, comedy; history, oratory, philosophy, medicine, and law. And finally, a miscellaneous section for the works that didn't fit into any of the main genres. This section featured, for example, four books on baking. The alphabetical organization of books by genre, which persists in our libraries today, obeyed merely formal criteria—useful, but essentially arbitrary. Ever since then, hybrid, experimental, borderline, genre-defying books—which existed even in ancient times—have brought with them the inconvenience of being unclassifiable.

Despite its formalism, *The Pínakes* became an essential search tool, the first great map of literature, a portolan chart for navigating the great ocean of the Library of Alexandria. And, in Aristotle's wake, a bold taxonomy of knowledge and invention. Callimachus's catalog was consulted and updated constantly throughout ancient times. It was an immense success and laid the foundations of bibliography and the creation of encyclopedias, branches of knowledge in the service of all the others.

I imagine Callimachus must have dreamed of saving all the little worlds encapsulated in books from oblivion, even the most obscure, and from here must have drawn strength and patience for the gargantuan effort required. After all, he himself was a writer concerned with the future of words. In an ironic twist of fate, his own work was almost completely lost.

To the best of our knowledge, he was a groundbreaking poet who fiercely defended creative experimentation. He was bored by those who dutifully aped an irrecoverable literary past. He was a lover of brevity, irony, wit, and fragmentation. There's nothing like a sound knowledge of the classics to show us where new paths can be forged.

59

Silently, gradually, libraries began to spread across the world. Between 1500 and 300 BC, there were fifty-five libraries with restricted access in certain Near Eastern cities, but none in Europe. According to statistics from 2014, 97 percent of the population of Spain has access to at least one public library where they live, and there are a total of 4,649 libraries in the country at large. These figures tell the story of an enormous change, an extraordinary proliferation. Though the fact has gone somewhat unnoticed, libraries are one of the ancient phenomena to have colonized us most effectively. If we asked ourselves, like the bedraggled members of the People's Front of Judea in the *Life of Brian*, "What have the Greeks and Romans ever done for us?" we would answer without hesitation: roads, sanitation, democracy, the rule of law, theaters, aqueducts. We might include in our list the epic of the gladiators, that collection of noisy, half-naked wrestlers that so fascinate Hollywood scriptwriters, or the chariot drivers, but the quiet success of public libraries, more alive today than ever, could hardly be farther from our minds.

I've never forgotten the first library of my childhood. I knew from a very young age that in every story, there was a forest; as soon as the main character sets out on its mysterious paths, they stumble upon something magical and make a marvelous discovery. I too walked among trees on long July afternoons, holding my father's hand. We used to go to a little library in Parque Grande together. It was in a tiny house whose façade and tiled roof made it look like a house from a story, or perhaps somewhere in the Alps. I would go inside into the shadows, choose a comic, then emerge into the sunny park grasping my treasure and choose a spot on a bench to read it. And I read it thoroughly, from the first letter to the last, drinking in the pictures and words as the afternoon waned and the bicycles passing us made their metallic music. When I finished, I would return the comic I'd clasped in my hands for a few hours, make my way out of the forest, and return home, my imagination humming in the cool evening air.

The wonders of that park that rose to the status of forest in my young eyes were of course pure fantasy; the books and the heroes that lived inside them; the mysterious murmur of the poplars that seemed to promise a story; the library. I had become a comic junkie, and every afternoon I demanded a higher dose.

The more than ten thousand librarians working in Spain—hundreds of thousands all over the world—feed our addiction to words. They are the ones who dispense the drug, the ones we entrust with the sum of our knowledge and our dreams, from fairy tales to encyclopedias, from erudite treatises to the coarsest of comic strips. Now that many publishers destroy their stock to avoid storage costs, libraries are the storehouses of out-of-print works. They are a treasure trove of words.

Each library is unique, and as someone once told me, it always resembles its librarian. I have immense admiration for those hundreds of thousands of people who still believe in the future of books, or rather, in their ability to dissolve time. Who advise, encourage, plot activities, and devise pretexts for the reader's gaze to awaken the words that slumber, sometimes for years, in a book lying on a shelf. Who know that this act, though commonplace, fundamentally implies the resurrection—rise up, Lazarus—of a whole world.

Librarians descend from a long line that begins in the Fertile Crescent of Mesopotamia, but we know hardly anything about those distant ancestors of the guild. The first of them to speak with his own voice was Callimachus, whom we can picture clearly in his patient cataloguing labor and his long nights of writing. Many writers after Callimachus have served as librarians for some period of their lives, among walls of books at once inviting and daunting: Goethe, Casanova, Hölderlin, the brothers Grimm, Lewis Carroll, Musil, Onetti, Perec, Stephen King. The Spanish poet Gloria Fuertes wrote, "God made me a poet, and I made myself a librarian."

And Borges, the blind librarian who almost became a literary genre unto himself. One of his friends tells of a time when he toured the National Library in Buenos Aires alongside the writer. Borges darted among the shelves as if in a habitat all his own. He caressed every shelf with his eyes, no longer able to see them clearly. He knew where to find every volume, and on opening one could immediately find the exact page he was seeking. Lost in aisles lined with books, slipping through almost invisible spaces, Borges made his way through the library's gloom with the delicate precision of a tightrope walker, just like Jorge de Burgos, the blind guardian—and stealthy assassin—of the abbey library in *The Name of the Rose*, whom Umberto Eco, somewhere between homage and irreverence, dreamed up with the Argentine writer in mind.

In the early twentieth century, this profession, which had been occupied by men from the times of Nineveh, Babylon, and Alexandria onward, began to transform into a territory peacefully occupied by women. In 1920, almost 80 percent of librarians were women. And since only single women were allowed to work, the caricature of the spinster librarian entered the collective imagination—mean and sour, with a grey bun, glasses, old-fashioned clothes, and a grouchy disposition. In those days, not so long ago, it was thought that all a woman who worked among books could do was bitterly lament the absence of the suitor who never put a ring on her finger, and the children she never had. We find a reflection of this stereotype in *It's a Wonderful Life*, which came out in 1946. To me it seems highly parodic, but, alas, the scene is filmed without a hint of irony. One Christmas Eve, George Bailey—the protagonist, played by James Stewart—is on the verge of suicide when his guardian angel swoops in to show him what the world would be like if he'd never been born and to convince him that his life is not in vain. After contemplating how all his friends and relatives would have been less fortunate without him, George asks after his wife. "Where is Mary?" "No . . . don't ask me that," the angel stammers. George imagines the worst and grabs the angel by the lapels in a fit of anguish. "If you know where she is, tell me where my wife is." "I'm not supposed to tell." "Please." "You're not going to like it, George." "Where is she?" George asks desperately. "She's an old maid, George . . . she's just about to close up the library." George drops the angel and runs to the library. Then Mary appears on-screen, closing the door to the Pottersville Public Library. She's wearing the full uniform: a nunlike suit, hair in a bun, thick glasses. She clutches her purse to her chest, neurotic and miserable. The soundtrack makes for a mournful atmosphere. And on seeing George's expression full of horror, the viewer is expected to raise their hands to their face and gasp: Oh no, not a librarian!

The researcher Julia Wells has demonstrated that this stereotype remains present in contemporary film. Many fictional librarians still appear as dour women who shoot a furious "Shhhh!" at anyone who dares speak in their domain. And this brings me to a sad historical irony. In the years immediately before Frank Capra's movie was filmed, in post–Civil War Spain, most of the women who worked as librarians were considered dangerous revolutionaries and were subjected to political purges. They were generally quite the opposite of Mary in *It's a Wonderful Life*: modern, forward-looking girls, forging their own paths in Spanish universities. The Francoist authorities investigated their public activities, their professional lives, and their private behavior. Those who managed to keep their jobs in the public system suffered humiliating wage reductions, were forced to take certain posts, and were denied access to management positions. I think of María Moliner, author of the *Diccionario de uso del español*, who was demoted by eighteen ranks and excluded from positions of trust or authority throughout her entire career. Relegated first to the Archivo de Hacienda de Valencia and then to the Escuela de Ingenieros de Madrid, she wrote her extraordinary dictionary in isolation. The library of my mother's childhood wasn't a tiny, enchanted house in the forest; it was a building where two women who'd been victims of reprisals were employed.

Libraries and librarians have their own universal history of infamy: attacks, bombings, censorship, purges, persecution. They have inspired a gallery of legendary characters like Jorge de Burgos in *The Name of the Rose*, who can turn a book by Aristotle into a criminal weapon; or Mary, who lives in two spatiotemporal dimensions at once, as a happy housewife and as a tormented librarian (we have no idea which of these lives she prefers). But the most remarkable thing of all is the path traveled from their Eastern origins—with their guilds of scribes and priestly castes who safeguarded knowledge—to the libraries of today, open to anyone who wishes to read and learn.

On their shelves sit books written in enemy countries, sometimes even countries at war with each other. Guides to photography and the interpretation of dreams. Essays about microbes and about galaxies. The autobiography of a general next to the memoirs of a traitor. The hopeful work of a misunderstood author, and the somber work of a best-selling one. The brief notes of a female travel writer, next to the five volumes it takes a sedentary author to describe his daydreams in meticulous detail. A book printed yesterday, and beside it, one that is twenty centuries old. Here, temporal and geographical borders are unknown. And in our times, finally, we are all invited in: foreigners and locals, those with glasses or contact lenses or sleep dust in their eyes, men with their hair in a bun, and women in ties. This is what a utopia looks like.

60

In the nineteenth century, Mallarmé wrote, "The flesh is sad, alas, and I have read all the books." He was probably referring to the tedium of a stale and jaded life. But read from the era of Amazon and the Kindle, his words remind us ironically that aspiring to read all books is an impossible dream harbored only by the most delirious bibliophiles. Every half minute, a new book is published. If we assume a price of twenty-two dollars and a thickness of two centimeters, the annual addition to Mallarmé's library would cost over twenty-two million dollars and take up some twenty kilometers of shelves.

Callimachus's catalog was the first complete atlas of known books. The continent he mapped was enormous, and the Greeks felt at least as overwhelmed as we do. No single person would ever read all the scrolls stored in the Library of Alexandria. No one could possibly ever know it all. The knowledge of each person would increasingly be a tiny archipelago in the fathomless ocean of their ignorance.

The anxiety of selection came into being: what should one read, see, or do before it's too late? For the same reason, we are still obsessed with lists to this day. Just a few years ago, Peter Boxall published the umpteenth list of books—in this case, 1,001, like the nights of Scheherazade—that you must read before you die. These days, there is a proliferation of essential albums, unmissable movies, and must-visit places. The internet is the great list of our times, fragmentary and with infinite branches. Any self-help guide worth its salt—meant to make you a millionaire, bring you success, or help you conquer obesity—includes the basic advice of making lists. Persevere at your list of goals and improve your life. The list-making impulse is related to the idea that order is like a tranquilizer, a defense mechanism for neutralizing the spread of chaos. It is also related to anxiety, fear, and the painful certainty that our days are numbered. And so, we try to reduce the things that overwhelm us to ten, fifty, or a hundred items.

As they cast their eyes over the boundless catalog, the scholars of the Great Library were undoubtedly consumed by the same frenzy for lists. What were the indispensable titles in every genre? Which stories, poems, and ideas ought to reach future generations?

In the era of the handwritten reproduction of texts, the survival of an ancient book required immense effort, since the material would deteriorate and it was periodically necessary to copy it all over again. These successive copies also meant the scribes had to revise the edition and provide a commentary so its meaning could not be eclipsed by the passage of time. The Library's scholars, with their limited number of days, could not guarantee such dedication to all the books in the catalog. They were forced to choose. Their lists, like most of ours, were a working agenda, but they also created a reference system that has endured to this day. In *The Infinity of Lists*, Umberto Eco maintains that lists are in fact the origin of culture, part of the history of art and literature. He adds that what we find in encyclopedias and dictionaries are also elaborate forms of lists. And all of them—catalogs, bibliographies, indexes, tables of contents, glossaries—make infinity easier to grasp.

The Greeks had a word for the authors included in lists: *enkrithentes*, "those who have passed through the sieve"—in other words, those who have been screened. The word suggests the rural metaphor of sifting the wheat from the chaff. Though on a smaller scale than now, there were also a great many lists of authors in ancient times, authors you had to read before you died. We know the titles of a few guides from the imperial age that sound just as up-to-date as contemporary publications: *Expertise Concerning Books* by Telephus of Pergamum; *On the Purchase and Selection of Books* by Philo of Byblos; and *The Bibliophile* by Damophilus of Bithynia. These treatises guide readers through book selection, identifying the most important works. Some of these ancient lists have reached us today, and though there are differences among them—the selections are continually updated—they share the same basic traits. Having combed through and compared them, I believe they all date back to the scholars of Alexandria and Callimachus's catalog. And I think the original point of those selections was for readers to join forces to ensure that a handful of beloved and extraordinary books didn't fade into oblivion.

In some ways, to choose is to protect. Today we make lists of landscapes and monuments that we designate as World Heritage Sites to try to shield them from the onslaught of destruction.

Alexandria is a point of departure. There, the money of kings and the efforts of scholars sustained a great project of preservation and rescue. Perhaps for the first time, the Greeks understood that their children and their children's children would need the legacy of the fragile words in books to make sense of existence; that something so ephemeral—a sketch of a puff of air, the musical vibration of our thoughts—must be preserved for future generations; that the ancient histories, legends, stories, and poems bear witness to hopes and dreams and to a way of understanding the world that refuses to die.

I believe the great innovation of the scholars at the Library of Alexandria has little to do with their love of the past. What made them visionaries was their understanding that Antigone, Oedipus, and Medea—those beings made of ink and papyrus in danger of being forgotten—should travel through the centuries; that millions of people still unborn should not be deprived of them; that they would inspire our rebellions, that they would remind us how painful certain truths can be, that they would reveal the darkest recesses of our selves; that each time we became too proud of our status as children of progress, they would be there to give us a slap in the face; that they would continue to matter to us.

For the first time, they considered the rights of future generations—like us.

61

As I write, December draws to a close amid the usual frenzy of lists of the year's best sellers and best-dressed people. The last twelve months are summarized in these roundups published by all the newspapers and splashed across the internet. Reality has turned into a great competition, and we're dying to know who the winners are.

For once, the internet isn't to blame. The Greeks were pioneers of classification with their famous lists: the Seven Sages and the Seven Wonders. Swept up, like us, in culinary fever, they created their own gastronomical record book, a precursor to the *Michelin Guide.* In a curious second-century essay entitled *The Deipnosophists*, we find a list of the Seven Great Greek Cooks. An erudite cook teaches his apprentice the names of the seven most illustrious chefs and their specialties: Agis of Rhodes and his perfectly roasted fish; Nereus of Chios, who made an eel dish worthy of the gods; Charides of Athens, the master of eggs in white sauce; Lamprias and his black broth; Afthonetus, inventor of the sausage; Euthunus, a great cook of lentils; Aristion, the inventor of various kinds of stew, among them a recipe involving an evaporation method, which today we might call his signature dish. The chef concludes, "They have become our second Seven Sages." There are flashes of irony characteristic of present times, too: in the same essay, an illustrious artist of the stove affirms mockingly that "the most important of all condiments in the kitchen is boastfulness."

Of course, writers were also fodder for lists, even before the Library of Alexandria was founded. In the fourth century BC, the great masters of tragedy were already a definitive trio: Aeschylus, Sophocles, and Euripides. Half a century after the death of the last of these, productions of their celebrated plays had become the main feature of theatrical offerings and drew larger audiences than the works of their living successors. The Athenian government decided to create a state archive to protect, as a public good, the authentic versions of the tragedies of Aeschylus, Sophocles, and Euripides, and of these three alone.

Thus, the Greek tragedians would forever be a trio. It must

have been at the Great Library where other famous lists were established—the Nine Lyric Poets, the Ten Orators. Ever since those distant times, the makers of lists opt for certain numbers imbued with a magic halo (three, seven, nine, ten).

There is undoubtedly pleasure in enumeration. I know; I have experienced it. In his final months, my father spent many hours and what little strength he had left surfing sports websites. He searched for photos of soccer games from the good old days—when he was young, of course—back in the late fifties and early sixties of the last century. For my father, any soccer in the past was always better. If anything got him excited, it was discovering some old lineup he'd memorized as a boy. First, he sang it aloud, reading it from the screen, savoring the precise order of the words. Then he wrote it down in a spiral graph-paper notebook I still have today. He proudly showed me his lists, teams of ghosts, rows and rows of names written in his lovely hand, now a little shaky from the strain of illness. Those verses—eleven surnames quickly memorized and then forgotten—had the power to take him back to his childhood. Lists are also an intimate part of each person's life story.

Experts say that writing was born to keep accounting records. In other words, to make lists of goats, swords, and wineskins. Perhaps this is why literature has always kept coming up with new ways to take inventories. In the second canto of *The Iliad*, a long enumeration of Greek ships fighting the Trojans unfurls. The Bible wouldn't be the same without the Ten Commandments or its endless genealogical lists. The tenth-century Japanese writer Sei Shōnagon included 164 lists in *The Pillow Book*. She noted down everything that could be cataloged, in descending order. She headed her enumerations with suggestive epigraphs like "Things That Make the Heart Beat Faster," "Things That Should be Short," "Things that Lose by Being Painted," "Things That Are Near Though Distant," "People Who Look Pleased with Themselves," "Clouds," and "Splendid Things."

In the last chapter of *Ulysses*, Joyce makes a detailed, exhaustive list of the utensils found in a drawer in Leopold Bloom's kitchen. I can't resist Italo Calvino's six proposals for the next millennium. Or Borges's enumerations, especially in his "Poem of the Gifts." Or

Perec's *Attempt at Exhausting a Place in Paris*, as he sits at a café in Saint-Sulpice.

In 1975, Joe Brainard published the book *I Remember,* where he threads his memories into a moving list that lasts a hundred and fifty pages: "I remember when I thought that anything old was very valuable." "I remember reading twelve books every summer so as to get a 'certificate' from the local library. I didn't give a shit about reading but I loved getting certificates. I remember picking books with big print and lots of pictures." "I remember keeping a list of states visited." "I remember fantasies of someday reading a complete set of encyclopedias and knowing everything."

I can't possibly leave out "A Contribution to Statistics" by Wisława Szymborska:

Out of a hundred people
those who always know better
—fifty-two / doubting every step
—nearly all the rest,
glad to lend a hand
if it doesn't take too long
—as high as forty-nine,
always good
because they can't be otherwise
. . . . .
capable of happiness
—twenty-something tops,
harmless singly, savage in crowds
—half at least,
cruel
when forced by circumstances
—better not to know
even ballpark figures,
. . . .
mortal
—a hundred out of a hundred.
Thus far this figure still remains unchanged.

We spend our lives making lists, reading them, memorizing them, tearing them up, throwing them into the trash, crossing off the things we've done, loving and loathing them. The best lists are those that recognize their items' importance and try to give them meaning. Those that embrace the details and the uniqueness of the world, preventing us from losing sight of what matters. Even if right now, in the midst of the end-of-year bombardment, we've read so many we feel like blacklisting them.

WOMEN, WEAVERS OF STORIES

62

There is only one female presence in the Greek literary canon: Sappho. It's tempting to attribute this glaring imbalance to women not writing in ancient Greece, but this is true only in part. Though it was more difficult for them to be educated and learn to read, many overcame the obstacles to doing so. For some of these, we have broken fragments of poems, but for most, scarcely a name. Here is my provisional list of women writers almost erased: Corinna, Telesilla, Myrtis, Praxilla, Cleobulina, Boeo, Erinna, Nossis, Moero, Anyte, Moschine, Hedyle, Philinna, Melinno, Caecilia Trebulla, Julia Balbilla, Demo, Theosebeia.

I'm intrigued by the verses from each of these women we'll never read, because for me, Greek began in a woman's voice—the voice of my high school teacher. In the beginning, I remember her classes didn't make a great impression; how long it takes us to recognize those who will change our lives. In those days, I was a teenager determined not to give my admiration away for free. I expected charismatic teachers who were sure of themselves, the kind I'd seen in the movies, who strode into the classroom with a rebellious air, leaned against the edge of their desk, and launched into a brilliant, ingenious, captivating speech. On the outside, Pilar Iranzo didn't fit into this fantasy. She was tall and thin with slightly hunched shoulders, as if she were apologizing to everyone else for her height. She wore an old-fashioned white smock. Her slender pianist's hands fluttered nervously in the air when she spoke. Occasionally, she faltered when teaching the lesson, as if the words had fled her mind all at once. She listened with rapt attention, asked more questions than she made statements, and in fact seemed especially at ease when sheltered by a question mark.

But the surprising Pilar soon broke through my skepticism. Of those two years of study with her, I remember the thrill of discovery, of flight, and the astonishing joy of learning. We were such a small group of students we ended up sitting around a table, huddling together like co-conspirators. We learned by contagion, by illumination. Pilar didn't hide behind declensions, cold dates and figures, abstract theories, conceptual devices. She was transparent: without any gimmicks, without putting on a show, she straightforwardly revealed to us her passion for Greece. She lent us her favorite books, told us about the films of her youth, her travels, the myths in which she could see herself. When she spoke of Antigone, she herself was Antigone, and when she spoke of Medea, it seemed to us the most terrifying tale we'd ever heard. When we translated them, we felt like the classics had been written for us. We forgot all about our fear of not understanding them. They stopped feeling like a burden weighing on us. Thanks to Pilar, some of us annexed a foreign country to our inner worlds.

Years later, when I had faced the dizzying task of teaching a class myself, I understood that you have to love your students to reveal what you love in their presence; to take the risk of offering your authentic enthusiasm, your own thoughts, the lines of poetry that excite you, to a group of teenagers, knowing that they might make fun of it or answer you stone-faced with flagrant indifference.

When I was an undergraduate, I used to visit Pilar during her office hours at the school where she taught. When she retired, I continued to see her in a café near where she lived. I needed to show my gratitude for her unguarded teaching style, and the way she trusted us and believed we deserved to know. Sharing her intimate and mysterious way of listening to the voices of the past.

We would talk for hours at those meetings, leaping across time, from our present concerns to the ancient Greece that tied us together. But we came up against a paradox: we understood that it would have been terrible to live in the era that fascinated us so much, where women were kept so far from power, where they had no freedom, where they never ceased to be treated as minors. Pilar, who had spent so many years passing on the luminous legacy of Greece, knew that this era would have condemned her to a life in the shadows. She longed for the words of the lost women writers and their poems, born in silence.

63

Literary history begins in an unexpected way: the first author in the world to sign a text with her name is a woman.

Fifteen hundred years before Homer, the poet and priestess Enheduanna wrote a collection of hymns whose echoes are present today in the Psalms of the Bible. She claimed them proudly. She was the daughter of King Sargon of Akkad, who unified southern and central Mesopotamia into a great empire, and aunt of the future King Naram-Sin. When scholars deciphered her fragmentary verses, lost for millennia and recovered only in the twentieth century, they were so impressed by her brilliant, complex writing that they dubbed her "the Shakespeare of Sumerian literature." "What I have done, no one has ever done before," Enheduanna writes. The most ancient astronomical notations can also be attributed to her. Powerful and brave, she dared to take part in the turbulent political struggles of her age, and as a result suffered the punishment of exile and nostalgia. But she never stopped writing songs to her protectress, Inanna, the goddess of love and war. In her most intimate, best-known hymn, she reveals the secret of her creative process: the goddess of the moon visits her home at midnight and helps her "conceive" new poems, "delivering" verses that live and breathe. It's a magical, erotic, nocturnal happening. As far as we know, Enheduanna was the first person to describe the mysterious birth of poetry.

This promising beginning was not a sign of things to come. As I have described, *The Odyssey* shows Telemachus silencing his mother because her voice must not be heard in public. Mary Beard has analyzed this episode with exquisite humor. "Speech is for men," says Telemachus. He is referring to authoritative public discourse, not to the kind of chatter or gossip in which everyone—including, or especially, women—could engage.

The silencing of Penelope initiates a long list of rules governing women's lives repeated throughout Greek and Latin antiquity. For example, Democritus, an advocate of democracy and freedom whose thought was subversive in many respects, did not hesitate to state, "To speak but little becomes a woman." To be quiet in public, he wrote, should be considered the best adornment a woman could wear. Greek civilization had this idea engraved in its mind: in public, words belonged only to men. The realm of politics, oratory, and to a large extent literature were their domain. We should not forget that Athenian democracy was founded on the exclusion of all women, and of foreigners and slaves—in other words, of most of the population. As the protagonist of the 1980s British TV series *Yes, Minister*, said, "We must, in my view, always have the right to promote the best man for the job, regardless of sex."

It's true that this exclusion wasn't experienced equally in all Greek territories. And here, another paradox arises: Athens, the capital of political experimentation and intellectual daring, was perhaps the most repressive city for women. In this place we admire so much, women—if they'd been born into wealthy homes—could hardly set foot in the street; they were confined to their houses, weaving between the walls of the gynaeceum, far from public spaces and the ferment of the agora. It goes without saying that the poor had neither money nor resources to facilitate this family apartheid, but on the other hand, those austere lives, poverty, hard labor, and force of habit didn't allow for much freedom, either.

Like all Attic pastimes, theater was a boys' club. The playwrights, actors, and singers in the chorus were men, no matter how hard it is for us today to imagine a bearded Antigone or Electra. In the classical era, when Athens was the beacon of Greek culture, the absence of women creators was more glaring than ever.

On the coast of Anatolia and the nearby Aegean islands (Lesbos, Chios, Samos . . .), a land of Greek emigrants on the Asian border, there was another, more open world. Prohibitions were less strict in those parts and confinement less suffocating. Girls were educated, and as long as they were rich and from noble families, certain women could make their voices heard: some researchers have tried to find in this region the last embers of a lost matriarchy. According to Plato, on the isle of Crete, "*fatherland* was called *motherland*." In the famous Battle of Salamis, the only known female commander in chief fought at the head of a fleet. Her name was Artemisia and she came from the coastal city of Halicarnassus, in Asia Minor, where she was ruler. Though she was Greek, she was allied with the Persian invaders. It's said that the Athenians offered a reward of ten thousand drachmas for her head, "since they found it unacceptable for a woman to wage war on Athens."

And on the nearby island of Rhodes, we find the striking case of a young woman who, though not a prostitute, participated in banquets for men. Her name was Eumetis, meaning "of good counsel," but everyone knew her as Cleobulina, since she was the daughter of Cleobulus, one of the Seven Sages. Like Enheduanna, she was a king's daughter. Cleobulina was politically astute and knew how to wield her influence. It was said that she had turned her father into a kinder ruler who was more caring toward his subjects. As a little girl, she made up playful puzzles while she braided ribbons and nets. She wrote a book of riddles in hexameters that would still be remembered centuries later. An ancient text describes her at a symposium, freely rubbing shoulders with the men. She takes pleasure in her surroundings, intervenes in the conversation, and cracks jokes as she combs and musses the hair of one of the Seven Sages. Since she was witty and clever in an era that wanted its women silent, Cleobulina was easy to caricature. We know that one Athenian comic parodied her in a play titled—in plural—*The Cleobulinas*. It's fair to assume that this comedy, now lost, must have drawn characters similar to those in Molière's *Les Précieuses ridicules*: silly young women who lose their minds over word games and, though they believe themselves very smart, are in fact insufferably pedantic. Women writers had to face the threat of mockery, of a mirror that distorted their reflection. Perhaps that's why they loved secrecy, the power of suggestion, riddles, questions. As Carlos García Gual writes, "In the Greek world, expressing themselves through enigmas was something that belonged to women, who were also weavers of words."

64

Sappho was short, dark, and unattractive. She says so herself. She was born into an aristocratic family that had fallen on hard times. Unlike Cleobulina, she wasn't a king's daughter. Her older brother squandered the family fortune, or what was left of it. She was married off to a stranger, as was the custom, and had a daughter. All this put her on the path to anonymity.

Of course, Greek women didn't write epic poetry. They had no experience of war; battles were a dangerous sport played by aristocratic men. Furthermore, it was impossible for them to live the free and itinerant life of the *aoidos*, traveling from city to city to peddle their songs. Nor did they take part in banquets, or sporting competitions, or political matters. So what could they do? They gave shelter to memories. Like those nannies and grandmothers who told tales to the brothers Grimm, they passed ancient legends on from generation to generation. They also composed songs for female choruses (including wedding songs, songs to honor the gods, and songs for dancing). And they spoke of themselves in songs to be sung in just one voice, with the accompaniment of a lyre; this is where the term "lyric poetry" comes from. Their worlds were forcibly local and small, but even so, almost by miracle, some women gazed out from their corner with an original eye, glowering at the walls that imprisoned them. This was what Sappho did. It is what other groundbreaking women living in confinement, such as Emily Dickinson or Janet Frame, would also do.

Sappho wrote, "Some say there is nothing finer on this dark earth than an army of horses, or an army of men, or an army of ships. But I say that your lover is the most beautiful sight of all." These simple words conceal an intellectual revolution. When they were written in the sixth century BC, they represented a break with tradition. In a profoundly authoritarian world, the poem surprises the reader with its multiple perspectives, and even seems to celebrate the freedom to disagree. Furthermore, it dares to question what the majority admire: parades, armies, the deployment and praise of power. Surely Sappho would have sung the same as Georges Brassens about his bad reputation: "The day of the fourteenth of July, / I stay in my cozy bed. / Music marches to the beat of boots, / This is no concern of mine." Faced with tiresome displays of warriors flexing their muscles, Sappho preferred to feel and to conjure desire. "The most beautiful thing of all . . . is whatever you love best." This unexpected line maintains that beauty is in the eye of the beholder; that we desire not whoever seems most attractive, but rather that they seem most attractive because we desire them. According to Sappho, the lover creates beauty by loving, rather than surrendering to it, as people often believe. To desire is an act of creation, just like writing poetry. Gifted with musical talent, the diminutive, ugly Sappho could adorn with her passions the small world around her and make it beautiful.

At some point, Sappho's life took a different turn. Her marriage came to an end, and she changed her domestic routine for a different way of life, the details of which are hazy. Based on the damaged fragments of her poems that have reached us, and through sources that mention her, we can reconstruct the unconventional circles in which she spent those years. We know that she mentored a group of young women, daughters of distinguished families. We also know that she fell in love with some of them, one after another—Athis, Dika, Irana, Anactoria—and that together, they wrote poetry, made sacrifices to Aphrodite, wove wreaths of flowers, desired and caressed one another, and sang and danced, far away from the influence of men. From time to time, one of these young women would leave, perhaps to get married, and the separation would be painful to all of them. Finally, we're told there were other, similar groups on the isle of Lesbos, overseen by women whom Sappho considered enemies. And she felt excruciatingly betrayed by girls who left her to join a rival circle.

It's thought, though this is mere conjecture, that these circles were *thiasi* for women, a kind of religious club where adolescents, under the guidance of a charismatic woman, learned poetry, music, dancing, honored the gods, and perhaps engaged in erotic exploration before they were married. In any case, the love Sappho had for her protégées was not forbidden but recognized and even encouraged. The Greeks believed love was the main driving force of education. They had little respect for the teacher who taught for money, chasing after his clients and demanding to be paid. For their aristocratic mentality, to accept a job with compensation was beggarly. They were more well-disposed to the teacher who chose new disciples only when he discovered in them a special spark, fell in love, and seduced them—just as Socrates did. In Greece, this pedagogical homosexuality was viewed as worthier and more elevated than heterosexual relationships.

Sappho's best-known poem takes place at the wedding of a young woman who will not return to the group. For Sappho, this is the farewell: "He seems equal to a god that man / who, seated before you / listens, captivated / by the sweetness of your speech / your enchanting laughter / has made my heart pound in my chest: / if I gaze, my voice does not obey / my tongue splits / and embers burn beneath my skin / I am blind, my ears abuzz / sweat trickles, I tremble and shake / and I am pale, paler than grass / I feel as though death is near."

These lines throbbing with desire have scandalized many a reader. Over the centuries, Sappho has suffered a genuine avalanche of incomprehension, caricatures, and malicious comments probing her personal life. Seneca mentions an essay with the title "Was Sappho a Whore?" At the other end of the spectrum, one prudish nineteenth-century philologist, to keep up appearances and shield the world from pagan obscenity, wrote that Sappho was in charge of "a young ladies' finishing school." In 1073, Pope Gregory VII ordered that all her books be burned for their dangerous immorality.

In a fragment of just one line, which has reached us by chance, we read, "I declare that someone will remember us." And though that chance seemed almost nonexistent, almost thirty centuries later, we can still hear the voice of that diminutive woman.

65

I'd like to think that in Athens there was a current of female rebellion of which no Greek author writes and that doesn't feature in any history books. To uncover the tracks of this fanciful, forgotten movement, I have ventured to dive beneath the surface of texts and read between the lines. Though we'll never know for sure whether it existed, this conjecture has always appealed to me. What I will describe here is just a hypothesis, but one that fascinates me.

The first to revolt would have been hetaeras, in other words, high-class prostitutes, the only women in classical Athens who were truly free. Comparable in some respects to Japanese geishas, they occupied an ambiguous position on the social scale, marked by both the advantages and disadvantages of their bad reputation: they lived an exposed life, but were independent. Most of these women were Greeks born in Asia Minor and thus did not have the rights of citizens. In their homeland, they had received a musical and literary education that Athens denied its daughters. Obliged to pay taxes like men, they could, like them, manage their own affairs. They had access to political and cultural circles through their lovers. They were not subject to the pressures borne by Athenian wives, though in exchange, they knew themselves to be doubly excluded, both as foreigners and as whores.

These immigrant women, who belonged to a minority, desired but socially vulnerable, were more able to protest than the Athenian women shut away in their gynaeceums. And for over a decade their voices were heard, thanks to a transgressive infatuation that shook the halls of power to their foundations.

For Athenians in the fifth century BC, the distribution of roles followed an indisputable order. One orator of the period put it bluntly: "We have hetaerae for pleasure, concubines for the daily care of our bodies, wives to give us legitimate children and to be the faithful guardians of our houses." When the most powerful man on the Attic Peninsula violated this system of responsibilities, the city seethed with indignation.

Pericles was married to a woman "appropriate for his lineage," who was mother to his two children. But their coexistence was troubled, and he broke the bonds of matrimony to be with Aspasia, a hetaera born in Asia Minor. Almost five centuries later, the historian Plutarch transcribes a string of insults against the subversive Athenian first lady taken from writings of the period, where she is called immodest, a bitch-faced concubine, and a brothel keeper, among other charming labels.

For most of our history, marriage was first and foremost an

economic institution, a fusion of shared interests. For Greek politicians, even in democratic times, weddings sealed alliances between powerful families with a tight grip on the reins of government. And marriages were dissolved for commercial or strategic reasons, when there was some other, more prosperous clan with which to form a bond. But Pericles chose Aspasia, a foreigner with a bad reputation and lacking in pedigree, for an utterly ridiculous reason: love. Plutarch writes that the citizens watched agape how "each day when he returned from the agora, he kissed and caressed her sweetly." We can infer from his account that this display of conjugal love was considered a scandal at the time. We can well imagine the Athenians grumbling and laughing at their ruler's perversions. It was stupid enough to be in love with one's wife, but to demonstrate this in public verged on obscenity. Many thought that evil times were afoot and fondly remembered a more decent past. The fifth century BC in Athens, which for us is a golden age, seemed to them a dark era of misconduct, miscegenation, and debauchery.

What hearsay didn't reveal was that Aspasia's intelligence aided Pericles in his political career. We know little about her; she is a figure enveloped in mystery and slander, but extant texts lead us to believe that she was a true orator in the shadows. Socrates would visit her with his disciples and enjoy her sparkling conversation; he even went as far as to call her "teacher." According to Plato, she wrote speeches on her husband's behalf, among them the famous funeral speech that contains his passionate defense of democracy. Even today, Barack Obama's speechwriters, and those of John F. Kennedy before him, have been inspired by words probably woven together by Aspasia. And yet, in literary history, she is nowhere to be seen. Her writings were lost or attributed to others.

For fifteen or twenty years, until the death of Pericles in 429 BC, Aspasia wielded enormous influence in powerful circles. How she used this unexpected principal role is unknown. But in that period, something unprecedented happened: texts by the tragedians, the comedians, and the philosophers began to discuss—or to ridicule—the outlandish idea of female emancipation, a question that until then not a single Greek had mentioned.

In those splendid decades, Antigone, the girl who dares to challenge the unjust law of a tyrant in the name of humanity all by herself, spoke from the stage. So did Lysistrata, who in the midst of a war has the extraordinary idea to join with the women of the enemy to organize a sex strike until peace is assured, and Praxagora, who leads a group of Athenian women to supplant the men in the Assembly and use their votes to instate an egalitarian, communist regime, as well as the foreign rebel, Medea.

No one goes further than Euripides's Medea. I imagine the audience of men packing the theater on the morning of the first performance, in the year 431 BC. Eyes fixed on the stage, captivated by fear, they watched an aggrieved, vengeful woman unleash the ultimate horror. They witnessed the unspeakable: a woman murdering her children by her own hand to punish the husband who abandoned and condemned her to exile. They heard words that had never been heard before. Medea spoke aloud, for the first time, of the fury and anguish that dwelled in Athenian homes: "Of all creatures we women are the most wretched. First we must lavish riches on taking a husband, who is master of our bodies, and this is the worst affliction. To leave a husband is scandalous for women but not for men. When men are bored at home, they go out and entertain themselves. But if we wish to do the same it is denied us; they say we must care for our children. They assure us that we do well to stay at home, away from danger, while the men, poor souls, must go to war." Medea, wrestling with her confinement and motherhood, ends by saying that she would rather fight three wars than give birth a single time.

Stirred by Medea's speech, the women of the chorus also abandon their modesty and fear. At a certain point, one of them even dares to suggest that women should not be excluded from philosophy, politics, or from subtle reasoning and debate: "We too possess a muse, companion in our search for wisdom." In Greek tragedy, the chorus represented the voice of the community. This was not where the unruly foreigner spoke, but the Athenians living orderly, domestic lives. To make matters more complex, all of these bold speeches by Medea and her chorus were uttered onstage by men in drag with long wigs, teetering on high platform shoes. It's an irony of history that drag queens were invented in Greece, but not a single woman was allowed to be an actress.

I want to imagine that there were new ideas in the air, that some kind of social movement was stirring debate in the plazas of Athens. The theater has always provided a space for collective discussion. Particularly in Greece, comedies and tragedies revealed the age's most burning conflicts. They found their inspiration in the agora, the streets, and assemblies, taking the political concerns of the moment to the stage. It's plausible to imagine that Antigone, Lysistrata, Praxagora, and Medea were in some sense real presences in Athenian life during those years.

I'd like to believe that this current of change, surely sustained by Aspasia's charisma, permeated even the thought of Plato, who was far from being a preacher of equality. In fact, the philosopher claimed in one of his books that unrighteous men were reincarnated as women, and that this was why the female sex existed. It's almost impossible to believe that the same individual, in whose work we read that to be born a woman is a punishment and an atonement, could have written these extraordinary lines in *The Republic*: "No position in the government of the state belongs to a woman because she is a woman or to a man because he is a man. Rather, the natural talents are evenly distributed between them, and women naturally participate in all pursuits, just as men do."

Aspasia is one of the greatest mysteries and one of the greatest absences from ancient documents. The things she did, thought, and said reach us filtered through others. We're told that she spent her time writing and reading; I want to believe that with her power as a speaker, she sparked the first emancipatory movement on record. I like to imagine that thanks to her, the women of Athens and other cities dared to darken the doorways of the great schools of philosophy. In Plato's Academy there were at least two female disciples: Lastheneia of Mantinea and Axiothea of Phlius. It's said that the latter dressed as a man. A hetaera named Leontion was a philosopher at the Garden, and Epicurus's lover. She wrote a book on the gods, today lost without a trace, where she tried to demolish the theses of highly respected philosophers. Centuries later, Cicero sourly decried her: "Even a little whore like Leontion had the gall to write a riposte to Theophrastus?"

The most well-known and transgressive of all was Hipparchia of Maroneia, who belonged to the school of the Cynics. As far as we know, she is the only female philosopher to whom the ancients dedicated a brief biography. She left no writings but was famous for jettisoning all conventions in her public conduct. She renounced her family fortune and lived in the streets with her husband Crates, dressed in rags. Since both believed that bodily functions were good and should not be a source of shame, they had sex in view of everyone, without shooing away their voyeurs. On one occasion, a man pointed at Hipparchia and asked, "Is this the woman who has abandoned her shuttle?" Hipparchia replied, "Yes, I am she. Do you think me wrong to spend on my own education the time I would have wasted on weaving?"

After all, perhaps Hipparchia thought, with playful humor, that the mind is a great loom on which to weave words. The literary terms we use today still rely on the same image of storytelling as a tapestry. We keep speaking—with textile metaphors—of the warp and weft of a narrative, of spinning a tale, of weaving a plot. What is a text for us, if not a collection of verbal threads knotted together?

This is how the Portuguese poet Sophia de Mello Breyner Andresen described herself: "I belong to the race of those who go through the labyrinth, without ever letting go of the linen thread of words."

66

Myths are woven and unwoven, as Penelope's legend tells. For the twenty years she spent waiting for Odysseus to return, the palace of Ithaca filled with suitors eager to declare the death of the king and take his place in the marriage bed. She promised them that she would choose a husband when she had finished making a funeral shroud for her father-in-law, Laertes. For three years, she wove the shroud during the day and then unwove it craftily during the night. Sitting at her loom, she moved the shuttle and wove the deception that saved her, then every morning, she began once more.

The ancient writers soon understood that the most fascinating paths are those born in the cracks, blind spots, and manipulations of a story. Did Penelope wait faithfully for Odysseus, or did she deceive him in his absence? Was Helen at Troy or not? Did Theseus abandon Ariadne, or was she kidnapped? Did Orpheus love Eurydice more than life itself, or was he the earliest pederast? All of these versions coexisted in the tangled labyrinth of Greek mythology. Just like in *Rashomon*, we must choose between mutually incompatible stories. From this primitive European literature, we inherited our taste for multiple points of view, for variations and different readings, for narratives woven and unwoven, over and over again.

Century after century, we continue to wind and unspool the legends the Greeks told as if looking through an ambiguous kaleidoscope. In Joyce's *Ulysses*, the singer Molly Bloom, a peculiar, foul-mouthed Penelope, sets forth her version of the myth in a long, unpunctuated sentence that can be counted not in lines but in pages—over ninety—and is laced with obscenities. The book ends with the rush of her stream of consciousness as she lies in bed beside her husband. She recalls her childhood in Gibraltar, her early lovers, motherhood, her desire, bodies, voices, things that cannot be said. The last word of the novel, "yes," is hers. Finally, Penelope can express an emphatic, affirmative eroticism: "First I put my arms around him yes and drew him down to me so he could feel my breasts all perfume yes and his heart was going like mad and yes I said yes I will Yes."

The Canadian writer Margaret Atwood has also traveled into the Homeric landscape of *The Odyssey*, where feminine monsters allow for a comic rereading. Atwood gives voice to a siren, a mocking bird-woman who according to the myth dwells on a nameless, rocky island teeming with skeletons and corpses. In the poem, the great seductress reveals her sweet and deadly secret, the words with which she lures the sailors who dare to come near her reefs toward shipwreck and death. What are the ingredients of her powerful spell? The siren sees that one needn't be a fatal mythological creature to entrap heroes; it's enough to call to them with her whispering voice, to beg them for help, to flatter their vanity.

The poet Louise Glück gives Circe, the sorceress and Medea's aunt, a chance to explain herself. Homer accused her of using her magic potions to turn the companions of Odysseus into hogs, but the story Glück's Circe tells is infinitely more sarcastic: "I never turned anyone into a pig. / Some people are pigs; I make them / look like pigs. / I'm sick of your world / That lets the outside disguise the inside." And, when her love Odysseus decides to abandon her, the witch, alone on the beach, speaks to the sea, where all stories dwell: "The great man turns his back on the island. / Now he will not die in paradise / . . . / . . . Time / begins now, in which he hears again / that pulse which is the narrative / sea, at dawn when its pull is strongest. / What has brought us here / will lead us away; our ship / sways in the tinted harbor water. / Now the spell is ended. / Give him back his life, / sea that can only move forward."

The legends come from an archaic world, but we weave them together with new threads, on our own loom. No matter how hard Telemachus tries to rule over words and impose silence, sooner or later, versions of the myth are born from the point of view of Penelope and her sisters, the weavers of stories.

THE OTHER TELLS ME MY STORY

67

Astonishing words were heard on the stages of Athens. There, desperate women, slaves, the sick, the insane, the murderous, and the suicidal all had a voice. The audience couldn't avert its gaze from those extraordinary characters. In Greek, "theater" meant precisely "a place to watch." For generations, the Greeks had heard tales, but to peer into a story like spies through a crack in the door was a different experience altogether, and a strangely intense one. There, the audiovisual language by which we're still entranced began to flourish. The tragedies, grouped into trilogies, caused the same kind of addiction as contemporary series and sagas. As Aristotle knew, they were works of horror, and the best of them were also journeys deep into the night, where ancestral fears, taboos, bloodshed, intrafamilial crime, the anguish of unresolved conflict, and the silence of the gods all lie in wait.

Little is left of those chilling works (seven tragedies by Aeschylus, seven by Sophocles, and eighteen by Euripides). We know they wrote several hundred plays altogether, most of which have disappeared. And we know the titles of at least three hundred lost plays by other authors. Today, the landscape of Greek tragedy is barren. Only a handful of works have reached us, but they are among the favorites of the Athenians at the time. They had no doubt about who the best were. Around the year 330 BC, bronze statues of the three tragedians were placed in front of the Theater of Dionysus, on the slope of the Acropolis. And as I mentioned before, the Greeks decided to preserve official copies of their texts, and theirs alone. The destruction has been terrible, but not indiscriminate.

The surviving tragedies present a remarkable fusion of violence and sophisticated verbal debate. Beautiful words coexist with bloodied weapons. Somehow, mysteriously, the tragedies manage to be savagely delicate. In general, they tell primitive myths from a legendary past—the Trojan War, the fate of Oedipus—whose echoes could still be heard in the fifth century BC. But there is one curious exception, a tragedy based on real events. It is also the oldest preserved piece of theater in the world. This is *The Persians*, where Aeschylus opened the way for Shakespeare and perhaps, unknowingly, invented the historical novel.

During Aeschylus's life, the Persian Empire launched various conquests against Greece's myriad tiny constituent cities, which were in perpetual dispute. The defense of Athens depended on a citizen army, and Aeschylus fought on several battlefields—among them Marathon, where he lost his brother, and perhaps also the naval Battle of Salamis. In those days, war was very different. I try to imagine that close, body to body combat, in a period when bullets and explosives hadn't yet been invented. The fighters looked one another in the eye as they tried to kill each other. They plunged spears and swords deep into the enemy's flesh, mutilated bodies, trampled on corpses, heard deathly cries, were spattered with mud and entrails. It's said that in his epitaph, Aeschylus mentioned his battles but said nothing of his enormous body of literary work. He was prouder of having participated in the tiny Greek resistance against the powerful Persian invasion than he was of his verses.

I do not think our idea of the clash of civilizations would have sounded strange to his ears. The struggle between East and West is an old story. The Athenians felt the constant threat of a tyrannical, dictatorial state. If that enemy was successful at subduing Greece, it would wipe out its democracy and way of life forever. The Greco-Persian Wars were the great conflict of the era, and Aeschylus decided to take this conflict to the stage, when the Greek victories were still a fresh memory.

He might have just written a patriotic pamphlet, but the poet and former soldier made a series of unexpected decisions. The most surprising of these was to adopt the point of view of the vanquished, like Clint Eastwood in *Letters from Iwo Jima.* The action takes place in Susa, the Persian capital, and there isn't a single Greek character in the play. Aeschylus seems to have researched Persian society—he demonstrates familiarity with real genealogies, Iranian words, and aspects of the pomp and ceremony of the court. But what's most remarkable is that we detect no trace of hatred, but rather an unexpected comprehension. The play begins on the palace esplanade. The Persians are worried, having received no news of the war expedition. Then a messenger arrives and tells of a dreadful defeat and of the Asian heroes fallen in battle. Finally, King Xerxes, who has been humbled along the way, returns home in rags, leaving behind him a pointless massacre.

This is a singular vision of an enemy who came close to destroying Greece. The Persians are not described as part of an axis of evil, or as natural-born criminals. Aeschylus invites us to contemplate the helplessness of the elderly advisers who opposed the war but went unheard, the anguish of those waiting at home for the army's return, the internal divisions between the hawks and doves of the regime, the pain of the widows and mothers. We can appreciate the tragedy of the soldiers led off to be slaughtered by the megalomania of their king.

The messenger of *The Persians* tells a painful and moving tale of the Battle of Salamis, which has become a symbol in our time. *Sol-*

diers of Salamis, the novel by Javier Cercas, alludes to the Greeks who stopped the Persian Empire's invasion and also to the soldiers of the anti-Nazi resistance. Cercas knows there can be soldiers of Salamis in any era: those who face a decisive and apparently losing battle to defend their country, their aspirations, and democracy. Salamis is no longer just a little island in the Aegean Sea, two kilometers from the port of Piraeus; it exists beyond maps, anywhere people rise up, in smaller numbers, against crushing aggression.

Theater is older than Aeschylus. He himself wrote other plays before *The Persians.* But they have all been lost, so for us, this work is a beginning. I've always been fascinated that Aeschylus, after fighting the Persians in close combat, staring them in the face, after seeing his brother die near him in battle, brought to the stage the sorrows of his defeated enemies. He did so without mockery, hatred, or generalized blame. Between grief and scars and the will to understand strangers, this is where the known history of theater began.

68

Aeschylus and his contemporaries believed that their war against the Persians formed part of a great confrontation between East and West, with capital letters. Influenced by the tragic experience of battle, they considered their enemies bloodthirsty and hungry for conquests. They believed the Greek victory represented the triumph of civilization over barbarism.

On the Anatolian Peninsula, the crossroads of several cultures, a Greek was born with mixed blood and a curious mind who was obsessed with this old conflict. Why were these two worlds—Europe and Asia—enmeshed in a life-and-death struggle? Why had they been at odds since time immemorial? What were they seeking, how did they justify themselves, what were their reasons? Had it always been this way? Would it be this way forever?

This man who was so fond of questions spent his whole life looking for answers. He wrote a long work of travels and chronicles, titling it *Historíai,* which in Greek meant "inquiries" or "studies." We still use the word he redefined when he gave a name to his task, untranslated: "history." With his work, a new discipline was born, and perhaps a different way of looking at the world. Because the author of *The Histories* was a person with inexhaustible curiosity, an adventurer, a seeker of wondrous things, a nomad, and one of the first writers able to think on a planetary scale; I might almost say, a precursor of globalization. This is, of course, Herodotus.

In a time when the vast majority of Greeks scarcely set foot outside their native village, Herodotus was a tireless traveler. He enlisted on merchant ships, moved in slow caravans, struck up conversation with many people, and visited a great number of cities in the Persian Empire, to give an account of the war with knowledge of the terrain and a range of perspectives. When he met the enemy in his daily life, he offered a different and more precise vision than any other writer. In the words of Jacques Lacarrière, Herodotus strove to topple his Greek countrymen's prejudices, teaching them that "the line between civilization and barbarism is never a geographic border between countries, but a moral border within every people, and beyond that, within each individual."

It's curious to note, so many centuries after Herodotus wrote his work, that the earliest history book begins in a ferociously modern way. There are wars between East and West, kidnappings, mutual accusations, differing versions of the same events, and alternative facts.

In the first paragraphs of his work, the historian wonders when the fighting between Europeans and Asians began. He finds echoes of the original conflict in the ancient myths. It all began with the kidnapping of a Greek woman called Io. The story goes that a group of merchants, or rather traffickers—the differences between the two were always unstable in ancient times—disembarked in the Greek city of Argos to show their wares. Some women came down to the shore, lured by the exotic goods. As they browsed, crowded about the stern of the foreign ship, the merchants, who were Phoenician, set upon them. Most of the women fought tooth and nail to defend themselves and escaped, but Io wasn't so lucky. She was captured and taken to Egypt, turned into goods herself. According to Herodotus, this kidnapping marked the beginning of all the violence. A detachment of Greeks in pursuit of revenge soon disembarked in Phoenicia—present-day Lebanon—and abducted Europa, daughter of the king of Tyre. The balance in offenses didn't last long, since the Greeks also abducted the Asian Medea in the territory of what is now Georgia. In the next generation, Paris decided to procure a woman by kidnapping, snatching the beautiful Helen on his way to Troy. This assault tried the Greeks' patience: war broke out, and so did the irrevocable enmity between Asia and Europe.

The beginning of *The Histories* displays a fascinating, hybrid mentality that is at once ancient and astonishingly modern. It's clear that Herodotus thinks legends, oracles, fantastic tales, and divine interventions should feature alongside documented facts. He lived in a world where a king's nightmare, caused by indigestion, might be interpreted as a message from the gods and change the course of an empire or the strategy of a war. The borders between the rational and the irrational were diffuse. But Herodotus was neither gullible nor reverent. I'm fascinated by the boldness with which he turns some of the great mythical episodes of his culture—the abduction of Europa, the voyage of the Argonauts, the beginning of the Trojan War—into a series of petty misdemeanors. I admire the clarity with which he discards the glitter of legend to denounce how easily women become victims when violence is unleashed in times of war and revenge.

Thereupon, Herodotus makes an unexpected statement about his sources. He says he heard the explanations he has just offered for the genesis of the conflict from educated people in Persia. The Phoenicians, on the other hand, tell another story, and "for my own part, I will not say if this or that story is true." After years of travels and conversations, Herodotus discovered that the witnesses he questioned offered him contradictory stories about the same events, that they often forgot what had happened and instead remembered things not as they occurred in reality, but as they occurred in the parallel world of their desires. He thus discovered that truth is elusive, that it's almost impossible to unravel the past exactly as it happened since we have only distinct, biased, contradictory, and incomplete versions of events. *The Histories* is stuffed with phrases like "as far as I know," and "I believe," and "according to what I heard from the mouth of . . . ," and "I don't know if this is true, I write only what is said." Millennia before contemporary multiperspectivism, the first

Greek historian understood that memory is fragile and tenuous, and that when someone evokes their past, they distort reality to justify themselves or to find relief. Therefore, just like in *Citizen Kane* and in *Rashomon*, we never learn the deepest truth but only its traces, its versions, its long shadow, its infinite interpretations.

And most incredible of all: our author does not record the Greeks' version, only that of the Persians and the Phoenicians. Thus, Western history was born with an explanation of the point of view of the other, of the enemy, of those who are unknown to us. Even twenty-five centuries later, to me this seems a profoundly revolutionary approach. It is essential to get to know different, distant cultures, since we will see our own reflected in them. We can only understand our identity by contrasting it with others. It is the other who tells me my story, who tells me who I am.

69

Many centuries later, the philosopher Emmanuel Levinas, an intellectual relative of Herodotus who was Lithuanian, Jewish, French by preference, and who survived a German concentration camp after losing his entire family at Auschwitz, would write, "My welcoming of the other is the ultimate fact, and in it the things figure not as what one builds but as what one gives."

70

I'd like to pause along the way and tell the Greek version of the abduction of Europa. For Herodotus, it's merely another episode in a tumultuous succession of legendary kidnappings, but I myself feel drawn to the story of the mysterious woman who gave her name to the continent where I live.

As all Greeks knew, the god Zeus was a womanizer, constantly on the prowl for young mortal girls. When he found one to his liking, he put on the most extravagant disguises to claim his particular droit du seigneur. The rapes he committed in the form of swans, golden rain, and bulls are notorious. This last transformation was the trick he chose to ensnare Europa, daughter of the king of Tyre.

There isn't what you'd call love and harmony—the poet Ovid comments wryly—in the house of the father of the gods. Zeus has had a domestic quarrel with his wife, Hera, and leaves the palace, slamming the door behind him. Once away from Mount Olympus, he resolves to have an affair with a mortal woman to offset the bitter taste of the argument and his unhappy marriage. He descends to the shore of Tyre, where the king's lovely daughter wanders with her retinue of maidservants. To approach his prey, the god appears in the guise of a snow-white bull with a muscular neck and, as Ovid tells us, a splendid dewlap that hangs to his hooves. Europa spots the calm, milk-colored creature near the water's edge and watches him graze, not suspecting that before her eyes is a crafty, malicious animal, like the white whale Melville will imagine centuries later.

The seduction begins: the bull nuzzles Europa's hands with his white snout, frolics and leaps in the sand, offers his chest for her to stroke. The maiden laughs, loses her fear, starts to play along. She delights in disobeying her elderly servants, who wave and try to warn her, but she throws caution to the wind, mounting the back of the bull. No sooner does the bull feel her thighs astride him than he heads for the water and gallops boldly across the waves. A terrified Europa looks back at the shore, her light tunic fluttering in the wind. Never again will she see her city or her home.

Zeus's gallop across the waves takes her to the island of Crete, where the couple's children will forge the dazzling civilization of the palaces, the labyrinth, the menacing Minotaur, and the luminous frescoes that today's tourists, spilling from cruise ships, flock to photograph among the ruins of Knossos.

Europa's brother Cadmus is commanded to find her wherever she might be. His father, the king, threatens him with exile if he fails to bring her back. Cadmus, a mere mortal, does not discover the hideout Zeus has chosen for his secret misdeeds. He scours Greece from end to end, calling to Europa until her name is carved into the rocks, the olive trees, and the wheat fields of this unknown continent. Exhausted by his interminable search, Cadmus founds the city of Thebes, cradle of the ill-fated line of Oedipus. The legend tells that it was Cadmus who taught the Greeks to write.

Ever since the linguist Ernest Klein proposed its etymology, many philologists maintain that the word "Europa" is in fact of Eastern origin, connecting it to the Akkadian *Erebu*, a relative of the modern Arabic term *ghurubu*. Both these terms mean "country where the sun dies"; the land of twilight; the West, from the point of view of those who live east of the Mediterranean. In the time the Greek myths evoke, the privileged land of great civilizations lay in the region of the Levant, between the River Tigris and the Nile. Our continent, by contrast, was a savage territory—the dark and barbaric Far West.

If this hypothesis is true, our continent has an Arabic name—one of those ironies of language. I try to imagine the face of the woman called Europa—a Phoenician, whom today we would describe as Syrian Lebanese, undoubtedly dark-skinned, with pronounced features and curly hair. The kind of foreigner who in our times awakens suspicion among those Europeans who frown upon the waves of refugees reaching their shores.

In fact, the legend of Europa's abduction is a symbol. Behind the story of the princess snatched from her home lies a distant historical memory: the journey of Eastern knowledge and beauty from the Fertile Crescent to the West, and in particular the arrival of the Phoenician alphabet to Greek lands. Europe—Europa—was born when it embraced written culture, books, and memory. Its very existence is indebted to knowledge kidnapped from the East. We must remember that there was a time when, officially, we were the barbarians; the barbarians were us.

71

In the midfifties of the last century, in a Europe divided by the Iron Curtain, traveling beyond Allied territories was an even more difficult mission than in Herodotus's time. In 1955, a young Polish journalist called Ryszard Kapuściński longed above anything else to "cross the border." It didn't matter which border or where; he didn't aspire to visit places like London or Paris, imbued with a capitalist aura beyond his reach. He simply longed to carry out the almost mystical, transcendental act of crossing a border. To break free. To experience the other side.

He was lucky. His newspaper, which answered to the exalted

name of *Banner of Youth,* sent him to India as a correspondent. Before he left, the editor in chief gave him a thick, hardcover tome: *The Histories*, by Herodotus. Hundreds of pages long, it wasn't exactly a light volume to drag around in his luggage, but Ryszard took it anyway. It gave him a sense of certainty at a time when he felt bewildered and scared. His first layover on the way to New Delhi would be Rome. He was about to set foot in the West, and as he'd been taught in his communist homeland, the West should be feared like the plague.

The Herodotus book was his vade mecum, a foundational guide in his discovery of the mysterious outside world. Decades later, with extensive international wanderings under his belt, Kapuściński wrote the marvelous *Travels with Herodotus*, a book overflowing with affection for the restless Greek in whom he found a fellow traveler and kindred spirit: "I was grateful for his being by my side in India during moments of uncertainty and confusion, for helping me with his book . . . I set off into Herodotus's world, the wise, experienced Greek as my guide. We wandered together for years. And although one travels best alone, I do not think we disturbed each other—we were separated by twenty-five hundred years and also by distance of another kind, born of my feelings of respect. For although Herodotus was always straightforward, kind, and gentle in relation to others, there was always with me the feeling of rubbing shoulders undeservedly, perhaps presumptuously, but always thankfully, with a giant."

In Herodotus, Kapuściński finds the temperament of a journalist in the making, gifted with the eye, ear, and intuition of a true reporter. In his view, *The Histories* is the first work of reportage in world literature, the work of a fearless man who sails seas, crosses steppes, and roams deserts, possessed with a passion and thirst for knowledge bordering on obsession. Herodotus had set himself the extraordinary goal of making world history immortal, and he let nothing deter him. In the distant fifth century BC, it was impossible to read up on foreign lands in archives and libraries, so his method was essentially that of the journalist: travel, observe, ask questions, draw conclusions from what others told him and from what he saw for himself. This was how he amassed his knowledge.

The Polish writer and journalist imagined his Greek master in situations such as this. After a long day of trudging along dusty roads, he reaches a seaside village. He lays down his staff, shakes the dirt from his sandals, and with no further ado, strikes up a conversation. Herodotus was born into a Mediterranean culture of long, welcoming tables, where many would gather on warm afternoons and evenings to eat cheese and olives, drink cool wine, and talk. In these conversations—dining beside the fire, or al fresco, beneath an age-old tree—stories, anecdotes, old tales, and legends would blossom. If a guest appeared, he was invited to the table. And if this guest had a good memory, he would glean an endless amount of information.

Hardly anything is known about Herodotus's private life. It's remarkable that in a book overflowing with characters and anecdotes, he tells us so little about himself, offering only a bare-bones account. He came from Halicarnassus, today known as Bodrum, in Turkey, a crowded port city overlooking a beautiful bay, a crossroads of trading routes between Asia, the Middle East, and Greece. At seventeen, Herodotus had to flee his native city when his uncle played a principal role in a failed rebellion against a pro-Persian tyrant. He became stateless at a young age—in those days, one of the worst fates to befall a Greek. Unperturbed, with little concern for the future, he decided to venture forth on the roads and seas and find out as much as he could about the known world, from India to the Atlantic, from Ethiopia to the Urals. We know nothing of how he subsisted in exile. He traveled, dedicated an immense amount of energy to his task as researcher, and gave himself over to the spell of the countries he traversed. He met hospitable foreigners and fueled his mind by speaking with them of customs and traditions. He wrote of distant, rival peoples without a single offensive overtone or negative judgment about them. He must have been as Kapuściński imagines him: a straightforward, friendly, understanding man, open and chatty, someone who could always charm others and make them talk. Despite his banishment, he harbored no rage or resentment. "He tries to understand everything, find out why someone behaves in one way and not another. He does not blame the human being, but blames the system." Like his rebel uncle, he became a fervent defender of freedom and democracy and an enemy of despotism, autocracy, and tyranny. He believed that only under the former system could humans live in a dignified way. Take note, Herodotus seems to say: an insignificant cluster of small Greek states has defeated the great Eastern power, only because the Greeks knew themselves to be free, and for that freedom, they were willing to give everything they had.

One passage in *The Histories* has amazed and captivated me ever since I first read it. In this section, it's suggested that each of our personalities is shaped—more than we'd like to admit—by mental habits, repetition, and chauvinism: "If it were proposed to all people to select which seemed the best of all customs, and they were invited to choose the most perfect, each would choose his own; so convinced is each that his own customs are the most perfect. During Darius's reign, the king summoned the Greeks in his court and asked them what price would persuade them to eat their fathers' dead bodies. They answered that they would not do it for any price. He then summoned the Indians who are called Callatiae, who eat their progenitors, and asked them in the presence of the Greeks, who were following the conversation helped by an interpreter, what would make them willing to burn their fathers' mortal remains on a pyre. The Indians protested loudly and begged him to desist from this blasphemy. Pindar was right to say that custom is lord of all things."

Some authors believe that this text by Herodotus contains the seed of the tolerance and the need to understand, know, and reflect that centuries later would form the basis of ethnography. In any case, it reveals an immense degree of insight into the peoples he visited, and also his Greek homeland. The customs of every culture are distinct, but everywhere they are deeply ingrained. What human communities have in common is that which inevitably pits them against one another: the tendency to believe themselves to be better than others. As the ironic gaze of this nomadic Greek discovered, we are all inclined to think we are superior. In this, we are equal.

If for Kapuściński, Herodotus's book weighed heavily in his baggage, it would have been far more unwieldy for ancient readers. In fact, it was one of the first enormous tomes on record and definitely the first extensive work of prose in Greek. It has reached us divided into nine parts with the names of the Muses, and each of those nine parts would have occupied an entire papyrus scroll. To lug those nine volumes around together, you would have needed a slave to carry them.

The invention of scrolls was undoubtedly a great step forward in its time. They were more practical reading devices than any of their predecessors. They had more space than clay tablets and were far more portable than smoke signals or inscriptions on blocks of stone, but even so, they were cumbersome. As we have already seen, only one side of the papyrus could be written on, so the scrolls became very long strips, their usable side crammed with columns of writing squeezed into a tiny space. To gain access to this jumbled labyrinth of words, the reader had to go through the troublesome maneuver of constantly rolling and unrolling meter upon meter of text. Furthermore, to make the most of the costly papyrus, books were written without any spaces to separate words or phrases, and without any chapter divisions. If, with the help of a time machine, we could hold a fifth-century BC copy of *The Histories* in our hands, it would look to us like a single, uninterrupted, endless word spread across nearly a dozen papyrus scrolls.

Only brief texts such as a tragedy or a Socratic dialogue fit comfortably onto a single scroll. The longer the scrolls, the more awkward and fragile, and the more likely they were to break. Searching for a specific passage in a forty-two-meter volume—the longest of which we know—might easily give the reader a cramp in the arm and quite a stiff neck.

The vast majority of ancient works thus occupied more than one scroll each. In the fourth century BC, Greek copyists and booksellers developed a system to ensure the unity of works distributed across multiple books. The same system had been used with tablets in the Middle East and consisted of writing at the end of a scroll the first words of the one that followed, to help the reader find the new volume they were about to start. Despite all these precautions, a work's integrity was always under threat from an uncontrollable march toward disintegration, chaos, and loss.

There were boxes made especially for storing and transporting scrolls. These containers were an attempt to protect the books from damp, from gnawing insects, and from the ravages of time. Each box could house between five and seven works, depending on their length. Oddly enough, many of the texts, by numerous ancient authors, were preserved in multiples of five and seven—for example, we have seven tragedies by Aeschylus and as many by Sophocles, twenty-one comedies by Plautus, and scrolls with parts of Livy's history preserved in tens. Some scholars believe that on the haphazard, twisting path across the centuries, these copies were saved precisely because they were stored together in one or several of those boxes.

I go into all this detail to explain just how fragile and difficult books were to preserve in those days. There were few copies of a given title in circulation, and their survival required gargantuan efforts. Fires and floods, which destroyed books beyond repair, were relatively frequent catastrophes. The wear and tear of use, the appetite of moths, and the toll of the seasonal damp climate meant that every so often, all of the scrolls in libraries and private collections had to be copied out anew, one by one. Pliny the Elder wrote that in the best possible conditions and with the most meticulous care, a papyrus scroll could withstand two hundred years of use. In the vast majority of cases, it would last far less than that. Losses were constant, and as the number of surviving copies of a particular work decreased, it became more and more complicated to locate a scroll so as to make a replacement copy. Throughout ancient times and the Middle Ages, up to the invention of the printing press, books were continually disintegrating, or teetering on the edge of the abyss before they vanished.

Let's imagine for a moment that each of us had to spend whole months of our lives making copies by hand, word for word, of our most beloved books, to avoid their extinction. How many would be saved?

We should therefore consider it a small miracle—thanks to the unknown passion of many anonymous readers—that a work as long, and therefore as vulnerable, as *The Histories* of Herodotus has managed to reach us, skirting the chasm of the centuries. As

J. M. Coetzee writes, a classic is a work that "survives the worst of barbarism, surviving because generations of people cannot afford to let go of it and therefore hold on to it at all costs."

THE DRAMA OF LAUGHTER

Our Debt to Rubbish Dumps

72

A series of grisly crimes begins to unfold inside the walls of a medieval abbey perched atop a mountain in Italy. The deadly trail leads to the great monastic library where, hidden like a tree in a forest or a diamond in a block of ice, a manuscript lies for which the monks are willing to kill or die. The abbot entrusts the investigation of the thorny issue to a visitor passing through the monastery, William of Baskerville, who has learned to interrogate people in his work as an inquisitor. All this occurs in the turbulent fourteenth century.

The Name of the Rose is a remarkable detective novel set in the ritualistic, secretive world of a convent full of hidden corners. Umberto Eco plays with the conventions of the genre, and in a nod to bookworms of every era, replaces the usual femme fatale with a fateful book that tempts, perverts, and kills anyone who dares read it. Needless to say, the reader wonders what dangerous secrets this prohibited text, which we're told has "the power of a thousand scorpions," might conceal. A hidden, seditious Gospel? Catastrophic prophecies made by some medieval Nostradamus? Necromancy, pornography, blasphemy, esotericism, satanic rituals? No, nothing as trifling as any of this. When William of Baskerville puts the pieces of the puzzle together, we learn that the book—great heavens—is an essay by Aristotle.

Seriously? One might easily feel cheated. After all, Aristotle isn't exactly a radical author known for subversive ideas. Today it's hard to imagine the theorist of the golden mean, the meticulous encyclopedist and founder of the Lyceum writing a book that carries a curse. Yet Umberto Eco speculates on the dangerous meanings of an Aristotelian work we will never read: the lost treatise on comedy, the legendary second part of the *Poetics*; in other words, the essay that—as we know from allusions made elsewhere by the author himself—explored the revolutionary world of laughter.

As we approach the dénouement of *The Name of the Rose*, we come upon one of those classic serial killer speeches, the moments of glory on which all villains pride themselves, during which they squander their chance to bump off the detective and win the game and instead choose to spend their time boasting of their intelligence. This is where the murderous monk explains, in sensational, apocalyptic style, why Aristotle's writings on laughter are dangerous and must be eliminated:

> Laughter frees the villein from fear of the Devil, because in the feast of fools the Devil also appears poor and foolish, and therefore controllable. But this book could teach that freeing oneself of the fear of the Devil is wisdom. When he laughs, as the wine gurgles in his throat, the villein feels he is master, because he has overturned his position with respect to his lord; but this book could teach learned men the clever and, from that moment, illustrious artifices that could legitimatize the reversal . . . This book could strike the Luciferine spark that would set a new fire to the whole world . . . But if one day—and no longer as plebeian exception, but as ascesis of the learned, devoted to the indestructible testimony of Scripture—the art of mockery were to be made acceptable . . . then we would have no weapons to combat that blasphemy, because it would summon the dark powers of corporal matter, those that are affirmed in the fart and the belch, and the fart and the belch would claim the right that is only of the spirit, to breathe where they list!

Eco's imagined assassin provides clues for understanding the curse that apparently pursues comedy. Ancient humor suffered a major shipwreck. Every copy of Aristotle's treatise on laughter disappeared, whereas the other half of the work, devoted to tragedy, survived. Dozens of Greek comedy writers had their work performed in theaters packed with rapturous audiences, but only the plays of one were preserved: those of Aristophanes. Most of the literary genres collected in the Alexandrian catalog (epic, tragedy, history, oratory, philosophy) were serious, even solemn.

Today, the canon still tends to exclude laughter. A comedy has a far lower chance of winning an Oscar than a drama. It's surprising to see an author of a humorous bent touch down in Stockholm. Publicists and TV producers know humor sells, but academia is reluctant to elevate it to the status of art. Mass culture exploits laughter and degrades it. We're entertained by reality shows and comic sketches, while high culture rejects its crass aesthetic with a raised eyebrow. So much trivial enjoyment—and the success of all this comic relief—seems to reduce laughter to a form of individual therapy, a fleeting distraction.

The researcher Luis Beltrán Almería maintains that "it's a common mistake to consider humor an odd or marginal phenomenon. What's odd," he adds, "is seriousness, which triumphed in this recent period of cultural and economic inequality we call history." Let's not forget that this phase is only the visible tip of the iceberg. For hundreds of thousands of years, we lived differently. Primitive culture, which came before writing, monarchies, and the accumulation of wealth, would have been essentially egalitarian and joyful. The Russian theorist Mikhail Bakhtin describes how our remote ancestors, in their festivities, clad in masks and costumes, celebrated their triumphs in the struggle for survival all together in joyful confusion. According to him, this kind of spirit of equality held sway while societies were inevitably poor and their systems of organization very simple. But as soon as the new agrarian societies, which introduced money, made it possible to get rich, those whose granaries were fullest were quick to establish hierarchies. The ruling classes who've since run unequal societies have a preference for serious language. Because the most authentic laughter still contains the pulse of rebellion against domination, authority, and status, the contempt these forces so often fear.

I'm drawn to the vindication of laughter in Bakhtin's theory, but

I do not believe in that essentially egalitarian, happy world. I imagine it as terrifying, authoritarian, and violent. I'm more sympathetic to the scene imagined by Kubrick in *2001: A Space Odyssey*. I'm sure that as soon as the first protohuman realized a bone could serve as a tool, they promptly used it to bash a fellow protohuman over the head. Tribes were not collective paradises; they had rulers. While it's true that, compared to our times, there were few differences in wealth between groups, I'm afraid this wouldn't prevent cases of despotism: You can't come in here, I'm keeping the biggest piece of meat for myself, it's your fault we're having a streak of bad luck hunting, we're going to expel you from the tribe, we're going to massacre you, and so on. Nor do I believe laughter always endeavors to restore equality—it can also be cruel and reactionary: schoolyard mockery of the weakest kids, the jokes Nazis must have cracked amongst themselves as they huddled together and smoked. And yet . . .

And yet, there is a rebellious kind of humor that challenges power relations, that undermines the aura of an authoritarian world, that exposes the emperor, stripping him bare. As Milan Kundera explains in his novel *The Joke*, laughter has an immense ability to delegitimize power, which is why it perturbs and is often punished. In general, dear leaders in every period have loathed and persecuted those who dared to ridicule them. Humorists tend to clash with the most inflexible regimes and individuals. Even in contemporary democracies, heated debates break out over the question of how far humor and offense can go. The positions taken generally depend on whether the convictions under scrutiny are our own or those of the other. Tolerance is conjugated like an irregular verb: I am outraged, you are sensitive, he is dogmatic.

Like Charlie Chaplin, Aristophanes embodies rebellious, dissident laughter. In fact, I have always thought this pair's humor has the feel of a family, one where Chaplin would be the genial cousin and Aristophanes the sarcastic grandpa. Both were interested in ordinary, vulnerable people; their heroes are never among the elite. In the guise of the Tramp, Chaplin appears as a vagrant, as an escaped prisoner, as an immigrant, as an alcoholic, as a worker down on his luck, or as a famished miner in search of gold. The protagonists of Aristophanes's comedies are people—men and women—without the assets of nobility; they are tricksters, tax-dodgers crippled by debt, people weary of war, seeking sex and merriment, foul-mouthed and perhaps not starving, but always dreaming of stuffing their faces with lentils, meat, and pies. The Tramp identifies with orphans and single mothers, falls in love with beggar women, and, when he sees the chance, delivers a kick in the rear to an unsuspecting policeman. He has the audacity to ridicule the filthy rich, business tycoons, immigration officials, haughty World War I soldiers, and even Hitler himself. Aristophanes's creations, of a similar stripe, attempt to end a war by means of a sex strike, occupy the Athenian Assembly to decree the institution of communal property, make fun of Socrates, or propose to cure the god of wealth's shortsightedness so he can do a better job of distributing assets. After a series of unruly adventures and intrigues, all of these works end in a festive, teeming, Pantagruelian banquet.

Both Aristophanes and Chaplin ran into problems with the law.

The comedies of Aristophanes were stuffed with personal allusions and political caricature, like a satirical puppet show on TV. From the stage, actors made jokes using first and last names—or rather, using names and patronyms—about the people watching the show from their seats: they mocked one person for being lackadaisical and the next for being miserly, ugly, or corrupt. The city of Athens, where performances were held, was considered the world's metropolis, the most important city on the planet, but with its hundred thousand inhabitants, it would seem to us today like a small provincial capital. Everyone knew everyone and practiced the timeless sport of gossip. Aristophanes rubbed shoulders with his fellow citizens in the agora, where they would gather in the morning to shop, rant about their rulers, spy on their neighbors, and tattle. He was especially friendly with conservatives who were nostalgic for the past and had little fondness for novelty. Later, at the theater, with almost the same freedom as in the gossip mills in the street, he would put Pericles to shame or nickname another political leader the Sausage Maker. The intellectuals, new educators, and learned men who came together in Athens seemed no more than fools to him, but he was grateful for the material they provided for his comedies. He filled his plays with prominent figures, making them perform the most ridiculous acts. He would use the language of the street and the countryside, then suddenly turn to parodying the pompous phrasing of tragedy or epic. In Andrés Barba's words, he gave materialistic answers to idealistic questions: "For us, Aristophanes ushered in a new route, established and created through the magic of theater: a route to peace through laughter, to freedom through laughter, and to political action through laughter." This kind of comedy, known as Old Comedy, lasted as long as the Athenian democracy against which it so often railed.

There was no successor to the humor of Aristophanes. We might say it reached its end before him rather than with him. At the end of the fifth century BC, Athens was conquered by Sparta, which supported an oligarchic coup in the city. Decades of political turbulence and broken spirits followed the defeat. The time of brazen critique was over. Aristophanes himself went on writing comedies, but they became cautious, their plots more and more allegorical, without personal allusions or political satire.

In the next generation, the Greeks were annexed to the Alexandrian Empire and the kingdoms of Alexander's successors. These monarchs did not tolerate jokes. This was when a new kind of comedy was born—sentimental comedies of manners and intrigue, the kind of humor Ortega y Gasset had in mind when he wrote, "Comedy is the literary genre of the conservative parties." As far as we know, plot ingredients were repetitive: young protagonists, conniving slaves, chance encounters, twins mistaken for each other, strict parents, whores with a heart of gold. The most renowned author of this era was Menander.

Menander was a unique case in the story of ancient literature's preservation. Read with enthusiasm for many centuries, in the end he gradually but completely disappeared. Until Egyptian papyrus scrolls returned substantial fragments of his comedies to us, we knew his plays only through quotes. He is the only author canonized in his time whose work did not survive in manuscript form. He is part of the obliterated sphere of comedy, where so many authors were lost. There is a long list of names that were practically silenced: Magnes,

Mylus, Eupolis, Cratinus, Epicharmus, Pherecrates, a certain Plato who is not the philosopher, Antiphanes, Alexis, Diphilus, Philemon, Apollodorus.

Though the writers of the New Comedy tried to provide their audiences with innocuous entertainment, they ended up causing trouble. As ancient society became more puritanical, their repetitive plots were considered immoral and spectators took offense. Their depictions of youths seeking merriment, of whores, and of deceived parents had nothing edifying to teach the new generations. In schools, teachers chose only isolated maxims by Menander or select fragments of his works, taking care not to sabotage their innocent students' morality. Thus, as they were slowly censored, their words were lost along with the majority of ancient humor. The villainous monk from *The Name of the Rose* has had many helpers throughout the centuries. Here, we come upon the paradox and the drama of laughter: the best kind is that which sooner or later makes enemies.

73

It's as redundant to speak of "textbooks" as it is to say "wooden plank," "close proximity," "sum total," or "unnecessary cruelty." Despite the tautology, we all know what the word means: books meant for learning. The Greeks used and may have invented them. In these works, they compiled literary passages for dictation, commentaries, and writing exercises. This kind of anthology played an important role in the survival of books, since the vast majority that have reached us in the present were, at one point or another, texts used in education.

The children of Hellenistic globalization who were fortunate enough to access more than a rudimentary education received an essentially literary grounding. The first reason for this was that their parents valued words—what we would now call communication skills—including fluency of speech and the rich vocabulary one learns from reading great writers. Inhabitants of the ancient world were convinced that it was impossible to think well without writing well: "*Libri faciunt labra,*" was the Roman saying: "Books make lips."

The second was nostalgia. Many Greeks had followed Alexander's footsteps and settled in unknown territories, from the Libyan desert to the central Asian steppes. In those regions, wherever the Greeks appeared and established themselves, whether in the villages of the Fayum, Babylon, or Susiana, they immediately set up their institutions, their primary schools, and their gymnasiums. Literature helped migrants maintain a common language, a system of shared references, an identity. It was the most reliable tool for contact and exchange between Greeks scattered across the vast territories of their empire. Lost in such immense spaces, they found their homeland in books. And many among the local population wished to increase their status by adopting the Greek language and lifestyle. The orator Isocrates best summarized this new concept of cultural citizenship: "We call those people Greek who have the same culture as us, more than those who have the same blood."

What kind of education did those Greeks receive? They were steeped in culture in all its variety. Unlike us, they weren't remotely interested in specialization. They looked down their noses at knowledge of a technical nature. They weren't obsessed with employment; after all, they had slaves to work for them. Those who could avoided anything as degrading as having a trade. Leisure was more refined—in other words, it involved cultivating the mind, fostering friendships, making conversation, and leading a contemplative life. Only medicine, an unquestionable social necessity, demanded its own particular kind of training. As a result, doctors suffered from an overt cultural inferiority complex. All of them, from Hippocrates to Galen, repeated the mantra in their texts that a doctor is also a philosopher. They wished to avoid being confined to their field and tried to show themselves to be cultured, slipping the occasional quote by a key poet into their writings. For everyone else, teachings and readings were essentially the same across the empire, which made for a powerful element of colonial unity.

This educational model prevailed for many centuries—the Roman system was simply an adaptation of the same idea—and is at the root of European pedagogy. In an essay, the emperor Julian the Apostate explained the professional openings available to a student educated according to the Greco-Latin tradition, which valued broad general knowledge. Julian says that anyone who has received a classical, or in other words literary, education will be able to contribute to the advance of science or be a political leader, a warrior, an explorer, or a hero. In those days, keen readers enjoyed broad professional prospects.

As we have seen, literacy gained ground in the third to first centuries BC, even beyond the ruling classes. While the state became concerned with regimenting schooling, its structure was too antiquated and its administrative workings too decrepit to take on the challenge of a genuine public education. Educational establishments were overseen by municipal authorities, and cities relied on the generosity of benefactors—they were called *euergetes*—to fund this service and others of general interest. Like its Roman counterpart, Hellenic civilization was essentially individualist and liberal. In those days there were plenty of Bill Gateses who flexed the muscles of their immense fortunes by making donations for public works—roads, schools, theaters, baths, libraries, or concert halls—and footing the bill for public festivities. This practice was considered a moral obligation for the rich, especially those who aspired to political office.

An inscription from the second century BC found in Teos, a city on the coast of Asia Minor, remembers a benefactor who gave a sum large enough to ensure "that all children born free receive an education." The donor stipulated that three teachers should be hired, one for each level of instruction, and further specified that these three should teach both boys and girls. An inscription discovered in Pergamum, dated in the third or second century BC, also records the presence of girls in school, since they feature among the winners of school competitions in reading and calligraphy. I like to imagine those little girls as they traced the letters with serious faces, their tongues peeking out between their lips, about to receive one of history's first prizes for girls. I wonder if they had any idea they were pioneers, if in their wildest dreams they ever imagined that twenty-five centuries later, we would still remember their victories over ignorance.

74

Ancient landfills offer us a glimpse of texts written by regular people in Egypt. In some areas of Egypt—alas, not in the Nile delta, where Alexandria is located—writings have been recovered that were abandoned or thrown into the trash two thousand years ago. Thanks to the desert climate, these texts remained as they were across the centuries, neither damaged nor disintegrating, gradually becoming enveloped in a protective layer of Egypt's burning sand. And they were preserved intact. This is how thousands and thousands of papyrus scrolls have reached our hands, discovered by peasants or dug up by archaeologists, sometimes with the ink almost as fresh as the day they were written by an ancient hand. The content of these texts varies widely, from the correspondence of a proud official to his laundry lists. Almost all are written in Greek, the language of government and the educated population. Their dates span from 300 BC to 700 AD, from the Greek occupation of Egypt, through the years of Ptolemaic and Roman rule, up to the Muslim conquest.

The papyruses demonstrate that many Greeks who didn't hold administrative positions still knew how to read and write and took care of their own affairs, writing commercial documents and answering their correspondence without engaging the services of professional scribes. Furthermore, they read for pleasure. One bored man, in a letter to a friend, writes from the monotony of an Egyptian village: "If you've already copied the books, send them, so that we have something to help pass the time, because we have no one to talk to." Yes, there were people facing rural tedium who sought out books as a lifeline. We have excavated the remains of what they read, including fragments of books and even whole works. In humid Alexandria, which boasted of having more readers than anywhere else in the world, no papyruses have been found, but even so, the discoveries in drier regions give us a sense of what people were reading at the time. And if we trust the estimates based on the number of remains discovered of each work, we can even tell which were those readers' favorite books.

I admit to an unbridled curiosity about other people's reading habits. On buses, streetcars, and trains, I twist my neck into unlikely contortions to spy on what the people around me are reading. I believe that books describe the people who hold them and find it thrilling to peer into the private moments of those readers in the Egyptian backlands, across the distance of centuries. Judging by the chronology, these readers might be the same men and women depicted in the Fayum mummy portraits who examine us with their large eyes full of nostalgia and who seem so alive that they vaguely remind us of someone we know.

What do the papyruses reveal about them? Their favorite poet by far was Homer. They liked *The Iliad* more than *The Odyssey*. They also read Hesiod, Plato, Menander, Demosthenes, and Thucydides, but the second on the podium was Euripides. This reminds me of a marvelous anecdote about the power of books.

Let us look back into the tumultuous years of the Peloponnesian War. As if it weren't enough for them to already be fighting the powerful Sparta, the rulers of imperialist Athens launched an expedition that ploughed through the waves to Sicily, to lay siege to Syracuse. The campaign was a devastating failure: some seven thousand Athenians along with their allies were taken prisoner and condemned to forced labor in a stone quarry known as Latomia, which belonged to the victorious city. There, according to Thucydides, they left not only their broken hands but also their lives. Trapped in the quarry's depths and exposed to the blazing heat or the cold, sick and coexisting with corpses stinking of their own urine and feces, fed only half a pint of water and a pint of barley meal a day, they gradually perished. Plutarch tells that the Syracusans were so fond of poetry, however, that they pardoned those who could recite a few lines from Euripides and let them walk free: "They say that many of those who finally reached home in safety visited Euripides in their gratitude, and some told him that they had been freed from slavery for reciting fragments of his works they had memorized, and some that as they roamed and wandered after the battle, they had been given food and drink for singing some of his verses."

Homer and Euripides were the winners of the competition, the writers who shaped the dreams of the Greeks. As children, all of them learned to read and write by copying their verses, which explains the number of papyruses discovered. Children were not introduced to reading with easy phrases such as "My mama loves me." The educational method consisted of sudden immersion. Almost from the beginning, children were taken by the scruff of the neck and immersed in beautiful, difficult phrases by Euripides that they could barely understand ("Come to me sweet balm of sleep, comfort from my ills" or "Waste not fresh tears over old griefs"). Many fragments found were probably copies made by students. But there were also readers in love with the music of those verses. In one especially moving case, archaeologists discovered a papyrus scroll beneath the head of a female mummy, almost touching her body. The scroll contains a particularly evocative canto from *The Iliad*. I imagine this dedicated reader wanted to be sure she would have books with her in the next life and remember Homer's winged words beyond the river of forgetfulness, which, according to her beliefs, she would cross to reach the world of the dead.

Dozens of texts have appeared beneath the sands of Egypt that belonged to private collectors—comedies, philosophical works, historical studies, mathematical and musical treatises, technical handbooks, and even texts by authors unknown to us until these discoveries. I think of those anonymous bibliophiles and wonder how they got their hands on all those minor works. Scrolls by Homer, Euripides, and the odd other famous author could no doubt be easily obtained in the bookshops of Alexandria, but copies of uncommon books had to be made to order. This is the case with a copy of *The Constitution of Athens* by Aristotle. It's most likely that its owner commissioned a copy from a workshop, and the establishment may have had to send a copyist to the Library of Alexandria to work from the original, which was part of the collection there. The journey back and forth would surely have made the price of the order skyrocket. In those days, obtaining a rare book could turn into a minor odyssey and was certain to be a drain on the purse.

Readers whose pouches were filled with nothing but cobwebs had to be satisfied with going to libraries, which existed even outside

Alexandria and Pergamum. Small and local, they could not be compared to the extraordinary royal collections, but they at least offered their visitors the great authors' essential works. We are aware of these establishments thanks again to inscriptions in stone. We know, for example, that there was a library on the island of Cos, near present-day Turkey. A fragment has survived of an inscription listing a series of private donations. A father and son defrayed the cost of the building, and also donated a hundred drachmas. A further four people gave two hundred drachmas and a hundred books each. Two more contributed two hundred drachmas. The money was undoubtedly destined to purchase books. There is similar evidence in Athens and elsewhere.

It's likely that those libraries were associated with their city's local gymnasium. Originally, these were places for youths to practice athletics and wrestling. "Gymnasium" comes from the word "nudity," because the Greek custom—to the barbarians' outrage—was to exercise shamelessly, smothered in oil, with the splendor of the masculine physique on full display. By the Hellenic era, gymnasiums had become centers for education, with classrooms, spaces for lectures, and reading rooms. We know that at least the Athens gymnasium had a library because part of a catalog has been preserved in stone. This list of holdings was apparently carved into the library's wall, where readers could consult it quickly without the nuisance of having to open and close a scroll, which in addition would be in danger of quick deterioration from continuous use. According to the catalog, the library specialized in comedy and tragedy. There were over two dozen titles by Euripides, and over a dozen by Sophocles. Fifteen comedies by Menander also featured in the collection. Only two prose works are documented, one of which is a speech by Demosthenes. On the other hand, the library at Rhodes, a renowned center of rhetorical studies, had barely any plays and specialized in political and historical essays.

If the evidence from Athens and Rhodes can be extrapolated to all cities with gymnasiums, there would have been over a hundred libraries during the Hellenic era, a delicate network of veins pumping the oxygen of language out into every corner of the territory.

75

Demosthenes was orphaned at seven years old. His father, an arms maker, left him enough to live comfortably, but his tutors squandered his inheritance. His mother, financially ruined, had no funds to pay for a good education for her son. They suffered hardships. The neighborhood boys would laugh at him for his skinny, sickly, fragile appearance. They even gave him a nickname, Batalus, from a word meaning "anus" or "queer." On top of that, he had a speech impediment that made him feel awkward and tongue-tied. He must have stuttered or had trouble pronouncing certain consonants.

It's said that Demosthenes conquered his problems through sadistic discipline. He forced himself to speak with pebbles in his mouth. He went running through the countryside to strengthen his lungs and recited verses when he was out of breath, panting his way uphill. He wandered the seashore on stormy days to increase his concentration amid the roar of the waves. At home, he rehearsed in front of a full-length mirror, repeating defiant phrases and striking poses. The scene, recounted by Plutarch, seems to pave the way for Robert De Niro's "You talkin' to me?" scene in *Taxi Driver*. Poverty-stricken, orphaned, stuttering, and humiliated, years later he would become the most famous orator of all times. The ancient Greeks, like today's Americans, loved a good underdog story.

The number ten symbolizes perfection. It's the foundation of our decimal system. It represents excellence in the academic world, the highest qualification. For the Pythagoreans, it was a magic, sacred figure. It's no coincidence, then, that there were ten canonical Attic orators whose works were considered deserving of preservation and study. The ancients believed that the bewitching power of words found its highest expression particularly in speeches.

The Greeks always had a reputation for being incorrigible charlatans and tireless litigators. Unlike in the collective imagination of other cultures, the heroes of their myths weren't simply mute and muscular warriors; instead, they'd been trained as experts in words and could deliver a well-adorned speech when the opportunity arose. The democratic institutions of Athens broadened the sphere

of speeches: Athenian citizens—those who fulfilled the requirements of being free and male—could speak before their peers at
the Assembly, where political decisions were voted on, and decide
as members of popular juries on the soundness of the speeches of
others. They seem to have adored the uninterrupted chatter that was
the main ingredient of their daily lives, from the agora to the par-
liament. Aristophanes wrote a comedy parodying someone called
Philocleon, a genuine trial junkie. To help him overcome his obsession with the courts, his son sets up a tribunal in his home and offers
his father the presidency. In the absence of anyone to accuse, they
put the family dog on trial for having swiped a hunk of cheese from
the kitchen and make up long allegations and defenses. This farce
provides Philocleon with relief like a shot of methadone to an addict.

Herodotus tells that the night before the crucial Battle of Salamis, to which they needed to arrive refreshed and well rested, the
Greek generals got into a rowdy quarrel that lasted into the wee
hours of the morning, while the soldiers grumbled and criticized
their superiors' folly. Though they still won the battle despite the
altercation, Herodotus seems to lament their combative temperament, which in his view was the reason the Greeks never managed
to build a strong and unified state. Yes, they loved words and inci-
sive arguments. This was why they could write exquisitely crafted
poems. But it was also why they could turn any dispute into a vain
and destructive fight.

The oratory practiced by Greek lawyers and statesmen was quite
different from what we see today. In the absence of libel laws, orators hurled a plethora of slanderous insults at one another. Endless
personal accusations and the imputation of base motives on the part
of the adversary added a morbid interest to debates that made them
almost like boxing matches. The art of slaying opponents with ingenious takedowns was a skill so cultivated that it must have been hypnotic to watch. In the courts, which were all made up of juries, legal
questions mattered less than the brilliance of the arguments. For private trials, judicial practice demanded that the litigant himself defend
his case before the tribunal with two successive speeches. There were
no lawyers representing clients as there are in our times. Usually,
litigants weren't confident enough to compose their own defense or

prosecution and ended up engaging the services of a logographer who would study the case and write a convincing speech, as colloquial and direct as possible. The client would learn it by heart to recite before the tribunal. This was how most orators earned a living. Beyond this, they tried to lend their services in cases that could boost their prestige and help them launch their own political career.

The best political and legal speeches were published soon after being delivered, while the polemic was still a hot topic, and people read them with the same delight with which we now relish legal dramas. Indeed, one of my favorite of these is the movie *To Kill a Mockingbird*, which contains a nod to that era. The lawyer protagonist, created by Harper Lee but whom we will always remember with the mature, sweaty, fatherly face of Gregory Peck, answers to the name of Atticus Finch, a clear reference to the ten great Attic orators in the classical canon. And of course, like any good Attic worth his salt, little Scout's hero knows how to deliver a lively plea—in favor of a black man—before a hostile jury, in a racist Alabama impoverished by the Great Depression of the 1930s.

Those ten legendary orators were born in the course of a century—between the fifth and fourth centuries BC—and practically all of them were able to meet and viciously denounce one another. Their years of glory coincided with Athenian democracy, and the era of the Hellenic monarchies marked their end. In fact, among Demosthenes's most famous speeches are *The Philippics*, a series of furious, apocalyptic attacks on the imperialism of Philip, father of Alexander the Great. All those of us who have launched a philippic since then are mere apprentices to the awe-inspiring Demosthenes.

Another of the ten orators, Antiphon, was a true pioneer who could have been at the forefront of psychoanalysis and talk therapy. His profession had taught him that speeches, if they are effective, can alter people's state of mind and move, cheer, inspire, and becalm their listeners. Then he had a novel idea: he invented a method for dispelling pain and affliction, akin to medical treatment for the sick. He opened a storefront in the city of Corinth and hung up a shingle announcing that he could "console the sad with the appropriate speeches." When a client appeared, he listened with full attention until he understood the misfortune afflicting them. Then he "erased it from their spirit" with a consoling talk. He used the drug of persuasive language to heal their sorrow and, according to ancient authors, was renowned for his soothing logic. After him, some philosophers claimed that their task was to "expel rebellious grief through logic," but Antiphon was the first to intuit that healing with words could become a trade. He also understood that therapy should be an exploratory dialogue. Experience taught him that it helps to coax the sufferer into speaking of the reasons for their grief, since searching for the right words might yield a solution. Many centuries later, Viktor Frankl, a disciple of Freud and survivor of Auschwitz and Dachau, would develop a similar method for overcoming the trauma of the barbarism during that period in Europe.

Seduced by the beauty of words, the Greeks inaugurated the genre of the lecture, which was astonishingly successful during antiquity. The Sophists, itinerant teachers who traveled from city to city hunting for students, held exhibitions to introduce themselves, show the quality of their teaching, and demonstrate their skills before an auditorium. Sometimes they made speeches they'd already prepared, and sometimes they improvised on topics suggested in the moment by the audience—things as absurd as praise for mosquitos or baldness. At some of those lectures the doors stood open to all kinds of curious onlookers, but in general, attendance was limited to a more select, fee-paying audience. The Sophists prepared the set for their speeches with the utmost care, sometimes even appearing in the extravagant attire of the old wandering *aoidos*, declaring themselves the heirs to those poets who bewitched kings and country people alike with the spell of their verses. In the Hellenic period, the phenomenon spread. There was a veritable army of roving intellectuals—orators, of course, but also artists, philosophers, and doctors—who trod the paths of the empire, taking their shabby talent from here to there, certain of finding a keen audience even in the dustiest corners of the known world. The lecture became the liveliest literary genre, the one that, according to some specialists, best represents the originality of the era. This is where the road to the TED Talks of today begins, and to the multimillion-dollar business of lectures by former presidents.

In the fifth century BC, the formidable Sophist Gorgias wrote, "Speech is a powerful master; it achieves the most divine feats with a tiny, completely invisible body. It can allay fear, relieve pain, bring joy, and increase compassion." There is an echo of these Greek ideas in what I believe to be one of the most beautiful lines in the Gospel: "Only say the word, and my servant shall be healed."

But that genuine passion for language gave rise to a whole series of rhetorical devices that in the end corrupted its spontaneity. The orators worked to devise a method crammed with formulas, principles, and procedures, thoroughly prepared down to the tiniest detail. All those disquisitions on style, along with their stifling system of preambles, proofs, and refutations, had generally dire results. Unfortunately, throughout antiquity, there were hordes of pedantic teachers of eloquence and artists full of hot air. Their love of embellishment saturated and ruined too many works of literature. When I translate Greek or Roman texts, sometimes I can't help but laugh. The writer will be speaking of his deepest and most essential emotions—pain, desire, abandonment, exile, solitude, fear, suicidal urges—when, at the worst possible moment, the diligent student who memorized his stylistic devices makes himself known. The spell is broken. The world is sinking beneath his feet, and he describes it with antitheses, homeoteleutons, and paronomasias.

Ever since then, our naïve faith in formulas to guide us through life has kept a great many rhetorical fraudsters well-fed. Today we are inundated by self-help manuals offering miraculous lists for success: ten methods for saving our marriage, sculpting our bodies, or becoming highly effective people; ten keys to being great parents. Ten tricks for cooking the perfect steak, ten brilliant phrases for ending a chapter. This last one, alas, I decided not to buy.

76

In 2011, a publisher in Louisville released an edition of Mark Twain's two most famous novels—*The Adventures of Huckleberry Finn* and *The Adventures of Tom Sawyer*—eliminating the derogatory term "nigger" and replacing it with the more neutral "slave." The person responsible for this preventive measure, a university professor specializing in Mark Twain, said he had made the tricky decision to eliminate the word at the request of numerous high school teachers for whom *Huck Finn* can no longer be taught in its original form due to "racially offensive language" that causes visible discomfort to many students. According to him, performing this minor surgery is the best way to prevent the classics of North American literature from being removed from American classrooms for good. This isn't an isolated event. In recent years there has been a steady trickle of controversies related to children's classics, especially those forming part of school curriculums.

Hordes of parents, anxious about the irreversible trauma the brothers Grimm or Andersen might inflict on their fragile offspring, wonder what values—and terrors—"Cinderella," "Snow White," or "The Steadfast Tin Soldier" convey to twenty-first-century children. These evangelists for the protection of minors prefer saccharine adaptations from the Disney factory to the original stories, so cruel, violent, patriarchal, and outmoded. Many are in favor, if not of banning traditional literature written in an imperfect past, at least of adapting it to our postmodern consciousness.

In the mid-1990s, the writer and satirist James Finn Garner published a book called *Politically Correct Bedtime Stories*, his contribution to the debate. Garner's humor isn't aimed at children but is rather a comic monologue interwoven with euphemisms we use as adults in the twenty-first century. With impeccable irony, always just on the verge of nonsense, he rewrote the beginning of "Little Red Riding Hood" like this: "There once was a young person named Red Riding Hood who lived with her mother on the edge of a large wood. One day her mother asked her to take a basket of fresh fruit and mineral water to her grandmother's house—not because this was womyn's work, mind you, but because the deed was generous and helped engender a feeling of community."

In fact, the controversy is older than we think, and the hordes of furious censorship supporters and other decency-promoting squads can lay claim to a prestigious fellow believer—Plato. Educating the youth was always one of the aristocratic Athenian's great concerns, and in the end it became his profession. After his attempts in politics floundered, he devoted himself fully to teaching at the Academy, the school he'd founded in some woods on the outskirts of Athens. We're told he taught his classes sitting in a high chair, the *kathedra*, surrounded by symbolically smaller chairs occupied by his disciples, a white board for writing on, a celestial globe, a mechanical model of the planets, a clock he boasted of having built himself, and maps drawn by the foremost geographers. His school was meant as a training center for the ruling elites of Greek cities. Today we might think of it as more of an antidemocratic think tank.

Plato's teachings have always seemed to me amazingly fractured in their explosive mix of free thought and authoritarian impulses. Among his most often read passages is the myth of the cave, an ideal tale of what the process of critical education ought to be. Inside the cave, a group of people are chained to the wall, their backs to a fire. The prisoners see only the movements of shadows as they cross the walls, and those shadows are their only reality. Finally, one of them frees himself and ventures out of the cave, heading toward the world that unfolds beyond the hypnotic shadows. The tale contains a beautiful invitation to doubt, to not be satisfied with appearances, to break free from shackles, abandon prejudices, and stare reality in the face. The Matrix movie saga adapted the rebellious message of this allegory to the contemporary world of virtual reality, the global village, the parallel worlds of advertising and consumerism, fake news, and the airbrushed autobiographies we make up for social media.

But in the most famous Platonic utopia, *The Republic*, the very same text that includes the myth of the cave, lies the dark antithesis of its enlightened message. The third book could serve as a practical handbook for a dictator in training. Here Plato asserts that in an ideal society, education should above all instill seriousness, decorum, and bravery. Plato supports strict censorship of the literature young people read and the music to which they listen. Mothers and nannies should only tell children authorized stories, and even childhood games should be subject to rules. Homer and Hesiod must be prohibited as childhood reading for several reasons. First, their representation of frivolous, hedonistic gods who are prone to bad behavior is not sufficiently edifying. Young people must be taught that evil never comes from the gods. Second, certain lines by both of these poets speak of fear of death, something that troubles Plato, since in his opinion, youths should be ready to die in battle without complaint. "Then we shall do well," he says, "to get rid of the lamentations of famous men and make them over to women instead." Plato also has an unfavorable opinion of theater. In his view, the plots of most comedies and tragedies involve bad people, and actors therefore have to put themselves in the shoes of undesirable figures such as criminals or inferior beings, women and slaves included. This identification with the emotions of commoners can only be harmful to the education of children and youths. Works of theater, if tolerated, should include only heroic, masculine figures, irreproachable and of noble birth. Since not a single play fulfils these requirements, Plato proceeds to banish playwrights from his perfect state, along with all the other poets.

The passage of the years didn't calm Plato's censorial spirit. In his last dialogue, *The Laws*, he virtually proposes the creation of a poetry police to monitor any new literature: "The poet shall compose nothing contrary to what the city considers lawful, or just, or beautiful, or good; once he has written a poem, he shall not show the work to any private individuals, until it has been read and approved by the judges appointed by the guardians of the law for such a purpose . . . and to he whom we select as our director of education." The message is resoundingly clear: poetic texts must be subject to severe censorship—sometimes suppressed, sometimes expurgated or corrected, and when necessary—and it will often be necessary—rewritten.

Plato's utopia is a twin sister to the dystopia of *1984*. The Ministry of Truth that Orwell imagines harbors the Fiction Department, where all new literature is produced. We see the protagonist, Julia, who works there, prowling around the office, her hands always greasy and carrying an adjustable wrench. Her job is to maintain the machines that write the novels according to ministerial guidelines. The regime doesn't wash its hands of the classics, either. This is where Orwell seems to make the authoritarian Plato's dreams a reality. His Ministry of Truth has set an ambitious project in motion whose purpose is to rewrite all the literature of the past. This fabulous task is expected to be completed in the year 2050. By then, one of the plan's enforcers says enthusiastically, "the whole literature of the past will have been destroyed. Chaucer, Shakespeare, Milton, Byron—they'll exist only in Newspeak versions, not merely changed into something different, but actually changed into something contradictory of what they used to be . . . The whole climate of thought will be different. In fact there will be no thought, as we understand it now. Orthodoxy means not thinking—not needing to think. Orthodoxy is unconsciousness."

Though Plato's assertions could hardly be more drastic and decisive, I detect a certain resistance among his readers to taking his words literally. When his admirers come up against passages like this one, they begin to look around in search of a way out. A. N. Whitehead, in an often-repeated statement, famously dismissed all of Western philosophy as "a series of footnotes to Plato." To salvage his work, we're told that Plato got overexcited while he was writing, that he takes his positions to the extreme just like all of us do in political discussions around the table at Sunday lunch with our families.

But Plato knew perfectly well what he was saying. He never liked Athenian democracy, which for him was aptly portrayed by the execution of Socrates. He wanted to establish an immutable political model, in which social change and indecent tales that undermined society's moral foundations would no longer be necessary. He had lived through turbulent, traumatic times in Athens. He wanted stability, he wanted a government of the wise and not of the foolish majority. If that ultraconservatism could only be defended by a repressive regime, then so be it. This was how Karl Popper understood it when he titled the first part of his book *The Open Society and Its Enemies* "The Spell of Plato."

Plato was concerned with what young people were reading for reasons as much pecuniary as pedagogical. The founding teacher of the first academy for children of the elite, he was trying to discredit his competition. He disliked the educational system of his time, in which the Greeks were educated by poets—people with erratic and rarely edifying ideas. In his dialogue *The Laws*, he says that studying the poets "is a great risk" to the youth and instead suggests, in an astonishing exercise of virtue and humility, that his own works be used as texts on which to base classes: "When I reflected upon all these words of ours, I felt immense pleasure, for of all the reasoning which I have read in poetry, none has seemed more sensible or suitable for young men to read. There is no better model than this to present to the guardian of the law and education, and it would be best for teachers to teach the children these discourses, and any related to them which resemble them." This was fundamentally a struggle for the minds of the Greeks, with education as a battleground. It was also a matter of business.

At this point there is no need for me to tell you that I am interested in and annoyed by Plato in equal measure. His ideas often make me feel like unleashing one of those fantastic strings of insults I learned from Captain Haddock: Meddlesome cabin boy! Anacoluthon! Bashi-bazouk! Ectoplasm! I wonder how a philosopher of such irreverent intelligence could defend an educational system that condemns its students to reading only sterilized texts and fables of virtue. His program does away with literary grey areas, excursions into the abyss, anxiety, pain, paradox, troubling intuitions. It's a chilling abridgement. If Plato himself had written according to these aesthetic principles, his work would bore us to death. And yet, it continues to fascinate us because, unlike the kind of work it prescribes, it is clever, paradoxical, and unsettling.

But today, the matter remains an open question, as the Louisville professors who erased the insult "nigger" from Twain's work well know. Are books for children and young adults complex works of literature or codes of conduct? A sanitized *Huck Finn* can teach young readers a lot, but it robs them of an essential lesson: that there was a time when almost everyone called their slaves "niggers," and that, due to this history of oppression, the word has become taboo. We won't save the young from harmful ideas by excising everything we find offensive from books. On the contrary, we'll make young people less able to spot them. Unlike what Plato says, evil characters are an essential ingredient of traditional tales: they are there for children to learn that evil exists. Sooner or later, they'll find out about it, whether from bullies stalking them in the schoolyard or from genocidal tyrants.

The marvelous and disturbing Flannery O'Connor once wrote, "The lady who only read books that improved her mind was taking a safe course—and a hopeless one. She'll never know whether her mind is improved or not, but should she ever, by some mistake, read a great novel, she'll know mighty well that something is happening to her." Feeling a certain amount of discomfort is part of the experience of reading a book; the reader has far more to learn from being troubled than from being relieved. We can send all the literature of the past to the operating room for cosmetic surgery, but then it will no longer be able to explain the world to us. And if we start going down that road we shouldn't be at all surprised when young people give up reading, and, in Santiago Roncagliolo's words, "devote themselves to the PlayStation, where they can kill dozens of people without anyone interfering."

I have a recent newspaper article in front of me. At the University of London, the students' union of the School of Oriental and African Studies is demanding that racist, colonialist philosophers such as Plato, Descartes, and Kant be removed from the curriculum.

It's ironic: Plato, the hunter, now hunted.

POISON AND FRAGILITY

77

The librarians of Alexandria didn't expel the Greek poets or Plato. The palace of books on the banks of the Nile was hospitable to both opposing factions. Its shelves created one of those surprising cease-fire zones where hostilities pause, enemies touch in the promiscuity of shared space, borders are blurred, and reading becomes another form of reconciliation.

We know the Great Library welcomed the ideas, discoveries, and grumblings of Plato. Not without a certain dose of irony, since the wise Callimachus, author of *The Pínakes* and illustrious member of the Musaeum, wished to leave a record of the potentially murderous character of Plato's books.

The anecdote appears in a brief text in verse. Perhaps Callimachus, like the poet he was, wished to fire an arrow at Plato on behalf of his guild. His poem describes the death of a certain Cleombrotus of Ambracia, who threw himself into the void from the top of a wall. Nothing had happened to give the young man a motive for suicide, Callimachus tells us, except that "he had read a single treatise by Plato: *On the Soul*." The dialogue that led poor Cleombrotus to his demise is now known as the *Phaedo*. Many have wondered why he might kill himself after reading this work, which describes Socrates's final hours before he drinks his dose of hemlock. Some say that Cleombrotus couldn't endure the wise man's end, but others hold that his leap into the void was due to something said by Plato, who claims that the peak of wisdom will arrive only after death. In any case, Callimachus craftily drops in his criticism: in the end, perhaps the young are at greater risk from reading Plato than reading the poets.

We don't know if Cleombrotus's was an isolated case, or if perhaps the *Phaedo* inspired a spate of suicides like those *The Sorrows of Young Werther* would leave behind it centuries later. From its publication in 1774, Goethe's novel drove many lovelorn young Europeans to give themselves a bullet in imitation of the tortured protagonist. The author experienced with alarm the social—and sepulchral—phenomenon his book brought about, edition after edition. In some countries, authorities even banned it for the sake of public health.

Goethe was inspired by the real suicide of a friend, and by his own adolescent fantasies about death. More than fifty years later, in his autobiography, *Poetry and Truth*, he admits that he could only calm his self-destructive urge by making Werther shoot himself symbolically in his place. But the ghost the author managed to expel through this literary exorcism went on to torment his readers, some of whom succumbed to its macabre influence. Two hundred years later, in 1974, the sociologist David Phillips coined the term "the Werther effect" to describe the mysterious urge to imitate the act of suicide. Even a fictional character's actions can be contagious and unleash a string of identical cases. Another marvelous and distressing novel, *The Virgin Suicides* by Jeffrey Eugenides, explores the profoundly enigmatic psychological phenomenon of copycat suicides.

At any rate, the case of the reader of the *Phaedo* who jumped off a wall—the Greek version of a bridge—would unwittingly inaugurate a new literary trend: stories of deadly books. It's not surprising that the most famous of all of them, the *Necronomicon,* should have a Greek name. This cursed volume, the mere reading of which leads to madness and suicide, was invented by H. P. Lovecraft as part of the terrifying universe of his tales of Cthulhu. Of course, we never learn what the *Necronomicon* is about since no one has ever survived to tell the tale. There are persistent rumors that it contains obscure knowledge and sorcery that allow contact with the Old Ones, alien beings who possess malevolent powers. Expelled from the planet in ancient times for practicing black magic, these beings languish in space, awaiting their chance to take over the world that once upon a time was theirs.

Lovecraft wrote a meticulous, playful history of the *Necronomicon* and its translation, so rich in bibliographical details that some readers have blindly believed in its existence, and certain crooked antiquarian book dealers have pretended to own a copy, offering it for sale to unwary customers. The joke begins with the name of the supposed author, a mad Arab poet called Abdul Alhazred. In fact, this is a childhood nickname of Lovecraft himself, inspired by the tales of *The Thousand and One Nights.* Alhazred is a nod to the English phrase "all has read."

The tales in *The Call of Cthulhu and Other Weird Stories* contain abundant warnings of the deadly consequences of reading the *Necronomicon.* We are told that frightful things happened in the Middle Ages due to its influence, and that the book was condemned by the church in the year 1050. According to Lovecraft's telling, despite the curses, a Latin translation of this heretical work was printed in Spain in the seventeenth century. Four copies of this edition remained, one in the British Museum, one in the National Library in Paris, another at Harvard, and the last at the fictitious American Miskatonic University, in the also fictitious city of Arkham. Among Lovecraft's fans, pranksters have slipped fake entries into card catalogs at several libraries around the world, listing the city of Toledo as the prohibited volume's place of origin. Wherever an alleged edition surfaces, requests to borrow it skyrocket. Apparently, curiosity is stronger than fear of the trail of death and dementia the *Necronomicon* leaves in its wake.

Plato, the mad Arab Alhazred, and Goethe all wrote books that could lead to perdition with the dark sorcery of their words. Another intriguing facet of death by reading are poisoned books. As far as I know, the oldest appearance of one of these murderous volumes dates to *The Thousand and One Nights*. At the end of the fourth night and throughout the fifth, Scheherazade tells the story of King Yunan and the doctor, Duban. After curing the king's leprosy, Duban discovers that the ungrateful monarch intends to do away with him, so he concocts a plan to punish him. He gives him a book, *The Secret of Secrets*. It happens that the book's pages are steeped in poison, and the king dies: "When the king opened the book, he found the pages stuck. So he put his finger in his mouth, wetted it with his saliva, and opened the first page, and he kept opening the pages with difficulty until he turned seven leaves. But when he looked in the book, he found nothing written inside, and he exclaimed, 'Sage, I see nothing written in this book.' The sage replied, 'Open more pages.' The king opened some more pages but still found nothing, and while he was doing this, the drug spread through his body—for the book had been poisoned—and he began to heave, sway, and twitch."

Just as many of us who have seen *Psycho* feel a shiver run down our spine when showering in a hotel alone, this story from *The Thousand and One Nights* may cause similar chills in readers who often moisten a fingertip to turn a page. I have come across the motif of the book daubed in poison several times, as if it were becoming a classic of horror for bibliophiles. I recall the exquisite treatise on falconry with which the evil Catherine de Medici mistakenly kills her son Charles in *La Reine Margot* by Alexandre Dumas, and Aristotle's treatise on laughter—of which I've already spoken—which causes a bloodbath at the sinister abbey in *The Name of the Rose*. I am especially fond of the scene where the secret is revealed: when the Franciscan detective William of Baskerville solves the mystery of the crimes, he can't avoid a moment of admiration for the murderer. He admits that the book is an exemplary, stealthy weapon, with which "the victim poisoned himself when he was alone, and only to the extent that he wanted to read."

Sadly, the last chapter in this story of murderous books is strictly truthful. I am thinking of book bombs, volumes containing powerful explosives intended to kill the recipient when they are opened. The White House receives hundreds of book bombs a year, which are deactivated by security teams. Hundreds of postal workers, journalists, doormen, secretaries, and men and women in a whole range of professions have died in this way all over the world. Anyone could be a victim of such an attack. According to scholar Fernando Báez, there are dozens of clandestine instruction manuals on the internet teaching people to make bombs out of books. Apparently, terrorists express preferences for certain authors, and there are a great many lists of titles, categories, and sizes used in these attacks. Some groups find the Bible inadequate, and for some mysterious reason prefer *Don Quixote* instead. On December 27, 2003, the president of the European Commission almost died on opening a copy of Gabriele D'Annunzio's *Pleasure*. The lives of politicians and those in high-ranking positions are clearly less imperiled if they do not read.

78

We like to imagine books as dangerous, deadly, and disturbing, but above all they are fragile. As you read these lines, somewhere in the world a library is burning down. At this very moment, a publisher is pulping its unsold stock. Somewhere not far from you, a flood is submerging a priceless collection in water. Several people are unloading an inherited library into a nearby dumpster. An army of insects bore tunnels through pages so they can lay their eggs in a network of tiny labyrinths on infinite shelves. In an unstable region, a collection is being seized and destroyed. Someone is demanding a purge of works that are troublesome for those in power. Someone is condemning a book for blasphemy or sin and tossing it into the flames.

A long history of horror and fascination binds books and fire together. Galen wrote that fires, along with earthquakes, were the most frequent cause of their destruction. The flames that obliterate words sometimes flare by accident but are often intentional. Burning books is an absurd endeavor repeated stubbornly throughout the centuries, from Mesopotamia to present times. It is meant to lay the foundations of a new order on the ashes of the old, to reform and to purify a world polluted by writers.

When censors insisted on burning copies of *Ulysses*, Joyce remarked wryly that thanks to those flames, he was sure to endure a less severe purgatory. In those same years, the Nazis were carrying out their barbaric *Bücherverbrennung* ("book burning") in the public squares of dozens of German cities. Thousands of books were transported in trucks and piled up for destruction. Human chains were formed to pass them from hand to hand until they reached the fire. Researchers estimate that during the Nazi bibliocaust, works by more than fifty-five hundred authors whom the new leaders considered degenerate were burned—a prologue to the furnaces that were to come, just as Heinrich Heine had prophesied in 1821 when he wrote, "Those who burn books will in the end burn people." The famous line comes from a play titled *Almansor*, in which the work burned is the Koran and the arsonists are members of the Spanish Inquisition.

In 2010, when the world was preparing to commemorate the ninth anniversary of September 11, the pastor of a small Christian church in Florida announced his intention to burn copies of the Koran on the date of the terrorist attacks—at the peak TV viewing hours of seven to nine in the evening, to be precise. In those incendiary days, the face of Terry Jones, a vehement preacher with a horseshoe moustache and a look somewhere between a nineteenth-century dignitary and a Hells Angel with a suntan, appeared constantly in the international papers and on the TV news. He declared his wish to turn 9/11 into Burn a Koran Day, a gleeful international festival of vandalism. Authorities were unable to put a stop to his provocative appeal, since no law prohibits setting fire to a legally acquired book on private property. To prevent an outbreak of protests and riots in Islamic countries, President Barack Obama and the director of the CIA tried to dissuade him for the safety of troops in Iraq and Afghanistan. The issue became a national emergency. At first, Jones bowed to pressure, but by March 2011, he could no longer stand the weight of his own capitulation. Like the character in Aristophanes who holds court in his house to try his dog for filching a piece of cheese, Terry Jones staged a fake trial of the Koran. After eight minutes of deliberation, the self-appointed court condemned the book for crimes against humanity and proceeded to burn a copy, streaming for the world to watch on YouTube. Several people died or were seriously injured in Afghanistan during the uproar the recording unleashed.

Reverend Jones's rapid rise to fame—and infamy—shows that throwing a book on the fire, even if the work doesn't run the slightest risk of disappearing, is a powerful symbolic, almost magical, act. Our sophisticated, technological global society can still be destabilized by the shock waves of an act of such an ancient variety of barbarism.

The bonfires of papyrus, parchment, and paper are emblematic of an old failure repeating itself. The story of the earliest books often ends in fire. "Every few centuries the Library of Alexandria must be burned down," a sorrowful Borges character observes. This is the brief chronicle of a massive disaster: in the capital of the Nile delta, a great dream of antiquity went up in flames several times, until it was completely devastated. And those flames fed by books scattered darkness in their wake.

THE THREE DESTRUCTIONS
OF THE LIBRARY OF ALEXANDRIA

79

Cleopatra was the last queen of Egypt, and also the youngest. She took the crown of the Two Lands at barely eighteen years old. For a woman to rule over Egypt, she had to go through with a minor traditional requirement: marrying her brother, just as Isis had married Osiris. Not to be discouraged by trivial matters, Cleopatra was wedded to Ptolemy XIII, a ten-year-old boy whom she believed she could control. Despite the long years of prior coexistence, it was not a harmonious marriage. The child rulers were soon entangled in a feud, vying against each other for power. Cleopatra failed to scheme as well as the miniature pharaoh and was toppled and banished from her country on pain of death. The young woman in exile learned a valuable family lesson: her relatives were just as likely to kill her as anyone else.

That same year, Julius Caesar arrived in Alexandria. Rome was now a great power that assumed the role of the world's police and mediator in the conflicts of others. Cleopatra understood that if she wanted to rule again, she needed Caesar's support. She traveled in secret from Syria, eluding her brother's spies, who'd been ordered to kill her if she ever set foot in Egypt again. Plutarch tells with panache the comic episode of the encounter between the deposed queen and Caesar. At dusk on a warm October day in 48 BC, a vessel berthed silently in the port of Alexandria. From it, a carpet merchant disembarked with a long bundle. Once at the palace, he asked to see Caesar to give him a gift. Admitted to the Roman general's room, he unrolled his burden. From inside emerged a hot, slight, and sweaty girl of twenty-one, risking her life out of sheer lust for power. Plutarch writes that Caesar was "captivated by the young woman's boldness." He was a man of fifty-two, with the scars of a thousand battles. It wasn't desire that drove Cleopatra into his arms, but survival instinct. She had no time to spare: if her brother found her, she would die; if Caesar didn't take her side, she would die. That very night, Cleopatra came, saw, and seduced.

Julius Caesar settled into the palace. Under her powerful lover's protection, Cleopatra recovered the crown. She kept the little Ptolemy by her side, more as a hostage than as a king. Those were days of wine and intrigue in Alexandria. The child pharaoh would not resign himself to being a puppet and began to plot an Egyptian rebellion against the Roman soldiers. When the insurrection was sparked, the foreign guest remained shut away in the royal palace with his meager troops. As we've already seen, the Ptolemaic palace occupied a whole walled neighborhood by the sea, where the Musaeum and Library rose among other buildings. The learned men in the Birdcage of the Muses—accustomed to being left in peace to study and ruthlessly tear one another to pieces—found themselves suddenly under siege with the Roman general, in a highly unfavorable strategic position. The assailants attacked from both land and sea, with a thirst for destruction. The scholars' eyes, wide with terror, saw the bright curve of flaming projectiles arch through the air, one by one landing threateningly close to their treasured books.

Caesar's men counterattacked by hurling torches coated with tar at the boats poised to strike. Soon, the thick ropes of the rigging and the wax-caulked decks were ablaze, and the ships sank hypnotically into the sea, licked by flames. The devastation spread to the port and the nearby houses. Fire fanned by the wind leapt over the roofs at the speed of a shooting star. The Egyptian troops ran to smother the blaze. Caesar took the chance to dash to the island of Pharos to take control of the maritime entrance to the city and await rein-forcements. As always, the brilliant Roman general outsmarted his enemy. Ptolemy XIII conveniently drowned in the Nile, leaving his sister widowed and all-powerful.

Plutarch, writing a century and a half after the events took place, claims that flames from the fire caused by Caesar's followers leapt from the ships to the Great Library, turning it to ash—a decisive requiem for the Alexandrian dream. Is that how it all ended?

There are reasons to doubt that it was so. In *The Civil War,* Caesar writes of the burning of the boats, but doesn't mention the destruction of the Library, even to justify his actions. Neither does his officer, Aulus Hirtius, who wrote the chronicle *The Alexandrian War.* On the contrary, he claims, the city's great buildings were fire-proof because they were built from marble and mortar, without any wood in the roofs or floors. No contemporary figure weeps for the destruction of the palace of books. And Strabo, the geographer, who visited Alexandria just a few years after the rebellion against Caesar, described the Musaeum in detail, with no reference to any recent disaster. Other Greek and Roman writers—Lucan, Suetonius, Athenaeus—also have nothing to say on the matter. But Seneca, the philosopher, complicates the riddle by writing, "Forty thousand scrolls burned in Alexandria."

Like in a detective novel, every new voice tells a different ver-sion and provides contradictory clues. What conclusion can we draw from this bewildering puzzle? What blurred reality is hidden behind the stories and silences? One possible answer is based on a detail mentioned obliquely by two much later authors: Cassius Dio and Orosius. Both say the fire started by Caesar destroyed the arsenal, the granaries, and some of the storehouses in the port, where, coincidentally, several thousand scrolls were stored—books that may have been new library acquisitions waiting to be transported to the Musaeum or simply blank scrolls belonging to merchants who would send them out to be sold along the trade routes of the Mediterranean.

Perhaps Plutarch misinterpreted the sources describing the burning of that storehouse full of books—which in Greek would also be called a *bibliothéke*—and imagined an apocalyptic fire at the Musaeum. Maybe this first destruction of the Great Library is an invented memory after all, a prophetic nightmare, a mythical fire that ultimately symbolized the twilight of a city, an empire, and a dynasty that began with Alexander's conquest and ended in Cleopatra's defeat.

80

Cleopatra's political and sexual alliances—first with Caesar and later with Mark Antony—were meant to prevent the kingdom of Egypt from being swallowed up by Roman greed. They managed only to delay the blow. After the queen's suicide in the year 30 BC, the land of the Nile was annexed to the nascent Roman Empire. Alexandria ceased to be the capital of a proud territory and became an outpost of the new global empire.

Funds to finance the community of scholars, which until then had come from the Ptolemies, became a responsibility of the Roman emperors. The Musaeum and its Library overcame the dynastic crisis, but it was soon clear that the best times now belonged to the past. That ambitious center of knowledge and creation had lived out its golden age thanks to an explosive blend of wealth, vanity, and imperialist calculations on the part of the Macedonian line. But the emperors' money and vanity were engaged in other schemes beyond Alexandria. We don't know if Caesar's fire affected the Library, but the drying up of imperial funds undoubtedly set its slow decline in motion.

In the first two centuries, the Library still found generous supporters, such as Hadrian, but the third century began darkly, with the senseless threats made by Caracalla. The emperor believed he knew—from the distance of a mere six centuries—that Aristotle had poisoned Alexander the Great. To wreak his vengeance, he plotted to set fire to the Musaeum, where the philosopher's ghost still roamed. Our source, the historian Cassius Dio, doesn't specify whether Caracalla ever carried out this act of villainy, but he does say that he put a stop to free dining for the scholars and did away with many of their privileges. Later, in response to a trivial crime, he ordered his troops to sack Alexandria, killing thousands of innocent people, and—in a Mediterranean version of Cold War Berlin—to build a wall through the city that would be patrolled by guards at regular intervals to prevent the populations of different areas from visiting one another freely.

In the second half of the third century, the Roman crisis became more acute. The empire's economic situation progressively worsened, and the cultural interests of the emperors, overwhelmed by serious political and military challenges, began to wane. In a world where the glories of Alexandria were no more than a distant gleam, financial support for maintaining the Musaeum's collection suffered a series of cuts. There was less and less money for replacing lost, aging, or deteriorated scrolls and for acquiring new ones. By now, the decline was unstoppable.

What followed was a chaotic cycle of pillage and depredations. In the times of the emperor Gallienus, the governor of Egypt declared himself emperor and cut off the supply of goods to Rome. Since Gallienus couldn't do without the Alexandrian granaries, he sent his general, Theodotus, to take back the city. The violent attack ravaged Alexandria. Soon afterward, the city was conquered and lost by Queen Zenobia of the Palmyrene Empire, who claimed to be descended from Cleopatra. Emperor Aurelian, and Diocletian after him, joined a destructive orgy of sieges and uprisings that were quashed with fire and bloodshed. The soldier and historian Ammianus Marcellinus, perhaps exaggerating for dramatic effect, wrote that by the end of the third century the walled area where the Musaeum once stood had been completely wiped off the map.

We have no detailed account of that twilight, but I like to think this is exactly what Paul Auster was trying to describe in his post-apocalyptic novel *In the Country of Last Things*. The novel tells of the journey made by a woman, Anna Blume, to a nameless city in the midst of disintegration, shaken by a period of conflicts and purges. The street names in this oppressive territory—Ptolemy Boulevard, Nero Prospect, Diogenes Terminal, Pyramid Road—suggest the impossible map of a pillaged and ghostly Alexandria, the ruins that make up its memory.

Anna arrived in the city in search of her only brother, a young journalist who disappeared there without explanation. In this place where all certainties are vanishing and one final catastrophe seems imminent, her hope of reunion is condemned to failure. One day, during her wanderings, Anna walks along Ptolemy Boulevard and comes by chance upon the crumbling National Library. ("It was a splendid edifice, with portraits on the walls of governors and generals, rows of Italianate columns, and beautiful inlaid marble—one of the landmark buildings of the city. As with everything else, however, its best days were behind it. A ceiling on the second floor had caved in, columns had toppled and cracked, books and papers were strewn everywhere.")

Anna moves into the attic of the library with Sam, a foreign press correspondent who knew her brother and injects some life into her frail hopes of finding him. Though the Great Library is little more than a ruin, it serves as a refuge for castaways from better times and is home to a small community of persecuted scholars, who, in a temporary truce in their fierce disagreements, collaborate to protect the last remaining fount of words, ideas, and books.

> I don't know how many people were living in the library
> at that time, but well over a hundred I should think, perhaps
> even more. The residents were all scholars and writers,
> remnants of the Purification Movement that had taken place
> during the tumult of the previous decade . . . A certain wary
> camaraderie had developed among the different factions
> in the library, at least to the extent that many of them were
> willing to talk to each other and exchange ideas . . . Public
> colloquies were held every morning for two hours—the
> so-called Peripatetic Hours—and everyone who lived in

the library was invited to attend . . . At one time, they say, there had been more than a million volumes in the National Library. Those numbers had been vastly reduced by the time I got there, but hundreds of thousands still remained, a bewildering avalanche of print.

Chaos and catastrophe have also seeped into the Library. Anna observes that the system of classification has fallen into disarray and it's almost impossible to find a book in the seven floors of archives. If a book is lost in this labyrinth of musty rooms, it might as well no longer exist: no one will ever find it again.

The city is gripped by a harsh cold snap that endangers the lives of the Library's refugees. In the absence of other fuel, they decide to burn books in the iron stove. Anna writes:

> I know it sounds like a terrible thing to have done, but we really didn't have much choice. It was either that or freeze to death . . . The curious thing about it was that I never felt any regrets. To be honest, I actually think I enjoyed throwing those books into the flames. Perhaps it released some secret anger in me; perhaps it was simply a recognition of the fact that it did not matter what happened to them. The world they had belonged to was finished, and at least now they were being used to some purpose. Most of them were not worth opening anyway . . . Whenever I found something that looked palatable, I would hold on to it and read it . . . I remember going through parts of Herodotus that way . . . But in the end, everything made its way into the stove, everything went up in smoke.

This is how I imagine the scientists and learned men of the Musaeum, watching in horror as their treasured discoveries were systematically plundered and burned, and eventually collapsed. In an unforgivable anachronism, I imagine those wise intellectuals falling victims to a black, nihilistic burst of humor, like Bakhtin in the dark days of the Nazi siege of Leningrad. The story goes that the Russian writer, an inveterate smoker, was shut in an apartment amid the terror of daily bombings. Since he had a supply of tobacco but no way to obtain any papers, he rolled his cigarettes with the pages of an essay to which he had dedicated ten years of work. Page by page, puff by puff, he smoked nearly the whole manuscript, certain of having another copy stored safely in Moscow, which, as it turned out, would also be lost in the chaos of war. I remember William Hurt recounting this almost legendary anecdote in the fascinating movie *Smoke*, written by Paul Auster. I think the librarians of Alexandria would have appreciated the despairing comedy of that survival story. In the end, the books in their care were also being transformed into air and smoke: a sigh, a mirage.

81

Fourth-century Alexandria was a turbulent place. Its inhabitants, known for their culture and sensuality, also spent their time on more brutal activities. The city had a long history of rioting in the streets. Social problems, religious differences, and power struggles broke out in the form of bloody, tumultuous fighting in the open air. We can imagine something not unlike the neighborhoods riven with vicious urban battles that Scorsese portrayed in *Gangs of New York*.

In the Egyptian capital, the tremors of a major Roman imperial crisis were beginning to make themselves known. As if according to some mysterious law of recurrence, certain regions suffer the shock waves of global tensions and unsolvable conflicts again and again. Since time immemorial, the eastern Mediterranean has been one of these geopolitical lightning rods.

Fanatical leaders of varied creeds (Jewish, pagan, and Christian, which in turn split into opposing factions: Nicean, Origenist, Arianist, and Monophysite, among others) swarmed along the streets of Alexandria. Attacks among groups were frequent, with mixed rivalries of shifting alliances. But it wasn't all chaos, sound, and fury. Beneath the confusion and violence on the surface, enormous historical change was brewing. At the beginning of the century, Emperor Constantine legalized Christianity. In the year 391, Theodosius enacted a series of edicts banning pagan sacrifices in public and ordering the closure of the main centers of pagan worship. Throughout those dramatic decades, the persecutors and persecuted changed roles. Nothing would ever be the same again: the state had converted to the new faith and embarked on the demolition of paganism.

The Musaeum and the library branch at the Serapeum were focal points of these religious battles. The two buildings were shrines, and their librarians, priests. The intellectuals working at both institutions made up a *thíasos*, a community that worshipped the Muses—the nine goddesses who protected human creation. Their workdays passed among statues of gods, altars, and other liturgical symbols of pagan worship, since the Ptolemies had kept alive the ancient Eastern custom of storing books in the temples. The continued existence of libraries created in the service of classical pagan culture wasn't easy under a regime that persecuted it.

The Serapeum—or temple to Zeus Serapis—which sheltered the sister library, was one of Alexandria's architectural wonders. With its elegant porticoed courtyards, its sculpted gods, its works of art, and its old-fashioned ostentation, it was a place of worship and a meetinghouse for pagans who were losing a historical battle. There they gathered, like veterans of a forgotten war, to grumble, feed their nostalgia, and lament—just like in every era—that any time in the past was superior.

In the year 391, everything went up in smoke.

Theophilus, the bishop and spiritual leader of the Christian community of Alexandria, enforced Emperor Theodosius's edicts with violence. Groups of Christian zealots set about hounding the pagans. Panic and hatred permeated the atmosphere, which began to crackle with dangerous electricity. Amid this extreme tension, a scandal brought the situation to a tipping point. During the renovation of a Christian basilica built on top of a chapel to the god Mithra, the workers uncovered a collection of mysterious pagan objects. Theophilus ordered that these secret symbols of worship be displayed in a procession through the city center. It's possible to build a picture of this gesture's impact if we remember Ariel Sharon's provocative visit to the Temple Mount, which sparked the Second Intifada just two decades ago. When they saw their beliefs profaned and exposed to the mockery of the masses, the Alexandrian pagans—and according to sources, especially the philosophy teachers—ferociously attacked the Christians. The streets were stained with blood. Fearing possible reprisals, the rioters bolted to the Serapeum and barricaded themselves in the shrine's inner rooms. They had taken some Christians hostage to use as a shield and, once inside, forced them to kneel before the old forbidden gods. On the other side of the barricades, hordes armed with axes laid siege to the temple.

The siege ended after a tense wait of several days. Finally, when it seemed impossible, a massacre was averted. A letter arrived from the emperor, recognizing the Christians who'd lost their lives in the commotion as martyrs, pardoning the pagan rebels, and ordering the destruction of the images in the Serapeum, in accordance with the new religious laws. A detachment of Roman soldiers arrived from the desert with a troupe of valiant anchorite monks as reinforcements. They fought their way into the temple, smashed the famous marble, ivory, and gold statue of the god Serapis—which a furious mob dragged piece by piece to the theater to burn in public—and destroyed the facilities. On the foundations of the ruined building, another church was built.

The destruction of the statue of Serapis and the pillage of the temple shook the pagans of Egypt, even those who weren't especially devout, to their core. Something graver and more final than the profaning of an ancient altar and an attack on a priceless collection of books had taken place. The pagans took it as a verdict of collective doom. They understood that all of them, with their hedonistic polytheism, their philosophical passion, and their grounding in the classics, had been tossed into the dustbin of history.

The voice of one of these exiles in time, the pagan teacher and poet Palladas, still has the power to move us. He was born and died in Alexandria at the turn of the fourth and fifth centuries AD. His profound alienation is latent in his epigrams—some hundred and fifty—which are preserved in the *Greek Anthology*. He watched the city founded by Alexander the Great as a synthesis of East and West seethe with bloody unrest and intolerance. He saw the ruins of his defeated gods. He witnessed the destruction of the Library and the brutal murder of Hypatia, whom he called in his verse the "unsullied star of wisdom." He learned of the incursion of the Huns and the arrival of the Germanic barbarians in Rome. When we read him today, his account of this other apocalypse seems stunningly modern. After the trauma of the Serapeum, in his disconsolate poem "Specters," he asked, "Is it not true, Greeks, that in the depths of night, / as all is plunged in darkness, we only seem to stir, / imagining that this mere dream is life? / Are we alive, though life itself is dead?"

The last resident at the Musaeum was the mathematician, astronomer, and musician Theon in the second half of the fourth century. It's difficult to imagine what might have been left of the institution's former splendor by then, but Theon tried to salvage the embers. Amid violent street battles and sectarian fighting, he devoted himself to predicting lunar and solar eclipses and to preparing the definitive edition of Euclid's *Elements*. He educated his daughter Hypatia, whose name means "highest," in science and philosophy, as if she'd been born a man. She collaborated with her father, and in her peers' opinion, in the end surpassed him in intellectual brilliance.

Hypatia decided to devote her life to studying and teaching. She never wanted to marry, no doubt because she wished to remain independent, and not, as sources claim, due to her love of virginity. Though her works were lost in the chaos of those turbulent centuries, except for a few brief fragments, we know that she wrote about geometry, algebra, and astronomy. She gathered around her a highly select group of students who would end up in significant roles among the Egyptian elites. Under the influence of her Gnostic beliefs—and her aristocratic prejudices—those of lower status, unable to understand her lofty teachings, were not granted access to her circle. There is every indication that Hypatia was classist, but not sectarian. She did not practice paganism, considering it simply one more element of the Greek cultural landscape to which she belonged. Among her followers there were Christians (two of whom became bishops, like Synesius), pagans, and philosophical atheists. Hypatia encouraged friendship among all of them. Unfortunately, however, it was the beginning of one of those eras in which moderates and mediators, those who opt for measured consideration and whom fanatics accuse of indifference, are an easy target, far from the protection of the closed ranks.

Until her tragic end, she managed to live by her own rules, and with remarkable freedom. In her youth, she was a woman of legendary beauty, but as far as men were concerned, her ideas were crystal clear. It's said that a student fell madly in love and asked for her hand in marriage. Hypatia, a follower of Plato and Plotinus, explained that she aspired only to the elevated world of ideas, and that base and crude material pleasures held no appeal for her. With her suitor still down on one knee, she chose an unusual—and scatological—gesture to shut him up. The anecdote is known thanks to Damascius, director of the Neoplatonic school of Athens, who describes the odd scene, caught between disgust and admiration: "She gathered some rags that were stained with her menstrual blood and declared, 'This is what you love, young man, and it isn't beautiful!' So ashamed and alarmed was he at this terrible sight, that he experienced a change of heart and quickly became a better man." This is the moral of the story, as told by Damascius: overcome by the sight of the menstrual rag, Hypatia's student stopped loving the flesh in its rottenness and kept searching for the perfection of beauty itself, through philosophy.

In any case, Hypatia held out as a single woman, allowing herself no distraction from her intellectual passions. A former teacher of many of the city's rulers, she engaged in public life and commanded respect from the municipal authorities of Alexandria. It was common knowledge that functionaries in high places sought her counsel, and the political influence of a woman so sure of herself began to awaken envy. Slanderous rumors flew of her supposed magic powers. Her interest in astronomy and mathematics must be hiding something more sinister—namely witchcraft and satanic spells.

The atmosphere had become increasingly strained, and the moderate Christian governor Orestes broke ties with Cyril, the bishop and nephew of Theophilus. The explosive mood of that cursed year of 415 is well portrayed in the movie *Agora*, though Hypatia, who was indeed still teaching, would have been around sixty at the time. A new wave of riots had broken out in Alexandria, this time between Christians and Jews. The usual violent episodes ensued in the theater, the streets, and at the doors of the churches and synagogues. Cyril demanded the expulsion of the city's large Jewish community.

Orestes, with support from Hypatia and the pagan intellectuals, refused to accept the patriarch's meddling. The gossip mill hummed with rumors that Hypatia was the true cause of the conflict between Orestes and Cyril.

In the middle of Lent, at the orders of a follower of Cyril's called Peter, an angry mob kidnapped Hypatia, accusing her of being a witch. She fought back and cried out as the attackers rushed at her cart but nobody dared to help her. The fanatics dragged her unopposed to a church called the Caesareum, which at another time had been a temple to the gods of the ancient religion. There, within view of all, they began to beat her brutally with pieces of broken tile. They gouged her eyes out of their sockets and cut out her tongue. When she was dead, they carried her body away from the city, cut out her organs and bones, and finally burned her remains on a pyre. They showed her body no mercy, attempting to obliterate all that Hypatia represented as a woman, pagan, and teacher.

Sources differ on the degree of Cyril's responsibility as instigator of the crime. Proof of what we would call intellectual authorship is always elusive, but suspicions immediately fell on him. There was no real investigation. Orestes was transferred to a new location, and the atrocity went unpunished. A few years later, another mob assassinated Orestes's successor as governor. Today, Cyril is considered a saint by the Catholic, Orthodox, Coptic, and Lutheran Churches.

The lynching of Hypatia marked the extinction of hope. The Musaeum and its dream of gathering together all the books and ideas in the world had succumbed in the brutal ring of the Alexandrian riots. From then on, the Great Library is shrouded in darkness, as if its great collection had vanished forever.

We don't know what became of the remains of the wreckage in those silent centuries. Libraries, schools, and museums are fragile institutions and cannot survive for long when surrounded by violence. In my mind, the old Alexandria is tinged with the sorrow of so many gentle, learned, peaceful people who felt stateless in their own city when faced with the horror of those years of fanaticism, from which they had no way out. Palladas, the old teacher of literature, wrote: "I spent my whole life among peaceful books, convers-

ing with the departed. I tried to spread admiration in a disdainful
era. From beginning to end I have been nothing but a consul for the
dead."

82

Just when we were no longer expecting any more news,
the Library appears for the last time in two Arabic chronicles. The
point of view is no longer Christian but Muslim and brings us forward in time to the twentieth year of the Hegira—the year 642 of
the Christian era. "I have conquered Alexandria, the great city of the
west, by force and without a treaty," writes the Arab commander
Amr ibn al-As, in a letter to Mohammed's second successor, the
caliph Umar I. After conveying this happy news, Amr lists the
city's charms and assets: "It has four thousand palaces, four thousand public baths, four hundred theaters or places of entertainment, twelve thousand fruit sellers, and forty thousand tax-paying
Jews."

The chronicler and thinker Ibn al-Qifṭī and the scholar ʿAbd al-
Laṭīf claim that a few days later, a wizened Christian scholar asked
the Muslim commander's permission to use the books from the
Great Library, which had been seized and held since the invasion.
Amr listened with curiosity to the old man's account of the ancient
splendor of the Musaeum and its collection, diminished by the passage of time, yet still valuable despite it all. Amr, far from being an
uncultured warrior, understood the significance of that dusty, moth-
eaten treasure, but didn't dare use it freely, preferring to write again
to ask Umar for instructions.

Before we go on, I must issue a warning. It's true that Amr conquered Alexandria in the year 640, and the general outline of events
also seems credible, but many specialists believe that Ibn al-Qifṭī and
ʿAbd al-Laṭīf invented the story of the Great Library's tragic end.
Both were writing several centuries after the events occurred and
seem to have had a stake in discrediting Caliph Umar's dynasty, to
flatter the learned Sultan Saladin. Perhaps any similarity between
this tale and reality is sheer coincidence, or perhaps not.

A letter took, on average, twelve days at sea and an equivalent length over land to reach Mesopotamia from Alexandria. Amr and the old man waited over a month for the caliph's response. Meanwhile, the commander asked to visit the dilapidated Library building. He was guided through a network of narrow, filthy lanes and alleys, to a palace in an advanced state of neglect guarded by a group of soldiers. Their steps echoed inside, and the whisper of all of those sleeping words could almost be heard. Manuscripts lay on the shelves like great chrysalises cocooned in cobwebs and dust. "It is advisable," said the old man, "for the books to be kept and preserved by rulers and their successors, until the end of time."

Amr took a liking to the old man and visited and talked with him every day. Like a story from *The Thousand and One Nights*, from the old man's lips he heard the incredible tale of a Greek king who tried to gather a copy of every book in the world in his palace, and of the searches carried out by his diligent servant Zamira—this was the name Ibn al-Qifṭī gave Demetrius of Phalerum—across India, Persia, Babylonia, Armenia, and other places.

Finally, Omar's emissary reached Alexandria with the caliph's answer. Amr read the message with bated breath. "Concerning the books in the Library, here is my response: if their content agrees with the [Koran], they are superfluous; and if not, they are sacrilegious. Go ahead and destroy them."

Amr obeyed, disillusioned. He distributed the books among Alexandria's four thousand bathhouses, where they were used as fuel for the stoves. It's said to have taken six months to burn that treasure of imagination and wisdom. Only the books of Aristotle were spared. Amid the steam of the bathhouses, the final utopia of his disciple Alexander crackled and burned into the silence of voiceless ashes.

83

After twelve years of construction and $225 million, the new Bibliotheca Alexandrina opened with spectacular pomp in October 2002, on the same spot where its predecessor once stood. The building represents the star of knowledge illuminating the world; it houses an immense reading room spread across seven floors with a single ceiling made up of thousands of colored panels that filter the sunlight during the day. The president of Egypt and around three thousand dignitaries from all over the world attended the ceremony. The speeches proclaimed with timely emphasis that this was a proud moment for the Egyptian people; that an ancient space of dialogue, understanding, and rationality was being reborn; that there, the critical spirit would take flight. And the resurrection of past glories was made official. But the stubborn ghosts of intolerance were also present at the festivities. The BBC journalist covering the event scoured the brand-new shelves for books by the Egyptian writer Naguib Mahfouz, banned by the country's religious authorities, and couldn't find a single one. When questioned about their absence, a senior official replied that "difficult books would be acquired only slowly." The young Macedonian's crazy dream continues to wage its endless battle with the prejudices of old.

LIFEBOATS AND
BLACK BUTTERFLIES

84

The three destructions of the Library of Alexandria may seem comfortingly ancient, but aversion to books is sadly a tradition firmly rooted in our history. Devastation never goes out of style. As a cartoon by the Spanish satirist El Roto said, "Civilizations grow old; barbarity is reborn."

In fact, the twentieth century was one of horrifying biblioclasm (bombed libraries in both world wars, the Nazi bonfires, the Chinese Cultural Revolution, the Soviet purges, McCarthyism, European and Latin American dictatorships, bookstores burned down or attacked with explosives, totalitarianism, apartheid, leaders with messianic tendencies, fundamentalism, the Taliban, the fatwa on Salman Rushdie, among other subsections of the overarching catastrophe). And the twenty-first century began with the looting of the museums and libraries of Iraq, where the earliest strokes of writing made their mark on the world.

I am working on this chapter in the last days of August, twenty-five years after the brutal attack on the National Library in Sarajevo. At the time I was a girl, and in my memory the war implied the discovery of a world beyond—a world bigger, but also darker than I had imagined. I remember that summer I began to get interested in those crisp books the grown-ups read that had never mattered to me before. Yes, that was when I read my first newspapers, holding them up to my face with my arms stretched out, like a cartoon spy. The first news, the first photos that made an impression on me were of those massacres in the summer of 1992. At the same time, here in Spain, we were living through the pageantry and euphoria of the Barcelona Olympics, the World Expo in Seville, and the sudden triumphalism of a country that modernized and got rich in a hurry. Little is left of that hypnotic dream, but the grey, bullet-ridden cityscape of Sarajevo is still engraved on my retinas. I remember one morning our ethics teacher told us to close our notebooks—there were only three or four of us in the class—and surprised us by suggesting we talk about the war in the former Yugoslavia. I've forgotten what we said, but we felt grown-up, important, only a step away from becoming qualified international experts. I remember one day I opened an atlas and traveled from Zaragoza to Sarajevo with the tip of my index finger. I thought the two cities' names shared a single melody. I remember the pictures of its library wounded by firebombs. A photo by Gervasio Sánchez of a shaft of sunlight crossing the ruined atrium, touching the piles of rubble and mutilated columns, is the iconic image of that shattered August.

The Bosnian writer Ivan Lovrenović has told of how, on one of those summer nights, "Sarajevo was brilliantly illuminated by the fire raging in the Vijećnica," the imposing building that housed the National Library by the edge of the river Miljacka. First, twenty-five incendiary shells hit the roof, even though the facility was marked with blue flags to signal its status as a cultural heritage site. When the blaze—so Lovrenović says—reached Neronian proportions, an unceasing, frenzied bombardment began, meant to cut off access to Vijećnica. From the hills overlooking the city, snipers shot at the gaunt and exhausted inhabitants of Sarajevo, who emerged from their shelters to try to save the books. The intensity of the attacks kept firemen at a distance. Finally, the building's Moorish columns collapsed, and the windows shattered and let out the flames. By dawn, hundreds of thousands of volumes had burned—rare books, manuscripts, irreplaceable documents. "There is nothing left here," said Vkekoslav, a librarian. "I saw a column of smoke, and paper flying everywhere, and I wanted to cry and scream but I kept kneeling with my head in my hands. All my life the memory will weigh upon me of how they burned down the National Library of Sarajevo."

Arturo Pérez-Reverte, a war correspondent at the time, witnessed the shelling and the blaze. The next morning, on the floor of the ravaged library, he could see the rubble from the walls and stairs, the remains of manuscripts no one would ever read again, demolished works of art. "When a book burns, when a book is destroyed, when a book dies, something inside us is irremediably maimed . . . When a book burns, with it also die all the lives that made it possible, all the lives it contains and all the lives to which the book could, in the future, have given warmth and knowledge, intelligence, pleasure, and hope. To destroy a book is literally to murder the soul of man."

The embers kept burning for days, smoldering and floating over the city like a dark smattering of snow. "Black butterflies," the residents of Sarajevo called the ashes of books that fell on pedestrians, on bomb sites, on sidewalks, on half-demolished buildings, and that finally decayed and mingled with the ghosts of the dead.

A curious coincidence: the captain of the arsonist firemen whom we met in *Fahrenheit 451* used the same metaphor. With a book in his hands, he dictated his poetic instructions for destroying it: "Light the first page, light the second page. Each becomes a black butterfly. Beautiful, eh?" In the dismal future Bradbury's novel describes, reading is strictly prohibited, and books are reported and destroyed. Here, fire brigades, instead of putting out fires, start them and fan the flames to burn down the homes that hide these dangerous clandestine objects. Only one book is legal: the rule book of the very brigade whose job is to set fire to all the others. From this sole permitted text, we learn that the corps was founded in 1790 to burn English books in the United States, and that the first fireman was Benjamin Franklin. No writings survive to refute these claims and nobody questions them. Where documents are destroyed and books cannot circulate freely, it's all too easy to modify history with impunity.

In the case of the former Yugoslavia, the goal of razing the past was driven by ethnic hatred. From 1992 until the end of the war, 188 libraries and archives were attacked. A grim report by the United Nations Commission of Experts established that there was an "intentional destruction of cultural heritage that cannot be justified by military necessity." Juan Goytisolo, who traveled to the Bosnian capital in response to a call from Susan Sontag, wrote in *Landscapes of War: From Sarajevo to Chechnya*, "When the library burned, victim of the sterile hatred of stubborn rocket launchers, it was worse than death. The rage and pain of those moments will go with me to my grave. The attackers' goal—to sweep away the historic substance of a land and mount in its place an edifice made of lies, myth, and legend—wounded us to the core."

A crooked version of events could be erected upon the ashes of the texts that were burned. Admittedly, the books destroyed by shells undoubtedly also contained their own biased interpretations. The works that make up library collections and lie on the shelves in bookstores are partial and sometimes even propagandistic—I remember the story of a London bookseller who, during the months of the Nazi bombings, covered the roof of his establishment with the copies of *Mein Kampf* he had in stock. But it's precisely because of the multiplicity of voices that speak, add nuance, and contradict one another on an incalculable number of pages that we can trust there will be no blind spots, that we'll be able to identify manipulation when it occurs. Those who destroy libraries and archives are advocating for a future with less diversity, less irony, and less dissent.

Though the Library of Alexandria was repeatedly burned and destroyed, not all was lost. Centuries of efforts to save its imaginative legacy weren't in vain. Many books that survive to this day still bear the textual hallmarks and symbols used by the Alexandrian philologists in their editions. And this means that to reach our hands, copies have traveled along a treacherous route, from copy to copy to copy, whose first link in the chain of transmission dates to the lost library. For hundreds and hundreds of years, the books available at

Alexandria were carefully copied and distributed through a network of humbler libraries and private collections, nurturing a burgeoning landscape of readers. Multiplying the number of copies represented the only remote possibility of safeguarding these works. If anything survived the devastation it was thanks to that slow, gentle, fertile irrigation of handwritten texts that were disseminated with great effort, reaching far-flung places that were hidden and safe, lowly places that would never be turned into battlefields. The works we still read endured in these corners—insignificant, marginal refuges—holding out against devastation through dangerous centuries, while great numbers of books, usually concentrated in centers of power, were ruined by waves of destruction, looting, and fires.

In Greco-Roman antiquity, a permanent community was born in Europe, a flame that, though it might flicker, never completely goes out, a minority inextinguishable to this day. Since then, over time, the passion of anonymous readers has protected the fragile inheritance of words. Alexandria was the place where we learned to preserve books from the ravages of moths, rust, mold, and from barbarians armed with matches.

85

The summer book review sections are always asking literary stars what book they would take to a desert island. I haven't a clue whose idea it was to include the famous island, or due to what strange mimetic impulse it remains part of the question, exotic and incongruous. We owe the best answer to G. K. Chesterton: *Thomas's Guide to Practical Shipbuilding*. Like Chesterton, I would also want to escape from a place like that. I have no interest in any desert island lacking a bookstore that stocks *The Odyssey*, *Robinson Crusoe*, *Story of a Shipwrecked Sailor*, and *Ocean Sea*.

It's possible to follow the life-saving trail of books anywhere in the world, even from the most sinister places. As Jesús Marchamalo explains in his delightful *Tocar los libros* (Touching Books), the poet Joseph Brodsky, imprisoned in Siberia for the crime of "social parasitism," was consoled by reading Auden; Reinaldo Arenas, locked away in Castro's jails, by *The Aeneid*. Leonora Carrington, confined to a psychiatric institution in Santander soon after the Second World War, survived her dire situation by reading Unamuno.

There were also libraries in Nazi concentration camps. They were supplied with books seized from prisoners on their arrival, and the money taken from inmates paid for new acquisitions. Though the SS invested a good part of the funds in propagandistic tracts, there was no shortage of popular novels or major classics, alongside dictionaries, philosophical essays, and scientific texts. There were even forbidden volumes whose bindings were disguised by prisoner librarians. These libraries began in 1933. In the autumn of 1939, there were six thousand titles just in Buchenwald; in Dachau there were thirteen thousand. The SS used them as a prop to show visitors that in those humanitarian work camps, not even the prisoners' intellectual interests were neglected. It seems that in the early days, the inmates had access to their own books, but the privilege was soon revoked.

Did the books in those libraries—close but inaccessible—bring the prisoners any relief? And, even more essentially, can culture serve as a lifeline for someone subjected to abuse, hunger, and the threat of death?

In *Goethe in Dachau,* we have conclusive, visceral proof. Its author, Nico Rost, was a Dutch translator of German literature. During the war, even after his country's invasion, he was involved in publishing German authors troublesome to the Nazis. He was also a communist—his second strike. Detained in May 1943 and sent to Dachau the following year, he went into the infirmary as a patient and ended up working there in administration. In this way, he avoided grueling days of outdoor work or enslavement in the arms factories. But staying in the infirmary was a dangerous blessing. If you were noticed and deemed a parasitic invalid, you were likely to be herded onto a train for extermination.

In a state of anguish, with no word of the Allies' progress, decimated by a lethal typhoid epidemic, and with dwindling rations—Rost describes a fellow prisoner who grew so thin that even his false teeth were too big for him—the prisoners were increasingly convinced that they wouldn't survive. Under these circumstances, Rost made several risky decisions. The first was to keep a diary, procuring paper with great difficulty, and hide away to scrawl a few lines each day before tucking his notes away in a nook. The curious thing is that this diary, published after the camp's liberation, is not a tale of his tribulations but rather a chronicle of his thoughts. He writes, "He who speaks of hunger ends up hungry. And those who speak of death are the first to die. Vitamin L (literature) and F (future) seem to me the best provisions." And later, "We're all going to get infected, and we'll all die of malnutrition. Read even more." Then, "In the end, it's true: the classics can help and give strength." And finally, "At the end of the day, living among the dead with Thucydides, Tacitus, and Plutarch, in Marathon or Salamis, is the most decent thing to do, when one isn't allowed to do anything else."

Rost's second dangerous decision was to organize a clandestine reading group. A friendly kapo and some doctors agree to borrow books from the library for the group members. When they can't get hold of texts, they recall phrases from things they've read in the past and discuss them together. They give brief talks on their national literatures, together belonging to a mosaic of European countries. They gather between the beds, frightened and trying to pass unnoticed with someone always on the lookout, sounding the alarm as soon as a guard appears. On one occasion, the kapo who used to turn a blind eye gets angry and scatters the circle, shouting, "Shut up! Enough chatter! You'd be shot for this in Mauthausen. There's no discipline here. It's like a damned nursery school!"

Two of the group members are writing books in their heads: a monograph on patent law and a story for the children who will grow up among the ruins. They talk about Goethe, Rilke, Stendhal, Homer, Virgil, Lichtenberg, Nietzsche, and Teresa of Ávila, while the bombs fall and the barracks shake, while the typhoid epidemic intensifies and a few doctors let their patients die—the more the better—to enter the SS officers' good graces.

Death constantly changes the composition of the group. Rost, who brings everyone together and keeps things going, tries to sound out and recruit the newly arrived sick inmates. His friends nickname him "the crazy paper-guzzling Dutchman." The secret diary is an act of rebellion through reading and writing, which were forbidden to him. As the bodies pile up, he clings stubbornly to his right to think. On March 4, 1945, scarcely a month before he would be freed, but unaware that salvation is near, he feels he is on the border between life and death. He writes, "I refuse to talk about typhoid, lice, hunger, or cold." He knows and suffers the existence of all these torments but believes the Nazis have invented them to animalize the prisoners and drive them to despair. Rost would rather not focus on the workings of the slaughterhouse; he clings urgently to his belief in literature, seeking a lifeline. There's something paradoxical about this communist who preaches a radical kind of materialism while surviving extreme conditions thanks to his faith in an idea.

Those with whom he shares conversation and readings are dissidents from a wide range of countries (Russians, Germans, Belgians, French, Spaniards, Dutch, Polish, Hungarians). In the July 12, 1944, entry he claims, "We make up a kind of European community—even though it is forced—and could learn a lot from our dealings with other countries." I like to think, contrary to the wisdom of history textbooks, that the European Union was really born in a dangerous reading group behind the wires of a Nazi concentration camp.

In those same years, beyond the fringes of Europe—wherever the continent's imaginary border lies—other voices, in the Soviet gulag, were discovering the meaning of culture in life-threatening circumstances. Galya Safonova was born in the barracks of a Siberian camp in the 1940s and spent her childhood as a prisoner at some notoriously fearsome mines amid the howling wind, in the land of everlasting snow. Her mother, a distinguished epidemiologist, was condemned to forced labor for refusing to inform on a colleague at her laboratory. In that freezing prison, where inmates were allowed to write no more than two letters a year and paper and pencils were scarce, the women made secret hand-sewn stories for the girl who knew only the gulag, with shaky pictures drawn in the dark and text scrawled with a quill. "Each one of those books made me happy!" an elderly Galya explained to the writer Monika Zgustova. "As a little girl, they were my only cultural points of reference. I have kept them all my life. I treasure them!" Elena Korybut, who served a sentence of over ten years in the mines of Vorkuta, in the tundra far beyond the Arctic Circle, showed Zgustova a book by Pushkin, illustrated with old engravings. "In the camp, this book of unknown origin passed through hundreds, maybe even thousands of hands. Books have their own lives, their histories and their ends, just as men do. You can't imagine what a book meant to the prisoners: it was salvation! Beauty, liberty, and civilization in the midst of total barbarity!" In *Dressed for a Dance in the Snow*, her fascinating book of interviews with women who survived the gulag, Monika Zgustova shows to just what extent, even at life's direst moments, human beings are creatures who thirst for stories. This is why we always carry books with us, or indeed inside us; we even take them into the terrain of horror, like first-aid kits to heal our despair.

Nico Rost, Galya Safonova, and Elena Korybut were not the only ones. In the disinfection chamber at Auschwitz, Viktor Frankl was robbed of a manuscript containing an entire career's research; the desire to rewrite it kept him tethered to life. The philosopher Paul Ricoeur, detained by the Vichy regime, devoted himself to teaching and organizing the prisoners' library. The sole possession the young Michel del Castillo had at Auschwitz was—aptly, given the circumstances—Tolstoy's *Resurrection*. "Literature is my only biography and my only truth," he later said. Eulalio Ferrer, the son of a Cantabrian socialist leader, was just eighteen when he entered a prison camp in France, where a militiaman suggested trading a book for some cigarettes. The book was *Don Quixote de la Mancha*, which he reread for months and which "kept me going and gave me personal solace amid the madness around me." All of them were like Scheherazades, saving themselves through the power of imagination and their faith in words. Frankl himself would later write that paradoxically, despite their being in worse physical shape, many intellectuals endured the hardships of life at Auschwitz more than other, sturdier prisoners. In the end, the psychiatrist says, those who could isolate themselves from their dreadful surroundings suffered less by taking refuge in their inner worlds.

Books help us survive major historical catastrophes and the small tragedies of our lives. As John Cheever, another explorer of the darkness beneath the surface, said, "Literature is the only consciousness we possess . . . Literature has been the salvation of the damned; literature has inspired and guided lovers, routed despair, and can perhaps, in this case, save the world."

86

The worst part was the silence. At the time, we didn't have a word to describe it. You could say, they laugh at me in class. Or, more dramatically, they beat me up at school. But that only scratched the surface of the situation. You didn't need X-ray vision to read the adults' minds and see the instant diagnosis they made: it was just kids' stuff.

It was the early revelation of a tribal, primitive, predatory mechanism. The protection of the group had been withdrawn. There was an invisible wire fence, and I was on the wrong side. If someone called me names or dragged me out of my chair, the others downplayed it. The bullying became routine, commonplace, unremarkable. I'm not saying it happened every day. Sometimes, there was an inexplicable lull; Pandora's box stayed locked for weeks, and the balls at recess were no longer aimed at me. Until suddenly, the teacher scolded one of my tormentors in class, and on the way out, in the blue-painted corridors amid the commotion of children impatient to play, they turned the humiliation back on me: *Bitch, nerd, what are you looking at? You'll get what's coming to you.* And then it was open season again.

The bullies divided the roles: one was the ringleader, the others her loyal minions. They made up nicknames for me; they did disgusting impressions of me with my braces; they threw balls at me whose heavy thud left me so dazed I can still feel it today; they broke my little finger in gymnastics class; they relished my fear. The other kids probably don't even remember. Maybe if they dug around in their memory they'd say, Okay, we played a few practical jokes on her. That's exactly how they cooperated, with their indifference.

In the toughest times, between the ages of eight and twelve, there were other misfits. I wasn't the only one. There was a student who had to repeat a grade, a Chinese immigrant who barely spoke Spanish, and a curvaceous girl going through puberty early. We were the weakest of the flock, the ones the predator watches and sets apart from afar.

Many people idealize their childhood, turning it into a glorified land of lost innocence. I don't have a single memory of this alleged innocence in other children. My childhood is a strange jumble of keenness and fear, of weakness and endurance, of dismal days and moments of exuberant joy. The games, the curiosity, my earliest friends, the crucial love of my parents—they are all there. And so is the daily humiliation. I don't know how those two fractured parts of my experience fit together. My memory has archived them separately.

But again, the worst part was the silence. I accepted the prevailing code among children, the gag rule. Everyone always knows from the time they're four years old that it's wrong to snitch. A snitch is a chicken, a bad team player, and they deserve a beating. What happens in the schoolyard stays in the schoolyard. You don't tell the grown-ups anything, or at most just the bare minimum so they won't get involved. I scratched myself by accident. I lost things that had really been stolen from me and turned up floating in the yellowish toilet water. I internalized the idea that the only shred of dignity left for me was to endure it, to keep quiet, to not cry in front of the others, to not ask for help.

I'm not the only one. Violence among children and teenagers is protected by a barrier of murky silence. For years I took comfort in not having been the class snitch, the tattletale, the coward. Not to have stooped that low. Misplaced pride and shame made me follow the rule that certain stories aren't told. Wanting to be a writer was a belated rebellion against that law. The stories that go untold are exactly the ones you must tell. I decided to become the snitch I was so afraid to be. The roots of writing are often dark. This is my darkness, the darkness that nurtures this book, and perhaps nurtures everything I write.

In those humiliating years, in addition to my family, I was helped by four people I've never met: Robert Louis, Michael, Jack, Joseph. Later I would discover that they are better known by their last names: Stevenson, Ende, London, and Conrad. Thanks to them, I learned that my world is just one among many simultaneously existing worlds, both real and imaginary. Thanks to them, I learned how to store comforting fantasies in a room inside me, a place to seek shelter when the hail was pummeling down outside. This revelation changed my life.

I dig through my old papers in search of a story titled "The Savage Tribes" that I wrote in my early years of literary exploration. Rereading it after so long I find the writing green, but refrain from sticking my scalpel in. It's an odd exercise of personal archaeology, digging down to a layer of the past where my proximity to events still protected me from the well-meaning but deceptive filters of memory. And among the text's amateur lines, I find that I too, in my own small tragedy, found a lifeline in books.

I was the captain of the boat. I was out on deck when I hear a cry. Land ahoy! I go to the prow and take out the telescope. On the island, there are palms and coconut trees and strangely shaped rocks. Treasure Island! Helmsman, three degrees starboard. Lower the sails. We'll dock. I'll explore the island alone since the whole crew is afraid. Sailors tell terrifying tales of the savages on the island.

"What are you doing there?"

"She's eating a sandwich. She has to eat a lot to be the smartest and know everything."

"Hey look, a cheese sandwich."

"Is it good?"

"Ha, you'll see. Now it'll be good."

"Good one."

"Here, look, you spit on it too."

"Now give it back. Make her eat it."

"That's right. Eat it. Come on, eat. Let us see you eat it. And don't start crying."

"No, she won't cry. Everyone says how smart she is. She's going to eat it all and she's not going to snitch."

I meet a tribe and steel myself to be brave. It had to happen. It's better not to annoy them. They call me crafty and a white devil in their language. Now they're taking me to their chiefs. There are two. They invite me to eat their food and say if I don't, they'll kill me. They can be friendly, and they can be very cruel. I see the skeletons of their victims around me. They give me live worms on the leaf of a large tropical plant. My stomach turns with disgust, but I have to put up with it and chew. Then I swallow. I finish it all. They laugh gleefully and let me go. Saved! According to the map, the tribe's village is near where the treasure is hidden. I reach a cave with damp and uneven walls, moving cautiously in case there are traps. After several days of wandering through tunnels dug into the rock, I find the treasure just as I hear the bell saying recess is over.

HOW WE BEGAN TO BE STRANGE

87

In reality, we are quite strange, and as Amelia Valcárcel tells us, this strangeness began with the Greeks. Certain oddities occurred in Alexandria for the first time and on a large scale that today are part of our normal lives. What the Ptolemies brought into being in their city on the banks of the Nile is an idea at once amazing and familiar to us. After the technological revolution of writing and the alphabet, Alexander's successors set an ambitious project in motion to stockpile and provide access to knowledge. The Musaeum attracted the era's best scientists and inventors with the promise that they could dedicate their lives to research; it also appealed to their tunic pockets with the added incentive of tax exemption. The Great Library and its branch at the Serapeum sprang open the locks that kept all ideas and discoveries behind closed doors. The electrifying atmosphere around those written scrolls and their accumulation in the gigantic library must have been something like the creative explosion the internet and Silicon Valley represent today.

What's more, those in charge of the Library developed effective systems for finding their way amid all the information beginning to burst the banks of memory. The invention of methods like catalogs, the alphabetical classification system, and training the staff who would take care of the scrolls—philologists to clean up errors, scribes to make copies, and librarians both pedantic and cheerful to guide the uninitiated through the veritable labyrinth of written texts—were as important a step as the invention of writing. Many writing systems appeared independently across cultures distant from one another in space and time, but relatively few managed to survive. Archaeologists have discovered traces of numerous forgotten languages that died because they lacked efficient methods to catalog texts and optimize searches. What is the point of accumulating documents if they get jumbled up and the information needed at any given moment is like a needle in an infinite haystack? What set the Great Library apart in its time, as with the internet today, was its sophisticated yet simplified techniques for finding the thread you sought in the chaotic tangle of written knowledge.

In the new technological era, organizing information is still fundamental, just as it was in the time of the Ptolemies. It's no coincidence that in several languages—French, Catalan, and Spanish—we call our computers "orderers." It was Jacques Perret, a professor of ancient languages at the Sorbonne, who on the eve of the new machines' launch in 1955 proposed to the French directors of IBM that they replace the English "computer," which describes only calculation, with the French *ordinateur*, which stresses the far more important and decisive function of ordering information. The history of the vicissitudes of technology from the invention of writing to computers is fundamentally a story of the methods created to provide access to knowledge, and to archive and call it up when necessary. The route of this progression against confusion and forgetting began in Mesopotamia. In ancient times, it reached its pinnacle in the palace of books at Alexandria, then meandered all the way up to our present-day digital networks.

The royal collectors took another unusual, genius step: translation. Never before had anyone tackled a universal translation project with such broad curiosity and such an abundance of means. Heirs to Alexander's ambition, the Ptolemies weren't content just to map the unexplored world but wished to open the way into the minds of others. And this was a pivotal moment, since European civilization was built on translations—from Greek, Latin, Arabic, Hebrew, from all the different languages of Babel. Without translations, we wouldn't have been the same. Divided by mountains, rivers, seas, and linguistic borders, Europeans would have been ignorant of the discoveries made by others, and these limitations would have isolated us even more. It's impossible for us all to know every language that gives voice to literature and knowledge, and, sadly, not all doves can bestow the gift of tongues. But our ancient habit of translation has built bridges, blended ideas, given rise to an endless, polyphonic conversation, and shielded us from the greatest perils of our provincial chauvinism, teaching us that our language is one more among many, and in fact is more than one.

The act of translation, which all of us take for granted, has mysterious elements. In *The Invention of Solitude,* Paul Auster reflects on this almost mystical experience, this game of mirrors. Auster is intrigued by its hidden details because for many years he earned a living translating the books of other writers. He would sit at his desk, read a book in French, and then, with great effort, write the same book in English. In fact, it both is and is not the same book; this is why the task has never ceased to amaze him. For a split second, every translation comes close to vertigo, a disturbing face-to-face meeting with its own double, where different states overlay one another in subtle and bewildering ways. Auster sits down at his table to write someone else's book, and though there is only one presence in the room, there are really two. Auster imagines himself as a kind of living ghost of another person—often dead—who is both present and absent, and whose book both is and is not the one he is translating in that very moment. Then he tells himself that it is possible to be both alone and not alone at the same time.

The transfer between languages is the child of a concept that to a large extent was invented by Alexander and that we still give a Greek name: cosmopolitanism. The best part of Alexander's megalomaniac dream—its realization, like in any self-respecting utopia, clearly faltered—was that it brought about a lasting union of all the peoples of the *oikoumene*, creating a new political form with the potential to bring peace, culture, and laws to all human beings. Plutarch wrote that "Alexander did not treat the Greeks as leaders and the barbarians with despotism, as Aristotle had advised, nor did he behave toward others as if they were plants or animals. Rather, he commanded that all should consider the world their homeland, the good their kin, and the evil, foreigners." Undoubtedly, the text is a hagiographic summary that carefully conceals the thorniest aspects of the Greek imperial enterprise. Yet it reflects, albeit with some distortion, the exceptional process of globalization that Alexander set in motion.

The project of creating a kingdom that stretched to the edge of the inhabited Earth died along with the young Macedonian, but his conquests expanded the sphere of human relationships. Hellenic civilization was in fact the largest network of cultural and commercial exchange the world had ever known. And the new cities, founded by Alexander and by his successors as a living celebration of their glory, ushered in a new way of life at the dusk of classical civilization. While life went on according to traditional patterns in Greece, in the teeming streets of the great Alexandrian cities of the Middle East and Asia Minor, the daily mixing of people with varied origins, customs, and beliefs opened the way to bold new hybridities.

Many scholars believe that the person who best embodied the new horizons of Hellenism was Eratosthenes, whom Ptolemy III summoned to direct the Library of Alexandria in the third century BC. The new director based his updated geographical maps on the information brought from Alexander's expedition. According to the researcher Luca Scuccimarra, "Eratosthenes expressed, with unprecedented clarity, a full recognition of the ethnic and linguistic diversity of the human race." The Alexandria this new cartographer of global reality knew was a projection of the future world: a Greek city in Africa, the most extraordinary of all the Babels, the most prodigious point of contact for the ideas, arts, and sciences of our old world.

There, on the shores of the Mediterranean Sea, the first culture was born that tried to embrace the knowledge of all of humanity. Such fantastic ambition gave rise to the desire for contact with others to which Herodotus devoted his life and that spurred Alexander on in his dash toward the end of the Earth. George Steiner recalls that Herodotus once said, "Every year we send our ships at the risk of life and very expensively to Africa to ask: 'Who are you? What are your laws? What is your language?' They never sent one ship to ask us." Hellenism defined and expanded the idea of the voyage of discovery in two different forms: physical travel—in convoys, boats, carriages, and on horseback—and the motionless journey made by the reader who glimpses the world's immensity from the paths traced by ink in a book. Alexandria, represented by the lighthouse and the Musaeum, was the symbol of this dual quest. In this crucible city we find the foundations of a Europe that, with its light and shadows, with its tensions and delirium, even with its periodic barbaric inclinations, has never lost its thirst for knowledge or the impulse to explore. In *Vision from the Bottom of the Sea*, Rafael Argullol claims a simple epitaph for himself, made up of just two words: "He traveled!" He adds, "I have traveled to escape and to try to see myself from another perspective. When you can see yourself from outside, you contemplate existence with more humility and perceptiveness than when, like an idiot cheered on by other idiots, you imagined yourself as the best self, your city as the best city, and what you called life as the only conceivable life."

In its ambiguous state as a Greek city outside of Greece and the seed of Europe beyond the bounds of Europe, Alexandria came to see itself from the outside. During the Library's greatest era and following in Alexander's wake, the Stoic philosophers were bold enough to teach for the first time that all people belonged to a community without borders and were obliged to accept humanity wherever and under whichever circumstances they encountered it. We should remember the Greek capital of the Nile delta as the place where this effervescence was born, where the languages and traditions of others began to matter, and where the world and knowledge were understood to be a shared territory. In these aspirations we find a precursor to the great European dream of universal citizenship. Writing, books, and libraries were the technologies that made this utopia possible.

The norm is to forget, to let the legacy of words disappear, to allow chauvinism and linguistic borders to hold sway. Thanks to Alexandria, we have become exceedingly strange: we are now translators and cosmopolitans, and we remember. The Great Library fascinates me—a little misfit from a school in Zaragoza—because it invented a homeland made of paper for the stateless of every era.

Part Two

THE ROADS TO ROME

1

The new center of the world was a city with a very bad reputation. From the beginning, the Romans were plagued by a terrible black legend, a special feature of which was that they invented it themselves. It began with a fratricide. The myth goes that Romulus and Remus—brothers, and impatient grandsons of the king of Alba Longa—set out to found their own city on that legendary April 21 in the year 753 BC. They agreed on the choice of a site for the future city on the banks of the Tiber but were soon enmeshed in a power struggle. Since they were twins, neither brother had the advantage of age, and both alleged there were divine omens in their favor—the gods also know how to cover all their bases. Remus provoked his brother by leaping over the walls that Romulus had begun to build by himself. According to Livy, in the ensuing fight, the fever of ambition led to bloodshed. Romulus murdered his brother and cried as he trembled with rage, "So perish everyone that shall hereafter leap over my wall." He thus set a useful precedent for future foreign policy in Rome, which, having attacked, would always excuse itself by alleging a prior aggressive or illegal act by the other party.

The next step was to organize a genuine cadre of criminals. The recently founded city needed some citizens. Without thinking twice, the young king declared Rome a place of asylum for outlaws and fugitives, announcing that they would be safe from persecution within its walls. Indiscriminate hordes of convicts and people of shady origins—so Livy tells us—fled neighboring territories to become the first inhabitants of Rome. The most pressing problem became the absence of women. And so we come to the third nefarious episode: a mass rape.

Romulus invited the families from the neighboring villages to a celebration of games in honor of the god Neptune. The people of the surrounding area seemed keen to see the new city, though in those days it was still a quagmire of mud huts with the occasional sheep as the only major attraction. On the appointed day, a curious crowd appeared in Rome. Men came with their wives and children from nearby villages with names as eccentric as Caenina, Antemnae, and Crustumerium (had the latter become a great imperial power instead of Rome, today we would all be Crustumerians). But the religious festival was merely a ruse. When the time came for the games, and the eyes and minds of all guests were trained on the spectacle, the agreed-upon signal was given. Then the Romans kidnapped the girls who had come with their families. According to Livy, nearly all the men snatched the first woman to fall into their hands. Since there is always a hierarchy, though, the main patricians kept the most beautiful girls for themselves and paid for them to be delivered to their homes. Weaker in numbers, the kidnapped women's husbands and fathers fled, bewildered and stricken, bitterly decrying their violent neighbors.

To clear things up, Livy is quick to explain that if the Romans were to guarantee their city's survival, the abduction was necessary. Furthermore, he depicts them as promising the terrified young women affection, love, and reconciliation. "These arguments," the historian adds, "were reinforced by the endearments of their husbands, who excused their conduct by pleading the irresistible force of their passion—a plea effective beyond all others in appealing to a woman's nature." On top of that, this legendary, collective barbaric deed served as a model for the Roman marriage ceremony, which for centuries dramatized the women's abduction. The ritual demanded that the bride take refuge in her mother's arms and that the groom pretend to drag her away as she wept, screamed, and refused.

The myth makes an appearance in *Seven Brides for Seven Brothers*, a harmless romantic comedy from 1954, in which an amusing song about the Sabines, an early Italic tribe, helps the coarse male protagonists solve the problem of their bachelorhood once and for all. And the gleeful friends sing together in their relief, reflecting on the women taken captive by the Romans,

Seems they cried and kissed and kissed and cried
All over that Roman countryside
. . . .
Oh they acted angry and annoyed
But secretly they was overjoyed.

Apparently, the prudish Hollywood of the Hays Code, which censored kisses and double beds on-screen, considered this old story of mass abduction an ideal step toward a happy and cozy domestic life.

But Rome's enemies saw in their murky foundational myths a foretaste and a warning of their later predatory disposition. One of those adversaries would write, centuries later, "From the very beginning, the Romans have owned nothing apart from what they have stolen: their home, their wives, their land, their empire." In just fifty-three years, according to Polybius's estimate, the descendants of the sinister and unscrupulous Romulus conquered the majority of the known world.

2

In fact, the making of the great Mediterranean empire took several centuries. But those fifty-three years during the second century BC mark the period in which everyone else understood with shock and horror that Rome had built the most devastating war machine ever known.

The first historically documented Roman battles date from the fifth century BC. These were local skirmishes—sometimes defensive, sometimes aggressive—that took place daily in the adjoining territories. Only in the fourth century BC did Roman expansion begin to catch the attention of the Greeks, the dominant power of the period. By the year 240 BC, after a dizzying string of victories, Roman territory already encompassed nearly all of Italy and Sicily. A century and a half later, the Romans controlled almost the entire Iberian Peninsula, Provence, Italy, the whole Adriatic coast, Greece, western Asia Minor, and the coast of North Africa between present-day Libya and Tunisia. Between 100 and 43 BC Gaul was annexed, followed by the rest of the Anatolian Peninsula, the coast of the Black Sea, Syria, Judea, Cyprus, Crete, the coastal strip of Algeria, and part of Morocco. The inhabitants of a small city in the marshes of the Tiber had gone from being stuck in their fetid quagmire to having all the Mediterranean Sea at their disposal, as if it were an inland lake for their use only.

Military campaigns became a feature of everyday life for the Romans. A fifth-century Hispanic historian records, as an unprecedented rarity, only one year without war through that long period of imperial expansion. Those unusual months of military indolence occurred in the year 235 BC, during the consulship of Gaius Atilius and Titus Manlius. But the norm was to devote immense effort and resources to waging war, and though they counted their battles as victories, they left a terrible trail of casualties from their own ranks, not to mention those from the other side. Mary Beard claims that during the conquest phase, "somewhere between 10 and 25 per cent of the Roman adult male population would have served in the legions each year, a greater proportion than in any other pre-industrial state and, on the higher estimate, comparable to the call-up rate in World War I." In the Battle of Cannae against Hannibal, which lasted a single afternoon, the pace of Roman deaths was an estimated hundred a minute. And many soldiers would later succumb to their wounds, since ancient weapons were better at maiming than killing, and death came later from infection.

The sacrifice was immense, but the rewards surpassed the most covetous fantasies of those ruthless legionnaires. Halfway through the second century BC, the spoils of so many victories had turned the Roman population into the wealthiest in the known world. The war greased the wheels of the supremely profitable trade of the era: slavery. Thousands and thousands of captives were turned into slaves who labored in Roman fields, mines, and mills. Carts loaded with bullion looted from Eastern cities and kingdoms packed the Roman treasury to the point of overflowing. In the year 167 BC, the abundance of gold was so great that the state chose to halt direct taxes for citizens. It's true that this sudden wealth was also destabilizing for the Romans—especially those who couldn't get their hands on any of it. The usual situation was repeated: the rich got richer and the poor even poorer. Patrician families profited from large estates, which were cheap to run with slave labor, while small-scale free farmers, whose lands Hannibal razed during the Second Punic War, became even more impoverished due to unfair competition. The best of all possible worlds is never the best for everyone.

Since time immemorial, wars have been waged with the purpose of capturing prisoners for enslavement and trade. Global wealth has often gone hand in hand with slavery. This is the true link between antiquity and more recent times. From the Great Wall of China to the Kolyma Road of Bones, from the Mesopotamian irrigation system to the cotton plantations of the United States, from the Roman brothels to sex trafficking today, from the Egyptian pyramids to the fast fashion manufactured in Bangladesh. In ancient times, slaves were undoubtedly one of the main reasons—and often the only one—to launch a conquering expedition. They represented such a powerful economic resource that there wasn't even any attempt to conceal it. On one occasion, Julius Caesar, famous for his clemency, sold the entire population of a recently conquered village in Gaul of no less than fifty-three thousand people on the spot. The deal was done so quickly because the slave traders made up a second army that straggled behind the legions, buying fresh merchandise as soon as night fell on the battlefields.

Prisoners, neighbors, and adversaries suffered the efficiency of Roman organization. The new empire achieved the unifying ambition the Greeks could never fulfill because at the moment of truth they always turned out to be inept politicians. As we have seen, Alexander's successors created rival dynasties that became entangled in a series of internecine wars, breaking up the inherited empire and plunging it into the ongoing strife of shifting alliances and outbreaks of brutal violence. All the contending sides grew accustomed to turning to the Romans as allies in their local struggles or as arbitrators in their conflicts, and they finally ended up devoured by such dangerous friends.

While it can't be claimed that the Romans invented globalization, since it already existed in the fragmented Hellenistic world, they raised it to a degree of perfection still impressive today. From one edge of the empire to another, from Spain to Turkey, a broad constellation of Roman cities were connected by roads so solid and well mapped out that many of them still exist. These cities embodied a recognizable, convenient kind of urban planning: wide avenues that intersected at right angles, gymnasiums, baths, a forum, marble temples, theaters, Latin inscriptions, aqueducts, sewage systems. Wherever they went, outsiders came upon the features of a standardized layout, just as today tourists find chains with the same brands of clothing, computers, and fast food on identical streets all over the world.

As a result of these transformations, swarms of people began to travel to and fro in a way never seen before in the ancient world. At first, this was mostly due to the movement of armies and forced mass migrations. It's estimated that at the beginning of the second century BC, an average of eight thousand slaves captured in wartime reached the Italian Peninsula every year. In the same period, Roman travelers, traders, and adventurers set out across the sea, journeying for long periods outside Italy. The waters of the Mediterranean, which, getting straight to the point, they began to call *mare nostrum,* or "our sea," were teeming with businessmen taking advantage of commercial opportunities opened up by the conquest. Selling slaves or dealing in arms became high-demand jobs. In the mid-second century BC, more than half of adult male Roman citizens had seen the horizons of the world beyond and contributed with gusto to ethnic diversity, leaving behind them—and to their fate—a great many mixed-race children.

All of Rome's military might, its wealth, its incredible transportation networks and feats of engineering made up a powerful machinery that was invincible but barren without the irrigation of poetry, stories, and symbols. In the absence of these elements, Oedipus, Antigone, and Odysseus filled in the cracks in unforeseen ways and set out for the highways of the globalized world.

3

The Romans achieved their extraordinary chain of victories thanks to a highly effective combination of violence and adaptability, in the finest Darwinian tradition. Romulus's uncivilized followers soon learned to imitate the best traits of their enemies, to adopt the things they liked without a shred of bigotry and to combine all these copied ingredients, creating new customs of their own. From the earliest skirmishes, they developed the habit of plundering not just the material goods but also the symbols of their vanquished opponents. During the fighting with the Samnites, they copied their military strategies—in particular, the maniple as the basic unit of the legion—and used these highly effectively to defeat them with their own weapons. In the First Punic War, the Roman bumpkins came up with a way to build a fleet as similar as possible to the Carthaginian one and used it to win their first naval battles. Italic landowners of the most ancient stock with the most traditional ideas quickly adapted to modern Hellenistic farming methods.

Thanks to all these appropriations, they created an invading force as invincible as Alexander's army and carried out their conquest more effectively. But beyond their indisputable skills for war and barbarity, they showed an astonishing burst of humility in accepting that Greek culture was highly superior. The most lucid members of the ruling classes understood that any great imperial civilization must devise a unifying and triumphant story sustained by symbols, monuments, architecture, sophisticated forms of speech, and myths that could forge identities. To achieve this quickly, as was their wont, they decided to imitate the best. They knew where to find their model. Mary Beard sums up the situation of those times with a punchy aphorism: "Made in Greece—wanted in Rome." The Romans set out to speak the language of the Greeks, to copy their statues, to reproduce the architecture of their temples, to write poems in the Homeric style, and to copy their refinements with the zeal of the parvenu.

The poet Horace captured this paradox when he wrote that Greece, once conquered, had invaded its ferocious adversary. It's difficult to tell today to what extent Rome borrowed all of Greek culture and to what degree the Romans were—or weren't—savage barbarians until they were civilized by the Greeks, but that is how both sides told the story. Roman intellectuals and creators always presented themselves as disciples of the Greek classics. The vestiges of native cultural forms were swept aside or erased. And many wealthy Romans learned to hold their own in the language of their Hellenistic subjects—though we know that the true Greeks mercilessly mocked the macaronic Roman vernacular. There is evidence that at the beginning of the first century BC, a Greek delegation spoke before the Roman Senate without any need for a translator. The effort made by the conquerors to speak the language of one of their many colonies in their most cultured spaces is an astonishing and extraordinary gesture, diametrically opposed to the usual cultural arrogance of the imperial metropolis. Imagine the British striving to hold their literary soirées in Bloomsbury in Sanskrit, or Proust sweating to strike up a refined conversation in Bantu with the Parisian aristocrats who so fascinated him.

For the first time, a great ancient superpower took on the legacy of a foreign—and defeated—people as an essential ingredient of their own identity. The Romans recognized Greek superiority without losing any sleep over it and were bold enough to explore its discoveries, interiorize them, protect them, and prolong their reverberation. This seduction has had enormous consequences for all of us. There, the thread was born that weaves our present together with the past, the strand that keeps us tied to a brilliant, extinguished world. Upon it, ideas, scientific discoveries, myths, thoughts, and passions walk as if on a tightrope, as do the errors and misfortunes of our history. We call this filament of words balancing above the void the classics. Owing to the fascination they still awaken in us, Greece persists as the first mile of European culture.

4

Latin literature is a peculiar case: it wasn't born spontaneously, but was developed on demand, in vitro. The birth was induced on a specific day in the year 240 BC, to celebrate the victory of Rome over Carthage.

Long before that inaugural day, the Romans had learned to write—naturally—in imitation of the Greeks, who from the eighth century BC had lived in the prosperous colonies of southern Italy, in the region known as Magna Graecia. Their culture and alphabetic writing had journeyed along trade and travel routes and disembarked in the north. The first northern Italians to learn the Greek alphabet and adapt it to their language were the Etruscans, who controlled the middle of the peninsula from the seventh to the fourth centuries BC. Their neighbors to the south, the Romans—who though they were loath to admit it, lived under an Etruscan dynasty for several decades—pounced eagerly on the marvelous innovation and adopted Etruscan writing with certain adjustments tailored to Latin. The alphabet of my childhood, the one looking up at me now from the dark rows of my computer's keyboard, is a constellation of the wandering letters the Phoenicians stowed in their ships. These letters plowed the waves toward Greece, set sail for Sicily, sought the hills and olive groves of what is now Tuscany, and lay in wait in Lazio, gradually changing as they were passed from hand to hand, until they became the lines touched by my fingers today.

The oldest accounts of this traveling alphabet leave no room for romanticizing. The Romans—pragmatic, born to organize—limited its use to factual records and regulations. The earliest texts—from the seventh and especially the sixth century BC—are a group of brief inscriptions (for example, records of ownership scribbled on pottery). In the following centuries, we find only laws and written rituals. There isn't a single trace of fictional writing. A life-and-death power struggle was afoot on the battlefields and times were hard as far as poetry was concerned. Roman literature had to wait; it was a belated event and took shape when the warriors were at rest. Only when their most dangerous enemy had bitten the dust, once the task was complete and they were at leisure and basking in victory, did the Romans allow themselves to think of the games of art and the pleasures of life. The First Punic War ended in the year 241 BC. Scarcely a few months later, the Romans enjoyed the first literary work in Latin. The public saw it in September of the year 240 BC on the boards of a theater in the capital, on the occasion of the Ludi Romani, a significant Roman holiday. It was a major attraction of the festivities: a play translated from Greek. Whether it was a comedy or a tragedy is unknown, and its title has been forgotten. It's no coincidence that a translation should mark the genesis of Roman literature, always bewitched by the Greek masters, always caught in an ambiguous game of echoes, nostalgia, envy, reverence, and all the nuances of love with an inferiority complex.

The story of that first performance is an odd one. Literature arrived in Rome amid the din of weapons, from the opposing side, by way of a foreign slave. Livius Andronicus, the unlikely founder of Latin literature, was not a Roman by birth. He made his living as an actor in Taranto, one of the main enclaves of Greek culture in Southern Italy, a refined and sumptuous city of theater lovers. He fell prisoner as a young man during the conquest in the year 272 BC and tasted the bitter fate of the vanquished: to be sold as a slave. I picture him catching sight of the metropolis for the first time, through the cracks in the cart that carried him as if he were livestock for sale. He was placed by a skillful trader in the wealthy Livius mansion, where his intelligence and silver tongue relieved him of the most arduous tasks. It's said that he tutored his master's children and that years later, the grateful family emancipated him. He kept the family name of his former owners—this was the custom among liberated slaves—and added a Greek nickname to mark his divided identity. Under the protection of the powerful family that bought and then freed him, he opened a school in the capital. In the absence of local poets, this foreigner, bilingual by necessity, would be entrusted with literary commissions in Rome. I wonder what conflicted feelings must have assailed him as he wrote in the language of his defeat. We know that he translated the first tragedies and comedies performed in the imperial capital, and also Homer's *Odyssey*. Thanks to him, a troupe of writers and actors was founded under the protection of the Temple of Minerva on the Aventine Hill. Scarcely any fragments of his inaugural verse have survived, but I find one of the truncated phrases from his *Odusia* evocative: "the steep hills and the dusty fields and the enormous sea."

One small mystery remains to be solved. There is every indication that in those days, Rome was a cultural backwater with hardly any books, public libraries, or booksellers. So how did Livius Andronicus obtain the originals for his translations? Wealthy patricians could afford to send messengers to the Greek cities of Southern Italy, where there were people who traded in books, but this was an unthinkable solution for a humble freed slave.

Today's bibliophiles can hardly imagine the book desert of the era. In the twenty-first century, the deluge of printed matter flows unchecked. A new book is published every half minute, 120 every hour, 2,800 a day, 86,000 a month. The average reader manages to read in a lifetime what the publishing industry can produce in a single day, and every year, millions of orphaned books are destroyed. But all this abundance is very recent. For centuries, to obtain books you had to be well connected, and even with the right contacts, it took time, effort, and expense, and sometimes even meant facing the dangers of the open road.

With his own resources and the stigma of his origins, Livius Andronicus could never have devoted himself to reading, translating, and running a school without the support of his powerful protectors. The Livius family probably funded a small Greek classics library, so they could display their wealth and boast of their culture. Their former servant would have had to rise at the crack of dawn to pay his respects—the *salutatio matutina*—waiting in boredom until his patron deigned to appear, and, availing himself of the acting skills acquired in his youth, bow his head and speak in just the right tone, grateful every day that they allowed him to hold the scrolls from their opulent collection in his Greek and until recently enslaved hands.

5

Roman nobles soon took a fancy to books, those rare and unique objects within the reach of only a select few. At first, they peacefully sent their servants to Alexandria and other major cultural centers and tasked them with commissioning copies from expert sellers. They soon found it far more practical to make off with entire libraries during their military expeditions on Greek territory. Literature thus turned into the spoils of war.

In the year 168 BC, the general Aemilius Paullus defeated the last king of Macedonia. He gave permission to Scipio Aemilianus and another of his sons, both lovers of knowledge, to take back to Rome all the books of the royal house of Macedonia, to which Alexander had belonged. Thanks to this invaluable loot, the Scipios became owners of the city's first great private library and served as patrons to the young generation of literary Romans. One of the satellite writers orbiting around their books was Terence, a playwright said to have been a slave. His nickname Afer ("the African") hints at his skin color and origins. In those days, a division of cultural labor was established: powerful patricians took on the responsibility of pillaging books to enrich their private collections—sometimes, to flaunt their honesty, they even bought them—and to gather the most talented authors together around them. Those who were writers, strictly speaking, were with some exceptions tatterdemalions bound to the service of the rich (slaves, foreigners, prisoners of war, poor men moonlighting at various jobs, and other dregs of society).

In the wake of the Scipios, other generals followed suit and took the easy path of literary plunder. The merciless Sulla took possession of perhaps the most enticing trophy: the collection of Aristotle himself, which had long lain hidden and reappeared as treasured booty. In Rome, the library of Lucullus was also famous and was acquired by methodical looting during his triumphant military campaigns in northern Anatolia. In 66 BC, his power was usurped, and from then on, Lucullus devoted himself to a life of sumptuous idleness, supported by the wealth he'd accumulated in his marauding years. It's said that his private library followed the architectural model of Pergamum and Alexandria, with scrolls stored in narrow rooms, arcades for reading, and rooms for meetings and discussion. Lucullus was a generous thief: he made his books available to family, friends, and scholars residing in Rome. Plutarch says coteries of intellectuals met and conferred in his mansion, as if in an endless gathering of the Muses.

Most of the texts gracing the libraries of the Scipios, Sulla, and Lucullus were Greek. In time, some would be added in Latin, but they would be a minority. The Romans had learned to write late, and the sum of their literature would represent an embarrassingly tiny fraction of available holdings.

I imagine that Roman artists of the time must have felt overwhelmed and belittled by the avalanche of works arriving in the luggage of rapacious conquerors. Dazzling masterpieces made up most of the booty. By then, Greek literature and art had half a millennium of history behind them. It's not easy to compete with five hundred years of inspired creative activity.

The Roman collecting frenzy is reminiscent of that of the American robber barons, who, captivated by long centuries of European art, took possession of altarpieces, frescos torn out of walls, entire cloisters, church doorways, fragile antiquities, and canvasses by the great masters, all for a fistful of dollars. Not to mention whole libraries. This is how F. Scott Fitzgerald imagined the young millionaire, Jay Gatsby. His fortune, a product of clandestine bootlegging activities, shone in a great Long Island mansion where no refinement nor luxury was spared. Gatsby was known for the lavish parties he hosted but never attended. In fact, a poignant childhood love lay behind his displays of opulence. The extravagance, the light, the dancing till dawn, the flashy cars and European art were all fireworks meant to dazzle the girl who had left him years earlier, when he wasn't yet rich enough. The palace Gatsby had built as a kitsch celebration of his social ascent would not be complete without "a high Gothic library, paneled with carved English oak, and probably transported complete from some ruin overseas."

The Romans' and Greeks' perceptions of each other were based on stereotypes much like our own of Americans and Europeans. On the one hand is pragmatism and economic and military power, and on the other, a long history, a great culture, and nostalgia for the splendors of the past. They were like Mars and Venus. Though they generally expressed mutual respect, they each had a repertoire of quips and caricatures for making fun of the other behind their back. I can imagine the Greeks privately joking about brutish and brainless legionnaires who couldn't write even a paltry inscription without a spelling mistake. On the other side, the old conservative Romans also ranted and raved. Juvenal declares in one of his satires that he can't stand the city being full of Greeks, those parasitic, charlatan lowlifes who brought their vices along with their language, corrupting local traditions and displacing the true citizens of Rome.

Indeed, not all was admiration. Globalization always awakens complex and contradictory reactions. Some of the most caustic voices of the third and second centuries BC attacked the influence of foreign cultures in general and Greek culture in particular. These voices were troubled by new phenomena becoming dangerous fads, like philosophy, culinary indulgences, and hair removal. The champion of these critics was Cato the Elder, a contemporary and rival of Scipio Africanus, whom he ridiculed for prancing around in Greek gymnasiums and consorting with the unwashed masses in Sicilian theaters. According to this curmudgeonly official, the decadent ways of foreigners would end up undermining the Romans' strength of character. On the other hand, we know that Cato himself taught his son Greek, and the remaining fragments of his speeches show that he was quick to imitate the Greek rhetorical devices he so reviled in public.

All these contradictions of Roman identity are reflected in early Roman literature. By now, the plays of Plautus and Terence go beyond simple translations cribbed from Greek. While they are presented as faithful adaptations that respect the plot of the Hellenistic originals and maintain the Greek setting, they are in fact hybrid works meant to satisfy rowdy, festive Roman audiences. Unlike in classical Athens, theater in Rome had to compete with other forms of popular entertainment such as wrestling, tightrope walking, and gladiatorial combat. Nearly all the comedies therefore turned on a basic, infallible story line: boy meets girl. In every comedy, the audience expected to see the typical crafty, swindling slave who caused a thousand intrigues. To please the crowd, a happy ending was guaranteed. But beneath the frivolous surface of these Roman plays lay a new ingredient. Through them, viewers peered out at the cultural complexity of the brand-new, wide imperial world.

The action of all these comedies took place in Greece and thus demanded certain notions of distant geography from the audience. In one performance, Plautus was bold enough to give a main part to a Carthaginian who speaks in his authentic Punic tongue—in fact, present-day linguists find in this work a unique source for studying that dead language. In another, two characters disguise themselves as Persians. In the prologues to several comedies there is a repeated joke about the adaptations. Plautus says of his translation, "A Greek wrote this, Plautus barbarized it." This line, as Mary Beard explains, is "a clever challenge to the audience. For those of Greek origin, it no doubt gave the opportunity for a quiet snigger at the expense of the new, barbaric rulers of the world."

Amid the jokes and laughter, theater helped its viewers to better understand the new reality of broadened horizons. The audience learned that the old traditions could no longer maintain their ancestral purity; that, despite conservative resistance, the smartest way to travel these new roads was to adapt to the wisdom of the world they had conquered. The new, hybrid literature was at the vanguard of an increasingly mixed society. Rome was discovering the mechanisms of globalization and its fundamental paradox: that the things we adopt from elsewhere also make us who we are.

6

Young empires have straightforward appetites: they simply want it all. They aspire to military strength, economic power, and to the splendors of the old world. With this ambition, the Scipios transferred the royal library of Macedonia to Rome, and, with the warmth of those valuable books, drew in a circle of Greek and Latin writers. Using weapons and money, they were trying to move the centers of gravity of literary creation. Throughout history, politics has redrawn cultural maps again and again.

Those wealthy Romans' thirst for appropriation wasn't so different at heart from the enthusiasm that led Peggy Guggenheim to transplant European abstract painting to the United States in the 1940s, outlining new artistic territories. Her father, the scion of a mining and smelting dynasty, died in the sinking of the *Titanic.* His daughter moved to Paris to lead a bohemian life from her comfortable position as an heiress. There, she began her famous avant-garde art collection. She was still in Paris when the Nazis invaded France.

Instead of leaving, she bought up artworks like there was no tomorrow. "A painting a day" was her motto, and with the German army advancing through the north of the country, there was no shortage of sellers. She often bought works from desperately fleeing Jewish families, or straight from the artists at bargain prices. Just two days before the fall of Paris, she hid her collection in a friend's barn and fled to Marseille, where she had a fling with Max Ernst, who'd escaped from a concentration camp. Her money allowed her to rescue Ernst and a group of artist friends, and together they absconded to the United States.

In New York, she opened a gallery where she exhibited art from the School of Paris. Around these works and the European refugees who found shelter in Peggy's New York gallery—Duchamp, Mondrian, Breton, Chagall, and Dalí, among others—the American avant-garde was born. Young artists saw and were influenced by the new works. The United States government, wishing to overtake Europe's artistic preeminence, had created a program called the Federal Art Project and offered unemployed painters a wage of twenty-one dollars a week to decorate public institutions. This was the meeting place for Pollock, Rothko, and de Kooning, who would become Peggy's new protégés. Jackson Pollock said in an interview, "The most important painting of the last hundred years was done in France. American painters have generally missed the point of Modern painting from beginning to end . . . Thus the fact that good European Moderns are now here is very important, for they bring with them an understanding of the problems of Modern painting." On many afternoons, these young painters met at MoMA to gaze at Picasso's *Guernica*, a refugee at the museum, where it would be safe from the wars and dictatorships of Europe. North American abstract expressionism was born in the shadows of the European avant-garde.

In May 1940, three weeks before the occupation of Paris, another exile fled to the United States on what would be the penultimate voyage of the SS *Champlain* before she was sunk. Like many persecuted European writers, Vladimir Nabokov found sanctuary in American universities. He even went into voluntary exile from his language, leaping into the void and writing his most essential books in English. He eventually said that he felt "as American as April in Arizona." At the same time, in his new country, he detected the aura of the Europe that revolutions and wars had taken away from him. In a letter to his literary agent, he wrote, "What charms me personally about American civilization is exactly that old-world touch, that old-fashioned something which clings to it despite the hard glitter, and hectic night-life, and up-to-date bathrooms, and lurid advertisements, and all the rest of it."

Cinema, invented in France, also transplanted its mecca to the United States. Most of the creators of the great studios of classic Hollywood cinema were central European émigrés, many of whom camouflaged their names and origins beneath an American patina. These men of humble origins who disembarked in New York with just a few dollars sewn into the linings of their waistcoats established the great film industry that soon drew a plethora of distinguished European directors, actors, and technicians—Fritz Lang, Murnau, Lubitsch, Chaplin, Frank Capra, Billy Wilder, Preminger, Hitchcock, Douglas Sirk, and so many others. Curiously, John Ford, in a reversal of the studio pioneers' new identities, fashioned himself as a European. The Homer of the American western, born in Maine, dreamed of a past in Innisfree, a nonexistent Irish village. He invented a consciously mythical tale of his family history, even claiming on more than one occasion that he had been born in a thatched cottage overlooking the Galway Bay. Ford, the father of American cinema, knew that the golden age of Hollywood was to a great extent a European invention.

All these examples, to which we could add the names of philosophers like Hannah Arendt, scientists like Einstein and Bohr, or Spanish writers like Juan Ramón Jiménez and Ramón Sender, who emigrated during Franco's dictatorship, show that in the mid-twentieth century, thanks to a highly calculated welcoming effort and at great expense, the epicenter of art and knowledge changed continents. In Greco-Latin antiquity, the cultural transfer occurred under less merciful conditions. There was no Roman dream, or art galleries, or universities eager to offer refuge to foreign talent. Instead, a staggering number of Greek artists and intellectuals set foot in Rome to be sold as slaves.

7

For Greeks and Romans alike, slavery was the monster lurking under the bed, the terror always lying in wait nearby. No one could be certain that they would never be enslaved, no matter how wealthy or aristocratic their lineage. A great many doors opened onto a hellish landscape, even for those who had been born free. If your city or country was ravaged by war—an almost daily experience in ancient times—defeat turned you into the spoils carried off by the winning army. *Vae victis* ("Woe to the vanquished") was a descriptive Latin motto. The most ancient legends made it clear that no thought would be spared for what's known today as the "civilian population." In *The Trojan Women* by Euripides, we walk among the smoking ashes of Troy as her disconsolate queen and princesses are raffled off among the invading generals. The previous evening, they still wore their finery and men bowed down before them. After a night of massacre and conquest, the Greeks drag them off by the hair, share them out amongst themselves, and rape them.

If, on the high seas, you were attacked by pirates—a catchall term for any kind of enemy or criminal in possession of a boat—your chances of escaping slavery were very slim.

If you were kidnapped on dry land, your captors were unlikely to ask your family for ransom. It was faster and safer to sell you to a slave trader. This cruel commerce in people torn from their homes became a highly lucrative business, a quick way of making money. Plautus's comedies often portray separated siblings, abducted children, and aged parents searching for them, only to find they've been turned into slaves or prostitutes.

If you fell on hard times, your creditors could sell you as a last resort to pay off your debts.

If someone powerful wanted revenge on you, they could choose between killing you or, if they were even crueler, handing you over to a trafficker. Plato suffered this fate himself. It's said that in Sicily, he enraged the tyrannical Dionysius I with an acerbic remark about his ignorance and the way he ruled. Dionysius intended to execute him, but his brother-in-law Dion, the philosopher's disciple, insisted his life be spared. Since his insolence deserved to be punished, they took him to the island of Aegina to be sold at the bustling slave market. Luckily for him, the story had a happy ending. He was bought by a fellow philosopher who followed a school of thought that opposed his own, though not too vehemently, and who let him go, chastened but free, back to his home in Athens.

According to Roman law, slaves belonged to their masters and had no legal personhood. They could be subjected to corporal punishment, and many were often flogged to discipline them or simply so that their masters could let off steam. The buyer had the right to separate them from their children, sleep with, sell, beat, or summarily execute them. Their owners could profit from them however they pleased, even by gladiator fighting or sexual exploitation—most prostitutes were slaves. A slave's testimony was valid at trial only if obtained by torture.

Shock. Anguish. Abyss. How to describe the excruciating change endured by all those free citizens forced into slavery by chance, debt, defeat, or ruthless trafficking? Hardworking people leading peaceful, even happy lives were violently torn from their refuge, deprived of their hopes and rights, left suddenly defenseless, and turned into human property. The film *12 Years a Slave* depicts a comparable situation many centuries later, in the plantations of the American South. Bound in chains in a dark cellar, Solomon Northup attempts to reconstruct the puzzle of his life. As memories emerge from the chaos of his bewildered mind, this African American man, born free, an educated violinist, comes to realize that he has been captured, deceived, and drugged to be sold as a slave. He searches in vain for his papers, the only proof of his freedom. Imprisoned beneath the city of Washington, in the shadow of the Capitol, Solomon sets out on a painful path of discovery. His jailers begin to torment the rebel in their charge with beatings, floggings, hunger, filth, foul and stinking clothes. One night, he is secretly sent south and handed over to a Louisiana slave trader. He will spend a decade of his youth picking cotton on the plantations of various southern masters who abuse him constantly to break his will, with no news of his loved ones. The movie, based on a true story, describes the odyssey of one stunned and defenseless man—as any of us would be, if all possible help was withdrawn, all legal protection—whose captors try to dehumanize him with fear.

In the ancient world, many were forced to cross that invisible threshold where they lost their status as free people and were transformed into salable goods.

For two hundred years, vast numbers of Greek slaves arrived in Rome, the result of victories over the Hellenistic kingdoms of Macedonia, the area that is now continental Greece, Turkey, Syria, Persia, and Egypt. The incursions of the Roman conquerors unleashed a long period of violence and chaos in the eastern Mediterranean, creating favorable conditions for the mass capture of slaves. The sea was crawling with pirates. Armies marched across sweeping territories, darkening the horizon with their menacing presence. Whole cities and states fell into a chasm of debt caused by the Romans' merciless taxes. The figures are chilling. In the mid-first century BC there must have been approximately two million slaves in Italy, around 20 percent of the census. In the early imperial period, when someone had the brilliant idea of making them wear a uniform, the Senate rejected the measure in horror. No one wanted the slaves to realize how numerous they were.

The Greeks weren't the only people enslaved by the Romans; a great many Hispanics, Gauls, and Carthaginians also fell into forced servitude. But the peculiarity of the Greeks was that many of them were more educated than their masters. Prestigious professions, today practiced by children of the middle and upper classes, were the terrain of slaves in Rome. Surprisingly, doctors, bankers, administrators, notaries, tax assessors, bureaucrats, and teachers were often Greeks deprived of their freedom. Roman aristocrats with cultural aspirations could go to any of the capital's well-stocked markets on a given morning and snap up the Greek intellectual of their choice, who would educate their children or simply confer on them the prestige of having a philosopher in residence. Outside the home, most schoolteachers were also Greek slaves or freedmen. They specialized in all kinds of white-collar and office work. They kept the administration of the empire going as well as its legal system.

Cicero implies in his letters that he owned some twenty slaves of this kind, between secretaries, workers, librarians, scribes, "readers"—who read books or documents aloud for their master's ease—assistants, accountants, and messenger boys. The famous orator had several libraries, one at his home in the capital and others distributed across his numerous rural properties. He needed highly qualified staff to run those collections and to assist him with his own work. His slaves took care of the daily chores, returning the scrolls to their respective shelves, repairing damaged volumes, and updating the catalog. Beautiful penmanship was also an essential part of the job. If the master's friends lent him books of interest, the slaves made handwritten copies, no matter how long. As soon as he finished writing a new speech or essay, they had to dash off a stack of manuscripts for the proud author to share with his friends and colleagues. It was an arduous task since Cicero was a highly arrogant, prolific author who had lots of friends.

For general library organization, his regular staff weren't enough. Cicero was enamored of his books and wished to engage the services of an expert. So he turned to Tiro, one of the many Greek scholars torn from his country to be sold as a slave. Despite his cruel fate, the captive writer stood out for his friendly nature. He had already developed a great reputation for cataloguing Sulla's famous library according to the Alexandrian model. Cicero writes to a friend, "When you come, you'll be able to see the marvelous organization Tiro has done of my books in the library." But not all of Cicero's slaves were so docile or made him so happy. In the autumn of the year 46 BC, the orator wrote a letter to his friend, the governor of Ilyria (a territory that today forms part of Albania, Croatia, Serbia, Bosnia, and Montenegro). He was annoyed and disappointed. His chief librarian, a slave called Dionysius, had been stealing and selling his books, and when he was finally caught and was about to get his just deserts, he took to his heels. An acquaintance thought he had seen him in Ilyria. Cicero begs his friend, general of the armies stationed in the region, to do him the small favor—a trifling thing—of capturing the culprit and bringing him home. But to Cicero's displeasure, book thieves weren't a priority for the provincial Roman governor, and the Roman legions weren't mobilized to trap the runaway slave.

In the story of books in Rome, slaves are the protagonists. They were involved in every facet of literary production, from teaching people to write to copying the manuscripts. The contrast between the hordes of erudite Greek slaves and the forced illiteracy of later civilizations is remarkable. In the United States, until the Confederacy was defeated in 1865, in many southern states it was illegal for slaves to learn to read and write, and those who could were considered a threat to the system's continuity. Doc Daniel Dowdy, a black man born into slavery in 1856, described the dreadful punishments reserved for those breaking this law: "The first time you was caught trying to read or write you was whipped with a cow-hide, the next time with a cat-o-nine tails and the third time they cut the first joint off your forefinger." Despite all this, some illiterate slaves learned to read in defiance of their masters and risked their lives. Since it was forbidden, the task took years of patience and secret study. There are many of these heroic stories of learning to read. Belle Myers, interviewed in the 1930s, explained that she'd learned her letters while taking care of her master's baby, who was playing with an alphabet puzzle. Her owner, suspecting his slave's intentions, gave Belle a few preventive kicks. But she persevered, studying the puzzle's letters and a child's spelling book. "One day, I found a hymn book . . . and spelled out 'When I Can Read My Title Clear.' I was so happy when I saw that I could really read, that I ran around telling all the other slaves."

In *12 Years a Slave*, Solomon must hide the fact that he knows how to read and write at all costs if he wants to avoid a savage beating. His tragedy is that at the same time, he is desperate to send a letter to his family in New York to explain where they can find and save him from that hell of hunger, exploitation, and brutality. For years, he takes any small chance to steal little bits of paper from his masters. Once he has enough, he makes a crude quill under cover of night and a substitute ink out of blackberry juice. The forbidden messages he manages to write with great effort and enormous risk represent his only feeble hope of one day recovering his old life as a free man. Alberto Manguel writes in *A History of Reading*, "Throughout the South, it was common for plantation owners to hang any slave who tried to teach the others how to spell . . . The slave-owners (like dictators, tyrants, absolute monarchs and other illicit holders of power) were strong believers in the power of the written word. They knew, far better than some readers, that reading is a strength that requires barely a few first words to become overwhelming. Someone able to read one sentence is able to read all . . . For all these reasons, reading had to be forbidden . . . An illiterate crowd is easiest to rule; since the craft of reading cannot be untaught once it has been acquired, the second-best recourse is to limit its scope."

Conversely, inhabitants of the Greco-Latin world thought it appropriate for their slaves to take on the work of copying, writing, and documentation, for reasons that today are surprising, to say the least.

As we have already seen, reading in ancient times was not the mute activity we practice today. Apart from some striking exceptions, back then people read aloud, even in private. In the eyes of the ancients, the act of sounding out the written letters involved a disturbing kind of bewitchment. The most ancient beliefs taught that a person's spirit dwelled in their breath. In early funeral inscriptions, the dead begged whoever walked by, "Lend me your voice," to come back to life and announce who lay in the tomb. The Greeks and Romans believed that any written text must take possession of a living voice to become complete. This is why the reader who scanned the words with their eyes and began to read them underwent a kind of spiritual and vocal possession: their throat was filled with the writer's breath. The reader's voice submitted and became one with the written word. The writer, even after his death, used others as a vocal instrument—placing them, in other words, at his service. Being read aloud meant having power over the reader, even across the distances of space and time. That's why—so the ancients thought—it was appropriate for professional readers and writers to be slaves. Their role was precisely to serve and submit.

A free man's love of reading was in turn viewed with suspicion. Only those who listened to a text and heard someone else read were saved, since they hadn't submitted their own voice to what was written. These were people like Cicero, who had slaves to read to them. These slaves, possessed by the book, ceased to belong to themselves for the duration of their reading. They placed in their mouths an "I" that didn't belong to them. They were mere instruments of a foreign music. Curiously, the metaphors used for this activity in the works of Plato and other authors up to Catullus are the same used to describe prostitution or a passive sexual partner. The reader was sodomized by the text. To read aloud is to lend one's body to an unknown writer and is a boldly promiscuous act. Though it wasn't considered completely incompatible with the rank of citizen, moralists of the era proclaimed that it ought to be practiced with moderation, so that it wouldn't become a vice.

IN THE BEGINNING WERE THE TREES

8

Books are the children of trees, which were the first home of our species and perhaps the oldest vehicle of our written words. The word's etymology contains an old origin story. In Latin, *liber*, which meant "book," originally described the bark of a tree, or, to be more precise, the fibrous film that separates the bark from the wood of the trunk. Pliny the Elder claims that the Romans wrote on bark before they discovered Egyptian scrolls. Over many centuries, various materials—papyrus, parchment—would supplant those ancient wooden pages, but with the triumph of paper, the circle would be complete and books would again be born from trees.

As we have seen, the Greek word for books was *biblíon*, recalling the Phoenician city of Byblos that was famous for exporting papyrus. In our time, the use of the term has evolved and is now reduced to the title of a single work, the Bible. For the Romans, *liber* evoked not cities or trade routes, but rather the mystery of the forest where their ancestors began to write to the sound of wind whispering among the leaves. The Germanic names—book, *Buch, boek*—descend from an arboreal word: the beech, with its whitish trunk.

In Latin, the term meaning "book" sounded almost the same as the adjective meaning "free," though the Indo-European roots of each word have different origins. Many romance languages, like Spanish, French, Italian, and Portuguese, have inherited this chance phonetic resemblance, which invites wordplay between reading and freedom. For the erudite in every period, these two passions always converge in the end.

Although today we have learned to write with light on an LCD or a plasma screen, we still feel the primal call of trees; we keep writing the scattered story of human love on their bark. On his walks through the *Campos de Castilla* ("fields of Castile"), from which he drew the title of his most beloved book of poems, Antonio Machado used to stop by the river to read a few lines:

> *I have once more seen the golden poplars,*
> *roadside poplars on the banks*
> *of the Duero, between San Polo and San Saturio,*
> *behind the old city walls*
> *of Soria . . .*
> . . . .
>
> *These riverside black-poplars, which accompany*
> *with the rustling of their dry leaves*
> *the sound of water, when the wind blows,*
> *bear, carved in their bark,*
> *initials standing for names*
> *of lovers, numbers standing for dates.*

Whenever a teenager carves their initials into the silvery bark of a poplar tree with a knife, they are unknowingly repeating an ancient gesture. In the third century BC, Callimachus, the librarian of Alexandria, mentions a love note on a tree. He isn't the only one. A character in Virgil imagines how the bark will swell as the years go by, erasing his name and that of his lover: "And carve my love upon the tender trees; the trees will grow, and you, my loves, grow with them." This custom—still alive—of tattooing letters onto the skin of a tree to preserve the memory of someone who lived and loved may have been one of the earliest instances of writing in Europe.

POOR WRITERS, RICH READERS

9

In the Roman world, access to books was mostly a matter of contacts. The ancients forged a peculiar version of a knowledge society based on who knew whom.

Ancient literature never resulted in the creation of a market or industry as we understand it today, and distribution always depended on friendships and copyists. In the era of private libraries, if a wealthy individual wanted an ancient book, he asked to borrow it from a friend—if that friend happened to have it—then ordered someone to copy it, sometimes a slave of his own, and sometimes a hardworking scribe at a workshop. New, contemporary works were distributed as gifts. In those days, when there were no publishers, if an author considered a book to be finished, they commissioned a certain number of copies and started giving them away to all and sundry. The fate of their work depended on the reach and status of their circle of acquaintances, colleagues, and clients who were willing to read it, out of affection, but mostly out of obligation. We're told that a wealthy orator named Regulus had a thousand copies made of a dreadful text he'd written about his dead son—Pliny remarks with spite that it was more like a book written by a child than about one—and sent them to his acquaintances across Italy and the provinces. He also contacted several decuriones in the Roman legions, paying them to select the soldiers with the best voices from among their ranks and organize public readings—a kind of book launch—all over the empire. The promotion and distribution of literature fell to the writer—if, like Regulus, he could afford it—or to his aristocratic protectors when he was a destitute foreigner, as was often the case.

Of course, there were people who wished to read a recently published book but didn't know the author personally, and therefore weren't on his distribution lists. In these cases, the only option was to turn to someone who was in the writer's circle and commission a copy of their scroll. As soon as a writer began to "distribute" a work, the book was considered to be in the public domain, and anyone could reproduce it. The Latin verb we translate today as "to edit" —*edere* (which in Spanish also means "publish")—in fact meant something closer to "donate" or "neglect." It implied abandoning the work to its fate. There was nothing remotely like royalties or copyright. In the entire chain of production and distribution, the only person to receive a fee per line of text was the one who made the copy (assuming he wasn't a domestic slave), just as today we're charged by the page for photocopies.

The great English intellectual Samuel Johnson said that "no man but a blockhead ever wrote, except for money." We don't know what the heads of the ancient writers were made of, but all of them knew from the outset that there wasn't the slightest hope of making money by selling books. In the first century, the satirist Martial complained, "My pages amuse only when they are free." Since his arrival in Rome, Martial, who was from Bilbilis, in what is now Aragon, had experienced firsthand the lack of profitability of writing, even for a successful author. On one occasion, he tells us, an affluent stranger stopped him in the street, just as people these days stop celebrities for selfies. "Are you, are you really that Martial, whose mischief and jests are known to all?" he asked, and then added, "Why then is your cloak so ragged?" "Because I am a bad poet," Martial answered, with a quip akin to the sarcastic humor for which his region is known today.

What did someone like Cicero want out of publishing his speeches and essays? To achieve his social and political ambitions; to increase his fame and influence; to fashion a public image in keeping with his self-interest; to make sure that his friends—and enemies—were aware of his success. The benefactors who provided for brilliant, poor authors were seeking something similar: glory, ostentation, and flattery. Books primarily served to create or cement certain people's prestige. Works of literature circulated freely and were shared voluntarily as gifts or personal loans, passed from hand to hand among interested parties. This system helped identify a small group of cultural elites, an exclusive community of the wealthy, to which certain favorites of humble origin or slaves were granted admission for their talent. Out in the cold, without friends in high places, both readers and writers found it impossible to thrive.

After the foreign and servile origin of literary culture, a few local authors had cautiously begun to emerge, provided they wrote in prose on respectable topics like history, warfare, law, agriculture, or morals. Cicero and Caesar were the two best-known figures in this first republican crop of Roman authors from well-to-do families. Unlike the slave poets brought from the Greek world, these were citizens who also happened to write. And they wrote about serious matters. Outsiders had not been allowed to write about Roman laws or traditions, nor was it favorably viewed for a Roman from a good family to devote their time to poetry—just as, in our times, many people would find it inappropriate for a head of state to write pop songs.

For a long time, there were thus two parallel, contemporary literatures. On one hand, the poetry Greek slaves or freedmen wrote to please their educated aristocratic patrons, and on the other, the dilettante work—always in prose—of respectable citizens. "Poetry occupies no place of honor, and anyone who devotes himself to it is called a vagabond," wrote Cato the Elder. Ever since then, puppeteers, musicians, and artists have had a lowly reputation, from Caravaggio to van Gogh, from Shakespeare to Cervantes and Genet.

Fully-fledged Roman citizens could devote themselves to artistic and literary activities if they liked, as long as this was occasional and, above all, disinterested. Trying to make a living from writing, on the other hand, was an undignified endeavor for members of high society. As we have seen, even the intellectual trades requiring the greatest wisdom, such as architecture, medicine, or teaching, belonged to the lower classes. Schoolteachers of the period, mostly slaves or freedmen, performed a humble and undervalued task. "He had shadowy origins," Tacitus said of someone, an upstart, who'd begun his career with such plebeian work. Patricians and aristocrats valued knowledge and culture but disdained instruction. The irony was that it was ignoble to teach the very things it was honorable to learn.

Who would have imagined that in the times of the great Digital Revolution, the ancient aristocratic idea of culture as a pastime for hobbyists would again take hold? The old refrain rings out, telling us that if writers, playwrights, musicians, actors, or filmmakers want to eat, they should find themselves a serious job and treat art as merely a pastime. Under neoliberalism, in the networked world, which bears a curious resemblance to slavery-dependent patrician Rome, creative work is expected to be provided for free.

10

In that wealthy universe of high society where culture began to take root, women also collected books. In Cicero's letters we meet Caerellia, a keen reader and owner of a library of philosophy. This rich noblewoman somehow obtained—perhaps by resorting to bribery—a pirated copy of Cicero's treatise *On the Supreme Good* (*De finibus malorum et bonorum*) before the author had officially released it into circulation. "Caerellia is clearly brimming with a burning passion for philosophy," wrote an irritated and sarcastic Cicero.

This wasn't the only case of an impatient woman reader. Well-educated women could often be found in high-ranking Roman families. In the second century BC, Cornelia, mother of the Gracchi, personally oversaw her children's studies, selecting only the most qualified teachers for them; her literary gatherings anticipated the French salons of Madame de Staël, where politicians and writers of the era came together. Servilia, the mother of Caesar's assassin Brutus, loved reading as much in Latin as in Greek. Cicero describes his daughter Tullia as "most learned." One of Pompey's several—though not simultaneous—wives was fond of literature, geometry, and the music of the lyre, and, furthermore, like Caerellia, "was pleased to attend philosophical discussions."

Roman aristocrats usually educated their daughters. In general, they didn't send them to school, preferring to have private tutors at home to keep watch on the girls' chastity. The ancients were always wary of the dangers that might befall their noble offspring in the street. As for boys, in a world where pederasty was commonplace, they couldn't be too careful. Noble families therefore kept a specific slave to escort their sons to school called the "pedagogue," *paedagogus*, which originally simply meant "child's companion." But the domestic solution also came with its perils. The relationship between a renowned teacher named Quintus Caecilius Epirota and his master's daughter became the talk of the town in the first century BC and ended in the lascivious freedman's exile.

The most advanced stages of learning were forbidden to women. Higher education was the exclusive preserve of men. Nor were they allowed to spend a year studying abroad in Athens or Rhodes like boys, which was something like the exchange programs of our times. Girls from well-to-do families did not attend rhetoric classes or travel to Greece to improve their language skills, or visit the Acropolis, or get a taste of freedom away from their parents. While their brothers were admiring Greek statues and enjoying Greek love, adolescent girls, who were married off young to older men, were husband hunting. The ancients believed that marriage was for women what war was for men: the fulfillment of their true nature.

Throughout the centuries we find traces of a heated debate on the merits and dangers of teaching literature to girls. Nightlife was a decisive factor in this controversy. Greek women stayed at home while the men went alone to banquets, where they were fêted by hired hetaeras until the wee hours of the morning. Roman women, meanwhile, attended dinners outside their mansions, and it was therefore important to their husbands that they know how to hold an intelligent conversation with other guests. This was why women proud of their brilliance, conversational skills, and knowledge could be found in aristocratic Roman homes.

A caustic and caricatured version of those educated women can be found in the satires of Juvenal. At the end of the first century, the comic poet wrote lines that in his own words were born of outrage. A curmudgeonly, reactionary humorist, he was gripped by nostalgia for a nonexistent past. It's no coincidence that so many medieval manuscripts of his *Satirae* were preserved; the monks adored his categorical condemnations of human depravity—an unbeatable subject for edifying sermons. In one of his poems, Juvenal warns men of the torments of marriage. He presents a catalog of the "evils" of women, including their dalliances with lice-ridden foreigners: "You will father an Ethiopian; a black heir will occupy your will, one whom you cannot look upon by the light of day." He goes on to rail against their lust for gladiators, their extravagant spending, their cruelty to slaves, their superstitions, their shamelessness, their ill humor and jealousy . . . and their education: "She who starts supper by quoting Virgil and weighing his merits against Homer is a tiresome woman. The grammarians make way for her, the teachers are defeated, all are silent. Not even the lawyer or the speechmaker can get a word in. I hate a Mrs. Know-it-all who studies the grammar and knows it by heart, who keeps to the rules of language and quotes verses I've never heard, correcting her dimwit friend for turns of phrase no husband would have any care about."

The misogyny of this satire is so virulent that some experts wonder if Juvenal was really a dinosaur with an ax to grind or if in fact he was giving voice to the most extreme views to ridicule them. It's almost impossible to judge the seriousness or irony of a text at a distance of twenty centuries. In any case, Juvenal's humor couldn't have been successful if there weren't certain elements of truth behind the mockery. There's no question that at the beginning of this era, many Roman women had embraced the pleasure of reading. And some of them, so enamored of literature and language, could give their husbands a run for their money. For the first time in noble families, there were mothers and daughters who conversed, read, experienced the freedom of books, and knew how to wield the indestructible power—"like a god or a diamond"—of words.

11

There is no evidence of anything remotely like universal education in ancient times. Only very recently in the modern era have some countries achieved general literacy, which has happened not spontaneously but through enormous collective effort. The Romans never tried to make literacy universal, nor did they establish a public school system. Education was voluntary, not compulsory. And it was expensive. It's tricky to reconstruct the extent of literacy in that period. There were those who could barely write their names and those who devoured the convoluted prose of Tacitus. Reading and writing skills were inconsistent between men and women and across rural and urban areas. Experts are generally cautious and vague in their conjectures. The historian W. V. Harris ventures to offer precise figures for the population of Pompeii, which was buried by the eruption of Vesuvius in the first century, and where thousands of instances of graffiti and wall paintings have been studied in detail—messages from ordinary people like advertisements for rentals, declarations of love, announcements of lost property, sundry insults and obscenities like those found on the doors of public restrooms, prostitutes' fees, even a fan cheering on his favorite gladiator. According to Harris, less than 60 percent of men and less than 20 percent of women would have been able to read and write in that city—a total of no more than two or three thousand Pompeiians. Though these numbers may seem low, they reveal a level of education never achieved before, and more access to culture than in any previous era.

The lives of boys who belonged to the privileged classes took a new path when they turned seven and stopped studying at home. Up until then, home had been a safe haven where their mothers had raised them and Greek slaves taught them their language, like the foreign governesses of nineteenth-century novels. But they now faced a harsh and even violent experience. From the age of seven to the age of eleven or twelve, they would suffer the obsessive and monotonous rote learning of primary school. Teachers hammered away unrelentingly at every step—letters, syllables, and texts—with no attempt to incite students' curiosity, and with total disregard for the workings of children's minds. As in Greece, the method was passive: memory and mimicry were the talents most highly valued.

Furthermore, rarely did the teacher make learning fun. For all the ancient writers, school conjures memories of beatings and terror. In the fourth century AD, the poet Ausonius sent his grandson a letter encouraging him to start his new life at school without fear: "A teacher isn't such a terrible thing. Though he may have an unpleasant voice and threaten harsh punishments with a frowning face, you will get used to him. Do not be afraid if the school shudders with many a blow. Do not be perturbed at the cries when he wields the cane and your little chairs shake with your trembling and fear." I imagine that these supposedly calming words must have given the poor child more than one nightmare. Saint Augustine, who never forgot the suffering of his school days, wrote at the age of seventy-two, "Who would not balk in horror if given the choice of death or life again as a child? Who would not choose to die?"

Primary school teachers were known as *litterators* in Latin—in other words, "he who teaches letters." These poor devils, who in general were strict, harsh, and poorly paid—it's no surprise that many worked multiple jobs—gave their name to "literature," another profession prone to penury. And the establishments where they taught their classes were less than grand: low-rent facilities, sometimes simple arcades separated from the noise of the street and curious onlookers by flimsy cloth curtains. The students sat on simple backless stools and wrote on their laps, since there were no tables. Horace describes them making their way to school, "having swung over their left arm a box with stones for counting and a tablet to write on." These were the contents of the earliest schoolchildren's backpacks.

Children needed cheap writing materials for their schoolwork, dictation, handwriting practice, and drafts. Since papyrus was a luxury product, wax tablets were the format used from Roman times on for the everyday, personal writing of childhood. With this tool, they learned to read and expressed their successes, their loves, and their memories. The tablets were generally simple, smooth pieces of wood or metal with a shallow dip which was coated in beeswax mixed with resin. On this soft layer, letters were drawn with a sharp stylus of iron or bone, which as we have seen, was topped with a kind of spatula used to smooth over the wax so that mistakes could be erased and the tablet reused. This format allowed for endless recycling simply by changing the layer of wax. Two portraits were found at Pompeii, almost intact, of women deep in thought with the tip of their stylus brushing their lips, just as a twentieth-century intellectual might have posed with his glasses, cigarette, and painstakingly disheveled beard. In the best known of the two—which, fantasizing about a nonexistent image, we have christened "the poet Sappho"—a young woman ruminates, a stylus resting on her lips and some tablets in one hand as she dreams up a line of poetry. Each time we chew on the tip of a pencil or ballpoint pen, lost in contemplation and gazing into space, we are perpetuating, unawares, a repertoire of gestures as ancient as writing itself.

The hand of the young Pompeiian Sappho holds a stack of five or six tablets. It was common to make small holes in a corner of the tablets to bind them together with rings, cords, or leather straps. Sometimes, diptychs or polyptychs were made, held together with hinges. Thanks to a great repository of artifacts discovered in Vindolanda, beside Hadrian's Wall in Great Britain, we also know of the existence of objects the size of a notebook, made from sheets of ordinary timber or strips of birch folded like an accordion. The wood was taken from trees in springtime, when the sap courses through them and the wood is more flexible, so that it could be folded like modern pamphlets. In these sets of tablets bound together like wooden pages—in Latin, *codices*—we find the link between writing's remote past and the present. These are the precursors of the book as we know it today.

Tablets were extremely common and had a wide range of uses. A great many birth certificates and slave manumission documents—two ways of marking the beginning of a new life—were written on them. They were also used for personal note-taking, domestic accounting and trade records of small businesses, as well as archives, letters, and the first drafts of the poems we still read today. In his erotic handbook *The Art of Love*, Ovid warns secret lovers to erase compromising phrases with the utmost care before they reuse a tablet. According to him, many infidelities were discovered due to such carelessness—apparently, ancient wax tablets were as likely to betray an affair as cell phones today. The matter undoubtedly caused our ancestors in the predigital era plenty of trouble; Vatsvayana's *Kama Sutra* gives ample space to instructing women in the art of hiding incriminating letters about their liaisons.

Sometimes, the tablets were coated in layers of plaster so they could be written on with ink using a stiff reed pen with a split tip like the nib of a fountain pen. This made it easier for an untrained hand to draw letters with downstrokes and simple lines. The poet Persius describes a grumbling schoolboy, exasperated by each drop of ink that fell from the tip of his pen and splattered onto his handwriting exercises. The scene has occurred over and over in classrooms for centuries, until very recently. My mother still remembers the sight of her schoolbooks sprinkled with those black tears.

I, on the other hand, belong to the era of the ballpoint pen, the genius invention of Hungarian journalist László Bíró. It's said that the basic idea of making a new writing instrument with a hard metal tip inside a hollow occurred to him while watching some boys play ball. He realized that after it passed through a puddle the ball left a trail as it rolled. I imagine that soccer match in a rainy city—the cries, the laughter, the grey sky, the ground dotted with mirrors, the ball's wet tracks like a newly invented alphabet. This is where the unforgettable hexagonal Bic Cristal pens of my childhood come from, with the blue cap and the little hole in the side. The long, dreary afternoons come flooding back to me, when we used them to shoot grains of rice at the back of our classmates' necks, and I would take aim, childish and clumsy, trying to get the attention of a possible crush.

12

The fascination with horror and extreme violence, which seems so modern to us, already had enthusiasts among the Romans. Greek mythology has its own repertoire of savage acts—rape, gouged eyes, human livers devoured by vultures, people torn viciously limb from limb—but at the pinnacle of the genre, the chronicles of Christian martyrs reign, with their explicit descriptions of torture, dismemberment, mutilation, and gallons and gallons of blood.

One of the great masters of sadism and gore was born in Hispania in the mid-fourth century, probably in Caesaraugusta, which means his childhood must have unfurled among the same winds and rivers as mine. Aurelius Prudentius Clemens was given a beautiful name by his parents and held a range of unadventurous positions as an imperial functionary, but behind this unassuming façade lurked the Roman forefather of Tarantino or Dario Argento. At around the age of fifty, this quiet man from Hispania experienced an intense burst of creativity, abandoning his official responsibilities and writing twenty thousand frenzied lines in seven years. Among other books, he published a poetry collection with a Greek name, *Peristephanon* (Crowns of Martyrdom), which describes, with richly detailed and stylized scenes of torture, the sufferings of fourteen Christians tormented to make them renounce their faith.

The chronicle of the death of Saint Cassian—a martyr in one of those morbid cases Prudentius found so stirring—is one of the most harrowing texts in Latin literature. Surprisingly, it is also an extraordinary—if macabre—document of daily life in ancient schools and the writing tools used by our Roman ancestors. Cassian was a primary school teacher, Prudentius tells us, who wasn't exactly kind to his charges. He oversaw the work of the youngest pupils, taught them to write by dictation, and often punished them harshly. Daily whippings caused a dangerous mix of fear, violence, and resentment to brew inside his students, like the eerie blond children with the icy stare in Michael Haneke's film *The White Ribbon*.

Those were dark years of religious persecution. When yet another wave of repression was unleashed against the Christians, Cassian was detained for his refusal to worship the pagan gods. According to Prudentius, the authorities handed him over unclothed, hands tied behind his back, so the little boys in his class could become his executioners. The tale, fairly predictable until then, suddenly takes a dark turn. Here, death and cruelty have the face of a child: "All of them let out the hatred and gall that has long built up inside them and turned into silent rage. They hurl and break brittle tablets against the teacher's face, and the pointer strikes his brow and then bounces off. They beat him with their waxed writing boards, and the slab splits and is soaked with blood from the blow. Others brandish the styluses with sharp metal pricks that they use to draw grooves when they write in the wax. Two hundred hands poke at his body all at once. Some dig into his guts, while others tear at his skin."

Prudentius wants the impressionable reader to shudder so that his faith may strengthen. He deploys the ingredients of terror with skill, lengthening the scene, dwelling on details, movements, sounds, and blows. He turns everyday objects into weapons, exploring the pain they can inflict and revealing that the scribers used to draw words in wax were as sharp as knives. This piercing writing symbolizes the violence that reigned in the bloody Roman school of letters. The poem thus becomes, paradoxically, a sinister indictment of the corporal punishment of children. The students all seem to have borne the teacher's sarcasm and aggressions, and the dreadful tale of their revenge forces us to behold children transformed into executioners, innocent boys into assassins. It's a gruesome, disturbing spectacle: "Why do you complain?" one boy says cruelly of his disgraced teacher. "You yourself armed us, putting these spikes into our hands. Now we're giving you back the thousands of letters you taught us. You cannot be angry with us for writing. So many times we asked you for breaks and you refused, so greedy were you for our efforts. Now use your authority; you have the right to punish the laziest pupil." The end of the poem is utterly ghastly. The children delight in drawing out their teacher's torment, as the warmth of life slips away through the wounds in his carved-up body.

Though Prudentius intended to condemn the crimes against Christians, the darkness of school life also seeps into his atrocious tale. Another man from Hispania, born in the mid-first century in Calagurris, in what is now Calahorra, was one of the first writers to question such brutal educational methods. In his *Institutes of Oratory*, Quintilian maintained that the desire to learn depended on the student's will, and that violence had no place at school. He opposed humiliating punishments, which he said were "fit only for slaves," thus showing that his humanitarian impulses were not without exception. Perhaps he was recalling the repeated thrashings of his own boyhood when he wrote that children who are often beaten are afflicted with fear and pain, and a shame so deep it shatters the joy of childhood. Children are vulnerable, he adds, and no one should be allowed unlimited power over the defenseless.

The blood-curdling tale of Cassian seems to show that whippings and beatings never disappeared from Roman classrooms, but we can also spot patches of light in this dismal landscape. Around the beginning of our era, proponents of a more compassionate and joyful kind of pedagogy appeared. This trend favored rewards over punishments and tried to awaken a thirst for learning in children.

We know that some teachers began to make educational toys for their pupils, and as a prize for their first faltering steps at reading, gave them cakes and cookies in the shape of the letters they learned. Such excessive indulgence caused an immediate reaction from leaders of the old tradition. A character in Petronius's *Satyricon* rails against the depraved and coddling customs of his time (Nero's reign, during the first century) and announces the imminent decadence of Rome if—heaven forbid!—little boys' studies were also to involve play. The battles waged between the old school and new are very ancient.

A YOUNG FAMILY

13

If we look back on our origins, we find that readers are in fact a very young family, a new group whose expansion has been meteoric. About 3.8 billion years ago, certain molecules on planet Earth joined together to make especially large and intricate structures called living organisms. Animals resembling modern humans appeared for the first time several million years ago. Three hundred thousand years ago, our ancestors learned to use fire. One hundred thousand years ago, the human species conquered words. Between the years 3500 and 3000 BC, under the scorching sun of Mesopotamia, anonymous Sumerian geniuses traced the first signs on clay, which overcame the spatial and temporal barriers of the voice, leaving the lasting imprint of language. Only in the twentieth century, over five millennia later, did writing become a widespread skill within reach of the majority—a long journey, and a very recent acquisition.

It wasn't until the last decades of the twentieth century and the threshold of the twenty-first that urban citizens of humble origins, members of gangs and subcultures, took hold of the alphabet and made it their own form of art, freely expressing their protests, nonconformity, and disillusionment. Contemporary graffiti is one of the most innovative developments the Roman alphabet has seen in centuries, an unanticipated icon of decades of effort to increase access to literacy. For the first time in our history, a group of young people—school-age children and teenagers, many born in blighted areas—had the means and the confidence to invent their own form of expression, creating an original art form based on scribbles and letters. Jean-Michel Basquiat, a young black man with Haitian roots, slept on the streets before he began to exhibit his graffiti in art galleries in the 1980s. Letters flow into many of his paintings like waterfalls, perhaps as a self-affirmation in a system that kept those who didn't fit in at bay. He wrote and then erased some words the better to highlight them; according to him, the mere fact of their prohibition forces us to read them with greater care.

It's interesting to note that graffiti—or "writing," as its practitioners called it—spread across the buildings, subway platforms, walls, and billboards of New York, Los Angeles, and Chicago, and later across those of Amsterdam, Madrid, Paris, London, and Berlin, in the same years when the Digital Revolution was taking place in the garages of Silicon Valley. While the new technology experts were exploring the frontiers of cyberspace, urban youths living in marginalized neighborhoods were experiencing for the first time the delight of drawing letters on walls and train cars, and the beauty of the physical act of writing. In those same years when keyboards were beginning to revolutionize the act of writing, alternative youth culture was engaged in the passionate discovery of writing by hand. Fascinated by the power of naming things, the creative possibilities held by letters, and the sense of risk inherent in writing—a dangerous act, always on the verge of flight—teenagers adopted the handwritten alphabet as a new way to express themselves, to occupy their free time, and to command the respect of their peers. The fact that this adoption is so contemporary is only explained by writing's relative youthfulness compared to the long trajectory of human existence. Writing is merely the latest flutter of the eyelid of our species, the most recent beat of an ancient heart.

Vladimir Nabokov was right to reproach us in *Pale Fire* for our lack of wonder at this marvelous innovation: "We are absurdly accustomed to the miracle of a few written signs being able to contain immortal imagery, involutions of thought, new worlds with live people, speaking, weeping, laughing." And he asks a disturbing question: "What if we awake one day, all of us, and find ourselves utterly unable to read?" It would represent a return to a not-so-distant world, a world before the miracle of written voices and silent words.

14

The spread of reading brought about a new balance of the senses. Until then, language traveled through the ears, but after the discovery of letters, part of communication migrated to the gaze. And readers were soon having problems with their sight. The complaints of some Roman writers reveal that daily use of waxed tablets fatigued and "darkened" their vision. The lines drawn on the waxed surface were simple cracks without contrast—laborious grooves of words. The poet Martial mentioned "the failing eyes" of those who read on tablets, and Quintilian recommended that those with poor eyesight read only books written in ink on papyrus or parchment, black on brown. The cheapest, most accessible format within our ancestors' reach took its toll.

In those days, there was no way of correcting poor vision. The tired eyesight of many readers and scholars was therefore often condemned to sink slowly into a mist with no return, or to become clouded with blotches that blotted out light and color. Glasses had yet to be invented. It's said that the emperor Nero looked through an enormous emerald to see his beloved gladiator fights in detail from his seat. He may have been short-sighted and used his immense cut jewels as a spyglass lens. In any case, giant precious stones may have been available to emperors, but not to intellectuals with an empty purse.

Long centuries later, Roger Bacon scientifically demonstrated that small letters could be enlarged and made clearer with precision-ground lenses. As a result of this discovery, factories in Murano, Italy, began to experiment with glass and became the birthplace of spectacles. Once the lenses had been discovered, light and comfortable frames had to be made to keep them in place. Though some of these early solutions were nicknamed pince-nez or "nose-pinchers," the new contraptions quickly became a desirable mark of social prestige.

In a scene from *The Name of the Rose*, William of Baskerville, to the amazement of Adso, removes a pair of glasses from the pouch that hangs at his chest and puts them on. In the fourteenth century, when the story takes place, glasses were still a rarity. The monks at the abbey, who had never seen anything like it, gaze curiously at the strange prosthetic glass object, not daring to ask a thing. The young Adso describes it as "a forked pin, so constructed that it could stay on a man's nose (or at least on his, so prominent and aquiline) as a rider remains astride his horse or as a bird clings to its perch. And, one on either side of the fork, before the eyes, there were two ovals of metal, which held two almonds of glass, thick as the bottom of a tumbler." William explains to his astonished assistant that the eyes harden with the passage of the years, and that without this extraordinary instrument, after their fiftieth summer many learned men "had virtually died, as far as reading and writing were concerned." Both praise the Lord that someone has discovered and made those fabulous discs that could bring the eyesight back to life.

Wealthy readers in ancient times couldn't yet buy glasses, but the most luxurious scrolls at their disposal were a feast for the eyes and also took less of a toll on them. Most books were made on commission and as in every era, the quality of the handmade product depended on the buyer's budget. For a start, there were different qualities of papyrus. As Pliny records, the finest came from sliced strips of the inner pith of the Egyptian reed. If the collector's coffers were nice and full, the copyist's handwriting would be larger and more beautiful, and the book would be more readable and also more durable.

Let's imagine the finest, most beautiful, most exclusive scrolls for a moment. The edges of the papyrus sheets, painstakingly smoothed with a pumice stone, were decorated with a colored border. To reinforce the books, small rods, known as umbilici, were made from ivory or valuable wood, which was sometimes covered in gold leaf. The rods were topped with highly decorated handles. The Torah scrolls used in synagogues keep the look of those first books alive. For Jews, those wooden cylinders with their knobs—"trees of life"— are indispensable for obeying the ritual injunction not to touch the parchment or the letters of the sacred books. Among the Greeks and

Romans, caressing the text was never a sacrilege, and the rods simply helped to unfurl and rewind the scroll with greater ease.

Craftsmen invented other costly accessories to satisfy book lovers' whims, like traveling boxes and leather cases to preserve papyruses from harm. In luxury editions the case was dyed purple, the color of wealth and power. There was also an expensive balm made of cedar oil for spreading on the papyrus to scare off the moths that devoured words.

Only Roman patricians and aristocrats could boast such opulent libraries. This was how they proudly showed off their fortunes, like people parading around in Rolls-Royces today. Though there were some exceptions, poets, learned men, and philosophers did not belong to those privileged circles. Some of them gazed at the beautiful books that lay out of their reach, and in their disgruntlement wrote vicious satires about their uncultured collectors. One of those spiteful screeds, titled *The Ignorant Book-Collector,* has reached us: "Of he who gains no benefit from books, why should he buy them except to give work to the mice, a nest to the moths, and beatings to the slaves who do not care well for them? Since you do not know what to do with them, you might as well lend them to those who would profit more. But you are like the dog in the manger, who neither eats the corn himself nor lets the horse eat it, though he would be able to do so." This masterpiece of invective angrily depicts the landscape of scarcity prior to the arrival of printing, when reading was all too often a mark of unearned privilege.

15

For a long time, books passed from hand to hand in closed circles of friends and the most exclusive clients. In republican Rome, reading was for the elites and their cronies. Long centuries passed during which, in the absence of public libraries, only the wealthy or those skilled at bootlicking could lay eyes on a book.

In around the first century BC, we glimpse the existence of people who read for pleasure for the first time, with no great fortune or social ambition. This opening was made possible by bookstores. While we know there was already a book trade in Greece, we have hardly anything on which to base an image of those early sellers. But when it comes to the Roman world, we have substantial details, including names, addresses, gestures, prices, and even jokes.

The young poet Catullus—he was always young, since he died at thirty—tells a revealing anecdote of friendship and bookshops set around the mid-first century BC. In something like a precursor of an April Fool's prank, at the end of a cold December, during the Saturnalia, he received a joke gift from his friend Licinius Calvus: a poetry anthology of the authors they thought the most terrible of the time. "Great gods, what a dire and cursed little book you have sent your Catullus, to make him drop dead at the sight," Catullus grumbles. He goes on to plot his revenge: "You jest, but this mischief will cost you dearly, since as soon as day dawns I shall dash to the bookshops and buy the worst literary poison there is to get back at you for this torture. Meanwhile, go back to the cave you came out of in evil hour, calamity of our times, you writers of dreadful doggerel."

From these playful lines we learn that by then, it was already a custom to give books from the Saturnalia market as gifts. What's more, the vengeful Catullus can be sure that at dawn the next day, he'll be able to find several bookshops open in Rome where he can buy the worst and most mind-numbing contemporary poetry with which to exact revenge on his friend for his antics.

Those early morning bookstores were mainly workshops where copies were made on commission, frequented mostly by riffraff who didn't even have a poor slave to whom they could delegate the task. With an original under their arm, they ordered a given number of handwritten copies, the quality of which would depend on their means. The workshop employees, mostly slaves, were quick with the pen. Martial, the standard-bearer of brief poetry in ancient times, claimed that a copy of his second book of epigrams—thirty pages long in my printed edition—could be done with a wait of only an hour. He argued the benefits of his fast and frugal work as follows: "Firstly, I waste less papyrus. Secondly, the copyist will do it all in only an hour, so will spend less time as a slave to my trifles. And in third place, though the book may be bad from beginning to end, it will be only a brief spell of boredom."

The same word, *librarius*, referred to both copyist and bookseller since the trades were one and the same. Before the invention of printing, books were reproduced one by one, letter by letter, word by word. The costs of material and labor were always the same. Producing a run of thousands of copies at once as we do today wouldn't have yielded any savings at all. On the contrary, producing numerous books without a guaranteed buyer would have put the business in danger of ruin. The Romans would have raised an eyebrow in disbelief at our modern concepts of readership and market expansion. But Catullus's anecdote shows that you could go to a bookshop for certain works ready for purchase, with no need to supply the original. This was most likely the case for a handful of new books and certain indispensable classics. Booksellers were beginning to take on a certain amount of commercial risk, offering ready-made books by authors they were confident they could sell.

Martial was the first writer to show that he had a friendly relationship with the booksellers' guild. He himself, who always protested the miserliness of his patrons, must surely have stocked up on books at the stores. Several of his highly modern poems contain covert advertising, for which he may have been paid: "In the Argiletum, opposite Caesar's forum is a bookshop whose door is completely covered in signs so that you can quickly read off the names of all the poets. Look for me there. Atrectus—such is the name of the owner—will take from the first or second shelf a Martial, smoothed with pumice-stone and adorned with purple, for five denarii."

Judging by the price of five denarii for his flimsy little book—one denarius was the wage for a day's work—Atrectus and his scribes must have been producing luxury goods, though we can assume they also made cheap books for less robust budgets.

Along with Atrectus, Martial also drops the names of three other booksellers into his poems: Tryphon, Secundus, and Quintus Pollius Valerianus. He dedicates a few sarcastic words of gratitude to the latter for keeping his early books on sale: "All the trivialities I wrote when I was young, reader, you may request from Quintus Pollius Valerianus, who is keeping my foolishness alive." He also advertises Secundus's bookshop, including the address: "So you won't fail to know where I am for sale, or wander aimlessly all over the town, follow these directions: Seek out Secundus, the freedman of learned

Lucensis, behind the temple of Peace and the Forum of Pallas." In a society that didn't recognize copyright, Martial received no royalties for the sale of his books in those stores or in any other, but he may have charged for advertising them in his poems, which would make him a precursor of contemporary TV product placement. He probably enjoyed wandering through those bookshops in his free time and wished to immortalize them in his epigrams. He must have felt more comfortable discussing the latest literary jokes in the company of those intelligent freed traders than in the mansions of the aristocrats who looked down on him and made him come in through the servants' door.

Martial's poems help us to reconstruct what those first bookshops must have been like: establishments with signs on their doors and rows of niches or shelves inside. Based on some businesses preserved in Pompeii, I can picture a bookshop with a solid counter and jumbled mythological frescoes on the walls; a back door would lead from the room where the owner served customers to the workshop where the copyist slaves toiled at a relentless speed, hour after hour, bent over papyrus or parchment pages, stoically suffering from backaches and cramps in their arms.

Thanks to booksellers, Martial's poems began to reach the hands of unknown readers beyond his patrons' circle, and the poet was delighted by his new literary promiscuity. Other writers, however, experienced this unchecked exposure to an increasingly wide and faceless audience with fear and embarrassment. Horace admits his reserve in an epistle where he converses with his own book. Here, he chastises his latest work as if it had a life of its own, or to be precise, as if it were a young exhibitionist too keen to go into the street and reveal itself in public. The argument becomes heated, and the poet reproaches his boastful creation, which wishes to go and prostitute itself at the Sosius bookshop: "You hate keys and seals, which are agreeable to those who are modest, you grieve that you are shown to few, and praise public places, although it goes against your breeding. 'Woe is me, what have I done?' you will say, when your lover is satisfied and grows tired of you. When, thumbed by vulgar hands, you begin to grow dirty."

Behind these jokes with erotic overtones pulses a historic change in access to reading. Between the first centuries BC and AD, a new addressee was born: the anonymous reader. Today it might seem sad to publish a book only friends and family will read, but this was the safe and comfortable scenario to which Roman authors were accustomed. Dissolving those borders, accepting that anyone could peer into their thoughts and emotions in exchange for a fistful of denarii was a traumatic experience for many writers. They felt as if they were being undressed.

Horace's epistle announces the end of the aristocratic monopoly on books. It also expresses a profound distrust of an audience made up of strangers—and even commoners—outside of his circles and distant in space and time. The author ends by threatening his impertinent little book with a humiliating fate: "You will be silent fodder for the crude moths, or age will catch up with you teaching boys their letters in some little corner, or you will be packaged up and sent to Ilerda [present-day Lérida, Spain]." Unless the shameless book behaves decently and stays at home among trusted acquaintances, it will suffer the grave indignity of becoming a textbook, or, worse still, the outrage of belonging to the library of a coarse Hispanic reader.

Next to that of Horace, Martial's open and irreverent attitude is remarkable. The latter was born even farther away than Lérida, in the Celtiberian Bilbilis (today Catalayud, in Aragon), and therefore was unprejudiced against those from the provinces. This was the beginning of a new era when it would no longer be necessary to court the rich to gain access to books. Martial and the booksellers applauded this expansion of the battlefield.

BOOKSELLING

A Risky Business

16

Helene was a daughter of immigrants. Her father, a humble shirtmaker, used to get tickets to the theater in Philadelphia in exchange for the garments he sold. Thanks to those trades, in the midst of the Great Depression, Helene could go and settle into the worn-out seats, and when the lights went down in the auditorium and the stage lit up, her heart would pound like a runaway horse in the darkened theater. At twenty, with a meager scholarship, she moved to Manhattan to begin her life as a writer. For decades, she lived in filthy rooms with shabby furniture and roach-infested kitchens, not knowing how she would pay her rent from one month to the next. She scraped out a living as a television scriptwriter while creating, one after another, dozens of plays that no one would agree to produce.

Her best work, which grew and developed slowly over the course of the next twenty years, was born in the most innocent and unpredictable way. Helene came across a tiny advertisement for a London bookstore specializing in out-of-print books. In the autumn of 1949, she sent her first order to 84, Charing Cross Road. The books, which the exchange rate made affordable to her, began to travel across the ocean to the orange-crate shelves that she set up in one apartment after another.

From the very beginning, Helene sent the bookstore something beyond spare lists and the payments she owed. Her letters described the pleasure of unpacking the latest arrival and caressing its beautiful cream-colored pages, smooth to the touch; her amused disappointment if the work failed to live up to her expectations; her impressions as she read, her financial woes, her quirks: "I do love secondhand books that open to the page some previous owner read oftenest." The initially arrogant tone of the answers sent by the bookseller, Frank, softened as the months went on and more letters arrived. In December, a Christmas package from Helene arrived at Charing Cross Road for the bookstore's workers. It contained ham, tins of preserves, and other items that could only be found on the black market in those hard years in postwar England. In the spring, she asked Frank to do her the favor of sending a small anthology of poets "who can make love without slobbering," for her to read outdoors in Central Park.

The extraordinary thing about these letters is the glimpse they allow of what's left unsaid. Though Frank never says so, there is no doubt that he bends over backward, going to great lengths, scouring every corner of remote private libraries for sale, in search of the loveliest books for Helene. She answers by sending him new gift packages, confiding new humorous details about herself, and making new urgent requests. Wordless emotion and quiet longing seep into this trade correspondence, which isn't even private, since Frank makes a copy of every letter for the shop's archive. The years go by and the books keep coming. Frank, who is married, watches his two daughters leave childhood and then youth behind. Helene, always hard up, gets by on the money from TV scripts. They exchange gifts, orders, and words, which come farther and farther apart. They have perfected a language of their own—reserved, unsentimental, full of ingenious turns of phrase that make light of their unspoken love.

Helene always said she would go to London—and to the bookstore—as soon as she scraped together the money for a ticket, but the ongoing penury of writing, a dental mishap, and the cost of her endless moves postponed the encounter summer after summer. In lines that were always discreet, Frank would lament that among all the American tourists and Beatles fans, Helene never arrived. In 1968, Frank died suddenly of a severe case of peritonitis. His widow penned a few lines to the American woman: "At times I don't mind telling you I was very jealous of you." Helene collected all the letters and published them in a book. Then the roaring success that eluded her throughout her years of hard work arrived: *84, Charing Cross Road* soon became a cult classic and was adapted for film and theater. After decades of writing plays that no one was willing to produce, Helene Hanff triumphed onstage with a work that was never meant to be. Thanks to the book's publication, she could finally travel to London for the first time, but it was too late: Frank was dead, and the bookshop, Marks & Co., had already disappeared.

Only half the story of the writer and her bookseller-confidant is included in their correspondence. The other half dwells in the books he sought out for her. To recommend and deliver a chosen text is a powerful way to seek closeness, communication, and intimacy.

Books haven't completely lost that primitive value they had in Rome, the subtle ability to draw a map of fondness and friendship. When we are moved by something we read, the first person we tell is a loved one. When we give a novel or collection of poetry to someone who matters to us, we know their opinion of the text will reflect on us. If a friend or lover places a book in our hands, we seek out their tastes and ideas in the text and feel intrigued, as if the underlined words refer to us; we begin a personal conversation with the written words, becoming more fully open to their mystery. We search the book's sea of letters for a message in a bottle just for us.

When they still barely knew each other, my father gave my mother a copy of *Trilce*, the poems César Vallejo wrote in his youth. Perhaps none of what happened next would have been possible without the feelings awakened by those lines. Some things we read serve to break down barriers; some things we read are a recommendation of the stranger who loves them. I am not related to the prodigious César Vallejo, but I have grafted him into my family tree. Just like my distant great-grandparents, his existence was essential to mine.

Despite the impact of blogs, criticism, and publicity campaigns, we almost always owe the most beautiful things we have read to someone we love—or to a bookseller who has become a friend. Books continue to tie us together, bonding us in mysterious ways.

17

Bookstores disappear quickly. The traces they leave behind are more subtle than those of great libraries. In his indispensable essay—and travel guide for bibliophiles—Jorge Carrión writes that "The dialogue between private and public collections, between the Bookshop and the Library, is . . . as old as civilization itself, but the balance of history always inclines toward the latter." While the librarian accumulates and hoards, lending their goods only temporarily, the bookseller acquires their stock precisely to let go of it, sending books into circulation. Their area is dealing, setting things in motion. While libraries are attached to power, to local governments, states, and their armies, bookstores pulse with the energy of the present; they are liquid, temporary. And, I would add, dangerous.

Bookselling was already a risky job in Martial's times. The poet witnessed the execution of Hermogenes of Tarsus, a historian who upset the emperor Domitian with certain allusions in his work. To teach the people an even harsher lesson, the copyists and booksellers responsible for the ill-fated book's circulation were also sentenced to death. Suetonius described their punishment with a handful of words that need no translation: *librariis . . . cruci fixis.*

With these crucifixion victims, Domitian inaugurated a grim program of oppression. Since then, countless censors have wielded the emperor's method, cracking down on those only indirectly responsible. This repressive machine's success lies precisely in extending the threat of reprisals, fines, or imprisonment to every link in the chain of distribution (from the scribes and printers of long ago to forum administrators or internet providers). Instilling fear in those who perform these roles helps to silence troublesome texts, since it's unlikely that they'll be willing to run the same risks as the author, who is more deeply committed to publishing his own work. Threats against booksellers are thus an essential part of this all-out war against the free circulation of books.

Almost nothing is known about the booksellers the emperor killed for copying and selling Hermogenes's history, which they may not even have liked. They are saved from oblivion only by a phrase dashed off by Suetonius in a paragraph on Domitian's reign of terror. They appear and are gone in a flash, leaving us with a lingering, unsatisfied curiosity. They are named for the first time only in death. What story might they have told? What trials did they suffer, and what pleasure did they take in their profession? Was their punishment arbitrary, or did they support the subversive spirit of the author whose writing cost them their lives?

A fascinating memoir gives voice to the booksellers of another uncertain, chaotic, authoritarian era: nineteenth-century Spain, as it was emerging from the despotic rule of Fernando VII. The author, George Borrow, whom the Madrileños called "Don Jorgito the Englishman," was sent to Spain by the British and Foreign Bible Society on a mission to distribute the Anglican versions of sacred books. Borrow traversed the peninsula along dusty, almost clandestine routes, leaving his copies of the Bible in the main bookstores of small towns and provincial capitals. Amid a motley landscape of peddlers, gypsies, wise women, laborers, muleteers, soldiers, smugglers, bandits, bullfighters, Carlists, and unemployed bureaucrats, he portrays the famished book world he came to know. When he published the tale of his pilgrimages, *The Bible in Spain*, in 1842, he asserted that "the demand for literature of every kind in Spain was miserably small."

The book offers up a priceless gallery of booksellers who speak in the first person, stubborn, disgruntled, downtrodden, and, in one case, disturbing. The Valladolid bookseller—"a kind-hearted simple man"—could only sell books in combination with other sundry occupations, since the bookshop wasn't enough to earn him a living. In León, Borrow convinced an intrepid bookseller to sell and advertise his Anglican Bibles, but the nearby Leonese, made up "with very few exceptions" of "furious Carlists," who were staunchly traditionalist, brought a trial before the ecclesiastical court against their unorthodox neighbor. Far from being cowed, the bookseller rose to the challenge and even nailed an advertisement to the cathedral door. In Santiago de Compostela, Borrow struck up a friendship with a veteran of the trade, who took him to explore the city's outskirts on pleasant summer evenings. After several walks, he dared to speak openly and confide in Borrow the persecution he'd suffered: "We booksellers of Spain . . . are all liberals . . . We love our profession, and have all more or less suffered for it; many of us, in the times of terror, were hanged for selling an innocent translation from the French or English . . . I was obliged to flee from Saint James and take refuge in the wildest part of Galicia . . . Had I not possessed good friends, I should not have been alive now; as it was, it cost me a considerable sum of money to arrange matters. Whilst I was away, my shop was in the charge of the ecclesiastical officers. They frequently told my wife that I ought to be burnt for the books which I had sold."

The most sinister of all was a Spanish Sweeney Todd, the mad bookseller-barber of Vigo who, according to hearsay, was as likely to sell you a book as he was to slit your throat under the pretext of shaving your beard. It's unclear what determined whether his approach would be friendly or murderous. I wonder if his dwindling clientele had risked their necks by proffering a literary opinion.

Nearly eighteen hundred years lie between Domitian and Fernando VII, but their booksellers' stories breathe a shared atmosphere. In periods of tyranny, bookstores tend to be places to access forbidden material, and therefore awaken suspicions. In periods when foreign influence is a source of fear, they serve as ports on dry land, border crossings that elude surveillance. In these places, the words of outsiders, words that are troublesome or condemned, find a hiding place. My mother has preserved intact her memory of the backrooms of certain bookstores during the dictatorship—the ritual at the door, the fear, and the childish, rebellious joy of being allowed to enter the hideout and finally touch the dangerous merchandise: exiled books, troublemaking essays, Russian novels, experimental literature, titles the censors had deemed obscene. You bought a book and also the need to hide it forever; you bought secrecy and danger; you paid to be branded an outlaw.

I remember one morning in Madrid with my father. We had gone into one of the secondhand bookstores he loved so much. (They are kingdoms of chaos and disarray.) He could spend hours there. He called it poking or sniffing around, but it looked more like he was digging through a mine. He sank his arms up to the armpits to reach the books at the bottom of a pile, causing avalanches as he groped around. If he stood directly under the light, you could see a halo of dust motes floating around him. He was delighted to be rummaging through the stacks, boxes, and shelves three rows deep with spines. The physical effort of the search was part of the pleasure of shopping. On that morning in Madrid in the nineties, my father unearthed a curious nugget. It was apparently a copy of *Don Quixote*. The skinny nobleman on the cloth cover, the first chapter with the ancient shield, the occasional stew of beef more often than lamb, the eggs and abstinence on Saturdays. But where chapter 2 should have been, another work began instead: *Das Kapital*. The smile on my father's face grew unusually wide. He lit up. The combined edition of Cervantes and Marx wasn't an exotic printing mistake, but a clandestine book, a living reminder, a ghost from the same years, ambiances, whispers, and deceits he had lived through as a young man. Suddenly, he was flooded with hundreds of brief memories. That strange graft—Karl spliced into Miguel—meant the world to him, perhaps because it awakened nostalgia for the camouflaged books he had read. It touched my memory too, and evoked the threat of those years I can't remember, years when I wasn't yet born: my parents swore not to have a child for as long as Franco lived.

18

Not long before I wrote this chapter, a copy of Françoise Frenkel's *A Bookshop in Berlin*, the riveting memoir of an exiled, nomadic Jewish bookseller, fell into my hands. I was immediately gripped by the book's first words: "It is the duty of those who have survived to bear witness to ensure the dead are not forgotten, nor humble acts of self-sacrifice left unacknowledged. May these pages inspire a reverent thought for those forever silenced, fallen by the wayside or murdered."

The more expressive original title—*No Place to Lay One's Head*—sums up her story of uprootedness. Françoise was born in Poland but her wandering took her to Paris, where she learned the bookselling trade and its subtleties ("By and by, after observing the way a book was held, almost tenderly, the way pages were delicately turned and reverently read or hastily and thoughtlessly leafed through, the book then put back on the table, sometimes so carelessly that its corners, its most precious part, were damaged as a result, I came to be able to see into a character, a spirit, a state of mind. I would place the book I considered appropriate down close to a reader—discreetly, however, so they wouldn't feel it had been suggested to them. If they happened to like it, I glowed.")

Years later, in 1921, she set up a French bookstore in Berlin, La Maison du Livre. There, she welcomed a cosmopolitan clientele and organized talks by writers passing through Germany (Gide, Maurois, Colette). The main customers for her business came from the White Russian community in Charlottenburg. Nabokov, who lived in the same neighborhood, must have spent melancholy afternoons there in winter, watching dusk fall. Those were exhilarating years for Françoise.

In 1935, with the Nazis at the helm, the hardships began.

First came the obligation to submit to a special service that assessed imported books. Sometimes the police would show up and seize a few volumes and French newspapers that appeared on their blacklist. The number of authorized French publications grew more and more limited, and the mere distribution of forbidden works sent booksellers straight to the concentration camp. It was Domitian's strategy, once again.

After the Nuremberg Race Laws were passed, the persecution became more severe. Françoise was interrogated by the Gestapo. As she lay in bed in the dark, she could hear the Brownshirts making their nightly rounds, brazenly singing songs that glorified strength, war, and hatred.

On Kristallnacht, Berlin crackled in the light of the torches and the burning synagogues. At dawn, Françoise sat on the steps of her bookshop and saw two people approach with long iron bars. They were stopping in front of certain store windows and smashing them, the shattered glass raining down. They entered the windows through the sharp hole they had made, to kick and stamp on the goods. Pausing in front of the Maison du Livre, they checked their list. "It's not on here," they said, before moving on. The precarious protection of the French embassy had prevented an attack on her shop, at least for the moment. Françoise thought that if it had happened that night, she would have defended every book with all her might, not just out of affection for her trade, but also out of revulsion, driven by "an infinite longing for death."

In spring 1939, she had to face the facts: there was no longer any place in Berlin for her little oasis of French books. The most sensible thing to do would be to escape. She spent her last night in Germany watching over the crowded shelves, the small space where her customers came to forget, to find comfort, to be able to breathe. Once in Paris, she learned that her collections of books and records, along with her furniture, had been confiscated by the German government on racial grounds. She had lost everything. War broke out. The monstrous military swarm Françoise had seen take shape in Germany was threatening to advance across Europe. Homeless, with hardly any luggage, with no place to rest, she was merely a drop in the oceanic wave of European refugees. Her memoir tells of her misfortunes as she fled, fearing for her life until she could cross the Swiss border in secret.

It's unlikely that Hitler ever set foot in La Maison du Livre. But literature had also been a refuge for him. The lung problems he suffered in adolescence turned him into a compulsive reader. According to friends from his youth, he was a regular at bookstores and lending libraries. They described him surrounded by piles of books, mostly treatises on history and German heroic sagas. On his death, he left a library of over fifteen hundred volumes. With *Mein Kampf*, he became the author of the best-selling German book of the 1930s. In that decade, his book sold more copies than any other after the Bible. He made millions from the sales, and with a new aura of success and wealth, managed to shed his image as a beer hall braggart. After the failure of the Munich Putsch, writing gave him back his self-esteem. From 1925 on, the year the first volume of *Mein Kampf* was published, he filled out the box corresponding to profession on his tax forms with "writer." By the time the war was over, an estimated ten million copies of the work had been distributed, translated into sixteen languages. Another hundred thousand copies have been sold in Germany since the book entered the public domain in 2016. Those responsible for the successive editions admit that "the figures are overwhelming."

In 1920—almost the same time as Françoise embarked on her Berlin endeavor, and as Hitler was delivering his first speeches to the masses with his characteristically wild gesticulations—Mao Zedong was opening a bookstore in Changsha. The business was so successful that it grew to have six employees—this early capitalist venture was so astonishingly profitable that for years it financed his incipient revolutionary career. Previously, he had worked at a university library, where he was remembered as a voracious reader. Forty-six years later and with inexplicable viciousness, he would launch the Cultural Revolution, which left in its wake a trail of burned books and intellectuals who were publicly humiliated, imprisoned, and murdered. As Jorge Carrión writes, "those who designed the biggest systems of control, repression and execution in the contemporary world, who showed themselves to be the most effective censors of books, were also individuals who studied culture, who were writers, *keen* readers. In a word: lovers of bookshops."

Bookstores may seem serene and far from the madding crowd, but their shelves quiver with the conflicts of every century.

19

Three years ago, the newspaper *Heraldo de Aragón* requested an article from me, and I decided to write about bookstores, about the magnetic fields that silently radiate out into the streets and neighborhoods around them. I began with a quote from bookseller Paco Puche, one of the authors of *Memoria de la librería* (Bookstore Memoir): "The effect a bookstore has on the city that hosts it, the energy it sends out into the streets and transmits to its inhabitants can't be measured. Customer and sales numbers or business statistics aren't enough, of course, because the influence a bookstore has on a city is subtle, secret, and hard to pin down."

I interviewed five booksellers from two cities—heirs to those whom Borrow met on his travels. I chose them for personal reasons, because I learned to read from them all at different times in my life. Ever since I was a child, I've loved stepping into these cavelike stores and finding their owners stationed like sentries amid mountains of books, organized or scattered, best sellers or tattered orphans, delicately crafted or cheaply produced, all waiting to be flipped through, sniffed, and caressed. I always breathe deeply when I peer at those pinnacles of paper and dust, like a mountaineer climbing the stacks. Though they may seem to be crowded, bookstores expand my sense of space.

It was thrilling to ask questions, listen, and fill my notebook with nervous scribbles. I'm flipping through it right now and looking at the arrows and brackets in the margins, teacup rings staining the pages, underlining, dog-eared corners, angrily crossed-out words. I made a note there that Chema, the bookseller at a little enchanted turret called Anónima, told me he was moved by support for lost causes. The literary version of that incorrigible romanticism was impossible to resist. Irony and passion, together or separately, were the most frequent registers in which the five booksellers spoke. There were hard times too, of course. Some still remembered how business was harmed by photocopiers; others lamented the damage done by internet sales. A risky business, they kept saying, remembering wonderful personal projects that had failed. How difficult it seems today to reach the kind of success Mao Zedong achieved, when he created six jobs in his bookstore and could devote himself freely to planning the destruction of capitalism.

In the mysterious, bacchanalian forest of Julia and Pepito's store, Librería Antígona, the pair said they felt like family doctors prescribing reading as medicine. They are jokers and anarchists, just as likely to assign you an obscure book as they are to forbid you a highly acclaimed one. "Therapist" was a recurring word in the mouth of Pablo at the mythical Librería París, which felt like a boat helmed by seasoned and jovial sailors. This remarkable likeness led me to consider the unique skills required by this ancient trade: managing the stock of literary medicine; understanding the tastes of readers, their opinions and inclinations, and the reasons a given work inspires their admiration, enthusiasm, joy, or dissatisfaction—in other words, slipping into the domain of individual whims and obsessions; and opening the blinds day after day for an often idealized job that consists of long hours, delivery notes, hauling boxes, and backache. George Orwell, who was a part-time bookshop assistant from 1934 to 1936, says in his *Bookshop Memories* that a bookstore is "so easily pictured, if you don't work in one, as a kind of paradise where charming old gentlemen browse eternally among calf-bound folios." In fact, the customers weren't as eccentric or endearing as Eric Blair—Orwell's true name—might have wished, and the author gritted his teeth to see titles he loved languish without ever finding a home. Eric's friends described him as a shy and sullen salesman. It seems he couldn't quite create a charismatic persona to oversee his paper kingdom with panache. Perhaps he didn't understand that a bookseller is, in addition to everything else, an actor, a conjuror in a magic theater.

In front of the big display window at Los Portadores de Sueños, where pools of light spill into their peaceful space, Eva and Félix spoke of the efforts of bookstores to take over from old cafés in hosting artistic and literary gatherings. What booksellers wanted was a place where things could happen: chance encounters, the possibility of reunions, exhibitions, plans; to be a cultural habitat for living, breathing ideas. What they wanted were rituals as inviting to the shy as to those who speak exuberantly. The vocation of our booksellers has created fertile ground for publishing houses, illustrators, and writers to thrive. When a haunt like Los Portadores de Sueños closes its doors, we experience a strangely bleak kind of solitude.

I live in a region with a harsh climate but hospitable bookstores, a happy place for the incurable tribe of repeat offenders to which we readers belong; we need to let time go by between well-chosen books, scanning, caressing, questioning, on the hunt for discoveries. Who knows, maybe it's the north wind unleashed in our winters—a wind that whips us, makes the trees creak, leaves us disheveled, makes us bend and blows dust in our eyes, forcing us to grow used to fighting with something unseen—that makes us, in the shelter of our homes, one of the regions of Spain that reads the most.

As I was pulling together the last of my material, just when the article seemed on course, I discovered a troubling corner, a forgotten nook, the shadow of another article yet to be written. It happened by chance, just like everything that later comes to seem inevitable. I was chatting to Paco at the bookstore Cálamo, without taking notes, without a voice recorder, both of us relaxed, gesturing that it was time to wrap up—some light coughs, the lid put back on a pen. In his hanging garden of books and origami birds in cages, Paco recalled Cálamo's opening thirty years earlier, his hunger to participate in the life of the city through books, but also his fear. From him I learned that we had our own nights of broken glass.

Whenever she speaks of the Transition in Spain, my mother raises a hand to her chest. The gesture emphasizes the words with which she always describes that part of her youth: "the heart-attack years." No one had ever told me that booksellers had been in the harrowing front lines of that historic tachycardia. For an interminable period of months—the height of the persecution lasted from 1976 to the spring of 1977—bookstores in Madrid, Barcelona, Zaragoza, Valencia, Pamplona, Tenerife, Córdoba, Tolosa, Getxo, and Valladolid, among other cities, were targeted by a series of attacks that recall the atmosphere of Françoise Frenkel's last days in Berlin. In fact, a group calling itself the Adolf Hitler Command claimed responsibility for several of these assaults. In their statements, they justified their actions by the presence of Marxist, liberal, and leftist books in the stores. "A Bookstore Attacked Every Two Weeks," a headline from those days declares. More than two hundred businesses were vandalized, and some were victims of multiple attacks—the Pórtico Librerías in Zaragoza, for example. The forms their aggression took were varied: anonymous messages, verbal threats, bomb threats via telephone, arson, gunfire, explosive devices, buckets of ink hurled at stores, or fecal matter smeared over the windows.

The Pórtico Librerías stood on the corner of calle Baltasar Gracián. One November night in 1976, a powerful device exploded. The steel armor plating protecting the doors and windows was blown apart, and the thick metal sheets transformed into shards of shrapnel, raining down in every direction. The impact scraped the stone porticos at the edge of the plaza. It was the fifth attack in just a few months. There were no arrests. José Alcrudo, the bookseller, told the press in a statement, "I just sell books . . . That's why I think these aren't attacks on me, even if I'm the one to suffer, but attacks on culture. And if no clear action is taken we'll end up having to close, because we know there's no possible armor or defense against bombs."

The fragile bookstore survived the violence. Years later, I would play hide and seek among its intricate islands of books, listening to Charlie Parker—without knowing who he was—while my father, his sleeves rolled up to his elbows, indulged his passion for mining books and had long, meandering conversations with José. Back then I was just a girl, and I listened to the flow of those strange, unhurried, indecipherable talks as if they were incantations. It seemed to me that talking was the point of adult existence.

Bookstores have always been a refuge under siege. They still are. Booksellers identify as doctors without a white coat, but they may have to wear a bulletproof vest to work in difficult times. When Salman Rushdie published his satirical novel *The Satanic Verses* in 1988, a rapid spiral of censorship and violence was unleashed, which for the first time had a global reach. An Indian parliamentarian started the fire by condemning the work for blasphemy. A week later, thousands of photocopies of the passages considered the most offensive began to circulate in Islamic institutes. In January 1989, images on TV showed Muslims burning copies of the book in the streets. The incidents spread across the whole world, and a few weeks later the author received death threats at his London home. A mob attacked the American cultural center in Islamabad, where five people were shot and killed as the crowd cried, "Rushdie, you are dead." In February, the Ayatollah Khomeini decided to do away with the book's profanities by declaring a fatwa that urged the faithful to execute the author and all those connected to the book's publication and distribution as soon as possible. A device exploded in a bookstore in Berkeley, and other establishments were attacked with firebombs in London and Australia. The book's Japanese translator, Hitoshi Igarashi, was murdered; the Italian translator, Ettore Capriolo, was stabbed; and the Norwegian editor, William Nygaard, was shot three times in his own home. Several bookstores were looted and destroyed. In another protest, thirty-seven people died. The publisher, Penguin, never considered withdrawing the novel from bookstores, even if this meant employees would have to wear bulletproof vests. Rushdie spent eleven years in hiding. In 1997, the price on his head reached two million dollars.

Days before *The Satanic Verses* appeared in bookstores, during the publicity campaign, an Indian journalist asked Rushdie, off the record, whether he was aware of the row that was coming. The writer's response was unequivocal: "It is a funny view of the world to think that a book can cause riots."

If we look back at the general history of book destruction, we'll see that in fact, the funny view of the world—the oasis, the strange paradise, the Shangri-La, the forest of Lothlórien—is freedom of expression. Over the centuries, the written word has been stubbornly persecuted, and the times when bookstores receive only peaceful visitors who do not wave flags or wag fingers, break windows or set things on fire, or give themselves over to the primitive zeal for prohibition, are in fact the unusual ones.

20

The chaos of bookstores is much like the chaos of memory. Their corridors, shelves, and thresholds are spaces inhabited by collective and individual views of the past. There, we come upon biographies, eyewitness accounts, and long shelves of fiction where writers uncover the truths of many lives. The thick spines of history books, like camels in a steady caravan, offer to guide us on a journey into former times. Research, dreams, myths, and chronicles drowse together in the same shadows. The chance of an encounter or of a rescue is always there.

It's no coincidence that in W. G. Sebald's *Austerlitz*, the protagonist recovers the repressed memory of his childhood in a bookstore. Raised in a small Welsh town by elderly adoptive parents who never revealed where he came from, Jacques Austerlitz always carried with him an inexplicable sorrow. Like a sleepwalker who fears waking, for years he had closed himself off to all knowledge of the tragedy from which the chapter of his own life was torn. He did not read newspapers, turned on the radio only at certain times, and perfected a system of quarantine that kept him away from any contact with his prior history. But his attempt to be immune to memory brought with it hallucinations and anguished dreams and finally exploded in a nervous breakdown. One spring day in London, on one of his despondent walks through the city, he went into a bookstore near the British Museum. The owner, who sat in a slightly tilted position behind a desk covered in books and papers, answered to the mythical name of Penelope Peacefull. Without knowing it, the reluctant traveler had found the road back to Ithaca.

The bookstore was calm. Penelope looked up occasionally, smiled at Jacques, then turned back to look at the street, lost in thought. Soft and crackling voices from an old radio captivated Jacques. Little by little, he became motionless, as if he couldn't miss even a syllable of the broadcast. Two women recalled how, in the summer of 1939 when they were girls, they had been sent to England from central Europe to escape Nazi persecution. Terror stricken, Austerlitz realized that the fragmentary memories of those women were also his. He suddenly saw again the grey waters of the port, the ropes and chains of the anchor, the prow of the boat taller than a house, the seagulls that flew overhead squawking furiously. There was no going back. The floodgates of his memory had burst open, unleashing a deluge of agonizing certainties. That he was a Jewish refugee. That his early childhood had taken place in Prague. That at the age of four he was separated from his real family forever. That he would spend the rest of his life in an almost certainly futile search for traces of all he had lost.

"Are you all right?" asked Penelope, the bookseller, concerned by his petrified look.

Austerlitz finally knew why he had always felt like a passerby everywhere he went, with neither home nor compass, lost and alone.

From that morning in the bookstore on, we follow the protagonist on a painful itinerary through a series of European cities as he wanders in search of the identity stolen from him. A series of epiphanies unfolds. Jacques pieces together the life of his mother, an actress and singer murdered in the Theresienstadt concentration camp. In Prague, he finds and speaks to an old friend of his parents. He recovers old photographs. He examines a Nazi propaganda film in slow motion, searching for a woman's face to wound his memory. He haunts places where voices echo—libraries, museums, archives, bookstores. The novel is a tribute to these realms where the past is invoked.

In Sebald's work, the line between fiction and nonfiction is often blurred. We have the impression that his characters come from the borderlands between the two. Though we can't know if the melancholy Austerlitz is a real or symbolic figure, we walk beside him, compelled by the horror and sadness in his words. Whatever the case may be, it's clear that the author, like his character, must give an account of a hellish era that is fading like mist dispersed in the wind. The story is shot through with a pain impossible to heal, and while the void at its center cannot be filled, the task of learning, of bearing witness, will never be in vain. Oblivion is unceasing and will swallow up everything in its path, unless we devote ourselves to keeping a record of what once was. Future generations have the right to demand the story of the past from us.

Books have a voice, and when they speak, they save eras and lives. Bookstores are magical places where, in an act of inspiration, we hear the soft and crackling echoes of unknown memories.

21

For a long time, alarmists have been making the direst predictions: books are an endangered species and at some point in the near future will disappear, devoured by the competition of other, lazier leisure activities and the cannibalistic expansion of the internet.

The feelings assailing us in the third millennium seem to bear out this forecast. Progress is getting faster and faster. The latest technologies are already pushing aside the triumphant inventions of the day before yesterday. The countdown to obsolescence gets shorter and shorter. Our wardrobes must be updated with seasonal trends, the newest cell phone replaces the old; our devices constantly ask us to update our software and apps. Things swallow up the things that preceded them. If we don't stand guard and watch out, the world will outpace us.

Mass media and social networks reinforce this perception with their dizzying speed. They urge us to admire all the innovations rushing toward us like surfers on the crest of a powerful wave. But historians and anthropologists remind us that in the water's depths, changes are gradual. Víctor Lapuente Giné has written that modern society suffers from a clearly future-oriented bias. When we compare something old and something new—like a book and an iPad or a nun sitting next to a texting teenager on a train—we believe that the new thing has more of a future, when in fact the reverse is true. The longer an object or custom has been with us, the greater its staying power. On average, the newest things die out first. It's more likely that nuns and books will exist in the twenty-second century than WhatsApp and tablet computers. There will be tables and chairs in the future, but maybe not plasma screens or cell phones. We'll be celebrating the winter solstice long after we stop using tanning beds. An invention as ancient as money has a strong chance of outlasting 3D cinema, drones, and electric cars. Many trends that seem irrevocable—from rampant consumerism to social networks—will subside. And old traditions that have been with us since time immemorial—from music to spiritual exploration—will never disappear. In fact, when we visit the world's most socioeconomically advanced countries, what's surprising is their fondness for archaisms—from monarchy, protocol, and social rituals to neoclassical architecture and outdated streetcars.

If Martial could come by a time machine and visit my house today, few of the objects would be familiar to him. He'd be amazed by the elevators, the doorbell, the router, the windowpanes, the fridge, the light bulbs, the microwave, the photos, the electrical outlets, the fan, the kettle, the flushing toilet, the zippers, the forks, and the can opener. The whistling pressure cooker would startle him, and the jolt of the washing machine would make him jump. Disturbed by the voices coming from the radio, he would try to work out where their owners were hiding. He'd be upset by the alarm clock's beeping—just like me, though for a different reason. He wouldn't have the slightest idea at first sight of the purpose of Band-Aids, spray bottles, the corkscrew, the drill, the blow-dryer, the lemon squeezer, the vinyl records, the electric shaver, Velcro fastenings, the stapler, lipstick, sunglasses, the breast pump, or tampons. But he would feel at home among my books. He would recognize them. He would know how to hold them, flip them open, and turn the pages. He would follow the lines with his index finger. He would be relieved—something of his world remains in ours.

This is why I say to the flood of doomsday predictions on the future of the book: hold on a minute. There aren't too many millenary artifacts left among us. The remaining ones are survivors and difficult to displace (the wheel, the chair, the spoon, scissors, the glass, the hammer, the book . . .). Something about their basic design and their pure simplicity leaves no room for dramatic improvements. They have passed many tests—mainly the test of the centuries—without our having found any gadget that does the job better, beyond minor adjustments to their materials or components. In their modest, utilitarian realm, they come close to perfection. This is why I believe that the book—or something very close to what the book has always been, even since before the invention of printing—will remain the essential format for reading.

Furthermore, long-lasting objects, those that have been among us for centuries, shape new inventions, leaving their mark on them. Ancient books were the model for our advanced personal computers. At the end of the 1960s, computers were so large that they occupied entire rooms and cost more than a house. These bulky contraptions that took up so much real estate had to be programmed with perforated cards. They were conceived for military and business use, but Alan Kay, a young computer scientist at Xerox's Palo Alto Research Center, had a vision that would cause our lives to take a spectacular turn. Reflecting on the relationship humans could establish with computers, he intuited their potential as a more personal tool. He understood that they could become a mass phenomenon, that they could be placed in the living room of any house and used by millions of people, regardless of their profession. Kay sketched out what his new computer might look like: it had to be small and portable like a book, accessible and easy to use. He built cardboard models, confident that in a few years the technology would have progressed enough for his idea to be feasible. At PARC, Kay kept developing his vision, which he called the Dynabook. The name indicates what it was going to be: a dynamic book. In other words, something resembling an ancient codex, but interactive and controlled by the reader. It would provide cognitive scaffolding, just as books and printed media had done in previous centuries, with the added advantage of new computing tools.

The first, provisional Dynabooks were called Altos. By the second half of the 1970s, the Alto computer was working. Almost a thousand of these devices were in use, not just at PARC but also in universities, in the United States Congress, and at the White House, all of them gifts from Xerox. A new world was emerging. Despite the Alto's numerous capabilities, in most of these places, they were largely used for dealing with text, design, and communication—essentially, as books with the capacity to compute. In 1979, Steve Jobs visited PARC and was astonished by what he saw. The Alto's aesthetic was integrated into all subsequent Apple computers, and today its essential appearance remains present in the newest products. Laptops, tablets, and smartphones have gone further in the quest for a computer as light, compact, and portable as a pocket-sized book.

In 1984, the calligrapher Sumner Stone became the first director of typography at Adobe. He hired a team of designers and asked them to find new sources, suggesting they seek inspiration in the most ancient traditions. The program Adobe Originals selected three stylistic exemplars in the evolution of calligraphy prior to printing. Lithos, a form inspired by Greek lettering—the designer studied the dedicatory inscription on the Temple of Athena Polias, now in the British Museum; Trajan, a meticulous attempt to re-create the letters from Trajan's Column in Rome; and Charlemagne, which, despite its name, was inspired by the capital letters in the Anglo-Saxon Benedictional of Saint Æthelwold. The Western manuscript tradition thus arrived in the digital era. In the 1980s, Adobe also developed the programming language PostScript, whose appearance on the screen was much like that of a paper page. With the introduction of the PDF or portable document format in 1993, Adobe took a step further, making it possible to mark up an electronic document just as one would a typed or handwritten original. And it consolidated an understanding of the whole architecture of a document that was inspired by ancient books.

These were smart decisions. Without introducing at least a certain connection between the look and feel of the ancient world (on paper) and the new one (on the screen) computers would have looked like alien artifacts to their earliest users. Without an identifiable kind of visual organization and an affinity to ordinary documents, no one would have understood so quickly just how useful the new medium could be. This is the paradox of technological progress: preserving a few traditional coordinates—page structure, typographical conventions, letterforms, and limited layouts—was key to opening the way to the digital realm's transformative changes. It's a mistake to think that every invention erases and replaces traditions. The future always progresses with one eye on the past.

22

In 1976, the Bosnian writer Izet Sarajlić wrote a poem called "Letter to the Year 2176." "What? / Do you still listen to Mendelssohn? / Do you still pick daisies? / Do you still have children's birthday parties? / Do you still name streets after poets? / And they assured me two centuries back, in the seventies, that the days of poetry were gone—just like matching suits, or studying the stars, or dances at the Rostovs' house / And I, being an idiot, nearly believed them!"

23

The "page book," which today is a book by definition—the kind we prop open, spine facing upward, like a pagoda roof; the kind in which we save our place by dog-earing the page when we don't have a bookmark; the kind we pile up in vertical stacks like stalagmites made of words—is around two thousand years old. It is a great anonymous invention for which we will never know whom to thank. It took centuries of searching and trial and error to make it happen. As with so many things, to reach the simplest solution, it was necessary to travel a tortuous path.

From the invention of writing onward, our ancestors looked around, wondering what surface would best preserve the transient imprint of letters (stone, clay, bark, reeds, animal skin, wood, ivory, cloth, metal . . .). They sought to defy the forces of oblivion by making the perfect book—portable, durable, and easy to use. In the Near East and Europe, papyrus or parchment scrolls and hard tablets were the protagonists of this early stage. The Romans used both methods in parallel, until, in a happy discovery, they invented the new hybrid object still with us today.

Scrolls were always an expensive luxury product. For the most ordinary writing—schoolwork, letters, official documents, notes, and drafts—the ancients generally used tablets. The reader who wished to consult them in a particular order kept them in boxes or bags or pierced their corners and tied them together with rings or straps. As we have seen, these sets of tablets strung together were known as codices. The revolutionary idea was to replace the small plaques of wood or metal with flexible sheets of papyrus or parchment, the materials used for scrolls. The initial result must have been little more than a notebook, which, though rudimentary, was ripe with possibilities.

That first hybrid opened the way for the more advanced codex, made of sheets of papyrus or pieces of animal skin folded over in two. The Romans tried sewing these folios together, and thus the art of bookbinding was born. They soon learned to protect these booklets with hard covers, generally made of wood covered with leather. The book's body gained a new anatomical component we call the spine, as if the object we read were a peaceful animal keeping us company. Since then, the title of each work is written on the tamed backs of those creatures, and our eyes can travel quickly along the library shelves, identifying the volumes that rest there by reading their spines.

We are indebted to the forgotten people who invented the codex. Thanks to them, the life expectancy of texts increased. With this new format, the written page, protected by its binding, could last longer than scrolls without tearing or disintegrating. Due to their flat and compact form, these new books could easily be stored on cabinet shelves. They were light, took up less space, and were easy to transport. On top of that, both sides of each page could be used. With the same surface, an estimated six times more text could fit into a codex than onto a scroll. The savings in material lowered the price of an item still only within the reach of a minority, and its flexibility allowed the first pocket-sized books we know of to appear: the *pugillares* codices, so called because they could be held in a fist. The codices could be as small as a miniature in size (Cicero claimed to have seen a parchment of Homer's *Iliad* that fit into a nutshell).

New inventions and advancements in materials usually go hand in hand with great revolutions in knowledge. In Roman civilization, more affordable books allowed many people beyond circles of privilege to read. Between the first and third centuries, there is abundant proof of the expansion of culture to readers who weren't part of the aristocracy. On the walls and houses of Pompeii archaeologists have found inscriptions including jokes, obscenities, political slogans, and advertisements for brothels. This graffiti reveals that there was a middle or lower middle class that could understand the written word. Furthermore, all over the empire, the mosaics, frescoes, and carvings of the era more and more frequently depict scenes of reading. In the same years, Roman public libraries flourished. We know of a bookseller who offered his wares from door to door, like the obsolete encyclopedia salesmen of modern times.

It's risky to speculate about figures, but it seems clear that the number of readers grew remarkably. Those first centuries of the millennium were a golden age for proselytizing pamphlets—notably the subversive texts of those rebelling against Rome's dominance. Nor is it coincidental that, beyond the traditional genres, escapist and consumerist texts also became popular (including treatises on sports and cooking, erotic tales with explicit illustrations, texts on magic or the interpretation of dreams, horoscopes, farces, and stories told in vignettes that were forerunners of the graphic novel). Some prestigious authors amused themselves by writing frivolous works or hybrid texts combining high and low culture. Ovid anticipated today's makeup tutorials by publishing a book in verse of cosmetic advice for women. Suetonius loved to mix history and sensationalistic, tabloid-style news in his biographies of emperors. Petronius scandalized polite society with the unscrupulous, foul-mouthed rogues who populated his work. All three were well-disposed to those new, free, nonaristocratic, untrained readers—men and women who read for pleasure.

24

Martial was a Hispanic immigrant to Rome. In the year 64, when he was about twenty-five, he moved to what was then the capital of opportunity—a precursor of the American Dream—to which waves of people were arriving from every province of the empire. He soon discovered that the city was a tough place. In his poems he speaks of the masses, pale with hunger. It wasn't easy to make a fortune or even to make a living. In one epigram, Martial says there were many lawyers in Rome who couldn't pay their rent, and many talented poets shivering without enough clothes on their backs. The competition was fierce; everyone wanted to strike it rich. The wealth of others was observed and envied. People were on the hunt for inheritance, stalking and sucking up to elderly plutocrats. The poet himself had this idea in mind, if we are to believe his words:

"Paula wishes to marry me; I don't want to marry Paula: she's old. I'd change my mind, if she were older."

Martial's teeth must have chattered when he wore his threadbare tunic in the Roman winters. Perhaps the cold, the sordid accommodations, and the difficulty of getting ahead explain his unusual literary choices. The poet decided to break the silence dictated by convention and direct his mockery at money. In his poetry, flouting the demands of gentility, he set out to satirize stingy patrons and the intellectuals determined to fleece them, society's taste for opulence and flaunting wealth, the vanity of the rich, and the great network of masters and minions in which the lives of all the imperial capital's inhabitants were embroiled. Martial was an irreverent and unsentimental comic poet, interested in the material dimension of things and their immense power to define those who possessed them. When he mentioned books in his poems, these weren't abstract symbols of literary talent, but concrete objects sold in bookstores or given as gifts in attempts at social climbing. In his epigrams, those books—which in the works of Horace and Ovid embodied the immortality of the creative act—whether cheap or expensive, were perishable volumes, well thumbed, and often defective due to the copyist's haste. These books that appeared for sale in Roman shops—shops that Martial takes the opportunity to advertise in his work—were books of all kinds (made of papyrus or parchment, scrolls or codices that could fit in one hand and travel around with their reader; books that earned or lost money for a freedman, their seller; successful books everyone wanted to read for free but for which they weren't willing to pay; unread books that ended up in a blackened kitchen, their pages used to wrap tuna or turned into a cone to store pepper).

Martial was the first author to show interest in the emergence of codices. He did so with one of his earliest books, ironically titled *The Apophoreta*, a grandiose word meaning "gift" in Greek. The poet had the brilliant idea of publishing catalogs of gift ideas in verse in December—the universal gift-giving season. Martial dedicated an epigram to each product (culinary treats, books, cosmetics, hair dyes, clothing, lingerie, kitchen implements, decorative objects . . .), informing the reader of its materials, price, characteristics, or uses. The repertoire of gifts in the book was organized in an order alternating between expensive suggestions (for the rich) and cheap ones (for the miserly rich): a gold brooch and an ear cleaner; a statue and a corset; a slave woman from Cádiz and a rattle; the latest fashionable extravagance—a beautiful bottle for drinking snow—and a clay urinal. These poems allow us to catch a glimpse of daily life in antiquity and to be amazed by Martial's shameless ease with erotic subjects. On the corset, he says, "Strap your chestful with the skin of a bull, for your own skin can't hold it in." And of the dancer from Cádiz: "Such sexy dances does she innovate that purity itself must masturbate."

The Apophoreta was a humorous handbook for the indecisive, a surprising poetic exercise applied to the needs of daily life. In a certain sense the poet was inventing the Christmas commercial, but he did so with a biting literary gesture. In his day, this entailed a base, transgressive, and frivolous use of verse. With this catalog book, Martial expressed his liking for the reading public who were new to the world of books, who appreciated easy poetry, a lack of snobbery, unrestrained humor, familiar touches of realism, and audacity; the readers who were a natural audience for the codices.

In *The Apophoreta*, Martial suggested fourteen literary works to the unsuspecting reader. Five of them, described as "pocket" codices on parchment—*pugillares membranei*—occupied the category of cheap gifts. Thanks to this document, we know that by the eighties of the first century, books with pages were on the market, and at an affordable price. Their advantages, beyond economics, were clear. Several epigrams express wonder at the codex's greater capacity, in implicit comparison with scrolls: "Virgil in parchment. How poor a parchment has contained the mighty Virgil!" "Titus Livius in parchment. The great Livy, squashed into scanty skins." Martial remarked that the fifteen books—equivalent to fifteen scrolls—of Ovid's *Metamorphoses* could fit into a single codex. This compression didn't just mean savings in space and money, but it guaranteed that the parts of a single work would not be scattered and lost. The codices therefore exponentially increased the survival chances of works of literature. This progress would turn out to be decisive on the difficult road ahead.

The poet recognized in the codex an easy and portable travel companion: "Cicero in parchment. If you should travel with this parchment, think of it as a long journey with Cicero." Years later, he would also promote the codex version of his own poems, with the same argument: "You, who wish my little books could be everywhere with you, and wish to have them as companions on a long journey, buy these which are squeezed into small parchment pages. Leave big books for the library; I can be grasped with only one hand."

The book as we know it, with pages, had burst onto the market. Some authors, like Martial, welcomed it with enthusiasm. Other, more old-fashioned intellectuals clung to the aristocratic papyrus scroll, lamenting that the times were changing and everything was in decline. Presumably, most Romans simply got used to the variety of formats. In the booksellers' workshops, both were available, and customers had a choice. For the centuries that followed, we no longer have a witness as attentive, curious, and open to novelty as Martial. We know that the codex gained ground on the scroll due to the Christians' marked preference for it. Victims of persecution for centuries, forced to suddenly end their meetings and go into hiding, they organized themselves in small clandestine groups. The pocket-sized book was easier to hide in a hurry in the folds of one's tunic. It allowed for a specific paragraph to be found more quickly—an epistle, a Gospel parable, a homily—and checked to make sure it was correct, since a mistake could endanger the soul's salvation. Notes could be made in the margin and important passages flagged with a bookmark. Furthermore, these books were easy to carry in secret on proselytizing journeys. All these were enormous advantages for communities of furtive readers. Beside this, the Christians wished to break with the Jewish and pagan symbolism of the scroll, affirming their own distinctive identity. Lightweight books with pages began to circulate in abundance through the eager hands of readers of average or below average education, where the Christian message was finding the most converts. The new format favored covert individual reading, as well as reading aloud at dangerous communal meetings. The faithful developed a profound link to those carefully selected religious texts. In fact, centuries later, the Koran would describe Christians as "People of the Book" (Ahl al-Kitāb) with a mixture of respect and astonishment.

Those of us who have ever read in secret, defying the grown-ups' prohibition—under the cover of night, when children ought to be sleeping, beneath the camouflage of the blanket with a flashlight, turning it off every time steps drew near—are direct descendants of those earliest furtive readers. We shouldn't forget that books with pages triumphed, to a certain extent, because they were the best format for clandestine, forbidden, unauthorized reading material.

25

The codex grew prevalent between the third and fifth centuries, first in the West and then in the East. Outside the Christian world, the change was spearheaded by lawyers, since the page format allowed them to locate specific articles more expeditiously in their legal catalogs. In fact, the compilation of laws ordered by the emperor Justinian was called the Code—in other words, the codex par excellence—a term inherited by all legal compendiums since. The codex was also a convenient format for textbooks due to its durability and capaciousness and was soon embraced by doctors for their often-consulted manuals. The invention of the contents page made it easier to search. In time, the codex became the preferred format for literary works, especially for long narratives, groups of tragedies or comedies, and anthologies. The scroll was unwieldy and required the use of both hands, but dreamy readers fell in love with the codex and its pages, which, to use Luis García Berlanga's description of erotic literature, could be read with just one hand. The codex could go anywhere with its reader. We know from literary sources that the Romans felt at liberty to read whenever they liked: while hunting, as they waited for their prey to fall into their net, or at night, to overcome the boredom of insomnia. Writings of the era describe a woman who reads as she walks, or a traveler in his carriage, or a reclining dinner guest and an adolescent girl in a gallery, all absorbed in their books.

But there was never a compulsive drive to replace the old with the new. Just as paper and electronic books coexist today, the scroll and the codex existed for centuries side by side. Those ancient writing cylinders were used for honorary and diplomatic texts—formal documents where the weight of tradition could still be felt. They were also part of the landscape of daily life in medieval times, when institutions and monastic orders used them out of fondness for ancient solemnity. Litanies and chronicles lent themselves to being copied in the old format. Scrolls even pop up in their rival's pages—they can be seen in the miniature illustrations that illuminated the most sumptuous medieval codices.

The so-called *rotuli mortuorum* were parchment scrolls on which the death of a person of note was announced. A messenger would travel along routes sometimes longer than a thousand kilometers, carrying the scroll to a range of institutions connected in some way to the deceased, at each of which a prayer or other expression of condolence was added. *The Mortuary Roll of Matilda,* which honored the daughter of William the Conqueror and abbess of Holy Trinity, Caen, grew to twenty meters long and was destroyed in the French Revolution. The keeper of the chancery records at the Senior Courts of England and Wales is still called Master of the Rolls. In the absence of a prompt, medieval theater actors would use scrolls to jog their memories during performances. This is the origin of the term for an actor's "role."

In fact, scrolls haven't completely disappeared. Their memory persists in our traditions, but also in our words, in our computers, on the internet, and in our visions of the future. Some universities still award their diplomas in this old-fashioned guise. When we speak of a book being "long" or "extensive," we have unwittingly inherited the specific terminology of the scroll. We call codices "volumes"—from the Latin *volvo*, "to turn" or "to roll"—though the term is unfitting, since we no longer roll them up. In colloquial Spanish, we still call something that bores us, that seems to unfurl on and on without end "*un rollo.*" And in English today, the word "scroll" is used to describe the act of moving text up and down on the screen of any electronic device, just as the old *rotuli* were handled. The most innovative technology companies are developing TV screens that can be rolled up and stored when not in use. Throughout the history of these different formats, the standard is coexistence and specialization, not replacement. The earliest books refuse to become completely extinct.

26

Martial and Perec were right: the materiality of objects, their characteristics, and the gestures that accompany them are more than just incidental details. In fact, they are decisive. In the fight for the survival of words—so fragile, just wisps of air—books' format and raw materials have always played a vital role, determining how long they last, how much they cost, and how often they need to be copied.

Changes in format leave enormous numbers of victims by the wayside. Anything not transferred from the old to the new disappears forever, and the danger still lingers today. After the arrival of the first computers in the 1980s, if we couldn't roll over our technological memory when we changed from the original floppy to the 3.5-inch disk, then to the CD, and later to the flash drive, we lost part or all of our information a thousand times over. No computer can now read the earliest disks, which belong to the prehistoric era of information technology.

In the twentieth century, cinema suffered a series of destructive changes in format. Agustín Sánchez Vidal offers an estimate of these losses: "The material most affected is from prior to 1920; around that year, those movies are destroyed when the transition is made from one or two reels (between ten and thirty minutes) to the standard length of an hour and a half. Emulsion is saved for its silver salts, and the cellulose substrate used for making combs and other objects. Approximately 80 percent of films were lost due to this shift. Around 1930, almost 70 percent of films were lost to another, even more systematic wave of destruction, due to the transition from silent film to movies with sound. The third wave takes place in the fifties, when flammable cellulose nitrate film is replaced with the safer acetate. In this case, the losses are difficult to quantify. Taking Spain as an example, only about 50 percent of the movies from the sound period up to 1954 were preserved." Every step of progress has also brought devastation.

Martin Scorsese re-created this tragic calamity in his film *Hugo,* based on the book *The Invention of Hugo Cabret* by Brian Selznick. I recall a particular melancholy scene where the celluloid of the delicious films of Georges Méliès ends up repurposed by the footwear industry to make heels for shoes. This is a curious chapter in the history of objects: the beautiful stories and images that lived in the minds of cinema's pioneers ended up being recycled into combs and heels. In the 1920s, people walked upon works of art, plunging them into puddles along the sidewalk. They combed their hair with these works, leaving traces of dandruff. Never did they suspect that these tools were in fact tiny tombs, daily monuments to destruction.

There is no doubt that with the replacement of ancient scrolls, a trove of poems, chronicles, adventures, stories, and ideas were lost to us forever. Throughout the centuries, carelessness and forgetting have destroyed more books than censorship and fanaticism. But we also know of great efforts to save the legacy of words. Certain libraries—it's impossible to know how many—embarked on the patient task of transcribing their holdings into the format that survived, copying them out again by hand, stroke by stroke, phrase by phrase, book by book. In the fourth century, the philosopher and statesman Themistius wrote that there were artisans working for Constantius II in the Constantinople library who were capable of "transferring thought from one worn out package to a new one, recently made." In the fifth century, Saint Jerome mentioned another library in the Roman city of Caesarea—on the Mediterranean coast of what is now Israel, between Tel Aviv and Haifa—where they had also carried out the task of transferring all their books to the codex format.

For twenty centuries, until the recent appearance of tablets and ebooks, readers suffered no other seismic change in format. The books with pages Martial welcomed enthusiastically in the first century remain with us in the twenty-first, simple and faithful, preserving our memory, holding our wisdom, and resisting the ravages of time.

27

On March 15 in the year 44 BC—the Ides of March, according to the Roman calendar—Julius Caesar was stabbed to death at the Senate in front of the statue of his old enemy Pompey, which was left spattered with blood. A group of senators sank their daggers repeatedly into the fifty-five-year-old's body—into his neck, back, chest, and belly—in the name of freedom. The last movement Caesar made, when he saw knives raised all around him, was a gesture of modesty. In his final throes and blinded by blood, he took the trouble to pull his tunic down over his legs, to die a nobler death without showing his sex. The daggers kept piercing him savagely as he lay defenseless at the portico steps. He was stabbed twenty-three times. According to Suetonius, only one of these wounds was mortal.

The conspirators liked to refer to themselves as "the liberators." To them, Caesar was a tyrant who aspired to be king. That political assassination, perhaps the most famous crime in history, has awakened as much admiration as disgust. It's no coincidence that, nineteen hundred years later, John Wilkes Booth used the word "ides" in his diary as a key for the day he killed Abraham Lincoln, or that as he fled the scene of the crime, Booth cried out a phrase in Latin, *Sic semper tyrannis*: ("Thus always to tyrants").

Was Julius Caesar a tyrant in the making? He was, without a doubt, a charismatic general and an unscrupulous politician. Some of his contemporaries labeled his campaigns in Gaul a genocide. It's true that, in his later years, he made less and less effort to disguise his gigantic ambition. He had declared himself dictator for life and granted himself the right to wear the attire of victory whenever he pleased—his laurel crown, the perfect solution for hiding his bald patch. Since then, his name has always indicated authoritarian power (caesar, czar). But his murder did not save the republic. The crime of the ides was a savage and bloody act that failed to achieve any of its goals. It unleashed a long civil war, more deaths, and even further destruction, upon the smoking ruins of which, in the end, Augustus founded the imperial monarchy. The young emperor, heir and successor to his uncle, had a concrete structure erected to mark and cover the scene of the crime. Today, all these centuries later, Roman street cats huddle in the Largo di Torre Argentina, the place where Julius Caesar breathed his last.

As collateral damage of the Ides of March, impoverished readers lost out. Among his other plans Caesar had envisioned building the first public library in Rome, more splendid than anything seen before it, and charged Marcus Terentius Varro with acquiring and organizing the books. It was a logical appointment, since Varro had written an essay titled *On Libraries,* of which only a few fragments survive.

Years later, one of Caesar's followers, Asinius Pollio, made his dream a reality with the substantial fruits of a military looting expedition. He established a library in the same building that housed—fittingly—a shrine to the goddess Libertas. We know of this first public temple of books only from passing references by several writers, since its remains have vanished without a trace. We know that the inner space was split into two sections, one for works in Greek and another for works in Latin. This bilingual two-part organization would be repeated in all subsequent Roman libraries. National pride dictated that the two sections have exactly the same dimensions, even though, for the moment, one was full to bursting and the other reproachfully empty. While some seven centuries of Greek texts existed, for the Roman section there were only two centuries of literature to choose from. Overlooking such trifles, the message Pollio's official library conveyed was double-edged: Greek works were incorporated into the Roman tradition in their own language; in exchange, it was necessary to pretend that the powerful empire's rulers were as worthy as their brilliant Hellenic subjects. No aspect of the staging ought to betray that in fact the colonizers had an inferiority complex about the overwhelming intellectual legacy of a conquered territory.

Another feature that all Roman libraries would inherit were statues of famous authors. In Rome, those busts in public spaces were the literary equivalent of the stars on the Hollywood Walk of Fame. Whoever received this homage had entered the canon. Pollio commissioned only one portrait of a living author for his library: Marcus Varro. Decades later, the foul-mouthed Martial, who kept a keen watch on the parade of ambitions at the Roman vanity fair, boasted that his bust already adorned several aristocratic mansions. In truth he longed for a statue in the galleries of distinguished figures at the public libraries. All evidence seems to suggest that, just as they have for those eternal Nobel Prize hopefuls, the doors remained closed to him. His epigrams are packed with cadging refrains, openly begging for honors, money, or flattery, but in general, as he said himself with humor and self-directed irony, his hopes led only to monumental disappointment.

Asinius Pollio's library is sure to have been open from dawn to midday and must have been used by a varied public: writers, scholars, general lovers of knowledge, but also copyists sent by booksellers or by their masters, with the task of making copies from the library's holdings. There were probably specialized staff to retrieve books from the cabinets. We also know that some libraries allowed borrowing, since the writer Aulus Gellius tells a story that proves it. Gellius had gathered with some friends to dine and converse. When the assembled company were served a drink of melted snow, a guest who was an expert in Aristotle warned them that, in the philosopher's view, it was bad for one's health. When someone denied that this was the case, the stubborn diner, his pride wounded, took the trouble to go to the city library, persuaded them to open it for him, and came back with a copy of the work containing the paragraph in question. In this laborious way, discussions were settled before the existence of search engines. The emperor Marcus Aurelius and his tutor Fronto mention taking borrowed books home in their letters. In addition to these casual accounts, an inscription in Athens from the imperial period states that the directors prohibited borrowing, from which we can deduce that in other establishments it was allowed. The inscription reads, word for word, "No book shall leave this place; we have thus decreed it."

The next two public libraries in Rome were built by Augustus, one on Palatine Hill and one in the Porticus Octaviae. Archaeologists have found remains of the Palatine library. Thanks to their excavations, we have a reliable picture of its architectural design and interior. Two adjacent rooms of identical size have been found that housed the bilingual collection. In both, the books were stored in large, recessed wood cabinets with shelves and doors, and were numbered with figures corresponding to the catalog. Given the height of the cabinet's niches, there must have been small portable ladders for reaching the highest shelves. As a whole, the building is more reminiscent of our contemporary reading rooms than of Greek libraries, where there were no facilities for readers. Greek readers would select a scroll from the shelves and take it into an adjacent portico. In Rome, the shelves were designed to offer a beautiful, ample, and luxurious ambiance. The books lay in the cabinets, within arm's reach but still out of the way. There were tables, chairs, carved wood, marble: a feast for the eyes, a lavishly appointed space.

As the collections grew, new cabinets were needed. Storage problems became difficult to resolve since the niches for books were integral to the buildings' architectural structure and therefore couldn't be fashioned ad hoc. New libraries had to be built. The emperor Tiberius added one or two during his reign, and Vespasian built another in the Temple of Peace, probably to celebrate, with books and fanfare, having quashed the Great Jewish Revolt with fire and bloodshed.

The best-preserved remains are those of the twin libraries built on Trajan's orders in the year 112 as part of his monumental forum. The Greek and Latin rooms faced each other, separated by a portico at whose center the famous Trajan's Column still stands. Archaeologists believe that the emblematic monument represents a great stone scroll, with its thirty-eight meters of full-color scenes of the Dacian Wars in low relief, like vignettes in a military comic. The story of the campaigns unfolds in a continuous strip that ascends in a spiral: thousands of painstakingly sculpted Romans and Dacians marching, building, fighting, sailing, fleeing, negotiating, begging, and perishing in 155 scenes—a veritable graphic novel.

The interior of the two libraries was an opulent wonder, open to the whole public: two floors of cabinets, columns, galleries, cornices, marble veneers from Asia Minor, and statues. I imagine the faces of ordinary people dumbstruck at a display of beauty and amenities that were until then a prerogative of the aristocracy, and a collection of some twenty thousand books accessible to any reader. Thanks to Trajan, the first Hispanic emperor, it was no longer necessary in Rome to court the rich to be able to read in a sumptuous setting.

28

Trajan's library was the last of its kind, since from the second century on, new reading rooms were incorporated into imperial public baths. Apart from offering all the services of thermal baths—a tepidarium, a caldarium, saunas, a cold plunge, and massage rooms—these buildings became genuine leisure complexes, forerunners of the community centers of today. Caracalla's thermal baths, inaugurated in the year 212, included gymnasiums, spaces for reading, conversation rooms, a theater, the baths themselves, gardens, dedicated spaces for exercise or games, eating establishments, and separate Greek and Latin libraries, all funded by the state.

By building these magnificent free baths the emperors conquered their subjects. "What could be worse than Nero?" Martial wondered, "but what could be better than Nero's baths?" All Romans, men and women, young and old, rich and poor, frequented them. Some of them bathed and stretched out on the massage beds, others played ball or passed judgment on their neighbor's game, proffering unsolicited advice. They went to lectures, chatted with friends, gossiped behind their acquaintances' backs, railed against municipal taxes, grumbled about the price of grain, stuffed their faces with sausages, and browsed in the library. The philosopher Seneca, who grew exasperated trying to concentrate in his office located right above some baths, wrote an amusing description of the merriment and joy at these facilities: "When the athletes lift their leaden weights, I hear them whistling, panting, and gasping for breath. I hear the masseur's hand as he slaps someone's back. Then if a ball player shows up and starts keeping count, I'm done for. Then add to that some rowdy fellow, a thief getting caught for his crimes, and the ones leaping into the pool making a great racket as they splash around. Think of the tweezer man's shrill cry to get the attention of customers, and the customers' pained cries when he plucks their armpits. And then come the drink seller, the sausage man, the pastry man, and all the other salesmen announcing their wares in their own peculiar tones." Undoubtedly the perfect conditions for the author of the reflections on serenity in *De tranquillitate animi*.

Unlike the exquisite forum libraries, the reading rooms at the baths catered to the tastes of a broad, varied, and frivolous public. Their readers must have been, first and foremost, curious people in search of entertainment who turned to books as an alternative to ball games, a dip in the water, or light conversation. We can assume that the book collections mostly contained renowned classics in both languages, fashionable contemporary authors, and perhaps the occasional philosopher. The establishment of libraries located in packed Roman baths was an enormous achievement. It brought together culture, entertainment, business, and education in a lively fusion, all under one roof. It implied an enormous drive to make books widespread, placing them in popular, bustling surroundings that did not intimidate inexperienced readers.

Furthermore, the libraries at the baths took reading to every corner of the empire. Leisure centers weren't limited to the capital but formed a robust network that covered the length and breadth of the territories conquered by the Romans. In fact, some specialists believe bath culture to have been the only shared public institution that united distant imperial citizens.

Enjoying the pleasures of the water became such a hallmark of pagan culture and Roman civilization that the strictest Christians disapproved of the baths as a symptom of sybaritism, sensuality, and spiritual corruption. A letter from a fifth-century country monk has been preserved that states, "We do not want to wash in the baths." Holy men understood stinking as a measure of ascetic devotion and rejected cleanliness in opposition to the Roman way of life. Simeon Stylites, affected by a serious illness, refused to be touched by water, and "so strong and fetid was the stench that it was impossible to go even halfway up the stairs without feeling unwell. Some of the disciples who wished to go close to him couldn't go up until they had smeared incense and fragrant ointments on their noses." After spending two years in a cave, Theodore of Sykeon emerged "with such a stink that no one could stand to be near him." Clement of Alexandria wrote that a good Gnostic Christian does not wish to

smell nice: "He rejects the pleasures of the theater and other refinements and luxuries, like perfumes that flatter the nostrils, or alluring
wines that seduce the palate, or fragrant garlands made of different
flowers that weaken the soul by way of the senses." In those days, the
"smell of holiness" was fetid.

Despite all this, leaving aside the stringent minorities, inhabitants of the imperial provinces enthusiastically embraced the pleasures of bathing, and the thermal baths brought with them, among
other pastimes and luxuries, a wave of books.

29

The city of the twenty-nine libraries: a catalog of Rome's
emblematic libraries dating to the year 350 mentions that precise figure. Outside the capital, on the other hand, it's difficult to follow the
trail of books. We have only patchy, incomplete, sometimes puzzling
information. In Pompeii, archaeologists discovered the remains of
a reading room. An inscription in the city of Comum (present-day
Como) recalls that the writer Pliny the Younger donated a library
and the sum of one hundred thousand sestertii for its upkeep to his
city of origin. Another inscription found on the coast not far from
Naples speaks of a library funded by Matidia, the emperor Hadrian's mother-in-law. There are also scattered traces of other donated
public collections in Tibur (now Tivoli) and in Volsinii (Orvieto).

The money that financed these collections generally came not
from the public treasury, but from the coffers of generous donors.
Throughout antiquity, an unwritten obligation fell on the rich to
spend part of their wealth on their community: to finance circus
games, build amphitheaters, pave roads, or construct aqueducts. If,
as Balzac wrote, behind every great fortune there is always a crime,
to the ancients, investing in collective improvements seemed like the
best compensation to society for those initial misdeeds. The initials
DSPF (*de sua pecunia fecit*) often appear beside a citizen's name on
public works. These philanthropic displays weren't always strictly
voluntary: magnates reluctant to contribute were pressured and
couldn't refuse for long, since they ran the risk of losing their prestige. If a stingy millionaire needed a gentle nudge to open his purse,

the plebeians would gather outside his door, singing sarcastic rhymes and mocking him. It's highly possible that the occasional provincial library originated in one of these ancient cases of public shaming.

In the Greek-speaking area of the empire, there had been public libraries since the Hellenistic era. The Roman emperors supported those prestigious centers of learning, investing in the collections at Alexandria and Pergamum. The venerable city of Athens gained two new libraries in the second century, one of them a gift from Hadrian and the other from a fellow citizen who funded a portico, a room full of books, and all of its decoration "with his own money"—so says an inscription—which he did emphatically and with a pocket apparently still smarting from the expense. In Ephesus, a Tiberian by the name of Julius Celsus erected a library in memory of his father, a great lover of books.

Meanwhile, by this standard, the West seems at first sight an enormous wasteland. In the entire region that today encompasses England, Spain, France, and the north coast of Africa, there is proof of the existence of libraries in only two places: Carthage, in what is now Tunisia, and Timgad, in present-day Algeria. We know of the first because a writer mentions it and the second thanks to archaeological excavations.

It's true that according to the stereotypes of the age, the heart of civilization lay in the East, while inhabitants of the West were mired in barbarity, hardship, and ignorance. In every era the most formidable powers construct geographical oppositions—north/south, east/west—not allowing the facts to spoil a good prejudice. In ancient times, western Europe was home to highly sophisticated cultures, nearly all of which were destroyed by their civilized invaders. In any case, by the beginning of the imperial age, Roman globalization had lessened the differences between territories. The architects and engineers of Rome thoroughly urbanized the West, replacing native villages with a network of cities large and small and furnished with sewers, aqueducts, temples, forums, and baths. There had to be books in those cities. In those years, written culture, though not as deeply rooted as in the Greek world, spread through Romanized communities. There were schoolteachers who taught Latin in the main villages, while in larger centers of population, secondary education and rhetoric were offered. In capitals like Carthage or Marseille, the richest inhabitants could take the equivalent of a university degree at the time. Martial, who was born in the Celtiberian Bilbilis and arrived in Rome at twenty, showed an exceptional command of the Latin tongue. If not in the town of his birth, he surely had access to a library in Caesaraugusta or in Tarraco. And just like Bilbilis or Caesaraugusta, dozens of significant Western population centers were home to citizens—men and women—who had wealth, cultural ambitions, and a thirst for books.

When I walk through the streets of my hometown, with their Roman layout, I think of how, like in the magical Oxford, a great library is sleeping somewhere underground. Flattened by the noise of the streets, beneath the asphalt and the rush, trampled upon and looted a thousand times over, the last remnants of the niches where our remote ancestors came to know books must undoubtedly survive.

TWO MEN FROM HISPANIA

The First Fan and the Aging Writer

30

The image of teenagers screaming, sobbing, and fainting at the arrival of their musical idols wasn't born with Elvis or the Beatles. In fact, the phenomenon didn't even emerge with rock and roll, but with classical music. The castrati of the eighteenth century were already awakening passions from the stage. And in the civilized concert halls of the nineteenth century, a Hungarian pianist who shook his mane as he hunched over the keys caused a genuine mass delirium known as Lisztomania, or "Liszt fever." If fans throw underwear at rock stars' faces, they threw jewels at Franz Liszt. He was the sex symbol of the Victorian era. It was said at the time that his swaying and studied poses as he played caused rapture in his audience. First a child prodigy and then a histrionic young artist, he starred in tours across the continent that made millions. At Liszt's public appearances, fans flocked around him, screaming, sighing, and swooning.

They followed him from capital to capital where he gave concerts, wearing his portrait on brooches and cameos. They tried to steal his personal effects, and some women even attempted to snip off locks of his hair. Each time a string snapped in the piano, fierce battles broke out to seize it so it could be fashioned into a bracelet. Some admirers stalked him in the street and in cafés, decanting the dregs from his coffee cup into glass vials they kept. On one occasion, a woman retrieved the butt of his cigar from beside the piano's pedal and wore it at her breast, inside a medallion, until the day she died. In its first use ever, the word "celebrity" was applied to him.

Despite all this, we can go even farther back in time. Without a doubt, the first international stars were a group of writers from the Roman imperial age: Titus Livius, Virgil, Horace, Propertius, and Ovid.

In fact, the first known fan in history was a Hispanic from Gades who was obsessed with meeting his idol, the historian Titus Livius. We're told he set out on a dangerous journey at the beginning of the first century, "from the remotest corner of the world"—present-day Cádiz—to Rome, to see his favorite artist with his own astonished eyes. Assuming he traveled by land, the devoted man from Gades needed over forty days for the pilgrimage to see his hero, enduring terrible food and the torture of lice in dusty inns, clattering along on old nags and in decrepit carts, shaking with fear at the highwaymen lurking in lonely forests. He traveled the roads of the empire, lined with the corpses of executed bandits impaled on stakes and rotting away at the scenes of their crimes. By night, he prayed that the slaves escorting him would not flee or turn against him in a foreign land. He emptied several bags of money along the way. He grew gaunt due to severe diarrhea caused by foul water. As soon as he arrived in Rome, he asked for the famous Livy. He caught a glimpse of him from afar, perhaps taking in how he did his hair and wore his toga, so as to copy him, and, not daring even to address him, he turned on his heel and went home—another forty-day journey. Pliny the Younger told the story in one of his letters, unaware that he was describing the earliest known celebrity stalker.

Roman globalization gave rise to readerships far away from the city of Rome. Horace boasted that his books were known in the Bosporus, in Libya, in what is now the Caucasus and Hungary, in the land of the Rhine, and in Hispania. Propertius affirmed that his glory had reached the wintry shores of the Borysthenes River, today's Dnieper in eastern Europe. Ovid wrote plainly and without a hint of false modesty that he was widely read "all over the world." In general, the Romans tended to confuse the borders of their empire with those of the planet. It's a typical feature of imperial visions. The Akkadian king Sargon the Great, whose domain extended from the Persian Gulf to the Mediterranean, boasted of having conquered the entire world. In the case of Roman writers, geographic inaccuracies and cockalorum aside, it was indeed true that the borders of reading were expanding at an astonishing pace: successful books were beginning to cross continents, seas, deserts, mountains, and jungles, during their authors' lifetimes. Ideas and words were circulating along modern roads. Martial's books could be bought in Vienna and Britannia; Pliny the Younger's in a bookstore in Lyon. Juvenal, a conservative averse to the new inclusive global culture, was outraged to imagine a filthy Cantabrian with Roman philosophy books in his barbarian hands: "These days, the whole world has its Greek and Roman culture. Eloquent Gaul has trained Britons as men of law, and now in Thule, they speak of hiring a rhetorician. Where was there ever a Cantabrian Stoic, in the age of old Metellus?"

In the capital, both natives and outsiders could spot the most famous writers in the street and stalked them just like the admirers and groupies of today. Virgil, who suffered from pathological shyness, often fled groups of followers who pestered and pointed at him. It wasn't all inconvenience, though. Among the Roman nobility, there was a custom of bequeathing large sums to individuals important to the community, and in those cases, they didn't forget about writers. In fact, it's said that the two great rival authors, Tacitus and Pliny the Younger, gauged their fame by the number of inheritances donated to one or the other. In a time when they couldn't compete over the number of copies sold—it was impossible to make a reliable calculation—the top ten stars in the literary firmament were measured by the gifts conferred on them in aristocratic wills.

From Livy to Liszt, there is a long, unknown history of fame and fetishism, aggressive fans, and unbridled passion for the classics.

31

Imagine this will be your last great journey. At almost sixty years old, as you leave Rome behind, you're thrilled by the swirl of adventure. The voyage from Ostia to Tarraco is calm; swayed by currents and favorable winds, the boat rocks you on the sea of memory. You have lived for thirty-five years in the city. You arrived in the imperial capital as a young man, where you managed to survive by writing books (and scrounging from the rich). You've been a witty and amiable moocher in the mansions of aristocrats, the indispensable joker at their parties. They treated you somewhat better than a butler, but significantly worse than a friend.

The journey goes smoothly, and the ship leaves you in Hispania on a clear day with a blazing sun. In Tarraco, you hire a guide with a cart and two mules. You set out at a steady pace: you'll spend six days on the road until you reach the land of your birth.

One afternoon, you're caught in a sudden storm while taking an unpaved shortcut. The cart gets stuck in the mud over and over, and you have to drag it like animals. When you pass the wall at Caesaraugusta, covered in dirt and with bloodshot eyes, you look more like a crusty beggar than a Roman celebrity. You go to the baths, where you sweat, talk, and doze. You wander amid the port's bustle, beside the yellowish river, snapping up two slaves in an auction while you're there. Someone who has found success abroad ought to arrive escorted by buff, broad-backed, hairy-chested men.

Back on the move, you're stirred by the sight of the lonely silhouette of Monte Cayo, which we'll call Moncayo centuries later and whose shadow will offer shelter and inspiration to other writers, like the poets Antonio Machado and Gustavo Adolfo Bécquer. When you draw near the Jalón River, you relive the raucous dips you took as a child in its shallow waters with other children. Grimy again with dust from the road, you dream of returning to the peaceful spa of Aquae Bilbilitanorum—the same warm waters that will later be given the Arabic name of Alhama. You recognize the landscape of your childhood: the hills, the bend in the river, the iron mines, tall ears of wheat awaiting the harvest, the pine trees, holm oaks, the shadows cast by tendrils on the vines. A hare vanishes behind a thicket, whetting your appetite for the delicacies of the hunt. Finally, the steep town of Bilbilis rises, the tiled roofs of houses that spill down the slope, the temple's silhouette, the memories. Your heart skips a beat. What awaits you in your homeland—the laurels of glory or the prick of envy? Knowing your neighbors, most likely a word of disdain muttered under their breath. At least the sleeplessness of Rome will be over, the symphony of cart drivers insulting one another by night, the obligation to get up at dawn and dash, sweating into your toga, to the homes of the rich, not to mention all the false words. Beneath the peaceful Celtiberian sky, dear Martial, you will sleep like a log.

You don't yet know it, but you will meet a wealthy old widow, Marcella, an admirer of your poetry. Flattered by the idea of having a lover who's famous in Rome, she will give you a country estate with meadows, a fountain that whispers splashing stanzas, covered ponds where eels swim, a vegetable garden, and a white dovecote. Thanks to her—she who has a warm and sturdy body, your final bedfellow, your most generous patron—you will at last escape the threat of penury, which never completely left you in peace in Rome. You will eat at a plentiful table. You will laze around. You will take long siestas, stretched out in the shade of trees that soften the cloudless summers. In winter, you will let the hours slide by enraptured by the hypnotic dance of the flames in your hearth. You will finally know peace, but you will stop writing. Your belly full, your rage will be pacified, and you will leave your disguise as an enfant terrible behind you.

In Rome, you were annoyed by the superficiality and the hypocrisy you saw. You were tired of flattering those with power. Then your nostalgia dictated poems in which you listed the coarse names of your homeland. Well, here you are, back in your little paradise of repose. Soon you'll be grumbling under your breath, muttering of your longing for the gatherings, theaters, and libraries of Rome, the wit of your social circle, the pleasures and bustle of the capital; in short, everything you left behind in your search for peace.

Preservation Amid Destruction

32

In the end, the majestic Roman libraries that filled Martial's nostalgic dreams in Hispania would succumb to a series of disasters, fires, accidents, pillage, and plunder. Paradoxically, the only ancient library that has been preserved survived thanks to the effects of destructive forces.

On August 24 of the year 79, under the reign of Titus, time came to a standstill in Pompeii and Herculaneum, two fashionable cities in the Bay of Naples, where the wealthiest citizens of the capital had built their mansions. The sun shone, the waters were the purest blue, the smell of myrtle sweetened the air, and strings of festivals were held for the summer residents' amusement. Life was relaxed, and pleasure was easy. But that late summer day, from the early hours of the morning, a menacing scarf of black smoke rose from the crater of Vesuvius into the sky. Soon, a kind of sludge—a mixture of rain, ash, and hardened lava—began to fall on the streets of Herculaneum, covering the rooftops and seeping through windows and cracks. Finally, a tide of pyroclastic flow of 700 degrees centigrade laid waste to the entire city. Only the bones of its inhabitants remained. Pompeii was wrapped in sulphureous vapors that made the air impossible to breathe. A fine drizzle of ash followed a hailstorm of tiny volcanic rocks, and then of pumice stones weighing several kilos. People came out of their houses in horror but it was already too late to flee.

The city, buried beneath a layer of solidified ash and lapilli, became a kind of time capsule. The temperature of 300 degrees centigrade caused a crust of volcanic ash to form around its inhabitants' twisted bodies. In the nineteenth century, archaeologists injected plaster into the ghostly hollows left by dead bodies in the ashes. These casts allow us to view Pompeiians eternally frozen in their final moments: a couple seeking refuge in an everlasting embrace, a man dying alone, his head sunk in his hands, a guard dog trying frenetically to get free from its leash, a little girl shaking and clinging to her mother's lap as if wanting to return to the womb. Two thousand years later, some of them still seem to be twitching, huddled in fear. In Roberto Rossellini's *Journey to Italy*, an estranged husband and wife watch in anguish as the plaster figures of two lovers who died together, swallowed up by the hot ash, are revealed.

Several generations before the catastrophe, Lucius Calpurnius Piso Caesoninus, Julius Caesar's father-in-law, commissioned the building of a palace with a two-hundred-meter façade in Herculaneum. When architects uncovered the remains of this sumptuous residence in the mid-eighteenth century, they found over eighty bronze and marble statues, and the only surviving library of the classical world. The collection contains some thousand carbonized scrolls, which the eruption at once preserved and destroyed. As a result of this unprecedented discovery, Piso's great villa is known as the Villa of the Papyri. This Roman mansion buried by lava made such an impression on the oil magnate Jean Paul Getty that he had an identical villa built for himself in Malibu. Today, the replica houses a branch of the Getty Museum.

For decades, Lucius Calpurnius's villa had been a meeting place for a renowned circle of Epicurean philosophers, among whom was the poet Virgil. Piso was a powerful magistrate and a keen reader of Greek philosophy. His political enemy, Cicero, portrayed him as a filthy-rich aristocrat singing smutty couplets and frolicking naked "amid the stench and mire of his beloved Greeks." Subtlety was scarce in the political invectives of the period. Regardless of whether Piso organized those sporadic orgies, it seems likely, judging by the content of his library, that guests at the villa spent their afternoons in Herculaneum engaged in thrilling, though perhaps less sensual, pastimes.

At the end of the republican and the beginning of the imperial periods, powerful Romans considered intellectual entertainment one of their most beloved privileges. Many spent long hours of their otherwise hectic lives skillfully and earnestly debating the gods, the causes of earthquakes, storms, and eclipses, the nature of good and evil, the legitimate goals of life, and the art of death. Pampered by slaves, in the comfort of their elegant villas, they clung to the treasures in their libraries and those civilized intellectual conversations as if somehow wishing to believe that their old world remained in one piece, despite civil wars, violence, social tensions, rumors of rioting, rising grain prices, and the columns of smoke steadily coughed out by Vesuvius. Those privileged men and women who lived at the epicenter of the greatest power in the world took refuge in their luxury mansions to forget about all these dangers, reducing them to remote threats, trivial matters that didn't merit interrupting a conversation about, for example, the beaver's testicles that so fascinated Aristotle. The Roman nobles' taste for lying back upon purple embroidered pillows on their cushy divans—tricliniums, or dining couches—as they were served drinks and delicacies and chatted calmly with one another, gave rise to the Spanish expression "to have a long, stretched-out chat."

Excavations at the Villa of the Papyri revealed that the sybaritic Piso's books were kept in a three-by-three-meter room lined with shelves and a freestanding bookcase in the middle with shelves on both sides. The scrolls were taken to the adjacent patio so they could be read in good light, among opulent statues. In this design, the villa's architect followed the Greek precedent.

That August 24, a blast of gas from the volcano carbonized the papyrus scrolls before the city was coated in fine volcanic ash that later cooled and solidified. When excavators and treasure hunters explored the city in the eighteenth century, they mistook the remains of the scrolls for pieces of coal and charred branches. In fact they used some of them as torches, burning the ancient words of lost books—a curious case of communication by smoke signal. When they realized what they had in their hands, they wondered if it would be possible to read them. In the euphoria of discovery, they resorted to clumsy methods (using their fingernails or, worse still, butcher's knives to slice them, with predictable and regrettable results). Soon afterward, an Italian invented a machine to try to open them delicately, but it was a desperately slow procedure. It took four years to unfurl the first scroll. And the fragments obtained with the machine, as black as a burnt newspaper, were fragile and difficult to preserve since they were prone to breaking into pieces.

Since then, researchers have sought new technology to decipher the hidden secrets of Piso's carbonized scrolls. On some of the pieces, nothing can be distinguished; on others, a few letters can be identified under a microscope. Constant handling brings with it the risk of the scrolls turning into nothing but black dust on the table. In 1999, scientists at Brigham Young University examined the papyri with infrared radiation and discovered that at a certain wavelength, they could achieve a high contrast between the paper and ink. Touched by invisible light, the letters began to blossom. Instead of black ink on black paper, the experts could make out dark lines on a pale grey surface. The possibilities of reconstructing the texts increased significantly. In 2008, multispectral imaging allowed for another step forward. However, none of the scrolls identified up until now—all in Greek—contain any of the destroyed treasures we covet: neither unknown poems by Sappho, nor long-lost tragedies by Aeschylus and Sophocles, nor missing dialogues by Aristotle. The books that have come to light are mostly philosophical treatises on highly specialized matters. The most remarkable discovery is probably *On Nature* by Epicurus. But many experts suspect that there was a Latin library in Piso's mansion that remains to be discovered. Meanwhile, the modern city of Ercolano shakes and roars above the ancient ruins, obstructing any deeper excavations. Maybe one day, fascinating lost books will be discovered and it will be possible to read them. Perhaps in the coming decades we will witness a minor literary miracle under the volcano.

The first archaeologists at Herculaneum discovered numerous scrolls scattered throughout the Villa of the Papyri, piled on the floor and tucked into traveling cases, as if the owner had made a last-ditch attempt to move the collection before it was blanketed beneath twenty meters of volcanic detritus. I picture that man, who, two thousand years ago, took the trouble to save his books while his world disappeared, carbonized by the scorching torrent of rock and burning air that rushed at Herculaneum at thirty meters per second, at a temperature of 700 degrees centigrade. For us, in a strange historical irony, this apocalyptic library is the only one that survives on a sweeping map of erasures.

33

Archaeological sites attracted pilgrimages by an army of new fans. When Charles III, king of Naples and the future king of Spain, ordered the excavations of Pompeii, Herculaneum, and Stabiae in the eighteenth century, a fever for antiquities was unleashed. The cities preserved by catastrophe sparked young passions in Europe. A world until then only imagined had suddenly come into view, and ancient civilization was all the rage on the continent. From that outpost of a lost era, certain features of modernity spread out and took shape: the Grand Tour and the beginnings of tourism, the specialization of archaeology as a scientific field, etchings of ruins, neoclassical architecture in centers of power, the aesthetic utopia of Johann Joachim Winckelmann, and the Greco-Latin influence that pulsed behind the revolutionary soul of the Enlightenment.

OVID CLASHES WITH CENSORSHIP

34

He was successful—highly successful—and he enjoyed it. He wasn't ashamed to have readers without aristocratic names. He was droll, sociable, hedonistic. He liked the Roman *dolce vita* just as it was—sometimes vulgar, sumptuous, gluttonous, other times melancholy, poetic, fragile. Writing came naturally to him, and he didn't suffer for his art, but even so he knew how to dazzle. It was hard to forgive such a happy man.

He had been born into a traditional, ambitious landowning family. His father sent him to study in Rome in the hope of turning him into a rich and respectable lawyer, but these hopes were dashed: Ovid liked poetry better than law. Tired of courts and good intentions, he soon abandoned his promising career to devote himself fully to literature. With his poems, not only did he disappoint his biological father, but sometime later he also displeased the symbolic one—the father of all Romans, Emperor Augustus. He would pay a high price for this second rebellion. But he savored the fame and applause in full before he slipped into the void.

Ovid was an explorer of new literary territories and the first writer to pay special attention to his female readers. As I've already mentioned, he wrote a specific treatise on cosmetics and makeup for women. His *Art of Love*, a hookup manual in verse, dedicated a long chapter—a third of the work's total length—to giving seduction advice to women and explaining the wiles used by womanizers to fool them into love. He established an intimacy until then unheard of between an author and his female readers. In a time of rapid expansion of reading horizons, Ovid gleefully joined in the transgression of old norms and archaic values. His young, nonconformist, erotic literature appealed to Roman women of the era; he knew this and played with its limits. But he failed to see the abyss over which he walked.

Some contemporaries accused him of being frivolous, but they forgot that frivolity can be profoundly subversive. Ovid trained his revolutionary gaze on certain essential matters in first-century BC Rome: pleasure, consent and its opposite, and beauty. In those days, marriages were an arrangement between families, who would typically hand over adolescent girls to powerful, aging men. These were times of conjugal duty, times when slaves of both sexes were available to their masters' appetites, like a would-be harem. Sexual relations were neither reciprocal nor egalitarian: you were either active or passive, you either penetrated or were penetrated. There were highly intricate distinctions, assumed rules, and codified limits—as always, it was mainly a matter of privilege. What was acceptable for a rich man was unacceptable for a poor man; what was permitted for men was prohibited for women. Pedophilia was allowed with someone of a lower rank—a slave, a foreigner, or a noncitizen. Martial was shamelessly public about his desire for a slave girl in his possession, whom he called Erotion in his poems, and who died at the age of six. Ovid shattered all these conventions and commonplaces, writing of his preference for older women over little girls, saying that his own pleasure required the pleasure of his female companion. Here, I loosely translate a passage from *The Art of Love*:

I would rather have a lover over the age of thirty-five,
with a few grey hairs: the hasty may drink fresh wine, but
I prefer a mature woman who knows her pleasure. She is
experienced, which is everything when it comes to talent,
and knows a thousand positions for making love. There is
no false voluptuousness in her. And when the woman feels
delight at the same time as her lover, this is the height of
pleasure. I hate the embrace in which man and woman do
not give themselves completely. I hate those unions that do
not leave both exhausted. I hate a woman who surrenders
because she must, who does not get wet, who thinks of her
work. I want no woman to pleasure me out of duty. No
woman must make love to me out of obligation! I like to
hear her voice translating her joy, for her to murmur that I
should slow down, that it isn't yet time to let go. I like to see
my lover delighted, an overcome look in her eyes, for her to
swoon, unable to take my touch anymore.

The traditional rules dictated that feeling was a weakness in free
men and that willingness to put oneself in another's place was insanity. As Pascal Quignard writes, Ovid is the first champion of mutual
desire and also the first Roman to support the claim that it was necessary to rein in the urgency of male lust and wait for the woman to
experience pleasure.

The Art of Love was considered an immoral and dangerous
book. Years later, as he recalled the beginning of his misfortunes,
Ovid would write that because of that work, many called him a
"teacher of obscene adulteries." It's true that he taught the practice
of extramarital erotic play. And it could hardly be any other way:
desire and attraction were rarely part of the panorama of married
life. The marriages of wealthy Romans were a dynastic decision first
and foremost, a calculated alliance, a pact between families. Fathers
used their daughters as pawns in their political maneuvers and didn't
hesitate to divorce them from one husband and marry them off to
another, even while they were pregnant by the first, if it suited their
political interests. It wasn't unusual for two patricians to cordially
trade wives: Cato the Younger, who is remembered as a paragon of

virtue, "lent" his wife, Marcia, to a friend—in other words, requested a divorce to make way for the new suitor—and married her a second time once she was widowed, acquiring an immense inheritance in the process. When he plotted this nuptial maneuver, Cato consulted Marcia's father but didn't ask her if she had an opinion on the matter: in the traditional mindset, women were subordinate, lifelong adolescents. The conduct of ambitious fathers did nothing to promote affection or loyalty between husbands and wives. Against this backdrop, passions flared beyond the confines of marriage, and Ovid had the audacity to express this reality in his verse. His timing was unfortunate, clashing directly with the emperor Augustus's moral program, and in particular with his Julian Laws, passed between the years 18 BC and 9 AD, which were meant to defend the family and old traditions, punishing adultery with exile and fining those who didn't have children.

In the eighth year AD, at barely fifty, Ovid was suddenly banished by imperial edict to the village of Tomis—now Constanta, Romania. His third wife remained in Rome to take care of their properties and beg for a pardon while the poet went into exile alone. They would never see each other again. Augustus had chosen to teach him a harsh lesson, with calculated cruelty. Not content to expel him to one of the Mediterranean islands normally used for such purposes, he cast him out to a savage land at the edge of the empire, bordering on the unknown, where Ovid would be separated from everything that in his view made life worth living: friends, love, books, conversation, and, above all, peace. Living in that desolate, godforsaken place, exposed to a cold, hostile climate, among people who spoke an unintelligible language, in constant fear of raids by nomadic armies, was a death sentence. Ovid survived nine years, sending constant petitions to Rome and writing *Tristia*, a precursor of the letter *De Profundis*, which Oscar Wilde, another great punished hedonist, would write from prison centuries later.

Of the reasons for his banishment, Ovid said that two crimes led to his downfall: "a poem and an error." He never explains what his error was so as not to add salt to the wound—it's possible that he witnessed the clandestine orgies of someone in a high place or was involved in some political conspiracy. As far as the poem goes, there can be few doubts—it's a handbook for lovers. "I am no longer love's master," he wrote from his exile, "that work has paid the price it deserved to pay." Two centuries later, a historian wrote cuttingly, "Augustus punished the poet Ovid with exile, for writing three little books on the art of love." Ovid cried when he learned that reprisals had been taken against his work in his absence. Augustus made sure to ban his verse from public libraries, following the banishment of their author.

As far as we know, this episode marked the beginning of moralizing in Europe, an obsession with control that found its first failure here. *The Art of Love*, that joyful little erotic book, persecuted by one of the empire's most powerful rulers and prohibited several times in later eras for being obscene and scandalous, has found its way into the libraries of today. Its story is one of an extended act of recovery, carried out century after century by the readers in whom Ovid put his faith, against the authorities. Classics can also be forged by subversion.

SWEET INERTIA

35

By the beginning of the second century, Rome had seen a long string of distrustful emperors somewhat lacking in sense of humor. Censorship and fear began to cleave the spirit of the times. The historian Tacitus touched the scars of this amputation and dared to name them. Nostalgic for a nonexistent past, he fantasized about "the rare good fortune of those times when one is allowed to think as one pleases and speak as one thinks." He decided to investigate what wounds the powerful, why those who are easily scandalized are scandalized, what they prohibit and what they fear, what they try to plunge into silence, and all that lurks behind the erasures in mutilated texts.

Tacitus describes in detail an episode of repression under Tiberius's rule, soon after Ovid's death in exile. The historian Aulus Cremutius Cordus, whose ideas were republican, was tried for a daring phrase in his *Annals*, where he described Brutus and Cassius, Julius Caesar's assassins, as "the last of the Romans." Accused of violating the *lex maiestatis,* or "laws of majesty," with these words, he had to appear before the Senate. Cordus defended himself bravely, but by the time he left the interrogation, he had already decided to starve himself to death to escape the punishment typical of the independent judiciary of the time. The trial went ahead according to custom, despite the minor inconvenience of the death of the accused. In the end, the verdict demanded that all copies of his work be burned. In Rome, the task was assigned to the aediles, and in the remaining cities of the empire, to the corresponding magistrates.

The *Annals* were saved from destruction thanks to the bravery of Cordus's daughter Marcia, who took the risk of hiding a single copy. A keen reader with a particular taste for philosophy, Marcia understood the value of books. Seneca dedicated an essay to her, in which he wrote, "Women have the same intellectual power as men, and the same capacity for noble and generous actions." No doubt he admired the young Marcia for daring to disobey. Though her life was endangered each time the house was searched, she kept her father's last manuscript until the new emperor, Caligula, lifted the prohibition. After obtaining a pardon, she commissioned new copies of the work and returned it to circulation. Subsequent generations eagerly read the historical chronicle that had been so offensive to those in power. A few fragments—the most controversial—have reached us.

In every era, censors risk producing the opposite of their desired effect. Their great paradox is that they draw attention to the very thing they intend to suppress. Tacitus wrote, "They are foolish, those who believe that they can, with their temporary power, extinguish the memory of events in those who come after them. On the contrary, talents that are punished only grow more revered, and those who act severely achieve nothing but their own dishonor and the glory of those they punished." In our times, the internet and social networks give instant attention to any message prohibited by authorities. If a work of art is removed from circulation, everyone starts talking about it. If a rapper is condemned for explicit lyrics, downloads of their songs skyrocket. If a complaint causes a legal decision for a book to be withdrawn, people rush out to buy it.

Though censorship rarely causes the ideas it targets to disappear—often giving them wings instead—those in power have a peculiar tendency to reoffend. Caligula had the idea of removing copies of Homer from libraries, in accordance with the ideas of Plato. Commodus banned the reading of Suetonius's biography of Caligula, on penalty of being torn limb from limb by wild beasts in the amphitheater. Caracalla, a keen admirer of Alexander the Great, believed that Aristotle had been involved in the Greek emperor's death and nursed the idea of setting fire to all his works. During the persecution of Diocletian in the early fourth century, there was a genuine frenzy for burning Christian books, comparable to that of the Nazis in 1933. We know of martyrs who gave their lives to protect their writings. Three sisters from Thessalonica—Agape, Chionia, and Irene—were burned at the stake for hiding banned books in their home. And, like them, Philip, Euplius, Vincenzo, Felix, Dativus, and Ampelius were martyred for refusing to give up their books. Later, when Christianity became an official religion, equally violent incinerations of pagan books were unleashed.

All these destructive efforts had little effect: emperors successfully influenced writers under their protection, but their prohibitions rarely prevailed, as their failed attempts to destroy Ovid's erotic poems or Cremutius Cordus's republican chronicle show. The system of book circulation in ancient times—with neither distributors nor publishers—was too difficult for censors to control. With slaves trained to copy books, and professional scribes, it was easy to reproduce condemned works in a clandestine way.

As Tacitus already understood, the most powerful effect of this drive to persecute is mainly to strike fear into others, into those less brave, but also into creativity itself. Self-censorship is always more decisive than censorship. The historian called it *inertiae dulcedo* ("sweet inertia"). He was referring to the abandonment of risk in favor of comfort, the personal temptation not to upset the status quo, to avoid conflict and strife, the perilous cowardice that can grip creators. Tacitus was witness to a submissive era, when even rebels stayed quiet and obeyed the rules. He wrote, "Without a doubt, we showed a great example of patience. We might have lost memory as well as voice, had it been as easy to forget as to stay silent." His texts rub salt in a painful wound and open our eyes: in every era, the battle is waged not only against the censorship meted out by power, but also against the fears we harbor within ourselves.

JOURNEY TO THE CENTER OF BOOKS
AND HOW TO NAME THEM

36

Until the invention of printing, books were handcrafted objects—in other words, they were painstaking to make, unique, and impossible to control. If books were copied one by one on demand, often in the reader's home by the hand of his private slaves, what kind of command could prevent their distribution?

Today's ebooks are the antithesis of those ancient manuscripts: cheap, ethereal, weightless objects, easy to reproduce infinitely, placidly stored on servers and in data-center storage units all over the world, but strictly controlled. In 2009, in a gesture easily interpreted as censorship, Amazon stealthily erased George Orwell's *1984* from its customers' Kindles, alleging a supposed conflict over copyright. Thousands of readers complained that the book had suddenly disappeared from their devices with no prior warning. A student from Detroit writing an academic paper protested when all their reading notes vanished along with the file. We don't know if Amazon was aware of the implicit literary symbolism. In *1984*, government censors erase every trace of literature that Big Brother finds bothersome, tossing it into an incinerator known as "the memory hole."

Internet forums are full of comments complaining about the disappearance of digital editions of a range of titles. In fact, when we click on "Buy now" to add a new book in ebook format to our account, we are not acquiring anything tangible. We have no rights to these texts that float behind a glass screen. The memory hole lies in wait; our virtual libraries are in danger of being devoured.

As a child, I believed all books had been written for me and that the only copy in the world was in my house, and I'm easily tempted to idealize ancient, irreplaceable manuscripts. In fact, those books were far less inviting than ours. Ancient writing had the look of an intricate, impenetrable forest, where words piled up without gaps, capital and lowercase were indistinguishable, and punctuation marks used only erratically. The reader had to hack their way through a thicket of letters, panting and uncertain, glancing back to make sure they didn't get lost. Why didn't the ancients let the text breathe? Partly to make the most of the papyrus or parchment, which were expensive materials at the time. Furthermore, the first books were made for people who read aloud, who used their ear to disentangle what for the eye was merely an uninterrupted succession of signs. And lastly, aristocrats, proud of their cultural superiority, had no interest in making things easier for readers they saw as upstarts—that is, those with less access to education—so that they could sneak into the exclusive fiefdom of books.

Progress toward the simplification of reading was slow, tentative, and gradual. The scholars at the Library of Alexandria invented a system of accents and punctuation. Both are attributed to Aristophanes of Byzantium, the librarian with the prodigious memory. When words were not separated, placing a few accents—like road signs along a winding route—was immensely helpful to the reader.

The separation of letters into words and phrases advanced little by little. There was a method of writing that consisted of dividing the text into lines whose meaning was complete, to help less confident readers raise or lower their voice at the end of a thought. In the late fourth century, on discovering this system in copies of works by Demosthenes and Cicero, Saint Jerome was the first to describe and recommend it. Even so, the method did not pass into common usage, and the vicissitudes of punctuation persisted. From the seventh century onward, a combination of dots and lines indicated a period; a raised or high dot was equivalent to our comma, and the semicolon was used as it is today. By the ninth century, silent reading was probably common enough that scribes and copyists began to separate each word from its intrusive neighbors, though they may also have done so for aesthetic reasons.

Manuscript illustrations were also hand done by necessity. From their origins in the Egyptian Book of the Dead, their purpose was more explanatory than ornamental. The image was born as a visual aid to clarify and complement texts, given how difficult they were to read. When the content was scientific, diagrams were used; when it was literary, there were narrative scenes. In the Greco-Latin tradition, the writer's head or bust sometimes appeared inside a medallion, as a mark of authorship. The first known example is Varro's *Imagines*, a lost work described by Pliny that detailed the lives of seven hundred Greek and Roman celebrities. Published around the year 39 AD, this ambitious book combined a portrait of each famous figure with an epigram and a description. The breadth of its distribution suggests that perhaps the Romans might have developed something akin to a printing method for use in the book trade.

Christian appropriation of the book as a theological symbol opened new decorative paths. Words themselves became ornamental forms. Pages were dyed Tyrian purple, and the writing was done in gold or silver ink. Books were no longer mere vehicles of information, but relics and works of art in their own right, and a mark of distinction for their owners. The work became specialized: the scribe would leave precise indications and set aside spaces for illustration; the parchments were then handed over to miniaturists and illuminators. By the thirteenth century, the space of the page had become like a jungle, complex and fanciful. This was the marginal origin of the comic. Literally: the first illustrated comic strips in history appeared in the margins of those ancient manuscripts. An incredible latticework of dragons, serpents, and creepers emerged around the letters, lacing together and intertwining in a wealth of twisted forms. People, animals, landscapes, and lively scenes unfurled in a series of illustrations. The small drawings were framed with a border of plants—this is the origin of the term "vignette," because each image was edged with fringes of vine leaves. From the medieval Gothic era onward, small ribbons emerge from characters' mouths bearing the phrases they utter, precursors of the speech bubbles in children's cartoon strips today. Beyond the text, miniatures were born to revitalize the human appetite for wonder. Meticulously detailed or fantastical, taken from the natural world or dreamed up by the imagination, these illustrations show how new artistic forms can find their beginnings in subordinate spaces and go on to flourish in their own right. The comic, heir to this elegant graphic past, has held on to features that harken back to its origins. Characters in today's comics, like the creatures who inhabited remote manuscripts, often belong to the outer fringes—strange, hypnotic, and distorted. And, like them, they demand our attention, fighting not to remain in a marginal space.

The great change in books' inner layout arrived with the printed page, which tried to facilitate nimble reading through a straight-forward structure. The text, which until then had been densely arranged in compact blocks, began to be separated into paragraphs. The headings, chapters, and page numbers served as a compass to orient oneself when reading. Since printing produced identical copies across a whole edition, a new apparatus was developed for looking things up: indexes with page references, footnotes, and lasting agreements on punctuation conventions. Printed books became easier and easier to read, and therefore more accessible. With indexes, readers now had a map of the insides of books. They could enter and navigate them with increasing freedom. As the centuries passed, the closed jungles of letters through which readers had forged a laborious path, machete in hand, were gradually transformed into tidy gardens of words through which they could take a peaceful stroll.

37

If a book is a journey, its title is a compass and astrolabe for those who venture along its paths. But the title hasn't always been there to orient explorers. The earliest stories, in the remotest times, arrived in the world unnamed and unchristened. Our ancestors might say, for example, "Mother, tell me the story of the girl who put a mountain in her basket" or "Do you want to hear the story of the crane who stole people's dreams?"

Certainly, in the earliest era of written poems and narratives, there was no single way of referring to them. The lists of books from the first libraries in history, in the ancient East, mention works by their subject. "When one supplicates the Storm-God," reads one clay tablet found in Hattusa. The next entry on the list says, "On the purification of a murder." Yet the most common method was to use the first words of the text: *Enuma Elish* (in Akkadian:

"When on high . . ."). Like these ancient clay catalogs, their Greek equivalents—*The Pínakes*, in the Library of Alexandria—offered lists of works identified by their opening line. In first-century Rome, we can still discern fluid approaches to naming books. *The Odyssey* is sometimes mentioned as "*Ulysses*," anticipating Joyce by twenty centuries. Martial calls *The Aeneid* "*Arma virumque*," while Ovid calls it "*Aeneas, Fugitive*." Though they have almost disappeared, these ancient ways survive in certain holdouts: papal encyclicals still take their Latin titles from the first words of the text.

Mênin áeide theá. The old way of naming stories by their beginning is beautiful. It's as if, unwittingly swept up in their enchantment, we were already beginning to tell the tale. Italo Calvino recovered that ancient method when he called one of his most beguiling novels *If on a Winter's Night a Traveler*.

The first fixed titles, unique and set in stone, belonged to plays. Athenian playwrights were pioneers in titling their works, with which they competed in public contests, thus needing to avoid any confusion when they were announced, promoted, or declared winners. *Prometheus Bound*, *Oedipus Rex*, and *The Trojan Women* never went by any other name. Meanwhile, prose took longer to acquire lasting titles, and when it did, they were often merely descriptive. *The History of the Peloponnesian War*, *Metaphysics*, *The Gallic Wars*, *On the Orator*.

In general, the names the Greeks and Romans gave their literary works are brief, accurate, and devoid of ambition. They sound monotonous, unoriginal, and bureaucratic. They perform an essentially identifying function. Almost without exception, they resort to common or proper names without verbs or conjunctions—we find nothing comparable to *The Man Who Was Thursday*, by Chesterton, or *As I Lay Dying*, by Faulkner. Neither the nouns nor the adjectives are expressively dense, and they usually lack poetic qualities—we find nothing like *Wide Sargasso Sea*, by Jean Rhys, or *A Universal History of Infamy*, by Borges. Despite all this, they left us a handful of titles that are mysterious and dazzling in their simplicity, like *Works and Days*, by Hesiod, which Alejandra Pizarnik rewrote in her book of poems *Works and Nights*; *Parallel Lives*, by Plutarch; *The Art of Love*, by Ovid, adapted by Erich Fromm; and *City of God*, by Saint Augustine, which gave Fernando Meirelles's chilling film about the Rio de Janeiro favelas its name.

In the times of papyrus scrolls, the preferred place for the title and author's name was at the end of the text, the most protected part of the book when it was rolled up—the beginning, on the outside of the cylinder, was especially prone to deterioration and often broke. It was in the codex format that the title achieved first place, on the face of the book, and took possession of the spine—its back. Saint Augustine makes it clear that in the fourth century it was already common to find that information "on the preliminary page," in other words, at the beginning, the doorway to the text. Today it's the first thing we read when the book is still unknown to us, and we expect it to define its universe in fewer than ten words. If the spell works, someone will pick up the book from the table and want to know more about it.

In fact, it wasn't until the nineteenth century that titles began to develop their own poetry and methods of enticement. When newspapers, the bookselling market, publishing competition, and thus the need to grab the reader's attention became established, writers set out to seduce from the cover. Without a doubt, the boldest and most beautiful have appeared between the nineteenth and twenty-first centuries. Here, I will sketch an incomplete, easily refuted catalog.

Poetically dense: *The Heart Is a Lonely Hunter* by Carson McCullers; *In Search of Lost Time* by Marcel Proust; *Tender Is the Night* by F. Scott Fitzgerald; *One Hundred Years of Solitude* by Gabriel García Márquez; *Tomorrow in the Battle Think on Me* by Javier Marías; *The General of the Dead Army* by Ismail Kadare.

Ironic: *Complete Works and Other Stories* by Augusto Monterroso; *A Confederacy of Dunces* by John Kennedy Toole; *Life: A User's Manual* by Georges Perec; *A Bad Night and Birthing a Female* by Angélica Gorodischer; *Will You Be Quiet, Please?* by Raymond Carver.

Disturbing: *Nip the Buds, Shoot the Kids* by Kenzaburō Ōe; *The Virgin Suicides* by Jeffrey Eugenides; *Death Will Come and Have Your Eyes* by Cesare Pavese; *To Kill a Mockingbird* by Harper Lee; *The Suicides at the End of the World* by Leila Guerriero; *Lying Bitch* by Marta Sanz.

Surprising and enigmatic: *By Grand Central Station I Sat Down and Wept* by Elizabeth Smart; *A Streetcar Named Desire* by Tennessee Williams; *All Our Yesterdays* by Natalia Ginzburg; *The Sound of Things Falling* by Juan Gabriel Vázquez; *Do Androids Dream of Electric Sheep?* by Philip K. Dick.

Secrets to be revealed: *I Should Have Said I Love You* by Juan Gelman; *Uninhabited Paradise* by Ana María Matute; *Closed Due to Melancholy* by Isidoro Blaisten; *The Age of Innocence* by Edith Wharton; *Games of the Late Age* by Luis Landero; *The Ridiculous Idea of Never Seeing You Again* by Rosa Montero.

How a good title happens is a mystery. Sometimes it is the first thing to appear—"In the beginning was the word"—and the whole book expands, like a linguistic big bang, from that crystal-clear explosion. At other times it holds back, tormenting the author on a long journey of indecision, or else it springs up where it was least expected—in a phrase heard in passing, or a suggestion by an inspired third party. There are several famous stories about books whose authors wanted to give them weak or impossible names, and which, thanks to other people—writers, editors, agents who were friends—found their way to their essential title. *All's Well That Ends Well* is what Tolstoy wanted to call *War and Peace*; Baudelaire considered *The Lesbians* for *Les Fleurs du mal*; Onetti proposed *The Big House* but someone suggested *When It Matters No More*; Bolaño was warned that *Shit Storm* wasn't a great idea, so he replaced it with *By Night in Chile*. On certain rare occasions, a free translation hits upon the right name, one the author himself couldn't come up with. *The Searchers* is a weak title for the novel and movie John Ford would turn into a classic. But in a flash of inspiration, an anonymous Spanish distributor decided to premiere it with the marvelous title *Desert Centaurs*. Leila Guerriero writes that when the epiphany of the perfect name occurs, the feeling is something akin to bliss; a book's title isn't just a string of ingenious words, but "a print soldered into the heart of a story, from which it will never be separate again."

After a long voyage through the indifference of centuries, titles have been transformed into tiny poems; barometers, spyholes, keyholes, bright posters, neon signs; the musical key defining the score to come; a pocket mirror, a threshold; a lighthouse in the fog, a premonition; the air that makes the windmill go round.

38

Modern artists have an obligation to be original; they must offer something new, something never seen before. The more pathbreaking a work seems in relation to tradition and norms, the better received it will be by critics. Every creator tries to be a rebel in their way—just like all the others. We cling to a set of romantic ideas: freedom is the lifeblood of true artists, and the literature that matters to us is the kind that builds its own worlds, a language free of convention, and unexplored narrative forms.

It was different for the Romans, who wanted their literature as much like the Greek as possible. That's why they copied their genres one by one—epic, lyric, tragedy, comedy, history, philosophy, oratory. That's why they adopted the Greeks' metric forms, which didn't fit into their language well and at first made their poems sound false and contrived. That's why they built double libraries—like twin towers—to highlight this brotherhood. They believed that they could outdo the best by overtly copying them. They voluntarily adopted an enormous set of limitations and imported models. And the surprising thing is that, even with such rigid rules, this divided culture created some extraordinary works.

This obsessive emulation is expressed in the literary criticism of a fascinating figure: Quintilian. He was born in Calagurris Nassica Iulia—I love the sound of this name—which today is Calahorra, just 120 kilometers from where I am writing. Coming into the world in a remote corner of the empire was no obstacle to triumph in the year 35: if you belonged to a wealthy family, geography did not determine your fate. Quintilian soon achieved professional success. A lawyer and rhetoric teacher, he was also the first professor in history whose salary was paid from the public coffers. The emperor Vespasian granted him this unprecedented honor, and Domitian chose him to educate his great-nephews. Quintilian shamelessly flattered the two emperors who gave him work. In those days, the language of flattery was required by palace protocol, and it was difficult to get ahead without resorting to sycophancy. In any case, Quintilian liked to rub shoulders with those in power. He was a peaceful conservative, fêted, and pleased with his accomplishments. Only later in life did personal misfortune strike. After losing his nineteen-year-old wife and his two children, he wrote, "I know not what secret envy rends the fiber of our hopes."

The twelve books of the *Institutes of Oratory*, the pedagogical essay where he distilled all his experience as a teacher, contained a series of trail-blazing ideas. As I have already mentioned, in an era that practiced systematic beatings, Quintilian rejected violent punishment in education. He believed that praise was more effective than violence, as was a love of the teacher, which little by little would be transformed into love of the subject. He did not believe in universally applicable principles, preferring to adjust his methods to circumstances and individual ability. He claimed that the purpose of education was to let the students find answers for themselves and make the teacher superfluous and was one of the earliest advocates of lifelong learning. He encouraged professional orators to read as much as they possibly could before finishing their studies, since he knew that reading helped improve speech. And, to provide them with a road map of literature, he wrote two parallel lists of the best authors of Greece and Rome (thirty-one on the first and thirty-nine on the second).

On Quintilian's lists, competition becomes obsessive. He tries to establish a perfect symmetry: every Greek author should have a Latin twin of equal stature. Virgil was the Roman Homer. Cicero was the Roman Demosthenes and the Roman Plato, too—who said one of their writers couldn't count for two Greeks? Livy was a reincarnated Herodotus, and Sallust the new Thucydides. The text gives the impression that it was a matter of national pride to clone the great Greek writers one by one. A curious experiment in programmatic imitation was underway. This helps us to understand the patriotic need for the *The Aeneid* even before it was written. It also explains the success of *Parallel Lives*, which the canny Plutarch wrote with the leitmotif of pairing great figures from Greece and Rome: Theseus and Romulus; Alexander and Julius Caesar, and so on.

This spirit of ambition and emulation was compatible with the mindset of elite Roman society. But the unbridled competition must have been exhausting for creators. For every writer spurred on by the challenge, another must have been oppressed by the weight of tradition. Comparisons were constant, to the point of suffocation. Poets and prose writers toiled endlessly in the shadow of a collective inferiority complex.

The paradox is that the Romans were original, after all. They created an unprecedented syncretism. For the first time, a civilization adopted a foreign literature and read, preserved, translated, cared for, and loved it, unhindered by the barriers of chauvinism. In Rome, a knot was first tied in a cord that still connects us to the past and to other cultures, languages, and horizons. Along it, as if on a tightrope, the ideas, scientific discoveries, myths, thoughts, feelings, and errors (which also inspire) walk from one century to the next. Some of them slip and fall; others manage to keep their balance (these are the classics). That link, that uninterrupted transition, that infinite conversation that continues today is a thing of wonder.

The nostalgic passion, the painful complex the Romans suffered, their military sovereignty, their envy, and their appropriations are fascinating phenomena. Because that complicated love, built with desire and fury, woven from different scraps of cloth, opened the way to the future we live in now.

39

Until recent times, only the wealthy and those who lurked around them waiting for commissions and money devoted themselves to literature. As Steven Pinker writes, "history is written not so much by the winners as by the affluent, the sliver of humanity with the leisure and education to write about it." We tend to forget the misery of other eras, partly because literature, poetry, and legends celebrate those who lived well, forgetting those who were smothered by the silence of poverty. Periods of hunger and scarcity have been mythologized and are even remembered as golden ages of pastoral simplicity. They were not.

What does the map of the origins of literary classics, the most admired writers and their emblematic works, look like? It shouldn't surprise us to learn that the word "classic" itself comes from the vocabulary of wealth and property. In the beginning, it didn't have the slightest connection to art or creation. These were serious matters, and the trivial details of arts and letters would come later. *Classici* comes from the specific terminology of the Roman census. It referred to the richest sector of society, in contrast with the rabble made up of the remaining citizens, who were known simply as *infra classem*. The census was immensely important in ancient Rome because it defined the rights and duties of each citizen and served to supply the legions with soldiers. The quantity of a person's assets—or, in most cases, their scarcity—decided the place each person occupied in society.

According to an old tradition, the census had been created by the ancient king Servius Tullius and had to be carried out every five years. When it was finished, a purification ceremony was performed, in which the gods were asked for blessings on the land and to stave off catastrophe. The ritual was called a lustrum; this is why a period of five years is called a *lustro* in Spanish. The head of each family had to attend and declare their assets under oath, as well as the number of members in their family—in other words, their children and slaves, with their corresponding value. This information determined who could participate in the assemblies and who could not. Those who lacked assets were proletarians; their only possessions were their descendants (*proles*). They weren't conscripted except in the greatest emergencies and were exempt from paying tribute. On the other hand, they did not participate in political life through voting. Those who declared assets were the *adsidui* and were suitable for military service and eligible members of the Assemblies. They entered the census class—of which there were six—that corresponded to their net worth. It was a straightforward system. The rich paid taxes and, in return, could influence politics. The poor, on the other hand, did not contribute and didn't count.

The lawyer and writer Aulus Gellius explains that the so-called classics were the economic crème de la crème, those with great fortunes, the blue bloods of the republic, the extravagantly rich who monopolized the first class. The word reached literature as a metaphor. Translating an obsession with business to art, some critics decided that there were first-class authors—in other words, reliable and solvent writers to whom one could lend attention, and in whom it was advisable to invest time. At the other end of the hierarchy were the "proletarian" writers, poor papyrus smudgers with neither property nor patrons. We don't know if the word "classic" was commonly used: it appears in only a couple of extant Latin texts. The word's true success came when it was rescued by various humanists from 1496 on, and when it later spread through all Romance languages. It no longer applies just to literature, nor even just to artistic creation. It has stayed alive for centuries and been adopted by other fields, used as a general term for a standard of excellence.

It's true that "classics" has a classist origin, as the word suggests. The concept has reached us from an era that saw the world through a hierarchical lens, imbued with arrogant notions of privilege—just like all other eras, as it happens. Yet there is something moving about considering words as a form of wealth—though only metaphorically—in the face of the always overwhelming dominance of money and real estate.

Just like the lineage of the wealthy, the classics aren't isolated books but networks and constellations. Italo Calvino wrote that "a classic is a book that comes before other classics; but anyone who has read the others first, and then reads this one, instantly recognizes its place in the family tree." Thanks to them, we discover origins, relationships, and dependencies. Some works hide in the folds of others: Homer shares genetic material with Joyce and Eugenides; the platonic myth of the cave returns in *Alice's Adventures in Wonderland* and *The Matrix*; Mary Shelley's Doctor Frankenstein was imagined as a modern Prometheus; the old Oedipus is reincarnated as the ill-fated King Lear; the story of Eros and Psyche, as *Beauty and the Beast*; Heraclitus as Borges; Sappho as Leopardi; Gilgamesh as Superman; Lucian as Cervantes and *Star Wars*; Seneca as Montaigne; Ovid's *Metamorphoses* as Virginia Woolf's *Orlando*; Lucretius as Giordano Bruno and Marx; and Herodotus as Paul Auster's *City of Glass*. Pindar sings, "Men are the dreams of a shadow." Shakespeare reformulates it: "We are such stuff / As dreams are made on, and our little life / Is rounded with a sleep." Calderón writes *Life Is a*

Dream. Schopenhauer enters the conversation: "Life and dreams are pages of the same book." The thread of words and metaphors travels through time, weaving the ages together.

The problem, for some, is how to approach the classics. Embedded in school and university curriculums, these books have become required reading, but as a result, we risk viewing them as an imposition and letting them scare us off. Mark Twain proposed an ironic definition in "Disappearance of Literature": A classic is "something that everybody wants to have read and nobody wants to read." Pierre Bayard borrows from this strain of humor for his essay *How to Talk About Books You Haven't Read,* where he examines the responses that lead to literary hypocrisy. Out of a childish fear of disappointing someone, so as not to be left out of a conversation, or to bluff our way through an exam, we say yes, and hardly notice the lie—yes, we have read the book that has never passed through our hands. To get closer to a new lover, says Bayard, we might pretend to have read their favorite books. But when we lie, there's no going back: we force ourselves to speak of certain texts without knowing them, fumbling through based on other people's opinions. This kind of pretense is easier to sustain when it comes to the classics, since they're somehow familiar to us. Even if they haven't come into our lives by some other route, they are present as background noise, as part of the atmosphere. They are part of a collective library. If we know the basic coordinates, we can get ourselves out of a tight spot.

But to return to Italo Calvino, the classics are books that, the more we believe we know them from hearsay, the fresher, more surprising, and more original they are when we finally read them. These books never finish saying what they have to say. This happens, naturally, when they excite and enlighten the reader. The people who have protected those texts like talismans through long periods of danger are not those who have been coerced into reading, but those who have fallen in love with it.

The classics are great survivors. In the ultracontemporary language of social networks, we might say that their power—their wealth, in census terms—is measured by their number of followers. They keep attracting new readers a hundred, two hundred, two thousand years after they were written. They elude variations in taste, mindset, and political ideas; revolutions, the changing seasons, the indifference of new generations. And along this journey, where it might be so easy to go astray, they gain access to the universe of other authors and influence them. They tread the boards of theaters the whole world over, are adapted to the language of cinema and broadcast on television; they have even left binding and ink behind to appear on the internet. Every new form of expression—advertising, manga, rap, video games—adopts these stories, giving them a new home.

A great, almost unknown story lies behind the survival of the oldest classics, the story of all the anonymous people who managed to preserve, with their passion, the fragile legacy of words; the story of their mysterious loyalty to those books. While the texts and even the languages of the earliest civilizations that invented writing in the Fertile Crescent—Mesopotamia and Egypt—were forgotten as the centuries passed, and, in the best-case scenarios, were deciphered long centuries later, *The Iliad* and *The Odyssey* have never been without readers. A chain of transmission and translation began in Greece that has never been broken and has kept the possibility of remembering and conversing across time, distance, and borders alive. Today's readers may feel alone, amid the rush of life, as we cultivate our slow rituals. But a long line of kin lies behind us, and we shouldn't forget that all of us, though we might be strangers to one another, have played a part in an extraordinary act of salvage.

40

Not everything new is worthwhile: chemical weapons are a more recent invention than democracy. Nor are traditions always conventional, rigid, and boring. The rebellions of today are inspired by crusades of the past such as abolitionism and the women's movement. A legacy can be revolutionary, just as it can also be regressive. The classics were sometimes profoundly critical of their world and of ours. We haven't come far enough to be able to do without their reflections on corruption, militarism, or injustice.

In the year 415 BC, Euripides presented his tragedy *The Trojan*

Women to a packed theater during a religious festival. The work re-created the end of the Trojan War—the Greeks' foundational myth, their ancestors' great patriotic victory. Most of the Athenians waiting on the steps before the performance and nibbling on bread, cheese, and olives were as proud of the feats of Achilles in Troy as we are today of having defeated the Nazis in the Second World War. But if they were expecting an Attic Spielberg to flatter their pride in being on the right side of history like in *Schindler's List*, they had a let-down of epic proportions ahead of them. Euripides unfurled a fero-cious massacre before their eyes, a frenzy of vengeful destruction, mass rapes, the cold-blooded murder of a boy thrown from the city walls into the void, defeated women enduring the horrors of war . . .

What the Athenians heard on that tumultuous afternoon in the fifth century BC was the rage and despair of the mothers of the enemy, railing against them for their cruelty. In the end, by the light of an apocalyptic fire, the elderly queen Hecuba decries with her toothless mouth the total orphanhood of the victims: "Woe is me, fire consumes the high citadel, the roofs of our city, the tops of the walls . . . Dust and smoke, blown on the wings of the wind, rob me of my palace. The name of this country will be forgotten, as every-thing is forgotten. Oh, how the earth shakes and shakes as Troy falls. Trembling, quaking limbs, carry me away. We shall live out our days in slavery."

It goes without saying that Euripides did not win the theater festival prize that year. During wartime—the ancient world was always at war—in a production financed with public money, he dared to take the side of the women instead of the men, the enemy instead of his compatriots, and the losers instead of the winners. He may not have won the prize, but the play has been performed after every major European war—recently, in honor of the widows and mothers of Sarajevo—and the toothless Hecuba has spoken anew from the warm trenches and still uncleared rubble, in the name of the victims of war, before we could begin to forget.

Our image of classical authors as consecrated and untouch-able makes it hard to imagine the immense interrogation to which some were subjected and the enormous uproar they caused with their works. If there was ever a controversial figure, it was the multimillionaire Seneca. A shrewd investor, he set up what today we would call a bank and enriched himself by charging exorbitant interest. He bought estates in Egypt, the prime real estate investment opportunity of the time. He multiplied his property holdings several times over, and, with the help of certain privileges and a network of contacts, amassed one of the century's largest fortunes, a tenth of the annual tax earnings of the entire Roman Empire. He could have dedicated himself to a life of luxury, to displaying his wealth in immense and costly mansions with thousands of tiles (in Rome, the size of a dwelling was measured not in square meters but by the number of tiles in the roof over its owner's head), to collecting antiques, slaves, and hunting trophies. Instead, his passion was philosophy—Stoic philosophy, the height of irony. He devoted pages brimming with conviction to his ideas, pages where he claimed that a man is rich when his needs are simple. Without any need for a list in *Forbes,* his contemporaries knew he possessed an extravagant fortune. It was highly tempting to crack jokes and poke fun at all those apologetics of detachment, frugality, and the virtues of settling for stale bread. Seneca was ridiculed over and over for defending his creed of austerity and philanthropy while administering his business with the methods of unbridled capitalism. It's hard to know what to make of this ambiguous figure, a banker and philosopher who never resolved the contradiction between what he thought and how he lived. Yet some of the texts that earned him so much mockery in his lifetime are the very ones that still challenge us today. A passage from his *Moral Letters to Lucilius* marks a point of no return in the history of Western pacifism: "We punish the murders of individuals, but what of wars, and the heroic crime of slaughtering entire peoples? Deeds that would merit a death penalty are praised when committed by generals in uniforms. Public authority demands that which is forbidden to private citizens, and violence is meted out by Senate decisions and plebeian decrees. Human beings, the gentlest among animals, are not ashamed to wage war or to entrust the waging of war to their sons."

These texts are centuries old, yet they re-create the world around us with astonishing accuracy. How is this possible? Because ever since Greece and Rome, we have not ceased to recycle our signs, our ideas, our revolutions. The three philosophers of suspicion—Nietzsche in metaphysics, Freud in ethics, and Marx in politics—studied the ancients as a point of departure for their shift toward modernity. Even the most innovative creation contains, among other things, the fragments and remains of previous ideas. The classics are those books that, like die-hard rockers, grow old onstage and adapt to new kinds of audiences. Devoted fans fork out for their concerts, the irreverent parody them, but no one ignores them. They show that the relationship between the old and the new is more complex and creative than it seems at first glimpse. As Hannah Arendt wrote, the past "does not pull back but presses forward, and it is, contrary to what one would expect, the future which drives us back into the past."

CANON

The History of a Reed

41

This story begins in the reedbeds of a river that sparkles beneath the sun in eastern climes almost devoid of woodland. Water licks the wet banks where tangled vegetation springs up, crickets sing stubbornly, and dazzling blue dragonflies dart. At dawn, a hunter lies in wait for his prey on the slope, listening to the faint lapping of the water and the creak of the reeds stirring in the breeze.

Somewhere like this, standing erect like cypress trees, the stalks of the giant reed (*Arundo donax*) grew. The name of this species contains an ancient Semitic root (in Akkadian, *qanu*; in Hebrew, *qaneh*; and in Aramaic, *qanja*). From this foreign root comes the Greek word *canon*, which means literally "straight like a reed."

What was a canon? It was a yardstick. Ancient builders used the term to refer to the simple strips of wood employed to draw straight lines and precisely measure size, proportion, and scale. In the agora, where merchants and clients argued loudly, accusing each other of being crooks, there was usually someone with weights and measures sculpted in stone. One person would grumble, "This piece of fabric isn't three elbows long, you drunkard, you dogface, you shall be my ruin!" and the person addressed would wail, "You beggar, you fleabag, how dare you call me a thief?" The majority of our Greek ancestors' haggling and disagreements were resolved with canons—precursors of the platinum meter we use today. In a leap toward abstraction, the sculptor Polykleitos titled his treatise on the ideal physical proportions *Kanón*. According to him, the perfect human figure measures seven times the size of a head. His sculpture *Doryphoros* seems to have exemplified these desirable masculine measurements—and marked the beginning of the tyranny of image: young men at the gymnasium were tormented by dreams of sculpting their body in the likeness of that marble model.

Through Aristotle, our humble reed arrived in the distant terrain of ethics. The philosopher wrote that the rule of action—the moral canon—should be not the absolute and eternal ideas of Plato but rather "the way an honorable and upright man behaves." This Aristotelian formula for resolving matters of conscience reminds me of a line spoken by Cary Grant in the movie *Holiday*: "When I find myself in a position like this, I ask myself, what would General Motors do? And then I do the opposite!" As archaic as it may seem, the Spanish Civil Code demands that we carry out our obligations "with the diligence of a good father."

Lists of the greatest writers and the greatest works were never called canons in Greek and Roman times. How did we arrive at the controversial concept of a "literary canon"? Through the filter of Christianity. Amid heated discussions of the authenticity of the Gospels, church authorities outlined the content of the New Testament: the Gospels of Mark, Matthew, Luke, and John—those four and no others—the Acts of the Apostles, and the Epistles. The debate among Christian communities that led to the exclusion of texts considered apocryphal was long and often acrimonious. In the fourth century, when the repertoire was almost set in stone, the historian Eusebius of Caesarea called the selection of books that the authorities had declared to be of divine inspiration and where believers could find a guide to life the "ecclesiastical canon." Over a thousand years later, in 1768, a German scholar used the expression "canon of writings" in the current sense for the first time. The problem is that the word arrived already loaded with characteristics and connotations. Due to the biblical analogy, the literary canon seemed to take the form of a vertical hierarchy, dictated by experts, resting on the authority of a select group, deliberately closed to entry. It also seemed permanent and impervious to the passage of time. It's hardly surprising that since then, in defense of their freedom, like Cary Grant in response to General Motors, many devoted readers have been tempted to do—and read—exactly the opposite.

In fact, many classics have become such by prevailing over the authorities that tried to destroy them. Ovid's books triumphed over Augustus, for example, and Sappho's verse over Pope Gregory VII. Plato's threats against poets never had any consequences, even in realms where the philosopher wielded political influence. Caligula couldn't do away with Homer's poems, nor Caracalla with the ideas of Aristotle. Works considered dangerous and heretical like Lucretius's *De rerum natura,* Rabelais's *Gargantua and Pantagruel*, or the writings of Sade, have survived as part of the canon. The Nazis failed to convince the world that no valuable work had ever been written by a Jew.

The literary canon has little in common with the religious one. The biblical repertoire, sustained by faith, is meant to be static; the literary one is not. For the latter, the metaphor chosen by the Romans is a better fit: the census—a hierarchical classification, yes, but one that is constantly being updated. If it can be a useful tool, this is precisely because its flexibility allows it to register change. There are no complete ruptures in culture, nor is there total continuity. Some works are positively or negatively received according to changes in historical circumstances. Enlightenment critics, in their obsession with didactic and moral works, were far less captivated by Shakespeare than we are today. These days, we have little interest in reading sermons and speeches, which were major genres in other eras. In the eighteenth century, intellectuals quite unanimously condemned the novel, never imagining its ascent to the heights of the canon today. Children's literature was never popular until childhood became valued—and reinvented—as a stage of life. With the rise of feminism, novels with persecuted heroines like those of María de Zayas in the Spanish Golden Age have ceased to be considered minor curiosities and have acquired a renewed importance. Like businesses, some authors open or close according to shifts in public sensibility. Baltasar Gracián had to wait until the 1990s, when aggressive executives in the United States and Japan made his work *The Art of Worldly Wisdom* into a bedtime book and an international best seller. The brilliant Nobel laureate Jacinto Benavente's plays are seldom performed, but we are fascinated by those of his contemporary Valle-Inclán, a marginal eccentric with an evasive relationship to his audience and to success. Martial had to fight accusations that his poems were too short, whereas now, the brevity of his epigrams—about the length of a tweet—works in their favor. Chivalric romances, for centuries all the rage, were swept aside, while their parody, *Don Quixote*, was consecrated. Humor and irony have gained ground—today we prefer books steeped in ambiguity to those that try to indoctrinate us.

Over time, numerous canons have coexisted, with infinite subbranches. In almost every period, different critics lock horns and build rival lists. Objectors must always have something to which to object. Each generation distinguishes between good taste (mine) and vulgarity (yours). Each literary movement vacates the pedestals to hoist its own favorites onto them. In the end, only time can have the last word. Cicero believed that the innovative Catullus was a vain youngster without any shred of talent, and Catullus detested Julius Caesar. But all three of them ended up in the Roman canon together. Emily Dickinson published just seven poems in her lifetime, and her editors found it necessary to correct her syntax and punctuation. André Gide rejected Proust's manuscript on behalf of Gallimard. Borges published a devastating review of *Citizen Kane* in the journal *Sur,* which he would later deny having written.

Like all taxonomies, canons reveal a lot about those who formulate them and their era. The choices blossom with prejudices, aspirations, feelings, blind spots, power structures, and self-validations. The study of classics no longer considered as such, of works that have emerged after being swept aside, and of those whose influence has persisted uninterrupted—in other words, the history of the canon's metamorphoses over the centuries—provides a fascinating perspective on our cultural life. The recognition that while we consider our judgments eternal, the context in which we make them is actually variable represents a step forward in historical understanding. According to J. M. Coetzee, this means understanding the past as a force that shapes the present. "What, if anything, is left of the classic after the classic has been historicized, which may still claim to speak across the ages?" the South African author wonders. A classic work transcends temporal limits, still holds meaning for the coming eras; it is alive. Every day it is put to the test and comes out unscathed. Though it may pass through dark ages, its continuity remains unbroken. It overcomes historical change, even survives the kiss of death of its consecration by fascism and dictatorships. In the propaganda films Eisenstein made for the Soviet communists, and in those Leni Riefenstahl made for the Nazis, something still has the power to make an impression on us.

The field of cultural studies has attacked the canon as oppressive and authoritarian and proposed alternative canons that give a central role to previously excluded works. The debate, begun in the seventies, was revitalized at the end of the twentieth century. In the context of an academic world that was newly conscious of multiculturalism, the American critic Harold Bloom condemned, in an elegiac tone, the moralizing focus of what he called "the school of resentment" and published his own shamelessly anglophone, white, male version of the Western canon. Never before had there been so much criticism and at the same time so much canonizing activity. The internet harbors infinite lists of books, movies, and songs. Cultural sections unceasingly classify what's new in a given year. Prizes and festivals announce their selections of the best works. Innumerable books are published with the title *The Hundred Best* . . . Social networks embrace millions of recommendations shared by expert readers and amateurs alike. We hate lists and at the same time are addicted to them. Indispensable but imperfect, the canon is an expression of this contradictory passion. And we find ourselves overwhelmed by the immeasurable flood of books.

But let's go back to the reed bed where this long excursion began. Peering between the reeds and bullrushes with their dark spikes, I believe we have chosen an imperfect metaphor. The stiff, straight stems that sprout from this bed of rushes do not evoke the winding path of the canon. Rather, it is the river that shifts, snakes, and meanders, the river whose tide swells and ebbs yet always remains, that seems always to be the same river, singing its inexhaustible stanza, but with different water.

42

When the last copy of a book was burning somewhere, or grew damp to the point of rotting, or was slowly devoured by insects, this meant the death of a world. No longer could anyone read, copy, or save it. Over the centuries, especially in ancient times and the Middle Ages, many voices fell silent forever. It's difficult to comprehend through what bizarre twists and turns certain tiny, innocent, or indecent works have reached us, while others have succumbed to the most extravagant processes of destruction.

The scholars of Alexandria were acutely aware of the fragility of words. Oblivion is in essence the most predictable fate of any story, any metaphor, any idea. Years of survival stolen from silence and disappearance are the exception, an exception that, prior to the printing press, could be sustained only by the gargantuan effort of copying texts by hand, letter by letter, to reproduce and keep them in circulation. The canon of the librarians of Alexandria was mostly a salvage program, a concentration of their available energy on a few chosen works, since keeping them all alive was unthinkable. It was a passport into the future for certain stories, verses, and thoughts, those that were most important to them.

The mechanisms of the canon were a matter of survival—in those days, the written word was a species in danger of extinction. There were more copies of the chosen books; their prestige translated into numbers, which were figures not of business but hope. All these were destined for public libraries, which sheltered them from the elements. The other great refuge was school. The texts used in reading and writing lessons were copied in every corner of the territory—a book's most reliable life insurance. In a school system without the slightest hint of centralization and without any academic authorities, each teacher was free to choose the titles he read with his students. That sum of individual decisions was inspired by the canon, at the same time influencing and transforming it.

There is only one genre in Greece and Rome that managed, without aristocratic origins or pretensions to high culture, to consecrate its own classics: animal fables. The hazy figure of Aesop of course had a Roman twin, the former slave Phaedrus. Ancient fables viewed reality from the bottom up, as a battle between humbler, more vulnerable animals such as sheep, hens, frogs, and swallows and more powerful creatures like lions, eagles, and wolves. The analogy is transparent, as is the moral: defenseless creatures usually end up getting fleeced. Rarely, and only by cunning, does the weak animal triumph; in general, he is trampled effortlessly by the strong. In one of these pessimistic stories, a crane peers down the throat of a lion to pluck out the bone that is choking him, but in the end doesn't receive his reward—isn't it enough that the lion didn't tear his head off in a single bite? In another fable, a lamb tries to refute a wolf's arbitrary accusations, but his reasoning serves only for the predator to creep up on him in the heat of the argument and gobble him down without a second thought. The genre seems ultimately to conclude that everyone must face up to their luck. The most vulnerable will get no help from the law, a kind of spider's web that may trap flies but lets dangerous birds pass through. Nothing else in the canon displays such harshness and disenchantment. And if these fables, so foreign to the elite, carved out a space for themselves, it was undoubtedly because for centuries, teachers used them in their classes.

One of those Roman teachers, Quintus Caecilius Epirota, made the revolutionary decision to study the work of living writers with his students. Thanks to schools, some first-century authors began to taste their status as classics without having to die to do so. Virgil was the most favored among them. As Mary Beard explains, more than fifty quotes from Virgil's poetry have been found scrawled on the walls of Pompeii. Most of these lines come from the first and second books of the *Aeneid*, undoubtedly the passages preferred by teachers. In the year 79, everyone seems to have known the poem's opening line, "*Arma virumque cano*" ("I sing of arms and the man"), without needing to have read the work in its entirety, just as today we needn't be experts in Cervantes to be able to mention the place in La Mancha whose name we don't care to remember. One joker parodied the *Aeneid* on the wall of a Pompeii laundry house to poke fun at the owners. Alluding to the bird they kept as a pet, the anonymous comedian wrote, "The fullers and their owl I sing, not arms and the man." The joke might have been obvious, but Beard emphasizes that it implies a remarkable shared frame of reference between the world of the streets and that of classical literature. Other vandals were less subtle in their insults and had more in common with those who decorate the doors of public restrooms today: "I fucked the landlady" an ancient Pompeiian scrawled on a tavern wall.

The first century BC was a hopeful period for writers. Certain select titles were copied and distributed across an immense territory and were incorporated into an unprecedented network of public and private libraries, as well as schools. Perhaps for the first time in history, the most celebrated authors had solid reasons to trust in a long future for their works. The condition for achieving this, of course, was to get onto the lists. In one of the most explicit passages of Roman canon anxiety, Horace suggests plainly to his patron Maecenas that he include him on the podium of the greats: "If you place me among the lyric poets, with head held high I'll touch the stars." Using the verb *inserere*, he translated the Greek *enkrínein*—"to separate the wheat from the chaff, to winnow"—the metaphor used in the language of the librarians of Alexandria to describe selecting an author. Delighted by his own work, Horace considered himself a worthy colleague of the nine famed Greek lyric poets and had no qualms about sharing such an impartial opinion of himself with his readers. In the same book of odes, he assures them that his poems, written on fragile sheets of papyrus, will survive metal and stone: "I have built a monument as durable as brass, higher than the royal tombs of the pyramids. The steady rains, the frigid winds, and the passage of time with its countless string of years cannot destroy it. I will not fully die." A few years later, Ovid expressed the same confidence that his *Metamorphoses* would endure: "I have completed a work that neither the wrath of Jupiter, nor fire, nor sword, nor the ravages of time shall ever ruin." Though these prophecies may seem rash, the truth is that so far they have been fulfilled.

Not all writers dared to dream of such a long life for their works. Martial, an author with no presence in schools, had less optimistic fantasies. In his *Epigrams,* he jokes about the fate of discarded books, the battered group of those excluded from the summit: *morituri te salutant.* He reveals that many have ended up as wrappers for food or destined for other less than solemn uses. And this is the end with which his own book is threatened: "Come, lest you get carried off to a sooty kitchen, where you'll wrap mackerel in your greasy paper, or be a cone for incense or pepper." His work is dotted with humorous images of literary failure: scrolls turned into togas for tuna, tunics for olives, and hoods for cheese. Martial may have feared his own entry into that underworld of literature that went into the kitchen to die among leftover scales and the stench of rancid fish.

For centuries, shopkeepers have wrapped their goods in pages torn from old books. The writer's dreams and the copyist's efforts—or later, the typographer's—perished as they were sold off for a paltry price. Cervantes tells the same story as Martial in *Don Quixote*, this time with a happy ending. Soon after the book begins, in a boldly metafictional chapter, we find the story's narrator wandering past the shops on calle Alcaná in Toledo, where he sees a young man loaded with folders bursting with secondhand papers to sell to a silk merchant. Though he doesn't yet suspect it, these old documents contain the chronicle of the adventures of Don Quixote de la Mancha. "As I am very fond of reading, even torn papers in the streets, I was moved by my natural inclinations to pick up one of the volumes the boy was selling," the narrator writes. Thanks to the curiosity of this reader in extremis, the manuscript is saved from wrapping up pieces of fabric, and the novel goes on. The episode is a literary game, a fiction concocted by Cervantes as a parody of the device of discovered manuscripts so common in the chivalric romances. But the image of the boy selling secondhand paper to the shops on calle Alcaná has an air of daily life and allows a glimpse into a parallel reality in which our great classic might have been destroyed, page by page, in an anonymous silk shop in Toledo.

On the eve of the twentieth century, the British bibliophile William Blades bought what was left of a valuable book saved from a scatological shipwreck. Blades tells that in the summer of 1887, a gentleman friend of his rented some rooms in Brighton. In the lavatory, he found some papers for wiping himself. He placed them on his bare knees and before using them for their hygienic purpose, scanned the text written in Gothic letters. He had a feeling that he had discovered something. In his excitement, he quickly saw to his bodily matters and the trifle of washing his hands and went out to ask if there were any more pages where those had come from. The landlady sold him the remaining unbound pages and told him that her father, who loved antiques, had at one time possessed a trunk full of books. After his death, she kept them until she tired of them taking up space. Imagining them to be worthless, she used them as bathroom supplies, where the final wreckage of the inherited library was about to drown. The book they had in their hands turned out to be one of the rarest and most unusual books from the press of Wynkyn de Worde, a work titled *Gesta Romanorum*, in which Shakespeare had found inspiration for his plays. The bibliographic treasures that supplied the lavatories on a daily basis in that English guesthouse can only be imagined.

In our times, we have organized the destruction of books with great efficiency. As Alberto Olmos says, our decent societies exterminate in one year as much printed matter as the Nazis, the Inquisition, and Shihuangdi put together. Stealthily, without the epic of the public bonfire, each year in Spain alone we get rid of millions of books. Publishers' warehouses have become funeral homes sheltering titles in their first death—in other words, when they are sent back from the bookstores. The deficit is immense: in 2016, 224 million books were printed in Spain, of which almost 90 million ended up in purgatory. Of the titles with best-selling pretensions, many more copies than readers can consume are knowingly printed, since in the publishing industry, gigantic piles of books are thought to sell books. The miscalculations and frustrated hopes of publishers also send hundreds of thousands of books straight to the funeral home. Due to the high cost of storage, those millions of evicted books end up in warehouses in suburbs, where they are shredded, compressed, and turned into an amorphous mass of paper pulp. They are then quietly transformed into other books born at the price of cannibalizing their failed predecessors, or recycled into other new products and supplies, like Tetra Pak cartons, napkins, tissues, coasters, shoeboxes, food packaging—the contemporary version of Martial's togas for tuna—or even rolls of toilet paper, which make us all into imitators of the guests at that Brighton boardinghouse.

The Czech writer Bohumil Hrabal worked as a paper packer in a recycling mill. Based on this experience, his novel *Too Loud a Solitude* transcribes the monologue of a worker shut away in a basement—with the mice and his musings—as he compacts bales of paper one by one, to be handed over to the carriers. His cave stinks to high heaven since the piles of paper aren't dry but damp and rotting and beginning to ferment, "in a way that makes manure seem sweet." Three times a week, the trucks take their bales to the station, load them into train cars, and haul them off to the paper factories, where workers plunge them into cloudy tanks of acid and alkali that dissolve them. The protagonist, in love with books, knows that wonderful works expire in his hydraulic press, but is powerless to stop the flow of destruction. "I am nothing but a refined butcher," he writes. His consolation consists of being these books' final reader and of carefully preparing their tombs, the bales he makes:

> I have a need to garnish my bales, give them my stamp, my signature . . . Last month they delivered nearly fifteen hundred pounds of 'Old Masters' reproductions, dropped nearly fifteen hundred pounds of sopping-wet Rembrandts, Halses, Monets, Manets, Klimts, Cézannes, and other big guns of European art into my cellar, so now I frame each of my bales with reproductions, and when evening comes and the bales stand one next to the other waiting in all their splendor for the service elevator, I can't take my eyes off them: now *The Night Watch*, now *Saskia,* here *Le Déjeuner sur l'herbe,* there the *House of the Hanged Man at Anvers* or *Guernica.* Besides, I'm the only one on earth who knows that deep in the heart of each bale there's a wide-open *Faust* or *Don Carlos*, that here, buried beneath a mound of

blood-soaked cardboard, lies a *Hyperion*, there, cushioned on piles of cement bags rests a *Thus Spake Zarathustra* . . . I am both artist and audience.

Hrabal wrote this novel when his work had been banned by the communist regime. In that period when writing was taken prisoner, he was obsessed with the dynamic of creation and destruction, with literature's raison d'être and the question of what leads to solitude. The old worker's monologue is a fable about the cruelty of time. It also indirectly bears informed witness to the fantastic and unlikely adventure required for a book to survive for millennia.

SHARDS OF WOMEN'S VOICES

43

In a landscape of shadows, she has a body, a presence, a voice. She is a unique case in Rome: an independent, cultured young woman who insists on her right to love; a poet who speaks of her own life and feelings, in her own words, with no mediation by any man.

Sulpicia lived in the golden age of the emperor Augustus. She was an exceptional woman for many reasons—the most significant of these was that she belonged to that 1 percent of the Roman population that today we classify as elite, at the summit of a harsh, hierarchical world. Her mother was the sister of Marcus Valerius Mesalla Corvinus, a powerful general and literary patron. At her uncle's mansion, she met some of the era's most acclaimed poets, such as Ovid and Tibullus. Favored by wealth and kinship, she was bold enough to write autobiographical verse, the only love poems written by a Roman woman in the classical era to have reached us. A feminine voice speaks in her poetry, laying claim to something unusual in the period: freedom and pleasure. Convinced that she could allow herself any boldness, she complains of her uncle's supervision of her, calling him—with irony and audacity—a "heartless relative."

Only six of Sulpicia's poems have reached us. A total of forty lines, six episodes of her passion for a man whom she calls Cerinthus. It's clear that he is not the suitor chosen by her family. On the contrary, her parents and her uncle and tutor fear her sleeping with him. She herself says that some suffer at the mere idea that she should succumb, allowing herself to be taken to an "unworthy bed." Cerinthus surely belongs to another world, another social class, and perhaps is even a freedman. Who knows? In any case, he seems to be an inappropriate suitor for the aristocratic Sulpicia, something that doesn't bother her in the slightest. If she suffers, and sometimes she suffers, it's for other reasons. For example, she chides herself for her cowardice, feeling anguished that the burden of her education prevents her from showing her desire.

The poem by Sulpicia that moves me most is a provocative and defiant public declaration of her feelings. Here is a loose translation of the elegy's lines:

> *Finally, you arrived, Love!*
> *Arrived with such intensity*
> *that it shames me more*
> *to deny you*
> *than to affirm myself.*
> *Love kept its word,*
> *it brought you to me.*
> *Swayed by my songs,*
> *love brought you to my lap.*
> *It brings me joy to have committed this offense.*
> *To reveal it and to shout it.*
> *No, I don't want to confide my pleasure*
> *to the stupid privacy of my notes.*
> *I shall defy the norm,*
> *it sickens me to pretend for the sake of what they say.*
> *We were each worthy of the other,*
> *let this be said.*
> *And may she who hasn't a story*
> *tell mine.*

What became of these lovers? We have no idea, but it's unlikely that their relationship managed to survive the family obstacles.

Sooner or later, she would have to give in. Among the upper classes to which Sulpicia belonged, the paterfamilias decided marriages based on strategic motives, when opportunity presented itself. Clans would unite two people for social, political, or economic convenience, not for passion. Surely, the beloved Cerinthus was expelled from Sulpicia's life, and only the memory and the poems remained—"deserted bed, / and cloudy mirror and empty heart!" as Antonio Machado wrote.

To rebel against sexual morality, if only for a brief, youthful interlude, implied a journey to the edge of the abyss for Sulpicia. She was committing a crime. Not long before, Augustus had passed a law—the *lex Iulia de adulteriis*—which condemned women who had sexual relations outside marriage, even if they were widows or spinsters, by public trial. Both they and their accomplices were punished severely. Only prostitutes and concubines were exempt. This is why, the sources tell us, patrician women of senatorial and equestrian rank began to declare themselves to be prostitutes in public. This was an act of civil disobedience, an open challenge to the courts. The protests resulted in the law being barely applied in practice. At the end of the first century, Juvenal exclaimed in exasperation in his fierce diatribe against the female sex, "Where are you now, *lex Iulia*, asleep?"

Sulpicia's other great transgression was to make her feelings and her rebellion public through her writing. Like the Greeks, the Romans also believed that words, the fundamental tool of political struggle, were a masculine prerogative. These ideas were also expressed in the religious realm through the cult of a silent goddess, Dea Tacita. The legend said that Tacita was a shameless nymph who talked too much and especially at the wrong time. To put a stop to this chattiness and make it clear to whom verbal authority belonged, Jupiter cut out her tongue. Unable to speak, Dea Tacita was an eloquent symbol. Roman women could not occupy public roles or participate in political life. A single generation allowed the existence of female orators, in the first half of the first century BC, but the activity was soon outlawed. Roman women from respectable families did have access to reading, but this was to be applied in their roles as mothers and teachers of future orators. Educated so that they could educate in turn, they learned to speak well for the benefit of their sons, not to use the skill themselves, which would mean going beyond the bounds of their private sphere and usurping a position in the field of men's work. They had few opportunities beyond the home to stand out or to make themselves heard. When the biographer Plutarch tried to repeat the success of his *Parallel Lives* with a work on the exploits of Greek, Roman, and barbarian women, the work met with an icy reception. In fact, the book received scant scholarly attention until recent times.

Studying the factors that helped Sulpicia's verse to survive is highly revealing. They arrived not under her name but spliced among poems attributed to a writer belonging to her uncle Tibullus's circle. Doubts over their authorship and Tibullus's great prestige contributed to the texts' preservation for centuries. Today, after careful philological analysis, academics accept almost unanimously that the poems are Sulpicia's work, though some skeptics still object that their content is too daring for a Roman lady. At the same time, until a few years ago, it was common to belittle her as a mere amateur—sadly redundant, since in those days no woman could make a profession of literature. Roman women of the time had no way to make their work known or have it distributed. Most didn't even consider it. And most significantly: those who assessed whether a book was worthy of passing into posterity didn't even take what women wrote into account. We shouldn't be at all surprised that these poems only survived embedded in someone else's book.

Despite the obstacles, Sulpicia wasn't the only one to try. We have brief fragments and quotes by or references to twenty-four female writers. They all had certain features in common: they were wealthy, they belonged to important families, and they wrote under the protection of powerful men. As Aurora López writes, they had a dowry, a fortune, and power over their slaves; the city provided them with leisure time; they ruled over a space that was always private—the home—but at the end of the day it was a space of which they were mistress. In other words, as Virginia Woolf came to desire, they had money and a room of their own, the requirements for a woman to be a writer. Julia Agrippina stands out among them—daughter of Germanicus, wife of Claudius, mother of Nero—whose lost memoirs we know only by allusion; or Cornelia, mother of the famous Gracchi, by whom two incomplete letters are preserved.

But the daring patrician ladies who set about invading the terrain of men were forced to respect certain boundaries. They were allowed to practice only genres considered minor or associated with inner life: the lyric (Hostia and Perilla), eulogy (Aconia Fabia Paulina), epigrams (Cornificia, Servilia, Clodia, Pilia, Attica, Terentia, Tullia, Publilia, Fulvia, Atia, Octavia Minor, and Julia Drusilla), and memoirs (Agrippina). We know the names of three women orators who practiced during the brief period when it was allowed—Hortensia, Mesia, and Carfania—but not a single paragraph of their speeches has survived. There is no trace of information about female authors of epic, tragedy, or comedy, since they couldn't possibly have presented their works onstage.

The texts these Roman women wrote have reached us in shards. All together, they can be read in one or two hours. This glimpse indicates the extent of our loss. Sulpicia benefited from a mistake and made her way into the future with an involuntary male pseudonym. The others were slowly stranded in silence. In the canon, these women are the fragmentary exceptions. Like Eurydice, when anyone tries to rescue them, they sink back into darkness. Following their erased footprints, we feel our way through a landscape of shadows where only the echoes can answer.

44

And yet, since time immemorial, women have told stories, sung songs, and threaded together lines of verse in the glow of the fireside. When I was a little girl, my mother unfurled before me a world of whispered stories. This was no coincidence. Throughout the ages, women have held the role of unraveling stories by night. Women have been the weavers of tales and tapestries. For centuries, they have unspooled their stories as they spun or threw the shuttle on their loom. They were the first to capture the universe as warp and weft. They knotted together their joys, hopes, sorrows, fears, and most private beliefs. They dyed drudgery, giving it color. They interlaced verbs, yarn, adjectives, and silk. This is why text and textiles share so many words: the thread of the story, the dénouement of the narrative, the fabric of the argument; weave a plot, embroider a tale, spin a yarn. This is why the old myths speak to us of Penelope's shroud, Nausicaa's tunics, Arachne's embroidery, Ariadne's thread, the thread of fate spun by the Moirai, the canvas of human fate sewn by the Norns, the magic tapestry of Scheherazade.

Now my mother and I whisper those nighttime stories in my son's ears. Though I am no longer that little girl, I write so the stories won't come to an end. I write because I don't know how to sew or knit; I never learned to embroider, but I am fascinated by the delicate warp and weft of words. I tell of my fantasies wound in a skein of dreams and memories. I feel like an heir to those women who have always woven and unwoven stories. I write so the old thread of voices will not be frayed.

WHAT WAS BELIEVED ETERNAL
TURNED OUT TO BE FLEETING

45

One day in the year 212, over thirty million people went to bed with a different identity from the one they woke up with early that morning. The reason wasn't a mass invasion of body snatchers, but an astonishing decision made by a Roman emperor. The sources do not tell us how the change was received, whether joy or suspicion prevailed. No doubt it was a great surprise: there was no historical precedent for anything of this nature, and I am convinced that I will see nothing remotely like it in the twenty-first century.

What was the cause of such sudden commotion? The emperor Caracalla had decreed that all free inhabitants of the empire, wherever they lived, from Caledonia to Roman Syria, from Cappadocia to Mauritania, from that moment on were granted Roman citizenship. It was a revolutionary decision that erased the distinction between natives and foreigners with the stroke of a pen. A long process of integration culminated in the instant the decree was approved. It was one of the largest concessions of citizenship ever recorded, if not the largest: dozens of millions of people from the provinces legally became Romans overnight. Historians still find this sudden gift disconcerting, because it broke with the ancient—and extremely contemporary—policy of granting citizenship to only a small percentage of those who aspired to it, in a gradual and restrictive way. The ancient politician and chronicler Cassius Dio suspected that beneath Caracalla's apparent generosity was hidden the need to collect money, since the new Romans acquired ipso facto the obligation to pay an inheritance tax and a duty on the manumission of slaves. As Mary Beard notes, if that was the motive, it was an extremely burdensome way of going about it. I don't think it would occur to any state in the present to legalize thirty million people at once, no matter how tantalizing the prospect of collecting taxes from them might be. The emperor's decision undoubtedly had a significant symbolic weight. In times of crisis, giving more people personal reasons to identify with Rome could be an intelligent step.

The extension of citizenship logically also reduced its value. When one barrier to privilege fell, another quickly rose in its place. Throughout the third century, the distinction between *honestiores* (the wealthy elite and army veterans) and *humiliores* (the humble ones, a timeless concept that needs no translation) became increasingly important. The law recognized unequal rights between these two groups: the *honestiores* were legally exempt from cruel or degrading punishments like crucifixion or flagellation, while the *humiliores* remained exposed to the humiliations formerly reserved for slaves and noncitizens. The border of wealth replaced that of geography.

Though in practice there was no lack of prejudice, conflict, or rapacity from the beginning, Roman civilization had a clear conciliatory drive. Caracalla represented the peak of an evolution that, according to legend, Romulus had begun a thousand years earlier, when he offered shelter, no questions asked, to all the outsiders who flocked to the recently founded Rome. What distinguished the new city was the welcome he gave to the most desperate fugitives and asylum seekers. And, in fact, Romulus's descendants practiced a politics of fusion with no precedent in the history of the world: they considered racial purity irrelevant, showed little concern for skin color, freed their slaves with straightforward procedures, and gave freedmen the status of quasi-citizens—the children of freedmen were citizens in their own right. We do not know to what extent the population of Rome was multicultural, among other reasons because no attention was paid to the matter; it was probably the most ethnically diverse society prior to the modern era. Of course, there was no shortage in Rome of those who lamented that so many slaves would end up eroding the national character, and many accused outsiders of making little effort to integrate. But even the most recalcitrant among those curmudgeons who wished to protest wouldn't have understood our modern concepts of "illegal" immigrants or "undocumented" migrants.

It is a fact that the population moved across the length and breadth of the Roman territories as it never had before: merchants, soldiers, administrators and bureaucrats, slave traders, wealthy provincials who dreamed of success in the capital. There were upperclass citizens in Britain who had come from North Africa. Each year, governors and senior officials were sent to far-off places. The legions were made up of soldiers from every background. Even the most penniless joined the flow of migration. The moral of one fable said, "The poor, who carry less baggage, travel easily from one city to another."

The emperors were obsessed with global iconography, which they used in their propaganda. It was proclaimed that Rome was not only the dominant world power, but also the shared homeland of all humanity; the great city of the world, the cosmopolis made real, that could hold and offer welcome to all the people scattered across distant territories. This ideal found perhaps its most characteristic expression in the pompous and adulatory "Roman Oration" by Aelius Aristides: "Neither the seas nor the whole expanse of the earth impede the granting of citizenship, and there is no distinction here between Asia and Europe. All things are open to all people. In Rome, no man worthy of trust is a foreigner." Philosophers of the era insisted that the empire was making the cosmopolitan dream inherited from Hellenism a reality. With his *Constitutio Antoniniana* in the year 212, Caracalla made these ideas a legal fact. Beyond this, he is remembered less than fondly as a ruler. Capricious and murderous, he was assassinated at twenty-nine by one of his bodyguards, while peeing in the gutter at the side of a road in Mesopotamia. Though he gave few signs of idealism during his reign, he admired Alexander and tried to imitate his project of an empire based on global citizenship. He himself, born in Lugdunum—present-day Lyon—was mixed-race: his father, Septimus Severus, was dark-skinned and descended from Berber stock, and his mother, Julia Domna, had been born in Emesa—now Homs—in Syria. And he was no exception. By the time he came to power, the emperors had not been natives of Rome, or even Italians, for quite some time. The Roman power elites' complexions were far less white than their marble statues.

If it wasn't race, skin color, or place of birth, what united the inhabitants of Caledonia, Gaul, Hispania, Roman Syria, Cappadocia, and Mauritania? What were the links that helped the Romans understand one another, share aspirations, and recognize one another as members of the same community, across the length and breadth of such enormous swaths of the world? An interweaving of words, ideas, myths, and books.

Feeling Roman consisted, as we have seen, of living in cities with wide avenues that intersected at right angles; of having access to gymnasiums, baths, forums, marble temples, libraries, Latin inscriptions, aqueducts, and sewage systems; of knowing who Achilles, Hector, Dido, and Aeneas were; of seeing scrolls and codices as a familiar part of the daily landscape; of paying taxes to the fearsome tax collectors; of having burst into guffaws at one of Plautus's jokes on the theater steps; of knowing the tales of primitive Rome told by Livy in *Ab urbe condita*; of having heard a Stoic philosopher speak of self-control; of being familiar with—or even having served in—the war machine of the legions. Mosaics, banquets, statues, rituals, façades, low-relief carvings, legends of triumph and pain, fables, comedies, and tragedies shaped—with air, stone, and papyrus—the Roman identity that stretched to unimaginable boundaries: the very first shared European story.

Along the roads of the globalized empire, essays and stories traveled from one end of the known world to the other. They found shelter in a constellation of public and private libraries such as had never been known before. They were copied and put on sale in bookstores in cities with great distances between them, like present-day Brindisi, Carthage, Lyon, or Reims. They seduced people of a wide range of origins, who were taught to read in Roman schools after generations of illiteracy. Like the aristocrats of the capital, the richest provincials bought slaves who specialized in copying texts—an inventory of the assets of an affluent Roman citizen, owner of an estate in Egypt, includes among his fifty-nine slaves five notaries, two scribes, a copyist, and a book restorer. There were many copyists who, whether in private or commercial service, spent their long days at a desk furnished with inkwells, rulers, and calamus pens, to satisfy the demands of the written word. Never had there been such a community of readers spread across several continents and united by the same books. It's true that they didn't amount to millions, nor hundreds of thousands; perhaps, at the best of times, there were several dozen thousand. But seen from the perspective of the period, these are extraordinary figures.

As Stephen Greenblatt says, "There was a time in the ancient world—a very long time—in which the central cultural problem must have seemed an inexhaustible outpouring of books. Where to put them all? How to organize them on the groaning shelves? How to hold the profusion of knowledge in one's head? The loss of this plenitude would have been virtually inconceivable to anyone living in its midst. Then, not all at once but with the cumulative force of a mass extinction, the whole enterprise came to an end. What looked stable turned out to be fragile, and what had seemed for all time was only for the time being." What was believed to be eternal was shown, in the end, to be fleeting.

46

The earth shook. Centuries of anarchy, division, barbaric invasions, and religious convulsions came. The copyists were probably the first to sense how serious things were: they were receiving fewer and fewer commissions. The work of copying almost completely came to a halt. Libraries went into decline, looted during wars and other disturbances, or simply neglected. In a succession of dreadful decades, they suffered pillage by the barbarians and destruction at the hands of Christian fanatics. At the end of the fourth century, the historian Ammianus Marcellinus complained that the Romans were giving up serious reading. With a moralistic view typical of his social class, he was outraged that his fellow citizens were dabbling in the most absurd trivialities while the empire was inexorably crumbling around them and the cultural bond was being dissolved: "Those few houses formerly admired for their serious cultivation of studies now give themselves over to idle pleasures. Instead of a philosopher, a singer is summoned, and instead of an orator, some master in the art of frivolous entertainment. And while the libraries are as tightly closed as a tomb, they spend their time making organs to be played with water-power, lyres so immense that they look like chariots, and flutes for buffoons to tinkle." Furthermore, he remarks with sorrow, people spend their time driving carts at a dizzying speed—as if on a suicide mission—through the packed streets. The anxiety leading up to the wreckage was palpable in the atmosphere.

In the fifth century, the community of classical culture suffered terrible misfortunes. The barbarian invasions gradually destroyed the Roman school system in the provinces of the West. The cities went into decline. The educated public dwindled into negligible figures—even at the best of times it had been a minority among the population, but it was such a considerable minority that in some places it was a genuine multitude. Readers were once again so scarce that, on their little islands, they lost contact with one another.

After its long and drawn-out death throes, the Western Roman Empire fell in the year 476, when the last emperor, Romulus Augustulus, quietly abdicated. The Germanic tribes that then came to power in the provinces did not feel drawn to reading. Those barbarians who attacked public buildings and seized private mansions surely weren't actively hostile to science or study, but nor did they have the slightest interest in preserving the books that housed the intangible treasures of knowledge and creation. The Romans whose mansions were confiscated, who were enslaved or shunted off to some remote and rustic estate, had needs more urgent and losses more profound than the nostalgia for their vanished libraries. Those who were readers in another time were consumed by distressing concerns: insecurity, illness, insufficient harvests, violent tax collectors who worked the poor to the bone, plagues, rising food prices, fear of ending up on the wrong side of the poverty line.

A period began, a long trajectory of hundreds of years, in which a large portion of the ideas that define us teetered on the edge of the abyss. Between the soldiers' torches and the slow and secret labor of moths, the dream of Alexandria was once again imperiled. Until the invention of printing, millennia of knowledge remained in the hands of very few people, who embarked on a heroic and almost implausible rescue effort. If not everything sank into nothingness, if the ideas, scientific achievements, imagination, laws, and rebellions of the Greeks and Romans survived, we owe it to the simple perfection books had achieved after centuries of searching and experimentation. Thanks to them and despite these journeys into the depths of night, European history is, as the philosopher María Zambrano wrote, a road always open to rebirth and enlightenment.

47

With the gradual collapse of the Roman Empire, a period of centuries began in which books lived dangerously. In the year 529, the emperor Justinian banned those who remained "under the insanity of paganism" from employment as teachers, so they could no longer "corrupt the souls of their disciples." His edict forced the closure of the Academy at Athens, whose origins proudly went back to the previous millennium, to Plato himself. Errant souls needed to be protected by the authorities from the dangers of pagan literature. From the early fourth century, zealous functionaries would burst into the baths and private residences to confiscate "heretical" and "magical" books, which went up in smoke in public bonfires. It's hardly surprising that the rate of copying of classical texts—or of any text at all—plummeted.

I imagine one of those prohibited philosophers roaming melancholically through a ghostly Athens. He has plenty of reasons for pessimism. The pagan temples are closed and crumbling from neglect, and the marvelous statues of other times have been disfigured or removed. The theaters have fallen silent, the shuttered libraries are kingdoms of dust and worms. In the capital of enlightenment, the last disciples of Socrates and Plato are banned from teaching philosophy. They cannot earn a living. If they refuse to be baptized, they must go into exile. The barbarians who invade and sack the old, collapsing empire set fire to the wonders of this ancient culture with ferocity, or, worse still, with indifference. What fate awaits the ideas no longer allowed to be taught, and the books condemned to burn?

This is the end.

Then, as if in a dream, the philosopher is assaulted by myriad strange visions. In a Europe controlled by illiterate warlords, when decline seems inevitable, the fables, myths, and ideas of Rome find a paradoxical refuge in the monasteries. Each abbey, with its school, library, and scriptorium, houses a glimmer of the Musaeum of Alexandria amid the era's fading light. There, the monks—and also nuns—become tireless readers, book preservers and binders. They learn the laborious art of parchment making. Letter by letter, word by word, they copy and preserve the best pagan books. They even invent the art of illumination, which transforms the pages of medieval codices into little windows gleaming with forests of figures, gold, and colors. Thanks to the scrupulous patience of these copyists and miniaturists—both men and women—knowledge will resist the onslaught of chaos, in isolated, well-fortified holdouts.

But all this is so unlikely—the philosopher says to himself, sinking back into fatalism—that it can only be a dream.

Suddenly he is gripped by the bustling scene of the first universities in the cities of Bologna and Oxford—the resuscitated Academy—a few centuries later. The teachers and students, thirsty for joy and beauty, as if they were returning home, once again seek the language of the old classics. And new booksellers open the doors of their workshops to feed them with words.

From improbable distances, along Muslim routes, across borderlands between various civilizations, dust-covered merchants bring something marvelous and new from China and Samarkand to the Iberian Peninsula: paper, so called because of its resemblance to the old papyrus. If everything happens at the right moment, this new material, much cheaper than parchment and easier to produce in large quantities, will arrive at the crossroads of Europe in time to supply the launch of the printing presses that will revolutionize Western culture.

But all these fantasies—the philosopher says to himself, resorting to cool logic—can only be hallucinations caused by indigestion, images engendered by a moldy piece of cheese or a foul fish stew.

Then, brandishing quills, some stubborn idealists appear before him, the humanists determined to restore the splendor of ancient times. All of them set about reading, copying, editing, and passionately commenting on the pagan texts within their reach—what's left of the wreckage. The bravest venture on horseback along remote routes, through snowy valleys, dark forests, and along almost invisible paths in the folds of the mountains, in search of the unique books still held in isolated medieval monasteries. With those castaway manuscripts that enclose ancient wisdom, they will attempt to modernize Europe.

Meanwhile, a cutter of precious stones by the name of Gutenberg invents a curious metal copyist who never rests. Books spread once again. Europeans recover the Alexandrian dream of infinite libraries and limitless knowledge. Paper, printing, and curiosity, liberated from fear and sin, will lead to the very threshold of modernity.

But all these visions—the philosopher tells himself, sinking back into his pessimism—are only nonsense.

And when his fervid imagination goes a few centuries further still, he glimpses some men in strange wigs who, in honor of the ancient *paideia,* embark on the adventure of the encyclopedia to spread knowledge and defeat the stubborn work of destruction. The intellectual revolutionaries of that distant eighteenth century will raise, on the foundations of ancient splendor, the edifice of their faith in reason, science, and law.

And although the people of the future twenty-first century will worship new inventions and technologies—especially strange luminous tablets they caress with their fingertips—they will continue to give shape to their fundamental ideas on power, citizenship, responsibility, violence, empire, luxury, and beauty in dialogue with books where the classics speak. This is how all that we love will be saved, along a turbulent and intrepid path, riddled with detours and forks in the road that will often threaten to be lost in nothingness.

But all this is as far-fetched as any dream, and no one in their right mind would believe such an outlandish hypothesis, the philosopher tells himself. Only a supernatural event—or one of those miracles with which the Christians delude themselves—could save our wisdom and give it shelter in the impossible libraries of tomorrow.

DARE TO REMEMBER

48

The invention of books was perhaps the greatest triumph in our tenacious struggle against destruction. With their help, humanity has undergone an extraordinary acceleration of history, development, and progress. The common ground made possible by our myths and knowledge multiplies our chances of cooperation, uniting readers from different parts of the world and successive generations throughout the centuries. As Stefan Zweig memorably writes at the end of "Buchmendel," "One only makes books in order to keep in touch with one's fellows after one has ceased to breathe, and thus to defend oneself against the inexorable fate of all that lives—transitoriness and oblivion."

In different eras, we have experimented with books made of smoke, of stone, of earth, of leaves, of reeds, of silk, of animal skin, of rags, of trees, and now, of light—the computers and ebooks of today. The actions of opening and closing a book, or of traveling through the text, have varied. Their format, their roughness or smoothness, their labyrinthine interior, the way they creak and whisper, their durability, the creatures that devour them, and the experience of reading them aloud have all changed. They have taken many shapes, but what's indisputable is the overwhelming success of their discovery.

We owe the survival of the greatest ideas dreamed up by humanity to books. Without them, we might have forgotten that handful of reckless Greeks who decided to give power to the people and called that bold experiment "democracy." We might have forgotten the Hippocratic doctors who created the first professional oath where they swore to care for slaves and the poor: "Keep your patient's means in mind. Sometimes, you should even offer your services free of charge; and, if you have a chance to help a foreigner in financial trouble, give him the maximum assistance." We might have forgotten Aristotle, who founded one of the earliest universities, and told his students that the difference between a wise man and an ignorant one is the same as the difference between a live man and a dead one; we might have forgotten Eratosthenes, who used the power of reason to calculate the Earth's circumference with a margin of error of less than 1 percent using only a stick and a camel; or we might have forgotten the legal codes of those Roman madmen who one day recognized the citizenship of all the inhabitants of their immense empire; or we might have forgotten that Greek Christian, Paul the Apostle, who gave the first egalitarian speech when he said, "There is neither Jew nor Greek, slave nor free, male nor female." Our knowledge of all these precedents has inspired ideas as outlandish in the animal kingdom as human rights, democracy, faith in science, universal healthcare, compulsory education, the right to a fair trial, and social concern for the disadvantaged. Who would we be today if we had lost the memory of all these discoveries, just as we lost the languages and wisdom of the Egyptian and Mesopotamian civilizations for centuries? The writer Elias Canetti, a German-speaking Bulgarian Sephardic Jew with a Spanish last name (his paternal ancestors changed Cañete to Canetti), answered that if every era lost contact with the previous ones, if every century cut the umbilical cord, we would only be able to construct a fable without a future. The result would be suffocation.

It is not my intention to omit the shadowy parts of this story. The word "cooperation" has a benevolent and altruistic halo that can sometimes conceal dark realities. Networks of collaboration can also serve to exploit and oppress. Many societies have organized themselves to guarantee the continuation of their system of enslavement, and the Nazis, to orchestrate their final solution. Books can also be vehicles for harmful ideas. Plato, who believed in reincarnation, invented a myth to explain the existence of the female sex: being born a woman is a punishment and atonement for those men who did wrong in a previous life. Aristotle wrote that slaves are inferior by nature. Martial seems to feel no moral scruples in his *Epigrams* when flattering a cruel emperor to the point of nausea or cracking jokes at the expense of those with physical defects. Most Roman writers considered gladiator combat, where the audience delighted in the agony of the fighters, part of their civilization. Books make us heirs to all stories: the best, the worst, the ambiguous, the problematic, the double-edged. Having access to all of them is vital for critical thought; it allows us to choose. It's difficult not to be shocked by the strange combination of creativity, splendor, violence, and abuses that built the foundations of Europe. This unease is almost an axiom of late modernity. In 1940, one of the darkest years in European history, Walter Benjamin, a fugitive in occupied France, wrote his famous incendiary reflection: "There is no document of civilization which is not at the same time a document of barbarism." Faced with the distressing evidence that barbarity persevered alongside the triumph of reason and that the Enlightenment had done nothing to expel evil, another ardent European, Stefan Zweig, committed suicide in 1942.

By now we know that any saccharine or reverential image of culture is not only naïve but fruitless. Petrarch, blinded by his sentimental admiration of ancient Rome, was enraged to discover the letters of Cicero, whom he had always considered a kindred spirit. The personal documents of his alter ego revealed an ambitious, sometimes mean-spirited, sometimes cynical character with little discernment when it came to political maneuvering. Petrarch settled the matter by writing a moralizing, reproachful letter to the deceased. All of us could hurl justifiable recriminations at our ancestors—and will no doubt take a beating from our descendants when it is their turn to diagnose the contradictions and callousness inside us. But if we resist the impulse to simplify literature with categorical judgments, we will be better at reading it. The sounder and more perceptive our understanding of history, the more capable we will be of protecting the things we value. As the poet and traveler Fernando Sanmartín writes, "The past defines us, gives us an identity, drives us to psychoanalysis or disguise, to narcotics or mysticism. Those of us who read have a past in books. For better or worse. Because we have read things that today would perplex or even bore us. But we have also read things that still provoke excitement or certainty. A book is always a message."

It's true that books have legitimized terrible events, but they have also nourished the greatest stories, symbols, knowledge, and inventions that humanity built in the past. In *The Iliad*, we saw the heart-rending encounter between an old man and his son's murderer; in Sappho's poems we discovered that desire is a form of rebellion; in Herodotus's *Histories* we learned to look for the other side of a story; in *Antigone*, we caught a glimpse of the existence of international law; in *The Trojan Women* we came face-to-face with our own barbarity; in one of Horace's epistles we found the enlightened maxim "Dare to know"; in Ovid's *The Art of Love* we took a crash course in pleasure; in the works of Tacitus we understood the machinery of dictatorship; and in the voice of Seneca we heard the first cry for pacifism. Books have bequeathed to us notions from our forebears that haven't aged at all badly: equality among human beings, the possibility of electing our leaders, the inkling that children might be better off in school than working, the choice to use—or to reduce—public funds to care for the sick, the weak, and the elderly. All these inventions were discoveries of the ancients, those we call classics, and they reached us along a treacherous path. Without books, the best things in our world would simply have vanished.

Forgotten Men, Anonymous Women

Every day, a small army of horses and mules ventures along the slippery slopes and through the ravines of the Appalachian Mountains, with saddlebags loaded with books. Those who ride in this troop are mostly female—literary horsewomen. At first, the people of eastern Kentucky, in their valleys isolated from the United States and the rest of the world, observe them with age-old suspicion. Who in their right mind would ride through that terrain without any paved highways in the dead of winter, a land of disappearing paths, rickety bridges swaying above the abyss, and streambeds where animals' hooves and paws skid among rolling pebbles? They sharpen their gaze and spit forcefully. In other times, they saw outsiders come to work in the mines or in the sawmills, but that was before the Great Depression. Of course they are unaccustomed to the sight of these women, young and alone, who give the alarming impression of being in the service of remote authorities, loitering like trappers. When one of them arrives, the air grows thick with foreboding. The families in these mountain counties feel a diffuse and primal fear at the arrival of strangers. Only a third of these decent rural people know how to read, but even they get scared when a stranger brandishes a piece of paper. An unpaid debt, a malicious report, or an incomprehensible lawsuit could have the power to obliterate what little they own. They would never admit it, but they are terrified of those women on horseback. The fear turns into surprise when they see them dismount, open their saddlebags, and remove—the suspense is palpable—stacks of books.

The mystery is solved, and the locals can't believe it. Really? Librarians on horseback? Literary delivery? They can't understand the strange technical language the women use: federal program, New Deal, public service, plans to encourage reading. They start feeling relieved. No one mentions taxes, courts, or evictions. And these young women librarians have a friendly look and seem to believe in God and kindness.

To combat unemployment, the economic crisis, and illiteracy through large doses of state-funded culture: this was one of the missions of the Works Progress Administration. In 1934, when the project was conceived, statistics recorded only one book per capita in the state of Kentucky. In the impoverished mountainous territory in the east, without paved roads or electricity, setting up the kind of vehicle-based mobile library system that was so successful in other parts of the country was unthinkable. The only alternative was to send those brave librarians out along the trails of Appalachia to carry books to the most isolated corners. One of them, Nan Milan, joked that their horses' hooves were shorter on one side than the other, so as not to slip on the steep mountain paths. Each rider covered three or four different routes every week, with distances up to thirty kilometers a day. The donated books were kept in post offices, barracks, churches, courts, or private residences. The women, who took their job as seriously as the tireless postal workers of the era, picked up their batches at the different depots and distributed them to rural schools, community centers, and country homes. There was no lack of adventure in their solitary rides: the documents contain anecdotes of horses exhausted in the middle of nowhere, in which case the women continued on foot, the heavy saddlebag full of imaginary worlds on their back. "Bring me a book to read," cried the children when they saw the unfamiliar women arrive. Even though in 1936, the circuit reached fifty thousand families and 155 schools, with a total of eight thousand kilometers covered each month, the mounted librarians of Kentucky could barely respond to a tenth of requests. Once they overcame the first surge of mistrust, the mountain people had become keen readers. In Whitley County, the literary porters were met by welcoming committees of up to thirty locals. On one occasion, a family refused to move to another county because there was no library service there. An old black-and-white photograph shows a young horsewoman reading aloud at the sickbed of an elderly man. The influx of books improved the health and habits of the region—families learned, for example, that washing their hands before eating was much more effective for avoiding an upset stomach than blowing tobacco smoke on a spoonful of milk. Adults and children fell in love with Mark Twain's sense of humor, but by far the title most in demand was *Robinson Crusoe*. The classics put new readers in touch with a kind of magic that had always been denied them. Literate schoolchildren read them to their illiterate parents. A boy said to his librarian, "Those books you brought us have saved our lives."

The program employed almost a thousand equestrian librarians over a decade. The funding dried up in 1943, the year the WPA was dissolved, when the Second World War replaced culture as an antidote to unemployment.

We are the only animals who imagine fables, who scatter the darkness with stories, who learn to live with chaos thanks to the tales we tell, who stoke the embers of fires with the air of their words, who travel great distances to carry their chronicles to strangers. And when we share the same stories, we are no longer strangers anymore.

There is something astonishing about having managed to preserve the fictions first woven millennia ago. Ever since someone narrated *The Iliad* for the first time, the vicissitudes of the old duel between Achilles and Hector on the beaches of Troy have never been forgotten. As Harari writes, a prehistoric sociologist who lived twenty thousand years ago could easily have concluded that mythology had little chance of survival. What is a story, after all? A string of words. A sigh. A breath of air that emerges from the lungs, passes the larynx, vibrates on the vocal cords and takes its definitive shape when the tongue touches the palate, the teeth, or the lips. It seems impossible to save something so fragile. But humanity defied the absolute sovereignty of destruction by inventing writing and books. These discoveries gave birth to an immense communal space, and a fantastical increase in the life expectancy of ideas occurred. Somehow, mysteriously, spontaneously, the love of books forged an invisible chain of people—men and women—who, without knowing one another, have rescued the treasure of the greatest stories, thoughts, and dreams throughout time.

This is the story of a choral novel that has yet to be written. The tale of a fabulous collective adventure, the quiet passion of so many human beings united by this mysterious loyalty: storytelling women, inventors, scribes, illuminators, librarians, translators, booksellers, traveling salesmen, teachers, scholars, spies, rebels, travelers, nuns, slaves, adventurers, printers. Readers at their clubs, in their homes, on mountaintops, beside the roaring sea, in capital cities pulsing with energy, and in distant enclaves where knowledge takes shelter in times of chaos. Common people whose names, in many cases, go unrecorded by history. Forgotten men, anonymous women. People who fought for us, who fought for the hazy faces of the future.

ACKNOWLEDGMENTS

Many people helped me on the writing journey in different ways. Here are my thanks to all of them:

Rafael Argullol, who imagined this book before I did, and unfolded the map of this voyage before my eyes.

Julio Guerrero, for offering me his hand.

Ofelia Grande, for that delicate generosity that has given me wisdom and hope.

Elena Palacios, for an unforgettable friendship and for making what I didn't dare dream into reality.

The editorial team at Siruela, for their extraordinary magic in the old office of infinite reeds.

Marina Penalva, María Lynch, Mercedes Casanovas, and so many people at Casanovas and Lynch, for being the wings on which this book has flown to a luminous constellation of countries and languages.

Alfonso Castán and Francisco Muñiz, for their unusual generosity.

Carlos García Gual, who guided me with his signals of light.

Agustín Sánchez Vidal, who shared his knowledge and the master key with me.

Luis Beltrán, for sharpening my gaze.

Ana María Moix, who welcomed me into a garden glimpsed from outside.

Guillermo Fatás, for his lessons in history, journalism, and irony.

Encarna Samitier, for the first opportunities and for lasting friendship.

Antón Castro, who supports our fragile literary landscape.

Fergus Millar, for opening the doors of Oxford to me, and for the time travel.

Mario Citroni, for his hospitality in Florence, his wisdom, and his attention.

Angel Escobar, for teaching me rigor.

The staff at the libraries of Oxford, Cambridge, Salamanca, Florence, Bologna, Rome, Madrid, and Zaragoza, for helping me to explore those regions of paper.

My unforgettable teachers, Pilar Iranzo, Carmen Romeo, Inocencia Torres, and Carmen Gómez Urdáñez.

Anna Caballé, who broadens horizons with her words.

Carmen Peña, Ana López-Navajas, Margarita Borja, and Marifé Santiago, for inspiring me.

Andrés Barba, for our conversations about laughter and the future.

Luis Landero, for believing in me.

Belén Gopegui, for the echoes of a conversation and for the mysterious beginning of a friendship.

Jesús Marchamalo, for his joviality and a shared hat.

Fernando López, for Dionysian days.

Stefania Ferchedau and Natalie Tchernetska, presences in the distance.

My creative friends Ana Alcolea, Patricia Esteban, Lina Vila, Sandra Santana y Laura Bordonaba.

The people who make life more welcoming: María Ángeles López, Francisco Gan, Teresa Azcona, Valle García, Reyes Lambea, Leticia Bravo, Albano Hernández, María Luisa Grau, Cristina Martín, Gloria Labarta, Pilar Pastor, María Jesús Pardos, María Gamón, Liliana Vargas, Diego Prada, Julio Cristellys, and Ricardo Lladosa.

The first readers, the booksellers Pepe Fernández, Julia Millán y Pablo Muñío.

All those schoolteachers who plant seeds of enthusiasm, especially Chus Picot, Ana Buñola, Paz Hernández, David Mayor, Berta Amella, Laura Lahoz, Fernando Escanero, José Antonio Escrig, Marcos Guillén, Amaia Zubilaga, Eva Ibáñez, Cristóbal Barea, Irene Ramos, Pilar Gómez, Mercedes Ortiz, Félix Gay, and José Antonio Laín.

The fabulous team at the neonatal unit at the Hospital Miguel Servet de Zaragoza, the nurses who gave us so much life, and all those children who are also fighting with all their might to hold on to life.

The caretakers: Esther, Pilar, Cristina, Zara, Nuria, and my tata María.

My mother Elena, who reins in the chaos.

Enrique, my lighthouse and my compass.

Little Pedro, who is getting a PhD in sabotage, and who has taught me what hope is made of.

My family, friends, and readers, who are another kind of family of friends.

NOTES

Unless otherwise noted, all translations of ancient sources are renderings by the translator of the author's original translations from Greek and Latin.

PROLOGUE

xiii   Mysterious bands of men: Apuleius, *The Golden Ass,* III, 28.

xiii   They've been forced: Horace, *Satires,* I, 5, 7.

xiv   They were searching: Casson, *Libraries,* p. 34.

xiv   The Lord of the Two Lands: *Letter of Aristeas,* 9.

xvi   The Egyptians paid: Galen, *Commentary on "The Hippocratic Humors,"* XVII, p. 607, ed. Kühn.

xvi   These books seized: Galen, *Commentary on "The Hippocratic Humors,"* XVII, p. 601, ed. Kühn.

xvi   In a sealed letter: Epiphanius, *On Weights and Measures,* XLIII, p. 252; Migne, *Patrologia Graeca.*

xvii   One wise man: Galen, *Commentary on "The Hippocratic Humors,"* XV, p. 109, ed. Kühn.

xvii   "What Thucydides Left Unsaid": Marcellinus, *Life of Thucydides,* 31–34.

xvii   He would ask the librarian: *Letter of Aristeas,* 10.

PART ONE: GREECE IMAGINES THE FUTURE

THE CITY OF PLEASURES AND BOOKS
CHAPTER 1

4   To conquer: Herodas, *Mimiambi,* I, 26–32.

CHAPTER 2

6   On one occasion: Pliny the Elder, *Natural History,* IX, 58, 119–21.

6   So Mark Antony: Plutarch, *Parallel Lives,* "Antony," 58, 5.

6   books served as fuel for passion: Plutarch, *Parallel Lives,* "Antony," 58, 27.

ALEXANDER: THE WORLD IS NEVER ENOUGH
CHAPTER 3

8   Plutarch tells: Plutarch, *Moralia,* "On the Fortune or the Virtue of Alexander," I, 5, 325C.

8   It's said that Alexander: Plutarch, *Parallel Lives,* "Alexander," 8, 2.

8   The Egyptian Alexandria: Plutarch, *Parallel Lives,* "Alexander," 26, 5.

8   Drawing to his side: Homer, *The Odyssey,* canto IV, 351–59.

9   Alexander himself traced: Strabo, *Geography,* XVII, 1, 8.

CHAPTER 4

10   He ordered that they continue: Plutarch, *Parallel Lives*, "Alexander," 21.

10   Alexander shook his head: Plutarch, *Parallel Lives*, "Alexander," 26, 1.

CHAPTER 5

11   But Alexander's men: Arrian, *The Anabasis of Alexander*, V, 25–29.

THE MACEDONIAN FRIEND
CHAPTER 6

13   Ptolemy and the remaining troops: Arrian, *The Anabasis of Alexander*, VII, 4.

CHAPTER 8

15   the Koran: Ash-Shura XVIII, verses 82–98.

15   the Bible: Old Testament, 1 Maccabees:1–9.

16   They never forgave: Diodorus Siculus, *Bibliotheca historica*, XVII, 72.

16   A traveler and geographer: Strabo, *Geography,* II, 1, 9.

CHAPTER 9

17   "The king is dead": *Astronomical Diaries from Babilonia*, vol. 1, ed. A. J. Sachs and H. Hunger, 207.

17   That was what many feared: Diodorus Siculus, *Bibliotheca historica*, XVIII, 1, 4 and ff.

17   Roxana murdered: Plutarch, *Parallel Lives*, "Alexander," 77.

17   Seleucus, one of Alexander's officials: Strabo, *Geography,* XV, 2, 9.

BALANCING AT THE EDGE OF THE ABYSS:
THE LIBRARY AND MUSAEUM OF ALEXANDRIA
CHAPTER 10

19   "The Earth": *Greek Historical Inscriptions, 404–323 BC*, ed. P. J. Rhodes and R. G. Osborne, p. 433.

19   "To renew the old world": Benamin, *Illuminations*, p. 61.

20   The young king: Diodorus Siculus, *Bibliotheca histórica*, XVIII, 4, 4.

20   It included the most important works: Tzetzes, *De comoedia*, ed. W. J. W. Koster, p. 43.

20   "From every village": *Letter of Aristeas*, 30 and ff.

20   The translation of the Iranian: Pliny the Elder, *Natural History,* XXX, 2, 4.

20   An Egyptian priest named Manetho: Flavius Josephus, *Against Apion,* I, 14.

20   Berossus, another bilingual priest: Flavius Josephus, *Jewish Antiquities,* III, 6.

20   The Library even had a treatise: Arrian, *The Anabasis of Alexander*, V, 6, 2.

CHAPTER 12

23   The lethal east wind: Lawrence Durrell, *Justine*, part 3.

24   With its flexible fibers: Pliny the Elder, *Natural History,* XIII, 22, 71.

24   Ancient stories recall: Old Testament, Exodus 2:3.

CHAPTER 13

25 One of the Companions: The Byzantine Encyclopedia, *Suda sub voce,* "Leontios."

25 Eumenes, a battlefield commander: Plutarch, *Parallel Lives,* "Eumenes," 13, 6–8.

25 Ptolemy started a rumor: Pausanius, *Description of Greece,* I, 6, 2; Theocritus, *Idyll XVII: Encomium of Ptolemy Philadelphus,* 20–34.

25 On one occasion: Diodorus Siculus, *Bibliotheca historica,* XIX, 15, 3–4.

26 In the autumn: Diodorus Siculus, *Bibliotheca historica,* XVIII, 15, 26–28.

26 They carried the body: Rader, *Tumba y poder,* 165–86.

26 There, Alexander was visited: Suetonius, *The Lives of the Twelve Caesars,* "Augustus," 18, 1.

26 Gossiping tongues would claim: Cassius Dio, *Roman History,* LI, 16, 5.

26 "the Reader": *Vita Marciana,* 6.

27 It was said that Aristotle: Strabo, *Geography,* XIII, 1, 54.

CHAPTER 14

28 "To the great King": *Letter of Aristeas,* 29.

29 He asked him: *Letter of Aristeas,* 35–40.

29 The Greek Bible: *Letter of Aristeas,* 301–7.

CHAPTER 15

30 Plutarch claims: Plutarch, *Moralia,* "On the Fortune or the Virtue of Alexander," I, 5, 328D.

31 A grammarian by the name of Apion: Flavius Josephus, *Against Apion,* II, 35.

31 xenophobia of the Jews: Diodorus Siculus, *Bibliotheca historica,* XL, 3, 4.

31 The historian Diodorus: Diodorus Siculus, *Bibliotheca historica,* I, 83, 8–9.

CHAPTER 16

32 The king longed: Thucydides, *The History of the Peloponnesian War,* II, 41.

33 For Ptolemy: Plutach, *Non posse suaviter vivi secundum Epicurum,* 1095d.

33 For a Greek, a musaeum: Strabo, *Geography,* XXII, 1, 8.

34 Furthermore, he made them: Cassius Dio, *Roman History,* LXXVIII, 7.

35 "sparring with one another in the Muses' cage": Athenaeus, *The Learned Banqueters,* I, 22D.

35 Historical sources reveal: Callimachus, *Iambus,* I.

CHAPTER 17

36 Though we cannot know: McKenzie, *Architecture,* p. 41.

CHAPTER 18

37 In his account: Strabo, *Geography,* XVII, 1, 6.

CHAPTER 19

40 Perhaps this is why: Saint Augustine, *Confessions,* VI, 3.

CHAPTER 20

41 It is said that Ptolemy X: Strabo, *Geography,* XVII, 1, 8.

42 "put the entire city": Aphthonius of Antioch, *Progymnasmata, XII.*

42   The Byzantine writer Tzetzes: Tzetzes, *De comoedia*, XX.

42   Of the Great Library: Epiphanius, *On Weights and Measures,* 324–29.

43   Aristaeus, 200,000: *Letter of Aristeas,* 10.

43   Aulus Gellius: Aulus Gellius, *Attic Nights*, VII, 17, 3.

43   Ammianus Marcellinus: Ammianus Marcellinus, *Histories,* XXII, 16, 13.

A STORY OF FIRE AND PASSAGEWAYS
CHAPTER 21

44   "For him that steals": Manguel, *A History*, p. 641.

46   They have to make room: www.bodleian.ox.ac.uk.

46   At that point, they told me: Clarke Price, "The Bod's Secret."

CHAPTER 22

47   One morning of steady rain: Vernon, *A History,* p. 15.

CHAPTER 23

48   The most ancient libraries: Casson, *Libraries*, p. 3 and ff.

CHAPTER 24

51   He claims to have seen: Diodorus Siculus, *Bibliotheca historica*, I, 49, 3.

51   From among the scribes: Báez, *Los primeros libros,* p. 108.

52   One of them, Esmet-Akhom: *Bulletin de la Société Française,* pp. 16–18.

55   Today there is an initiative: http://rosettaproject.org.

BOOKS AND SKIN
CHAPTER 25

57   They were imported: Lewis, *Papyrus*, p. 92.

57   The pharaohs and Egyptian kings: Pliny the Elder, *Natural History*, XIII, 23, 74–77.

58   It's said that when he discovered: The Byzantine Encyclopedia, *Suda sub voce*, "Aristophanes of Byzantium."

58   The measure might: Pliny the Elder, *Natural History*, XIII, 21, 70.

CHAPTER 26

59   "Now I know how cuneiforms": Akhmatova. *Selected Poems,* p. 151.

60   The historian Herodotus tells: Herodotus, *Histories*, V, 35, 3; Polyaenus, *Strategems,* I, 24.

CHAPTER 27

64   According to the historian Peter Watson's calculations: Watson, *Ideas*, p. 398.

CHAPTER 28

65   Experts believe: Nelles, "Renaissance Libraries," p. 151.

A DETECTIVE'S TASK
CHAPTER 29

67   The favored target: Seneca, *Moral Letters to Lucilius*, 88, 37.

67   Didymus was known: Quintilian, *Institutes of Oratory*, I, 8, 20.

68   Didymus's protégé Apion: Pliny the Elder, *Natural History*, preface.

HOMER: ENIGMA AND TWILIGHT
CHAPTER 30

68   Herodotus believed: Herodotus, *Histories*, II, 53, 2.

68   while other authors imagined him: Graziosi, *Inventing Homer*, p. 98 and ff.

69   "crumbs from the great banquet": Athenaeus, *The Learned Banqueters*, VIII, 277E.

69   Plato dedicated: Plato, *The Republic*, X, 606d–7a.

69   "the scourge of Homer": Vitruvius, *On Architecture*, VII, preface 8–9.

70   Achilles, the assassin: Homer, *The Iliad*, XXIV, 475 and ff.

71   "So, Odysseus, you wish": Homer, *The Odyssey*, V, 1–270.

THE LOST WORLD OF ORALITY: A TAPESTRY OF ECHOES
CHAPTER 31

73   If the conjectures about its age: Lane Fox, *The Classical World*, p. 19.

75   The ethnologist Mathias Murko: Murko, *La Poésie populaire*.

CHAPTER 34

82   "Mother, go to your chamber": Homer, *The Odyssey*, I, 356–59.

82   As far as the Greeks were concerned: Beard, *Women and Power*, p. 4.

82   In *The Iliad*, Zeus himself: Homer, *The Iliad*, 545–50.

83   "Son of Atreus": Homer, *The Iliad*, 212 and ff.

CHAPTER 35

84   When the Muse learned: Havelock, *The Muse*, pp. 98 and ff.

86   In the Gospel of John: John 8:8.

87   In 1933, an illiterate bard: Albert Lord, *The Singer*, pp. 272–75.

87   Film, which in the beginning: Sánchez Salas, *La figura del explicador*.

88   Heigo Kurosawa: Various, *No lo comprendo*, p. 41 and ff.

CHAPTER 37

90   A woman listens: Schlink, *The Reader*.

THE ALPHABET: A PEACEFUL REVOLUTION
CHAPTER 38

93   Six thousand years ago: Báez, *Los primeros libros*, p. 19 and ff.

CHAPTER 39

94   Primitive writing systems: Clayton, *The Golden Thread*, p. 9 and ff.

CHAPTER 40

97   "And the symbol of the white man's power": Achebe, *No Longer at Ease*, pp. 183–84.

CHAPTER 41

97   We don't know his name: Pérez Cortés, "Un aliento poético," pp. 5–40.

CHAPTER 42

100   The most ancient: Pérez Cortés, "Un aliento poético," pp. 5–40.

100   In *The Odyssey*: Homer, *The Odyssey*, VIII, 382.

VOICES FROM THE MIST, UNCERTAIN TIMES
CHAPTER 43

101   With his usual acerbic humor: Hesiod, *Works and Days*, 633–40.

101   The nine Muses appeared: Hesiod, *Theogony*, 22 and ff.

102   He rails against his brother Perses: Hesiod, *Works and Days*, 27 and ff.

CHAPTER 44

103   According to Eric A. Havelock: Havelock, *The Muse,* p. 88.

104   "The king, Thamus, asked": Plato, *Phaedrus*, 274d and ff.

105   An experiment conducted in 2011: Sparrow and Wegner, "Google Effects on Memory."

CHAPTER 45

106   "Of all man's instruments": Borges, *Borges oral*, p. 9.

CHAPTER 46

106   "In the shade of the plane trees": Hölderlin, "Grecia," p. 37.

CHAPTER 47

108   "It wasn't planned": Bradbury, *Fahrenheit 451,* p. 136.

108   In the year 213 BC: Baéz, *Nueva historia,* pp. 50 and 102.

108   At the same time Bradbury: Caballé, *El bolso,* p. 2.

109   In one of his books, Saint Augustine: Saint Augustine, *On the Soul and Its Origin,* IV, 7, 9.

109   "I am Plato's *Republic*": Bradbury, *Fahrenheit 451,* p. 137.

LEARNING TO READ THE SHADOWS
CHAPTER 48

110   The historian Thucydides: Thucydides, *The History of the Peloponnesian War,* I, 6, 3.

111   "They say that Cleomedes": Pausanius, *Description of Greece,* VI, 9, 6.

CHAPTER 49

113   In medieval Jewish society: Manguel, *A History*, p. 91.

114   "Where is the hard leather": Herodas, *Miniambi,* III, 59–73.

THE TRIUMPH OF UNRULY WORDS
CHAPTER 50

116   "That excellent shield": Archilochus, fr. 6, Diehl.

116   "If only I could touch": Archilochus, fr. 72, Diehl.

116   "No man is honored": Archilochus, fr. 64, Diehl.

116   "Europe's first pain in the neck": Jenkyns, *Classical Literature,* p. 30.

THE FIRST BOOK
CHAPTER 51

117   It's said that during that period: Diogenes Laërtius, *Lives and Opinions of Eminent Philosophers*, IX, 5.

117   "the Riddler": Diogenes Laërtius, *Lives and Opinions of Eminent Philosophers*, IX, 5–6.

117   "the Obscure": Cicero, *On the Ends of Good and Evil*, II, 5, 15.

118   "It is sickness that makes health": Heraclitus, fr. 111, DK.

118   We will never bathe: Plato, *Cratylus,* 402a.

118   "Our lives are rivers": Manrique, *Coplas,* 25–27.

118   "To Ephesus": Borges, "To Ephesus" in *The Selected Poems of Jorge Luis Borges,* trans. Robert Mezey and Richard Barnes (unpublished manuscript, August 1988), typescript.

CHAPTER 52

119   There is someone who wants: Strabo, *Geography*, XIV, 1, 22; Valerius Maximus, *Memorable Doings and Sayings* VIII, 14, ext. 5; Aelian, *On the Nature of Animals*, VI, 40.

120   On the moonless night: Plutarch, *Parallel Lives,* "Alexander," 3, 5.

TRAVELING BOOKSTORES
CHAPTER 53

121   It's in this period: Aristomenes, fr. 9K; Theopompus, fr. 77k; Nicophon, fr. 19, 4K.

122   For a drachma, Socrates says: Eupolis, fr. 304K; Plato, *Apology of Socrates*, 26 d–e.

122   The high figures mentioned: Lucian, *The Solecist*, 30.

122   "squeeze their works": Aristophanes, *The Frogs,* 943.

122   Heracles, who in Greek comedies: Alexis, fr. 135K.

123   "beds, small boxes": Xenophon, *Anabasis*, 7, 5, 15.

123   One disciple of Plato's: Zenobius, 5, 6.

123   "as far as we know": Strabo, *Geographies*, XIII 1, 54.

123   It's said that Aristotle: Diogenes Laërtius, *Lives and Opinions of Eminent Philosophers*, IV, 6.

CHAPTER 54

123   He adds that their books enjoy: Aristotle, *Rhetoric* 1413b, 12–13.

124   According to him, booksellers: Dionysius of Halicarnassus, *The Ancient Orators,* "Isocrates," 18.

124   In fact, as Jorge Carrión points out: "Librerías Nómadas," *El país*, November 24, 2014.

THE RELIGION OF CULTURE
CHAPTER 55

126   Some took refuge: Marrou, *Historia de la educación,* 136–37.

126   They wished to educate themselves: Pseudo-Plutarch, *The Education of Children,* 8.

126   "What strikes me is the fact": Dreyfus and Rabinow, *Michel Foucault,* p. 236.

126   The meaning of the word *paideia*: Aulus Gellius, *Attic Nights*, XIII, 17, 1.

127   The faithful believed: Pseudo Plato, *Axiochus,* 371 cd.

CHAPTER 56

127   During the third to the first centuries BC: Easterling and Knox, eds., *The Cambridge History of Classical Literature*, vol. 1, *Greek Literature*, 1–16.

128   Nevertheless, at least in European Greece: *Sylloge inscriptionum Graecarum*, 577–79, ed. Dittemberger.

A MAN WITH A PRODIGIOUS MEMORY
AND A GROUP OF AVANT-GARDE GIRLS
CHAPTER 57

130   This anecdote, recounted by Vitruvius: Vitruvius, *On Architecture*, VII, preface 4–7.

131   We know it took up: The Byzantine Encyclopedia, *Suda sub voce*, "Callimachus."

CHAPTER 58

131   For example, the true but now forgotten: Diogenes Laërtius, *Lives and Opinions of Eminent Philosophers*, III, 4.

132   Callimachus's catalog: Rudolph Pfeiffer, ed., *Callimachus I. Fragmenta* (Oxford: Clarendon Press, 1949).

132   For instance, the titles: Murray (ed.), *Aeschylus,* p. 375.

132   This section featured: Pfeiffer, *Callimachus I. Fragmenta*, fr. 434–35.

CHAPTER 59

133   Between 1500 and 300 BC: Báez, *Nueva historia,* p. 49.

133   According to statistics from 2014: Bibliotecas públicas españolas en cifras [Spanish Public Libraries in Figures], Ministry of Culture and Sports, Government of Spain, https://www.culturaydeporte.gob.es/cultura/bibliotecas/novedades/estadisticas-2014 .html.

135   Many writers after Callimachus: Esteban, *El escritor en su paraíso.*

135   One of his friends tells: Emir Rodríguez Monegal, *Borges por él mismo* [Borges by Himself] (Barcelona: Laia-Literatura, 1984), p. 112.

136   The researcher Julia Wells: Julia Wells, "The Female Librarian in Film: Has the Image Changed in 60 Years?," *SLIS Student Research Journal* 3, no. 2 (2013).

136   In the years immediately before: Rosa San Segundo Manuel, "Mujeres bibliotecarias durante la II República: De vanguardia intelectual a la depuración" [Women Librarians During the Second Republic: From the Intellectual Vanguard to Purging], *CEE participación educativa*, special issue 2010, pp. 143–64.

136   I think of María Moliner: Inmaculada de la Fuente, *El exilio interior,* pp. 175–98.

CHAPTER 60

138   Every half minute: Zaid, *Los demasiados libros*, p. 20.

139   The Greeks had a word: The Byzantine Encyclopedia, *Suda sub voce*, "Dinarchus" and "Lycurgus Focius, *Library,* 20b 25.

139   *Expertise Concerning Books*: The Byzantine Encyclopedia, *Suda sub voce*, "Telephus."

139   *On the Purchase and Selection of Books:* The Byzantine Encyclopedia, *Suda sub voce*, "Philon."

CHAPTER 61

140   In a curious second-century essay: Athenaeus, *Deipnosophistae*, IX, 379E.

141   The Athenian government decided: Plutarch, *Moralia*, 841f.

WOMEN, WEAVERS OF STORIES
CHAPTER 62

143   For some of these, we have: Alberto Bernabé and Helena Rodríguez Somolinos, eds., *Poetisas griegas* [Greek Women Poets] (Madrid: Clásicas, 1994).

CHAPTER 63

145   Literary history begins: Janés, *Guardar la casa*, p. 17 and ff.

145   Fifteen hundred years before Homer: Gwendolyn Leick, *The A to Z of Mesopotamia*, 2010, *sub voce,* "Enheduanna."

146   To be quiet in public: Democritus, Fragments B110 and B274 DK.

147   "*fatherland* was called": Plato, *The Republic*, IX, 575d.

147   Her name was Artemisia: Herodotus, *Histories*, VII, 99.

147   It's said that the Athenians: Herodotus, *Histories*, VIII, 94.

147   And on the nearby island: Plutarch, *The Banquet of the Seven Sages,* 3 = *Moralia*, 148 c–e.

147   She wrote a book of riddles: The Byzantine Encyclopedia, *Suda sub voce*, "Cleobulina."

148   We know that one Athenian comic: Diogenes Laërtius, *Lives and Opinions of Eminent Philosophers*, I, 89.

148   Perhaps that's why they loved secrecy: Carlos García Gual, *Los siete sabios (y tres más)*, p. 117.

CHAPTER 64

150   Seneca mentions an essay: Seneca, *Moral Letters to Lucilius,* 88, 37.

151   In 1073, Pope Gregory VII: Báez, *Nueva historia*, p. 441.

CHAPTER 65

152   "We have hetaerae": Pseudo-Demosthenes, *Against Neaera,* 122.

152   Almost five centuries later: Plutarch, *Parallel Lives,* "Pericles," 24, 8.

153   According to Plato: Thucydides, *The History of the Peloponnesian War,* II, 36 and ff; *Menexenus,* 236b.

153   Even today, Barack Obama's speechwriters: Carlos Iglesias-Zoido, *El legado de Tucídides. Discursos e historia* [The Legacy of Thucydides: Speeches and History] (Coimbra: Centro de Estudos Clássicos e Humanísticos da Universidade de Coimbra, 2011), p. 228.

153   "Of all creatures": Euripides, *Medea*, 230 and ff.

154   "We too possess": Euripides, *Medea*, 1088–89.

154   I want to imagine: Dueso, *Aspasia de Mileto* (Amazon ebook, 2014).

154   In fact, the philosopher claimed: Plato, *Timaaeus,* 90e–91d.

154   "No position in the government": Plato, *The Republic*, V, 455c–56b.

155   In Plato's Academy: Diogenes Laërtius, *Lives and Opinions of Eminent Philosophers*, III, 46.

155   A hetaera named Leontion: Diogenes Laërtius, *Lives and Opinions of Eminent Philosophers*, X, 4–6.

155   "Even a little whore": Cicero, *The Nature of the Gods,* I, 93.

155   The most well-known and transgressive: Diogenes Laërtius, *Lives and Opinions of Eminent Philosophers*, VI, 96–98.

THE OTHER TELLS ME MY STORY
CHAPTER 67

158   Around the year 330 BC: Pseudo Plutarch, *Lives of the Ten Orators: Lycurgus.* 10 = *Moralia*, 841F; Pausanias, *Description of Greece*, I, 21, 1–2.

159   It's said that in his epitaph: Pausanius, *Description of Greece*, I, 14, 5; Athenaeus, *Deipnosophistae*, XIV, 627C.

CHAPTER 68

161   Why were these two worlds: Herodotus, *Histories*, I, 1–5.

161   In the words of Jacques Lacarrière: Jacques Lacarrière, *Heródoto y el descubrimiento de la tierra* [Herodotus and the Discovery of the World], trans. Víctor Peral Domínguez (Madrid: Espasa-Calpe, 1973), p. 56.

CHAPTER 69

164   Many centuries later: Levinas, *Totalidad e infinito*, p. 100.

CHAPTER 70

164   There isn't what you'd call love: Ovid, *Metamorphoses*, II, 833.

165   Ever since the linguist Ernest Klein: Hatem N. Akil, *The Visual Divide Between Islam and the West* (New York: Palgrave Macmillan, 2016), p. 12.

CHAPTER 71

166   "I was grateful for": Kapuściński, *Travels with Herodotus*, p. 44.

167   In his view, *The Histories*: Kapuściński, *Travels with Herodotus*, p. 267.

168   He tries to understand: Kapuściński, *Travels with Herodotus*, p. 271.

168   "If it were proposed": Herodotus, *Histories*, III, 38.

170   The vast majority: Canfora, *The Vanished Library*, p. 39.

171   Pliny the Elder wrote: Pliny the Elder, *Natural History,* XIII, 26, 83.

172   As J. M. Coetzee writes: Coetzee, *Stranger Shores*, p. 16.

THE DRAMA OF LAUGHTER: OUR DEBT TO RUBBISH DUMPS
CHAPTER 72

172   "Laughter frees the villein": Umberto Eco, *The Name of the Rose*, pp. 277–80.

173   The researcher Luis Beltrán: Luis Beltrán Almería, *Anatomía de la risa* (Mexico City: Sin Nombre, 2011), pp. 14–25.

176   "For us, Aristophanes": Barba, *La risa caníbal,* p. 35.

177   "Comedy is": José Ortega y Gasset, *Meditations on Quixote,* translated by Diego Marín, and Evelyn Rugg (Champaign: University of Illinois Press, 2000), p. 159.

CHAPTER 73

178   "We call those people Greek": Isocrates, *Panegyricus,* 50.

179   In an essay, the emperor: Julian the Apostate, *Against the Galileans*, 229 E.

180   An inscription from the second century BC: *Sylloge inscriptionum Graecarum*, 578.2–13, Dittemberger.

180   An inscription discovered in Pergamum: *Sylloge inscriptionum Graecarum*, 577.4–5, 50–53, Dittemberger.

A PASSIONATE AFFAIR WITH WORDS
CHAPTER 74

182   "They say that many": Plutarch, *Parallel Lives*, "Nicias," 29, 2.

182   In one especially moving case: Turner, *Greek Papyri*, p. 77.

183   We know, for example: Casson, *Libraries*, pp. 57–58.

CHAPTER 75

184   It's said that Demosthenes: Plutarch, *Parallel Lives*, "Nicias" and "Demosthenes," 4 and 11.

184   He wandered the seashore: Quintilian, *Institutes of Oratory*, X, 3, 30.

185   Aristophanes wrote a comedy: Aristophanes, *The Wasps*, 836 and ff.

185   Herodotus tells that the night before: Herodotus, *Histories,* VIII, 74–83.

187   He opened a storefront: Pseudo Plutarch, *Lives of the Ten Orators,* I, 18.

187   The Sophists, itinerant teachers: Marrou, *Historia de la educación,* 248.

188   "Speech is a powerful master": Gorgias, *Encomium of Helen*, 8.

188   "Only say the word": Matthew 8.

CHAPTER 76

189   In 2011, a publisher in Louisville: Various, "Does One Word Change 'Huckleberry Finn'?," *New York Times*, January 5, 2011.

190   "There once was a young person": Garner, *Politically Correct Bedtime Stories,* 12.

190   We're told he taught: Pausanias, *Description of Greece*, I, 30, 1.

190   Among his most often read passages: Plato, *The Republic*, VI, 514a–17a.

191   Plato supports strict censorship: Plato, *The Republic*, III, 386a–98b.

191   "The poet shall": Plato, *Laws,* VII, 801d–2b.

192   By then: Orwell, *1984,* p. 56.

193   "When I reflected": Plato, *Laws,* VII, 811 c–e.

194   "The lady who only read": O'Connor, *Mystery,* 91.

194   And if we start going down: Roncagliolo, "Cuentos para niños malos."

194   At the University of London: Pasha-Robinson, "SOAS Students Call for 'White Philosophers to Be Dropped from the Curriculum.'"

POISON AND FRAGILITY

CHAPTER 77

195   His poem describes: Callimachus, *Epigrams,* 25.

195   From its publication in 1774: Andrés, *Semper,* pp. 325–28.

196   Lovecraft wrote: Lovecraft, "The History of the Necronomicon," *The Fiction*, pp. 621–22.

197   Among Lovecraft's fans: Rafael Llopis Paret in Lovecraft, *Los mitos*, 43–44.

197   "When the king opened the book": Hadawi, trans., *The Arabian Nights,* p. 57.

198   I recall the exquisite treatise: Dumas, *La reine Margot*, p. 245.

198   "the victim poisoned himself": Eco, *The Name of the Rose*, p. 276.

198   According to scholar Fernando Báez: Báez, *Nueva historia*, pp. 390–91.

CHAPTER 78

199   Galen wrote: Galen, *Commentary on "The Hippocratic Humors,"* XV, p. 24, ed. Kühn.

199   When censors insisted: Báez, *Nueva historia*, 297.

199   Joyce remarked wryly: Marchamalo, *Tocar,* p. 92.

199   In those same years: Báez, *Nueva historia,* 270.

199   "Those who burn books": Heinrich Heine, *Almansor*, lines 242–43, p. 314.

200   "Every few centuries": Borges, *The Congress*, p. 20.

THE THREE DESTRUCTIONS OF THE LIBRARY OF ALEXANDRIA
CHAPTER 79

201 "captivated by": Plutarch, *Parallel Lives,* "Caesar," 49.

202 When the insurrection: Lucano, *Pharsalia,* X, 439–54.

202 Caesar's men counterattacked: Lucano, *Pharsalia,* 486–505.

202 In *The Civil War:* Caesar, *The Civil War,* III, 111.

203 Neither does his officer: Aulus Hirtius, *Caesar's Alexandrian War,* 1.

203 But Seneca: Seneca, *On Tranquility of Mind,* 9, 5.

203 One possible answer: Cassius Dio, *Roman History,* XLII, 38, 2; Orosius, *Histories,* XLII, 38, 2.

CHAPTER 80

204 Our source, the historian: Cassius Dio, *Roman History,* LXXVII, 7, 3.

204 Later, in response: Cassius Dio, *Roman History,* 22, 1–23, 3.

205 The soldier and historian: Ammianus Marcellinus, *Histories,* XXII, 16, 15.

205 "It was a splendid edifice": Auster, *In the Country,* p. 94.

206 "I don't know how many": Auster, *In the Country,* p. 110.

207 "I know it sounds": Auster, *In the Country,* p. 116.

207 The story goes: Michael Holquist in Bakhtin, *The Dialogic,* p. 24.

CHAPTER 81

208 The city had a long history: Ammianus Marcellinus, *Histories,* XXII, 16, 15.

208 The Musaeum and the library branch: Rufinus, XI, 22–30; Sozomen, *The Ecclesiastical History,* VII, 15.

210 They fought their way: Socrates Scholasticus, *Historia ecclesiastica,* V, 16.

210 "unsullied star": Palladas, *Greek Anthology,* IX, 400.

210 The last resident: The Byzantine Encyclopedia, *Suda sub voce,* "Theon."

211 Hypatia decided: Dzielska, *Hypatia,* p. 41 and ff.

211 "She gathered some rags": Damascius, *Life of Isidore,* fr. 102.

212 Her interest in astronomy: John of Nikiû, *Chronicle,* LXXXIV, 87–103.

CHAPTER 82

213 Just when we were: Canfora, *The Vanished Library,* p. 83 and ff.

213 "I have conquered Alexandria": Eutychius, *Annals,* II, p. 316, ed. Pococke.

214 The chronicler: Ibn al-Qifṭī, *History of Learned Men.*

214 It's true that Amr conquered: Báez, *Nueva historia,* pp. 78–81.

CHAPTER 83

215 The BBC journalist: Wood, "Famous Egyptian Library Reopens."

LIFEBOATS AND BLACK BUTTERFLIES
CHAPTER 84

217 The Bosnian writer: Ivan Lovrenović, "The Hatred of Memory," *The New York Times,* May 28, 1994.

217 Arturo Pérez-Reverte: Pérez-Reverte, "Asesinos de libros," pp. 50–53.

218 "Light the first page": Bradbury, *Fahrenheit 451,* p. 68.

218 "intentional destruction": UN Commission of Experts, paragraphs 183–93.

218 "When the library burned": Goytisolo, *Cuaderno de Sarajevo,* pp. 56–57.

219   The works that make up: Carrión, *Bookshops*, p. 97.

219   Many books that survive: Reynolds and Wilson, *Scribes*, p. 10 and ff.

CHAPTER 85

220   As Jesús Marchamalo explains: Marchamalo, *Tocar*, p. 51.

220   Leonora Carrington: Carrington, *Down Below*, p. 128.

221   In *Goethe in Dachau*: Rost, *Goethe*, p. 35.

221   "He who speaks of hunger": Rost, *Goethe*, p. 237.

221   Rost's second dangerous decision: Rost, *Goethe*, p. 146.

222   "I refuse to talk": Rost, *Goethe*, p. 251.

222   "We make up a kind": Rost, *Goethe*, p. 56.

223   "Each one of those books": Zgustova, *Dressed*, p. 225.

223   "In the camp": Zgustova, *Dressed,* p. 123.

223   In the disinfection chamber: Frankl, *Man's Search*, p. 24.

223   The sole possession: Castillo, *Tanguy*, p. 104.

224   Eulalio Ferrer: Javier Barrio, "Eulalio Ferrer, la memoria de *El Quijote*."

224   Frankl himself: Frankl, *Man's Search,* p. 47.

HOW WE BEGAN TO BE STRANGE
CHAPTER 87

227   In reality, we are: Valcárcel, "Crisis de valores y ética democrática."

228   It was Jacques Perret: Berger and Ghernaouti-Hélie, *Technocivilisation*, p. 1.

229   In *The Invention of Solitude*: Auster, *The Invention*, p. 137.

230   "Alexander did not treat": Plutarch, *On the Fortune or Virtue of Alexander,* I, 6, 329cd.

230   "Eratosthenes expressed": Scuccimarra and Campione, *Los confines del mundo,* pp. 88–94.

231   "Every year we send our ships": Steiner, *The Idea*, p. 70.

231   "He traveled!": Argullol, *Visión*, p. 708.

PART TWO: THE ROADS TO ROME

A CITY WITH A BAD REPUTATION
CHAPTER 1

235   According to Livy: Livy, *The Early History of Rome*, I, 7.

235   Indiscriminate hordes: Livy, *The Early History of Rome*, 8.

236   According to Livy, nearly all the men: Livy, *The Early History of Rome,* 9.

237   "From the very beginning": Mithridates in Sallust, *Histories*, IV, 69, 17.

CHAPTER 2

238   A fifth-century Hispanic historian: Orosius, *History Against the Pagans*, IV, 12.

238   Mary Beard claims: Beard, *SPQR*, p. 162 and ff.

239   On one occasion, Julius Caesar: Caesar, *The Conquest of Gaul*, II, 33.

THE LITERATURE OF DEFEAT
CHAPTER 3

241   But beyond their indisputable skills: von Albrecht, *A History*, p. 78.

241   "Made in Greece": Beard and Henderson, *Classics*, p. 20.

242   The poet Horace: Horace, *Epistulae,* II, 1, 156.

242   There is evidence: Valerius Maximus, *Memorable Deeds and Sayings*, II, 2, 3.

CHAPTER 4

243   Latin literature is a peculiar case: Cicero, *Brutus*, 72.

243   Their neighbors to the south: Escolar, *Manual*, p. 88.

244   Livius Andronicus: von Albrecht, *A History,* p. 114.

244   In the absence of local poets: Livy, *The Early History of Rome*, XXVII, 37, 7.

245   A new book is published: Marchamalo, *Tocar*, p. 62.

CHAPTER 5

246   He gave permission: Plutarch, *Parallel Lives*, "Aemilius Paulus," 28, 6.

246   The merciless Sulla: Strabo, *Geography*, XIII, 1, 54.

246   the collection of Aristotle: Canfora, *The Vanished Library*, p. 29 and ff.

246   In Rome, the library of Lucullus: Isidore of Seville, *Etymologies*, VI, 5, 1.

246   Plutarch says coteries of intellectuals: Plutarch, *Parallel Lives*, "Lucullus," 42, 1.

247   "a high Gothic library": Fitzgerald, *Great Gatsby*, p. 51.

248   Juvenal declares: Juvenal, *Satires*, III, 60.

248   Unlike in classical Athens: Terence, *Hecyra*, second prologue.

249   This line, as Mary Beard explains: Beard, *SPQR*, pp. 202–3.

CHAPTER 6

250   Just two days before the fall of Paris: Prose, *Peggy Guggenheim*, p. 28 and ff.

250   Around these works: Sandler, *Abstract Expressionism,* p. 33.

250   The United States government: Guilbaut, *How New York Stole the Idea of Modern Art,* pp. 63–70.

250   "The most important painting": Pollock in Rose, ed., *Pollock,* p. 97.

251   "What charms me personally": Nabokov, "Letter to Altagracia de Jannelli on November 16, 1938," *Vladimir Nabokov Selected Letters.* pp. 28–29.

251   Most of the creators: Gubern, *Historia,* p. 117.

251   These men of humble origins: Gubern, *Historia del cine,* p. 117.

251   Curiously, John Ford: McBride, *Searching,* p. 21.

THE INVISIBLE THRESHOLD OF SLAVERY
CHAPTER 7

253   It's said that in Sicily: Diogenes Laertius, *Lives of Eminent Philosophers*, III, 19.

254   In the mid-first century BC: Beard, *SPQR*, p. 329.

255   Cicero implies: Casson, *Libraries*, p. 76 and ff.

255   In the autumn: Cicero, *Letters to Friends*, 13, 77, 3.

256   In the story of books: Hunt, *Ancient Greek,* p. 93 and ff.

256   Doc Daniel Dowdy: Duitsman, Manguel, *A History,* p. 280.

257   "Throughout the South": Manguel, *A History*, p. 280.

258   Curiously, the metaphors: Cavallo and Chartier, *Historia de la lectura*, pp. 45–46.

IN THE BEGINNING WERE THE TREES
CHAPTER 8

258   Pliny the Elder claims: Pliny the Elder, *Natural History,* XIII, 21.

259   "I have once more seen": Machado, *Fields of Castile,* p. 47.

259   In the third century BC: Callimachus, *Aetia,* fr. 73, Pfeiffer.

259   A character in Virgil: Virgil, *Eclogues*, X, 53–54.

POOR WRITERS, RICH READERS
CHAPTER 9

260   Ancient literature never resulted: Hedrick, "Literature and Communication," p. 190 and ff.

260   We're told that a wealthy orator: Pliny the Younger, *Letters*, IV, 7, 2.

261   "My pages amuse": Martial, *Epigrams,* V, 16, 10.

261   "Are you, are you really": Martial, *Epigrams,* VI, 82.

262   "Poetry occupies": Cato, cited by Aulus Gellius in *Attic Nights*, X, 2, 5.

262   Schoolteachers of the period: Manacorda, *Historia,* p. 131 and ff.

262   "He had shadowy origins": Tacitus, *Annals,* III, 6, 4.

CHAPTER 10

263   "Caerellia is clearly": Cicero, *Letters to Atticus,* XIII, 21a, 2.

263   In the second century BC: Valerius Maximus, *Memorable Doings and Sayings,* IV, 4.

263   her literary gatherings: Plutarch, *Parallel Lives*, "Gaius Sempronius Gracchus," 19.

263   Sempronia, the mother: Sallust, *The Conspiracy of Catiline,* 25, 2.

263   Cicero describes his daughter: Cicero in Lactantius, *The Divine Institutes*, I, 15, 20.

263   One of Pompey's: Plutarch, *Parallel Lives*, "Pompey," 55.

264   The relationship between: Suetonius, *On Grammarians*, 16, 1.

265   "You will father": Juvenal, *Satires*, VI, 434–56.

265   "like a god": Alonso, *Wendy*, p. 74.

CHAPTER 11

266   According to Harris: Harris, "Literacy and Epigraphy," pp. 87–111.

266   "A teacher isn't": Ausonius, *A Book of Exhortation to His Grandson*, 2, 15, and ff.

267   "Who would not balk": Saint Augustine, *City of God,* XXI, 14.

267   These poor devils: Marrou, *Historia de la educación,* p. 347.

267   "having swung over": Horace, *Satires,* I, 6, 74.

268   In his erotic handbook: Ovid, *The Art of Love,* II, 395.

268   Sometimes, the tablets: Ruiz García, *Introducción,* pp. 96 and 122.

268   The poet Persius: Persius, *Satires,* III, 10–14.

CHAPTER 12

270   "All of them let out": Prudentius, *Peristephanon*, IX.

271   "You yourself armed us": Prudentius, *Peristephanon*, IX.

271   In his *Institutes of Oratory*: Quintilian, *Institutes of Oratory*, I, 3, 14–17.

271   Around the beginning of our era: Marrou, *Historia de la educación,* pp. 352–53.

271   We know that some teachers: Horace, *Satires*, I, 25–26.

272   A character in Petronius's *Satyricon*: Petronius, *Satyricon*, IV, 1.

A YOUNG FAMILY
CHAPTER 13

272   About 3.8 billion years ago: Harari, *Sapiens*, pp. viii–ix.

273   It's interesting to note: Clayton, *The Golden Thread*, pp. 324–25.

273   "We are absurdly accustomed": Nabokov, *Pale Fire*, pp. 371–72.

CHAPTER 14

274   The poet Martial mentioned: Martial, *Epigrams,* XIV, 5.

274   Quintilian recommended: Quintilian, *Institutes of Oratory*, X, 3, 31.

274   It's said that the emperor Nero: Pliny the Elder, *Natural Histories*, XXXVII, 16, 64.

274   Long centuries later: Grom and Broitman, *Ensayos.*

275   "a forked pin": Umberto Eco, *The Name of the Rose*, p. 56.

275   As Pliny records: Pliny, *Natural History*, XIII, 23, 74–77.

275   The edges of the papyrus: Martial, *Epigrams*, I, 117, 16.

275   To reinforce the books: Martial, *Epigrams*, IV, 89, 2.

276   There was also an expensive balm: Vitruvius, *Architecture*, II, 9, 13.

276   "Of he who gains": Lucian of Samosata, *The Ignorant Book Collector,* translated from the Greek by Irene Vallejo, translated from the Spanish by Charlotte Whittle.

CHAPTER 15

277   "Great gods, what a dire": Catullus, *Poems*, XIV.

277   Martial, the standard-bearer: Martial, *Epigrams*, II, 1, 5.

278   "In the Argiletum": Martial, *Epigrams*, I, 117, 9.

278   Along with Atrectus: Martial, *Epigrams*, I, 2 and 113, and IV, 72.

279   Thanks to booksellers: Citroni, *Poesia,* pp. 12–15.

279   "You hate keys and seals": Horace, *Epistles,* I, 20.

BOOKSELLING: A RISKY BUSINESS
CHAPTER 16

281   "I do love secondhand books": Hanff, *84, Charing Cross Road,* p. 24.

281   "who can make love": Hanff, *84, Charing Cross Road,* 29.

282   "At times I don't mind": Hanff, *84, Charing Cross Road,* 173.

CHAPTER 17

283   In his indispensable essay: Carrión, *Bookshops,* pp. 54–56, p. 39.

284   Suetonius described: Suetonius, *The Lives of the Twelve Caesars*, "Domitian," 10, 1.

285   "the demand for literature": Borrow, *The Bible*, p. 260.

285   "a kind-hearted simple man": Borrow, *The Bible*, p. 295.

285   "We booksellers of Spain": Borrow, *The Bible*, pp. 383–84.

CHAPTER 18

287   "It is the duty of those": Frenkel, *A Bookshop in Berlin*, p. xiii.

287   "By and by, after observing": Frenkel, *A Bookshop in Berlin*, p. 4.

288   "It's not on here": Frenkel, *A Bookshop in Berlin*, p. 23.

288   "an infinite longing for death": Frenkel, *A Bookshop in Berlin*, p. 23.

289   Another hundred thousand: Sánchez, "*Mein Kampf,* un éxito de ventas en Alemania."

289   In 1920: Spence, *Mao.*

289   As Jorge Carrión writes: Carrión, *Bookshops,* p. 99.

CHAPTER 19

290   "The effect a bookstore has": Pascual, Puche, and Rivero, *Memoria.*

291   George Orwell: George Orwell, "Bookshop Memories," p. 242.

292   I live in a region: Federación de Gremios, *Barómetro.*

292   For an interminable period: Sarría Buil, "Atentados," pp. 115–44.

292   "A Bookstore Attacked": *El país,* "Atentados."

292   More than two hundred: *El país,* "Una librería asaltada."

293   When Salman Rushdie published: Salman Rushdie, *Joseph Anton,* Báez, *Nueva historia,* pp. 300–301.

CHAPTER 20

296   "Are you all right": Sebald, *Austerlitz,* p. 142.

THE BIRTH AND TRIUMPH OF BOOKS WITH PAGES
CHAPTER 21

299   Ancient books were the model: Maxwell, *Tracing.*

300   He hired a team: Clayton, *The Golden Thread,* p. 318.

CHAPTER 22

300   "Letter to the Year 2176": Sarajlić, *Después,* p. 90.

CHAPTER 23

302   With the same surface: Roberts and Skeat, *The Birth,* p. 76.

302   Cicero claimed: Pliny, *Natural History,* VII 21, 85.

302   In Roman civilization: Cavallo and Chartier, *A History of Reading,* p. 83 and ff.

302   We know of a bookseller: Turner, *Greek Papyri,* p. 204.

CHAPTER 24

303   "Paula wishes to marry": Martial, *Epigrams,* X, 8.

304   He did so with one of his earliest books: Martial, *The Apophoreta,* 183–96.

305   "Such sexy dances": Martial, *Epigrams,* trans. Wills, 14, 203, p. 194.

306   "You, who wish": Martial, *Epigrams,* I, 2.

306   We know that the codex: Cavallo and Chartier, *Historia de la lectura,* p. 143.

CHAPTER 25

307   The codex grew prevalent: Ruiz García, *Introducción,* pp. 120–35.

307   Just as paper: Escolar, *Manual,* pp. 99–100.

308   The most innovative technology: Fernández, "Así será la tele."

CHAPTER 26

309   "The material most affected": Sánchez Vidal, *Historia,* pp. 9–10.

310   In the fourth century: Themistius, *Speeches,* IV, 59d–60c.

310   In the fifth century: Jerome, *Letters,* 141.

PUBLIC LIBRARIES IN PALACES OF WATER
CHAPTER 27

311   According to Suetonius: Suetonius, *The Lives of the Twelve Caesars,* "Gaius Julius Caesar," 82, 2.

311   That political assassination: Strauss, *The Death.*

312   Among his other plans: Suetonius, *The Lives of the Twelve Caesars,* "Gaius Julius Caesar," 44, 2.

312   It was a logical appointment: Jerome, *Letters,* 33, 2.

312   We know of this first public temple: Pliny the Elder, *Natural History*, VII, 30, 115; Isidore of Seville, *Etymologies*, 6, 5, 1.

313   Whoever received this homage: Dix, "Public Libraries," p. 289.

313   In truth he longed: Martial, *Epigrams*, IX, preface.

313   We also know that: Aulus Gellius, *Attic Nights*, XIX, 5.

313   The emperor Marcus Aurelius: Fronto, *Letters*, IV, 5, 2.

313   The next two public libraries: Casson, *Libraries*, pp. 81–88.

314   Archaeologists believe: Coarelli, *La Colonna*.

CHAPTER 28

315   Trajan's library: Casson, *Libraries*, pp. 89–92.

315   "What could be worse": Martial, *Epigrams*, VII, 34, 4–5.

315   "When the athletes": Seneca, *Letters to Lucilius*, 56, 1–2.

316   Enjoying the pleasures: Toner, *Popular Culture*, p. 165.

316   After spending two years in a cave: *The Life of Saint Theodore of Sykeon*, 20.

316   "He rejects the pleasures": Clement of Alexandria, *Stromata*, VII, 7, 36.

CHAPTER 29

317   An inscription in the city of Comum: *Corpus inscriptionum Latinarum (CIL)*, 5.5262.

317   Another inscription found on the coast: *CIL*, 10.4760.

317   There are also scattered traces: *CIL*, 11.2704.

318   Meanwhile, by this standard: Casson, *Libraries*, p. 109 and ff.

318   In the entire region: Harris, *Ancient Literacy*, p. 273.

318   We know of the first: Apuleius, *Florida*, XVIII, 8.

TWO MEN FROM HISPANIA: THE FIRST FAN AND THE AGING WRITER
CHAPTER 30

319   And in the civilized concert halls: Hilmes, *Franz Liszt*.

320   We're told he set out: Pliny the Younger, *Letters*, II, 3.

320   Horace boasted: Horace, *Odes*, II, 20.

321   Propertius affirmed: Propertius, *Elegies*, II, 7.

321   Ovid wrote plainly: Ovid, *Tristia*, IV, 9 and 10.

321   Martial's books: Martial, *Epigrams*, VII, 88, and XI, 3.

321   Pliny the Younger's: Pliny the Younger, *Letters*, IX, 11.

321   "These days, the whole world": Juvenal, *Satires*, XV, 108.

321   Virgil, who suffered: Suetonius, *Life of Virgil*, 6, 11.

CHAPTER 31

323   Flattered by the idea: Martial, *Epigrams*, XII, 31.

323   Soon you'll be grumbling: Martial, *Epigrams*, preface to book XII.

HERCULANEUM: PRESERVATION AMID DESTRUCTION
CHAPTER 32

324   The city, buried: Beard, *Pompeii*, p. 1 and ff.

325   For decades, Lucius Calpurnius's villa: Greenblatt, *The Swerve*, p. 65 and ff.

325   "amid the stench and mire": Cicero, *Against Piso*, 22.

OVID CLASHES WITH CENSORSHIP
CHAPTER 34

328   His father sent him: Ovid, *Tristia*, IV, 10, 21–26.

329   Ovid was an explorer: Citroni, *Poesia*, pp. 459–64.

329   Martial was shamelessly public: Martial, *Epigrams*, V, 34 and 37, and X, 61.

329   "I would rather have": Ovid, *The Art of Love*, II, 665 and ff.

330   As Pascal Quignard writes: Quignard, *El sexo*, p. 15.

330   "teacher of obscene adulteries": Ovid, *Tristia*, II, 212.

330   It wasn't unusual: Plutarch, *Parallel Lives,* "Cato the Younger," 25.

331   "a poem and an error": Ovid, *Tristia*, II, 207.

331   "I am no longer love's master": Ovid, *Tristia*, I, 1, 67.

332   "Augustus punished": Aurelius Victor, *Epitome de Caesaribus,* I, 24.

332   Augustus made sure: Ovid, *Tristia*, III, 1.

SWEET INERTIA
CHAPTER 35

332   "the rare good fortune": Tacitus, *Histories*, I, 1.

332   The historian Aulus Cremutius Cordus: Suetonius, *The Lives of the Twelve Caesars*, "Tiberius," 45; Tacitus, *Annals,* IV, 34.

333   "Women have the same intellectual power": Seneca, *Consolation to Marcia*, XVI, 1.

333   "They are foolish": Tacitus, *Annals,* IV, 35.

333   Though censorship: Gil, *Censura*, p. 190 and ff.

334   Caligula had the idea: Suetonius, *The Lives of the Twelve Caesars*, "Caligula," 34.

334   Commodus banned: Aelius Lampridius, *Historia Augusta*, "Commodus," 10, 2.

334   Caracalla, a keen admirer: Cassius Dio, *Roman History*, LXXVIII, 7.

334   "Without a doubt": Tacitus, *Agricola,* 2.

JOURNEY TO THE CENTER OF BOOKS AND HOW TO NAME THEM
CHAPTER 36

335   In 2009, in a gesture: Houston, *The Book,* introduction; Brad Stone, "Amazon Erases."

336   Both are attributed: Reynolds and Wilson, *Scholars,* p. 9.

336   The separation of letters: Manguel, *A History*, pp. 48–50.

336   Manuscript illustrations: Ruiz García, *Introducción*, p. 283.

337   The first known example: Pliny, *Natural History,* XXXV, 11.

337   Christian appropriation: Báez, *Los primeros*, p. 501.

CHAPTER 37

338   Certainly, in the earliest era: Casson, *Libraries,* pp. 4–12.

339   In general, the names: Ballester, *Los mejores* and *La titulación*.

340   Saint Augustine makes: Saint Augustine, *Letters*, II, 40, 2.

341   "a print soldered into the heart": Guerriero, "El alma."

WHAT IS A CLASSIC?
CHAPTER 38

342   A lawyer and rhetoric teacher: Suetonius, *The Lives of the Twelve Caesars*, "Vespasian," 18.

343   "I know not what secret": Quintilian, *Institutes of Oratory*, VI, preface 10.

343 As I have already: Quintilian, *Institutes of Oratory*, I, 3, 14–17.

343 He claimed that the purpose: Quintilian, *Institutes of Oratory*, X, 1, 4, and II, 5, 13.

343 And, to provide them with a road map: Quintilian, *Institutes of Oratory* X, 1, 46–131.

CHAPTER 39

344 As Steven Pinker writes: Pinker, *Enlightenment*, p. 105.

344 It shouldn't surprise us: Vallejo, "Una fábula," pp. 335–55.

345 The lawyer and writer Aulus Gellius: Aulus Gellius, *Attic Nights*, VI, 13, 1.

345 Translating an obsession: Fronto cited in Aulus Gellius, *Attic Nights*, XIX, 8, 15.

346 At the other end of the hierarchy: Cicero, *Academica priora*, 73.

346 The word's true success: Rizzo, *Il lessico filologico*, p. 379.

346 Italo Calvino wrote that "a classic": Calvino, *The Uses of Literature*, p. 131.

347 A classic is "something": Twain, "Disappearance of Literature," Project Gutenberg.

347 Pierre Bayard borrows: Bayard, *How to Talk*.

CHAPTER 40

349 "Woe is me": Euripides, *The Trojan Women*, 1295 and ff.

350 "We punish the murders": Seneca, *Moral Letters to Lucilius*, 95, 30–31.

351 the past "does not pull back": Arendt, *Between Past and Future*, p. 10.

CANON: THE HISTORY OF A REED

CHAPTER 41

351 From this foreign root: Oppel, "Zur Bedeutungsgeschichte."

352 His sculpture *Doryphoros*: Pliny the Elder, *Natural History*, XXXIV, 19, 55.

352 "the way an honorable": Aristotle, *Nicomachean Ethics*, 1113a, 29.

352 "ecclesiastical canon": Eusebius, *Ecclesiastical History*, VI, 25, 3.

352 "canon of writings": Ruhnken, *Historia critica*, p. 386.

353 Some works are positively: Eagleton, *How to Read*. pp. 175–206.

355 "What, if anything,": Coetzee, *Stranger Shores*, p. 10.

CHAPTER 42

357 One of those Roman teachers: Suetonius, *On Grammarians*, 16, 2.

357 As Mary Beard explains: Beard, *SPQR*, p. 470.

358 "If you place me": Horace, *Odes*, I, 1, 35–36.

358 "I have built a monument": Horace, *Odes*, III, 30, 1.

358 "I have completed": Ovid, *Metamorphoses*, XV, 871.

359 "Come, lest you get carried off": Martial, *Epigrams*, III, 2.

359 "As I am very fond": Cervantes, *Don Quixote*, p. 67.

359 Blades tells that: Blades, *Enemies*, pp. 54–55.

360 As Alberto Olmos says: Olmos, "Los Nazis no quemaron."

360 Publishers' warehouses: González, "Así mueren."

360 The deficit is immense: Paula Corroto, "Hasta un 40% de los 225 millones de libros editados en España se devuelve," *El País*, July 10, 2018, https://elpais.com /cultura/2018/07/09/actualidad/1531163370_371133.html.

361 "in a way that makes manure": Hrabal, *Too Loud*, p. 34.

361 "I am nothing but": Hrabal, *Too Loud*, p. 9.

361 "I have a need to garnish": Hrabal, *Too Loud*, pp. 12–13.

SHARDS OF WOMEN'S VOICES
CHAPTER 43

362   "heartless relative": Tibullus, *Elégies*, III, 14, 6.

363   *"Finally, you arrived"*: Tibullus, *Elégies*, III, 13 (= IV, 7). Free translation of Sulpicia inspired by a rewriting by Leonor Silvestri.

364   This is why: Suetonius, *The Lives of the Twelve Caesars,* "Tiberius," 35, 2; Tacitus, *Annals,* II, 85, 1; and *Digest (Pandects)*, 48, 5, 11.

364   "Where are you now": Juvenal, *Satires*, II, 37.

364   The legend said: Ovid, *Fasti*, II, 583–616.

364   When the biographer Plutarch: Mirón, "Plutarco y la virtud."

365   They arrived not under: Cantarella, *Pasado próximo*, pp. 181–88.

365   As Aurora López writes: López, *No sólo hilaron*.

CHAPTER 44

366   This is why text: Sánchez Vidal, *La especie*, p. 38 and ff.

WHAT WAS BELIEVED ETERNAL TURNED OUT TO BE FLEETING
CHAPTER 45

368   The ancient politician: Cassiud Dio, *Roman History*, LXXVIII, 9, 4.

368   As Mary Beard notes: Beard, *SPQR*, p. 527.

369   It was proclaimed: Scuccimarra, *Los confines*, pp. 127–40.

369   "Neither the seas": Aelius Aristides, *Roman Oration,* XXVI, 60.

371   As Stephen Greenblatt says: Greenblatt, *The Swerve*, p. 81.

CHAPTER 46

372   "Those few houses": Ammianus Marcellinus, *Histories*, XIV, 6, 18.

372   The educated public dwindled: Auerbach, *Lenguage literario,* p. 289.

CHAPTER 47

373   In the year 529: Nixey, *The Darkening*, pp xxiv and ff.

374   Each abbey, with its school: Reynolds and Wilson, *Scribes*, p. 79 and ff.

374   They even invent: Báez, *Los primeros*, p. 501 and ff.

375   All of them set about: Reynolds and Wilson, *Scribes*, p. 118 and ff.

375   The bravest venture: Greenblatt, *The Swerve*, p. 23.

375   The intellectual revolutionaries: Wittmann, *A History of Reading*, pp. 285–99.

DARE TO REMEMBER
CHAPTER 48

376   "One only makes books": Zweig, "Buchmendel," p. 263.

376   "Keep your patient's": Hippocratic *Precepts,* Book VI, translated from the Greek by Irene Vallejo, translated from the Spanish by Charlotte Whittle.

377   The writer Elias Canetti: Steiner and Ladjlali, *Elogio*, p. 159.

378   "There is no document": Benjamin, *Illuminations*, p. 512.

EPILOGUE: FORGOTTEN MEN, ANONYMOUS WOMEN

381   Every day, a small army: Schnitzer, "Reaching Out." pp. 57–77.

383   As Harari writes: Harari, *Sapiens*, p. 102.

BIBLIOGRAPHY

Adichie, Chimamanda Ngozie. *The Danger of a Single Story*. TED Talk, 2009.

Aguirre, Javier. *Platón y la poesía* [Plato and Poetry]. Madrid: Editorial Plaza y Valdés, 2013.

Akhmatova, Anna Andreevna. *A Poem Without a Hero*. Translated and Annotated by Carl R. Proffer. Ann Arbor, MI: Ardis, 1976.

———. *Requiem*. Translated by Robin Kemball. Ann Arbor, MI: Ardis, 1976.

———. *Selected Poems*. Edited and Translated by Walter Arndt. Ann Arbor, MI: Ardis, 1976.

Alighiero Manacorda, Mario. *Historia de la educación, 1. De la antigüedad al 1500* [A History of Education, I: From Antiquity to 1500]. México: Siglo XXI, 2006.

Alonso, Martha Asunción. *Wendy*. Valencia: Pre-Textos, 2015.

Altares, Guillermo. *Una lección olvidada. Viajes por la historia de Europa* [A Forgotten Lesson: Travels Through the History of Europe]. Barcelona: Tusquets Editores, 2018.

Andrés, Ramón. *Semper dolens. Historia del suicidio en Occidente* [*Semper Dolens:* A History of Suicide in the West]. Barcelona: Acantilado, 2015.

Arendt, Hannah. *Between Past and Present*. New York: Penguin, 2006.

Argullol, Rafael. *Visión desde el fondo del mar* [View from the Bottom of the Sea]. Barcelona: Acantilado, 2010.

Aspasia de Mileto. *Testimonios y discursos* [Testimonies and Speeches]. Barcelona: Editorial Anthropos, 1994.

"Atentados del 'Comando Adolfo Hitler' contra cuatro librerías" [Attacks on Four Bookstores by the 'Adolf Hitler Command'"]. *El país*. November 26, 1976.

Auerbach, Erich. *Literary Language & Its Public in Late Latin Antiquity and in the Middle Ages*. Translated by Ralph Manheim. Princeton: Princeton University Press, 1993.

Auster, Paul. *In the Country of Last Things*. New York: Viking, 1987.

———. *The Invention of Solitude*. Los Angeles: Sun Press, 1982.

Báez, Fernando. *Nueva historia universal de la destrucción de los libros. De las tablillas sumerias a la era digital* [A New General History of the Destruction of Books]. Barcelona: Destino, 2011.

———. *Los primeros libros de la humanidad. El mundo antes de la imprenta y el libro electrónico* [Humanity's First Books: The World Before Printing and Ebooks]. Madrid: Fórcola, 2013.

Bakhtin, Mikhail. *The Dialogic Imagination*. Prologue by Michael Holquist. Austin: Texas University Press, 1981.

———. *Rabelais and His World*. Translated by Hélène Iswolsky. Bloomington: Indiana University Press, 1984.

Ballester, Xaverio. *Los mejores títulos y los peores versos de la literatura Latina* [The Best Titles and Worst Lines of Latin Literature]. Barcelona: Universitat de Barcelona, 1998.

———. "La titulación de las obras en la literatura romana" [The Titling of Works in Roman Literature]. *Cuadernos de filología clásica* 24 (1990): 135–56.

Barba, Andrés. *La risa caníbal. Humor, pensamiento cínico y poder* [Cannibal Laughter: Humor, Cynical Thought and Power]. Barcelona: Alpha Decay, 2016.

Barrio, Javier. "Eulalio Ferrer, la memoria de *El Quijote*" [Eulalio Ferrer, the Memory of the Quixote]. *El país*, April 26, 1990.

Basanta, A., ed. *La lectura* [Reading]. Madrid: Editorial CSIC and Los libros de la Catarata, 2010.

———. *Leer contra la nada* [Reading Against Nothing]. Madrid: Siruela, 2017.

Bayard, Pierre. *How to Talk About Books You Haven't Read*. Translated by Jeffrey Mehlman. London: Bloomsbury, 2007.

Beard, Mary. *Pompeii*. London: Profile, 2008.

———. *SPQR: A History of Ancient Rome*. New York: Liveright, 2015.

———. *Women & Power: A Manifesto*. London: Profile Books, 2017.

Beard, M., and J. Henderson. *Classics. A Very Short Introduction*. Oxford: Oxford University Press, 1995.

Beltrán, Luis. *Estética de la risa. Genealogía del humorismo literario* [The Aesthetics of Laughter: A Genealogy of Humor in Literature]. Mexico City: Ficticia, 2016.

———. *La imaginación literaria. La seriedad y la risa en la literatura occidental* [The Literary Imagination: Seriousness and Laughter in Western Literature]. Barcelona: Montesinos, 2002.

Benjamin, Walter. *Illuminations*. London: Bodley Head, 2015.

Berger, René, and Solange Ghernaouti-Hélie. *Technocivilisation* [Technocivilization]. Lausanne: EPFL Press, 2010.

Bernal, Martin. *Black Athena: The Afroasiatic Roots of Classical Civilization*. New Brunswick, NJ: Rutgers University Press, 1987.

Blades, William. *The Enemies of Books*. London: Elliot Stock, 1888.

Blom, Philipp. *To Have and to Hold*. London: Allen Lane, 2002.

———. *A Wicked Company*. New York: Basic Books, 2010.

Bloom, Harold. *The Western Canon: The Books and School of Ages*. San Diego: Harcourt Brace, 1994.

Boardman, John, Jasper Griffin, and Oswyn Murray. *The Oxford History of the Classical World*. Oxford: Oxford University Press, 1986.

Borges, Jorge Luis. *Borges oral* [Borges Speaks]. Madrid: Alianza, 1999.

———. *The Congress*. Translated by Norman Thomas di Giovanni. London: Enitharmon, 1974.

———. *Obra poética* [Complete Poetry]. Madrid: Alianza, 1993.

Borrow, George. *The Bible in Spain*. London: John Murray, 1896.

Bradbury, Ray. *Fahrenheit 451*. New York: Ballantine, 1953.

Brottman, Mikita. *The Solitary Vice: Against Reading*. Berkeley: Counterpoint, 2008.

Caballé, Anna. *El bolso de Ana Karenina* [Anna Karenina's Purse]. Barcelona: Península, 2009.

———. *Una breve historia de la misoginia* [A Brief History of Misogyny]. Barcelona: Lumen, 2005.

Calvino, Italo. *The Uses of Literature*. New York: Houghton Mifflin Harcourt, 1987.

Canfora, Luciano. *The Vanished Library: A Wonder of the Ancient World*. Translated by Martin Ryle. Berkeley: University of California Press, 1990.

Cantarella, Eva. *Pandora's Daughters: The Role and Status of Women in Greek and Roman Antiquity*. Translated by Mary R. Lefkowitz. Baltimore: Johns Hopkins University Press, 1987.

———. *Pasado próximo. Mujeres romanas de Tácita a Sulpicia*. Translated by Isabel Núñez. Madrid: Cátedra, Universitat de Valencia e Instituto de la Mujer, 1997. Originally published as *Passato prossimo: donne romane da Tacita a Sulpicia*, 1996.

Carrère, Emmanuel. *The Kingdom*. Translated by John Lambert. London: Hutchinson, 2017.

Carrington, Leonora. *Down Below*. New York: NYRB Classics, 2017.

Carrión, Jorge. *Bookshops*. Translated by Peter Bush. Windsor, Ontario: Biblioasis, 2017.

Carson, Anne. *Eros the Bittersweet*. Princeton, NJ: Princeton University Press, 1986.

Casson, Lionel. *Libraries in the Ancient World*. New Haven, CT: Yale University Press, 2001.

Cavallo, G., and R. Chartier, eds. *A History of Reading in the West*. Translated by Lydia G. Cochrane. Amherst: University of Massachusetts Press, 2003.

Cervantes, Miguel. *Don Quixote*. Translated by Edith Grossman. New York: Ecco, 2003.

Cervelló, Josep. *Escrituras, lengua y cultura en el antiguo Egipto* [Writing, Language and Culture in Ancient Egypt]. Barcelona: Ediciones UAB, Colección El Espejo y la Lámpara, 2016.

Citroni, Mario. *Poesia e lettori in Roma antica* [Poetry and Reading in Ancient Rome]. Ediciones, Rome: Laterza, 1995.

Clarke Price, Henry. "The Bod's Secret Underbelly." *Cherwell*, November 16, 2007.

Clayton, Ewan. *The Golden Thread: The Story of Writing*. London: Atlantic Books, 2013.

Coarelli, Filippo. *La Colonna Traiana* [Trajan's Column]. Roma: Colombo, 1999.

Coetzee, J. M. *Stranger Shores*. London: Penguin, 2002.

Cribiore, R. *Gymnastics of the Mind: Greek Education in Hellenistic and Roman Egypt*. Princeton, NJ: Princeton University Press, 2001.

de la Fuente, Inmaculada. *El exilio interior. La vida de María Moliner* [Interior Exile: A Life of María Moliner]. Madrid: Turner, 2011.

del Castillo, Michel. *Tanguy*. Vitoria-Gasteiz: Ikusager, 2010.

Devauchelle, Didier. "24 août 394–24 août 1994: 1600 ans" [August 24, 394 to August 24, 1994: 1600 Years]. *Bulletin de la Société Française d'Égyptologie* 131 (1994): 16–18.

Dix, T. Keith. "Public Libraries in Ancient Rome: Ideology and Reality." *Libraries and Culture* 29 (1997): 282–96.

Dreyfus, Hubert L., and Paul Rabinow. *Michel Foucault: Beyond Structuralism and Hermeneutics*. 2nd ed. Chicago: University of Chicago Press, 1983.

Dueso, José Solana. *Aspasia de Mileto y la emancipación de las mujeres* [Aspasia of Miletus and the Emancipation of Women]. Amazon ebook, 2014.

Duisman Cornelius, Janet. *When I Can Read My Title Clear: Literacy, Slavery, and Religion in the Antebellum South*. Columbia: University of South Carolina Press, 1991.

Dumas, Alexandre, and Auguste Maquet. *Marguerite De Valois*. Boston: Little, Brown, 1893.

Dzielska, Maria. *Hypatia of Alexandria*. Translated by F. Lyra. Cambridge, MA: Harvard University Press, 1995.

Eagleton, Terry. *How to Read Literature*. New Haven, CT: Yale University Press, 2013.

Easterling, P. E., and B. M. W. Knox, eds. *The Cambridge History of Classical Literature*. Vol. 1, *Greek Literature*. Cambridge: Cambridge University Press, 1985.

Eco, Umberto. *The Infinity of Lists*. Translated by Alistair McEwen. London: MacLehose Press, 2009.

———. *The Name of the Rose*. New York: Harcourt, 1983.

Eco, Umberto, and Jean-Claude Carrière. *Nadie acabará con los libros. Entrevistas realizadas por Jean-Philippe de Tonnac* [No One Will Destroy Books: Interviews by Jean-

Philippe de Tonnac]. Translated by Helena Lozano Miralles. Barcelona: Lumen, 2010.

Escolar, Hipólito. *Manual de historia del libro* [A Manual of the History of the Book]. Madrid: Gredos, 2000.

Esteban, Angel. *El escritor en su paraíso* [The Writer in His Paradise]. Cáceres: Periférica, 2014.

Federación de Gremios de Editores de España. *Barómetro de los hábitos de lectura y compra de libros en España en 2017* [Barometer of the Reading and Buying Habits of Spanish Readers, 2017]. https://www.federacioneditores.org/img/documentos/Habitos LecturaCompraLibros2017.pdf.

Fernández de Lis, Patricia. "Así será la tele del futuro: Tú eliges el tamaño y la forma, y la podrás enrollar" [This the TV of the Future: Choose the Size and Shape and Roll It Up]. *El país,* January 8, 2019.

Fitzgerald, F. Scott. *The Great Gatsby.* New York: Scribner, 1995.

Fränkel, Hermann. *Poesía y filosofía de la Grecia arcaica* [The Poetry and Philosophy in Archaic Greece]. Translated by Ricardo Sánchez Ortiz. Madrid: Visor, 1993.

Frankl, Viktor. *Man's Search for Meaning.* Boston: Beacon Press, 1992.

Frenkel, Françoise. *A Bookshop in Berlin.* New York: Atria, 2019.

García Gual, Carlos. *La muerte de los heroes* [The Death of Heroes]. Madrid: Turner, 2016.

———. *Los siete sabios (y tres más)* [The Seven Sages (and Three More)]. Madrid: Alianza, 2007.

Garner, James Finn. *Politically Correct Bedtime Stories: Modern Tales for Our Life and Times.* Hoboken, NJ: John Wiley & Sons Inc., 1994.

Gentili, Bruno. *Poetry and Its Public in Ancient Greece: From Homer to the Fifth Century.* Translated by A. Thomas Cole. Baltimore: Johns Hopkins University Press, 1988. Originally published as *Poesia e pubblico nella Grecia antica,* 1984.

Gil, Luis. *Censura en el mundo antiguo* [Censorship in the Ancient World]. Madrid: Alianza Editorial, 2007.

Gómez Espelosín, F. J., and Antonio Guzmán Guerra. *Alejandro Magno* [Alexander the Great]. Madrid: Alianza, 2005.

González, David. "Así mueren los libros que no se venden" [How Unsold Books Die]. *El confidencial,* June 27, 2015.

Goytisolo, Juan. *Cuaderno de Sarajevo, anotaciones de un viaje a la barbarie* [Sarajevo Notebook: Notes on a Journey to Barbarity]. Madrid: El País Aguilar, 1993.

Graziosi, Barbara. *Inventing Homer.* Cambridge: Cambridge University Press, 2002.

Greenblatt, Stephen. *The Swerve: How the World Became Modern.* New York: W. W. Norton & Company, 2011.

Grom, Edward, and Leon Broitman. *Ensayos sobre historia, ética, arte y oftalmología* [Essays on History, Ethics, Art, and Opthalmology]. Caracas, 1988.

Gubern, Román. *Historia del cine* [A History of Cinema]. Barcelona: Dánae, 1971.

Guerriero, Leila. "El alma de los libros" [The Soul of Books]. *El país cultural,* June 28, 2013, https://elpais.com/cultura/2013/06/26/actualidad/1372256062_358323.html.

Guilbaut, Serge. *How New York Stole the Idea of Modern Art.* Chicago: University of Chicago Press, 1985.

Hadawi, Husain, trans. *The Arabian Nights.* New York: Norton, 2008.

Hanff, Helene. *84, Charing Cross Road.* London: Penguin, 1990.

Harari, Yuval Noah. *Sapiens: A Brief History of Humankind.* New York: Harper, 2015.

Harris, W. V. *Ancient Literacy*. Cambridge, MA: Harvard University Press, 1989.

———. "Literacy and Epigraphy." *ZPE* 52 (1983): 87–111.

Havelock, Eric. A. *The Muse Learns to Write: Reflections on Orality and Literacy from Antiquity to the Present*. New Haven, CT: Yale University Press, 1986.

———. *Preface to Plato*. Cambridge: Cambridge University Press, 1963.

Hedrick, Charles W. "Literature and Communication." In *The Oxford Handbook of Social Relations in the Roman World*, edited by Michael Peachin. New York: Oxford University Press, 2011.

Heine, Heinrich, and Oskar Franz Walzel. *Werke*. Leipzig: Insel-Verlag, 1910–1915.

Hilmes, Oliver. *Franz Liszt: Musician, Celebrity, Superstar*. New Haven, CT: Yale University Press, 2016.

Hölderlin, Friedrich. "Grecia" [Greece]. In *Poesía completa. Edición bilingüe* [Complete Poetry, Bilingual Edition]. Barcelona: Río Nuevo, 1995, 37.

Houston, Keith. *The Book: A Cover-to-Cover Exploration of the Most Powerful Object of Our Time*. New York: W. W. Norton & Company, 2016.

Hunt, P. *Ancient Greek and Roman Slavery*. Hoboken, NJ: Wiley-Blackwell, 2017.

Hustvedt, S. *Living, Thinking, Looking*. New York: Picador, 2012.

Janés, Clara. *Guardar la casa y cerrar la boca. En torno a la mujer y la literature* [Keeping House and Keeping Quiet: On Women and Literature]. Madrid: Siruela, 2015.

Jenkyns, Richard. *Classical Literature: An Epic Journey from Homer to Virgil and Beyond*. London: Penguin, 2015.

Jullien, F. *La identidad cultural no existe* [Cultural Identity Does Not Exist]. Translated by Pablo Cuartas. Barcelona: Taurus, 2017. Originally published as *Il n'y a pas d'identité culturelle*, 2016.

———. *De lo universal, de lo uniforme, de lo común y del diálogo entre las culturas* [On the Universal, the Uniform, the Common, and on Dialogue Between Cultures]. Translated by Tomás Fernández and Beatriz Eguibar. Madrid: Siruela, 2010. Originally published as *De l'universel, de l'uniforme, du commun et du dialogue entre les cultures*, 2008.

Kapuściński, Ryszard. *Travels with Herodotus*. New York: Knopf, 2007.

Laín Entralgo, Pedro. *La curación por la palabra en la antigüedad clásica* [Healing with Words in the Ancient World]. Barcelona: Anthropos, 2005.

Landa, Josu. *Canon City*. Mexico: Afínita, 2010.

Landero, Luis. *El balcón en invierno* [The Winter Balcony]. Barcelona: Tusquets, 2014.

———. *Entre líneas. El cuento o la vida* [Between the Lines: Story or Life]. Barcelona: Tusquets, 2001.

Lane Fox, Robin. *Alexander the Great*. London: Penguin, 1973.

———. *The Classical World: An Epic History of Greece and Rome*. London: Penguin, 2007.

Leick, Gwendolen. *The A to Z of Mesopotamia*. Lanham, MD: Rowman and Littlefield, 2010.

Levinas, E. *Totalidad e infinito. Ensayo sobre la exterioridad* [Totality and Infinity: An Essay on Exteriority]. Translated by Daniel E. Guillot. Salamanca: Sígueme, 2006. Originally published as *Totalité et infini*, 1971.

Lewis, N. *Papyrus in Classical Antiquity*. Oxford: Clarendon Press, 1974.

"Una librería asaltada cada dos semanas" [A Bookstore Attacked Every Two Weeks]. *El país*. May 24, 1976.

Lledó, Emilio. *Los libros y la libertad* [Books and Freedom]. Barcelona: RBA, 2013.

————. *El silencio de la escritura* [Silence and Writing]. Barcelona: Austral, 2015.

————. *Sobre la educación* [On Education]. Barcelona: Taurus, 2018.

López, Aurora. *No solo hilaron lana. Escritoras romanas en prosa y en verso* [They Spun Not Only Wool: Roman Women Writers in Prose and Verse]. Madrid: Ediciones Clásicas, 1994.

Loraux, Nicole. *Los hijos de Atenea: Ideas atenienses sobre la ciudadanía y la división de sexos* [Athena's Children: Athenian Ideas on Citizenship and the Division of the Sexes]. Translated by Montserrat Jufresa Muñoz. Barcelona: Acantilado, 2017. Originally published as *Les enfants d'Athéna. Idées athéniennes sur la citoyenneté et la division des sexes*, 1981.

Lord, Albert. *The Singer Resumes the Tale*. Ithaca, NY: Cornell University Press, 1995.

Lovecraft, H. P. "The History of Necronomicón." The Fiction: Complete and Unabridged. New York: Barnes and Noble, 2018.

————. *Los mitos de Cthulhu* [The Myths of Cthulhu]. Prologue by Rafael Llopis Paret. Madrid: Alianza, 1969.

Machado, Antonio. *Fields of Castile*. Translated by Stanley Appelbaum. Mineola: Dover, 2012.

Madrid, Mercedes. *La misoginia en Grecia* [Misogyny in Greece]. Madrid: Cátedra, 1999.

Manguel, A. *A History of Reading*. London: HarperCollins, 1996.

Marchamalo, Jesús. *Tocar los libros* [Touching Books]. Madrid: Fórcola, 2016.

Marrou, Hénri-Irénée. *Historia de la educación en la Antigüedad* [The History of Education in Ancient Times]. Translated by Yago Barja de Quiroga. Madrid: Akal, 2004. Originally published as *Histoire de l'éducation dans l'antiquité*, 1948.

Martino, Giulio, and Marina Bruzzese. *Las filósofas: Las mujeres protagonistas en la historia del pensamiento* [Women Philosophers: Female Protagonists of the History of Thought]. Translated by Mercè Otero Vidal. Madrid: Cátedra, 1996. Originally published as *Le filosofe. Le donne protagoniste nella storia del pensiero*, 1994.

Maxwell, John W. *Tracing the Dynabook: A Study of Technocultural Transformations*. Vancouver: University of British Columbia, 2006.

McBride, Joseph, and Michael Wilmington. *John Ford*. London: Secker & Warburg, 1974.

McKenzie, Judith. *Architecture of Alexandria and Egypt 300 B.C. to A.D. 700*. New Haven, CT: Yale University Press, 2007.

Ménage, Gilles. *Historia de las mujeres filósofas* [A History of Women Philosophers]. Translated by Mónica Poole. Madrid: Cátedra, 2000. Originally published as *Historia mulierum philosopharum,* 1690.

Mirón, María Dolores. "Plutarco y la virtud de las mujeres" [Plutarch and the Virtue of Women]. In *Mujeres de la antigüedad. Texto e imagen* [Women in Antiquity: Text and Image], edited by Marta González González. Ediciones electrónicas de la Universidad de Málaga, 2012.

Morson, Gary Saul, and Morton O. Schapiro. *Cents and Sensibility: What Economics Can Learn from the Humanities*. Princeton, NJ: Princeton University Press, 2017.

Movellán, Mireia, and Juan Piquero Rodríguez, eds. *Los pasos perdidos. Viajes y viajeros en la antigüedad* [The Lost Steps: Travels and Travelers in Ancient Times]. Madrid: Abada, 2017.

Muñoz Páez, Adela. *Sabias* [Wise Women]. Barcelona: Debate, 2017.

Murko, Matías. *La Poésie populaire épique en Yougoslavie au début du XX e siècle* [Popular Epic Folk Poetry in Yugoslavia in the Early Twentieth Century]. Paris: Champion, 1929.

Murray, Gilbert (ed.), *Aeschylus: The Creator of Tragedy*. Oxford: Clarendon Press, 1955.

Murray, Stuart A. P. *The Library. An Illustrated History*. New York: Skyhorse, 2009.

Nabokov, Vladimir, "Letter to Altagracia de Jannelli on November 16, 1938." In *Vladimir Nabokov Selected Letters 1940–1977*, edited by Dmitri Nabokov. New York: Harcourt Brace Jovanovich, 1989.

———. *Pale Fire*, New York: Vintage, 1989.

Nelles, P. "Renaissance Libraries." In *International Dictionary of Library Histories*, edited by D. H. Stam. New York: Routledge, 2001, p. 151.

Nixey, Catherine. *The Darkening Age: The Christian Destruction of the Classical World*. New York: Macmillan, 2017.

O'Connor, Flannery. *Mystery and Manners: Occasional Prose*. Edited by Sally and Robert Fitzgerald. New York: FSG, 1970.

Olmos, Alberto. "Los Nazis no quemaron tantos libros como nosotros" [The Nazis Didn't Burn as Many Books as Us]. *El confidencial,* July 20, 2016.

Oppel, Herbert. "ΚΑΝΩΝ Zur Bedeutungsgeschichte des Wortes und seiner lateinischen Entsprechungen (regula-norma)" [Toward a History of the Word and its Latin Equivalent]. *Philologus Supplementband* 30 (1937): 1–116.

Ordine, Nuccio. *Clásicos para la vida* [Classics for Life]. Translated by Jordi Bayod Brau. Barcelona: Acantilado, 2017. Originally published as *Classici per la vita*, 2017.

Orwell, George. "Bookshop Memories." In *The Collected Essays, Journalism, and Letters of George Orwell*. Edited by Sonia Orwell and Ian Angus, 242–46. New York: Harcourt Brace Jovanovich, 1968.

Otranto, Rosa. *Antiche liste di libri su papiro* [Ancient Lists of Books on Papyrus]. Rome: Edizioni di Storia e Letteratura, 2000.

Padró, Josep. *Historia del Egipto faraónico* [A History of Pharaonic Egypt]. Madrid: Alianza Universidad, 1999.

Pascual, Carlos, Paco Puche, and Antonio Rivero. *Memoria de la librería* [Bookstore Memoir]. Madrid: Trama, 2012.

Pasha-Robinson, Lucy. "SOAS Students Call for 'White Philosophers to be Dropped from the Curriculum.'" *The Independent*, January 8, 2017, https://www.independent.co.uk/news/uk/home-news/soas-university-of-london-student-s-union-white-philosophers-curriculum-syllabus-a7515716.html.

Pennac, Daniel. *Como una novela* [Like a Novel]. Translated by Joaquín Jordá. Barcelona: Anagrama, 1993. Originally published as *Comme un roman*, 1992.

Pérez Cortés, Sergio. "Un aliento poético: el alfabeto" [A Poetic Breath]. *Éndoxa*. Series filológicas no. 8, 5–40. Madrid: UNED, 1997.

Pérez-Reverte, Arturo. "Asesinos de libros" [Book Killers]. In *Patente de corso (1993–1998)* [Letter of Marque (1993–1998)]. Madrid: Suma de Letras, 2001.

Pfeiffer, Rudolf. *History of Classical Scholarship. From the Beginnings to the End of the Hellenistic Age*. Oxford: Oxford University Press, 1968.

Pinker, Stephen. *Enlightment Now: The Case for Reason, Science, Humanism*. New York: Viking, 2018.

Popper, Karl R. *The Open Society and Its Enemies*. London: Routledge, 1945.

Prose, Francine. *Peggy Guggenheim: The Shock of the Modern*. New Haven, CT: Yale University Press, 2015.

Quignard, Pascal. *El sexo y el espanto* [Sex and Terror]. Translated by Ana Becciú. Barcelona: Minúscula, 2014. Originally published as *Le Sexe et l'effroi*, 1994.

Rader, Olaf B. *Tumba y poder. El culto político a los muertos desde Alejandro Magno hasta*

Lenin [Power and the Grave: Political Cults of Death from Alexander the Great to Lenin]. Translated by María Condor. Madrid: Siruela, 2006. Originally published as *Grab und Herrschaft. Politischer Totenkult von Alexander dem Großen bis Lenin*, 2003.

Reynolds, Leighton Durrell, and N. G. Wilson. *Scribes and Scholars: A Guide to the Transmission of Greek and Latin Literature*. Oxford: Clarendon Press, 1974.

Rhodes, P. J. and R. G. Osborne, *Greek Historical Inscriptions, 404–323 BC*. Oxford: Oxford University Press, 2007.

Rizzo, Silvia. *Il lessico filologico degli umanisti* [The Humanists' Philological Lexicon]. Rome: Edizioni di Storia e Letteratura, 1973.

Robert, Colin H., and T. C. Skeat. *The Birth of the Codex*. Cambridge: Cambridge University Press, 1987.

Robinson, Marilyn. *When I Was a Child I Read Books*. New York: Farrar, Straus, and Giroux, 2012.

Roncagliolo, Santiago. "Cuentos para niños malos" [Stories for Naughty Children]. *El país semanal,* December 14, 2013.

Rose, Barbara, ed. *Pollock: Painting*. New York: Agrinde, 1980.

Rost, Nico. *Goethe en Dachau.* [Goethe at Dachau]. Barcelona: ContraEscritura, 2016.

Ruhnken, David. *Historia critica oratorum Graecorum* [Critical History of Greek Orators]. Leiden: S. and J. Luchtmans, 1768.

Ruiz García, Elisa. *Introducción a la codicología* [Introduction to Codicology]. Madrid: Fundación Germán Sánchez Ruipérez, colección Biblioteca del libro, 2002.

Rushdie, Salman. *Joseph Anton: A Memoir.* New York: Random House, 2012.

Sánchez, Rosalía. "*Mein Kampf,* un éxito de ventas en Alemania" [*Mein Kampf,* a Best Seller in Germany]. ABC Cultura, January 18, 2018, https://www.abc.es/cultura /libros/abci-mein-kampf-exito-ventas-alemania-201801180148_noticia.html.

Sánchez Salas, Daniel. *La figura del explicador en los inicios del cine español* [The Explainer in Early Spanish Cinema]. Biblioteca Virtual Miguel de Cervantes, 2002.

Sánchez Vidal, Agustín. *La especie simbólica* [The Symbolic Species]. Pamplona: Universidad Pública de Navarra, Cátedra Jorge Oteiza, 2011.

———. *Historia del cine.* Madrid: Historia 16, 1997.

Sandler, Irving. *Abstract Expressionism: The Triumph of American Painting.* London: Pall Mall, 1970.

Sarajlić, Izet. *Después de mil balas* [After a Thousand Bullets]. Barcelona: Seix Barral, 2017.

Sarría Buil, Aránzazu. "Atentados contra librerías en la España de los setenta, la expresión de una violencia política" [Attacks on Bookstores in 1970s Spain, An Expression of Political Violence]. In *Sucesos, guerras, atentados.* Edited by Marie-Claude Chaput and Manuelle Peloille. Paris: PILAR editores, 2009.

Saunders, Nicholas J. *Alexander's Tomb: The Two Thousand Year Obsession to Find the Lost Conqueror.* New York: Basic Books, 2006.

Schlink, Bernard. *The Reader.* New York: Vintage, 1998.

Schnitzer, Jeanne Cannella. "Reaching Out to the Mountains: The Pack Horse Library of Eastern Kentucky." *The Register of the Kentucky Historical Society* 95, no. 1 (1997): 57–77.

Scuccimarra, Luca, and Roger Campione. *Los confines del mundo. Historia del cosmopolitismo desde la antigüedad hasta el siglo XVIII* [The Ends of the Earth: A History of Cosmopolitanism from Antiquity to the Eighteenth Century]. Oviedo: KRK, 2017. Originally published as *I confini del mondo. Storia del cosmopolitismo dall'Antichità al Settecento*, 2006.

Sebald, W. G. *Austerlitz.* New York: Modern Library, 2001.

Sparrow, B., J. Liu, and D. M. Wegner. "Google Effects on Memory: Cognitive Conse- quences of Having Information at Our Fingertips." *Science* 333 (August 2011): 776–78.

Spence, Jonathan. *Mao Zedong. A Life.* New York: Penguin Books, 2006.

Steiner, George, and Cécile Ladjali. *Elogio de la transmisión* [In Praise of Transmission]. Madrid: Siruela, 2005.

Steiner, George, and Rob Riemen. *The Idea of Europe.* New York: Overlook Duckworth, 2015.

Stone, Brad. "Amazon Erases Orwell Books from Kindle." *The New York Times*, July 17, 2009.

Straten, Giorgio. *Historia de los libros perdidos* [A History of Lost Books]. Translated by María Pons. Barcelona: Pasado & Presente, 2016. Originally published as *Storie di libri perduti*, 2016.

Strauss, Barry. *The Death of Caesar: The Story of History's Most Famous Assassination.* New York: Simon and Schuster, 2015.

Sullivan, J. P. *Martial: The Unexpected Classic.* Cambridge: Cambridge University Press, 2004.

Todorov, Tzvetan. *La literatura en peligro* [Literature in Danger]. Translated by Noemí Sobregués. Barcelona: Galaxia Gutenberg, 2009. Originally published as *La Litté- rature en péril*, 2007.

Toner, Jeremy Peter. *Popular Culture in Ancient Rome.* Cambridge: Polity, 2012.

Turner, E. G. *Greek Papyri: An Introduction.* Oxford: Clarendon Press, 1980.

Twain, Mark. "Disappearance of Literature." In *Mark Twain's Speeches,* Project Gutenberg, August 19, 2006.

UN Commission of Experts on the Former Yugoslavia, 1994, annex VI, paragraphs 183–93.

Valcárcel, Amelia. "Crisis de valores y ética democrática" [A Crisis in Democratic Values and Ethics]. Talk, part the of series "El mundo que queremos," November 22, 2013, https://www.youtube.com/watch?v=c_gZcZFq-YE.

———. *Sexo y filosofía. Sobre «mujer» y «poder»* [Sex and Philosophy: On "Women" and "Power"]. Madrid: Horas y Horas, 2013.

Vallejo, Irene. "Una fábula con porvenir" [A Fable with a Future]. In *La profanación del Olimpo* [The Profaning of Olympus]. Edited by Luis Marcelo Martino and Ana María Risco. Buenos Aries: Teseo, 2018, pp. 335–55.

Various authors. *No lo comprendo, no lo comprendo. Conversaciones con Akira Kurosawa* [I Don't Understand, I Don't Understand: Conversations with Akira Kurosawa]. Almería: Confluencias, 2014.

Vernon, H. M. *A History of the Oxford Museum.* Oxford: Clarendon, 1909.

Veyne, Paul. *Sexo y poder en Roma* [Sex and Power in Rome]. Translated by María José Furió. Barcelona: Paidós, 2010. Originally published as *Sexe et pouvoir à Rome*, 2005.

von Albrecht, Michael. *A History of Roman Literature.* Leiden: Brill, 1996.

Watson, Peter. *Ideas: A History of Thought and Invention, from Fire to Freud.* New York: Harper, 2006.

Wills, Gary. *Martial's Epigrams.* New York: Viking, 2008.

Wittmann, Reinhard. "¿Hubo una revolución en la lectura a finales del siglo XVIII?" [Was There a Revolution in Reading at the End of the Eighteenth Century?]. In *Historia de la lectura en el mundo occidental*, edited by G. Cavallo and R. Chartier. Madrid: Taurus, 2001, 497–537.

Wood, Paul. "Famous Egyptian Library Reopens." BBC News, October 16, 2002, http://news.bbc.co.uk/1/hi/world/middle_east/2334707.stm.

Zafra, Remedios. *El entusiasmo: Precariedad y trabajo creativo en la era digital* [Enthusiasm: Precarity and Creative Work in the Digital Era]. Barcelona: Anagrama, 2017.

Zaid, Gabriel. *Los demasiados libros* [Too Many Books]. Barcelona: Debolsillo, 2010.

Zambrano, María. *La agonía de Europa* [The Death Throes of Europe]. Madrid: Trotta, 2000.

Zgustova, Monika. *Dressed for a Dance in the Snow.* New York: Other Press, 2020.

Zweig, Stefan. "Buchmendel." In *Jewish Legends.* New York: Markus Wiener, 1987.

INDEX

'Abd al-Laṭīf, 214
accents and punctuation, system of, 336
Achebe, Chinua, 97
Achilles, 12, 69, 72, 73, 349, 370, 383
    Alexander's obsession with, 8
    death of, 117
    overview of, 70, 71
Aconia Fabia Paulina, 366
Adobe, 300
Adolf Hitler Command, 292
Adso, 275
"Adventure of the Dancing Men, The"
    (Doyle), 54
Adventures of Huckleberry Finn, The
    (Twain), 189–90, 194
Adventures of Tom Sawyer The (Twain),
    189–90
Aemilius Paullus, 246
Aeneid, The, 220, 339, 343, 357–58
Aeschylus, xvi, 69, 132–33, 141, 159–60,
    161, 171
Aesop, 357
Agamemnon, 83, 103
Age of Innocence, The (Wharton), 341
Agora, 212
Agrippina, Julia, 365–66
Ahiram, 96
Akhmatova, Anna, 59–60, 109, 110
Alcrudo, José, 293
Alexander, 14
Alexander Romance, The, 16
Alexander the Great, 7–12, 53, 109, 187,
    246, 343, 370
    Aristotle and, 8, 11, 28, 205, 230, 334
    birth of, 120
    children of, 17, 20
    conquests of, 8, 9–11, 204
    death of, 14–15, 17, 20, 205, 334
    founding of Alexandria, 7–9, 210

globalization and, 126, 230–31
Iliad and, 8, 10, 19, 32, 70–71
influence over generals, 25, 27, 30
legend of, 8, 13, 15–17
marriages of, 13, 20
mausoleum of, 26–27, 42
mutiny in the Ganges against, 11–12,
    13
Ptolemy I and, 12, 13, 14, 15, 18, 25, 26,
    41
slavery and, 10
Alexandria, Egypt, 32–34, 38, 68, 232,
    245–46
    Amr's conquering of, 214
    Bibliotheca Alexandrina in, 216–17
    building of, 23–24
    conflict between different communities
        in, 31
    decline of, 42, 205
    economic power of, xvi, 32
    fire in, 203–4
    founding of, 7–9, 210
    legend of, 4–5, 6–7
    Library of, Great, *see* Library of
        Alexandria
    Lighthouse of, 32, 35–36, 232
    Musaeum of, *see* Musaeum of
        Alexandria
    turbulence in fourth century in, 208–10,
        211, 212–13
    World War II and, 7
Alexandrian War, The (Hirtius), 203
Alexandria Quartet, The, 6–7
Alhazred, Abdul, 197, 198
Alice's Adventures in Wonderland (Carroll),
    45, 346
All Our Yesterdays (Ginzburg), 341
Almansor (Heine), 200
Almería, Luis Beltrán, 174

alphabet, 97, 104
Aramaic system of, 96
as building communal memory, 45
Greek, 77, 96, 99–100, 110–12, 114–15, 243
Hebrew, 96, 114
invention of, 77, 95–96, 99–100
Latin, 96, 243
Phoenician, 95–96, 166
Roman, 243, 272–73
see also letters
Altos, 299
Amazon, 335
Ambrose of Milan, 41
Ammianus Marcellinus, 43, 205, 372
Amon, Temple of, 51
Amr ibn al-As, 214, 215
Anatolia, 8, 28, 30, 69, 117, 147, 246
Andresen, Sophia de Mello Breyner, 156
Andronicus, Livius, 244–45
Angelico, Fra, 65
angels, 39
animal fables, 357
Annals (Cordus), 333
Anónima, 290
Antigone, 140, 153–54, 155, 240
Antigonus, 18
Antiphon, 187–88
antiquities, fever for, 328
Antony, Mark, 5–6, 204
Antyllus, 110
Anyte, 144
Aphrodite, 101, 150
Apion, 31, 68
Apollonius of Rhodes, 32, 34
Apophoreta, The (Martial), 304–5
Apple computers, 299
archaeology, 328
Archilochus, 115–17
Archimedes, 34
Arenas, Reinaldo, 221
Arendt, Hannah, 251, 351
Argullol, Rafael, 232
Aristaeus, 43
Aristagoras, 60–61
Aristarchus, 34
Aristeas, 30
Aristides, Aelius, 369

Aristophanes of Byzantium, 58, 122, 174
comedies of, 175–77, 186, 200–201
as director of Library of Alexandria, 129–30
system of accents and punctuation invented by, 336
Aristotle, 30, 85, 129, 132, 158–59, 215, 353, 377
Alexander the Great and, 8, 11, 28, 205, 230, 334
in Alexandria, 33
book collection of, 123–24, 246
on booksellers, 124
The Constitution of Athens, 183
death of, 27
on drinking melted snow, 313
fascination with beaver's testicles, 326
Lyceum of, 27, 33, 123, 172
on moral canon, 352
Poetics, 172–74, 198
on slaves, 378
Arrian, 16
Artemis, Temple of, 117, 120
Artemisia, 148
Art of Love, The (Ovid), 268, 329–30, 332, 339, 379
Art of Worldly Wisdom, The (Gracián), 354
Ashmole, Elias, 47, 48
Ashmolean Museum, 46, 47
Ashurbanipal, 19, 50
Asia Minor, 117, 128, 152
As I Lay Dying (Faulkner), 339
Aspasia, 152, 153, 155
Astypalea, 112
Athena Polias, Temple of, 300
Athens, xvi, 141, 176, 373
book trade in, 104, 122, 123
citizen army's defense of, 159
Dipylon Amphora in, 100
in Greco-Persian Wars, 160
gymnasium in, 184
marriage in, 152–53
oratory in, 185–86
public library in, 184, 313, 318
siege on Syracuse, 182
Sparta and, 177, 182
women in, 147, 151–52, 155
Atia, 366

Atrectus, 278

Attempt at Exhausting a Place in Paris
(Perec), 143

Attica, 366

Atwood, Margaret, 157

Augustine, 41, 109–10, 267, 339–40

Augustus, 26–27, 38, 362
building of public libraries, 313
City of God, 339–40
founding of imperial monarchy, 312
homage to Alexander the Great, 26–27
Julian Laws of, 331, 364
Ovid and, 328–29, 331, 332, 353

Aurelian, 205

Auschwitz, 91, 164, 224

Ausonius, 266–67

Auster, Paul, 205–6, 208, 230, 346

Austerlitz (Sebald), 295–96

Austerlitz, Jacques, 295–96

authors, *see* writers

autofiction, 101

Axiothea of Phlius, 155

Bacon, Roger, 274

Bad Night and Birthing a Female, A
(Gorodischer), 340

Báez, Fernando, 199

Bakhtin, Mikhail, 174, 207–8

Balbilla, Julia, 144

Ballad of Reading Gaol, The (Wilde), 26

Balzac, Honoré de, 317

Banner of Youth, 167

Barba, Andrés, 177

Basquiat, Jean-Michel, 273

Bassani, Giorgio, 33

baths, Roman, 315–17

Batrachomyomachia, 32

Baudelaire, Charles, 341

Bauman, Zygmunt, 119

Bayard, Pierre, 347

BBC, 216

Beard, Mary, 146–47, 238, 241, 249, 357,
358, 368

Beauty and the Beast, 346

Bécquer, Gustavo Adolfo, 322

Benavente, Jacinto, 354

Benedictional of Saint Æthelwold, 300

Benjamin, Walter, 19, 378

Bergman, Ingmar, 35

Berlanga, Luis García, 307

Berners-Lee, Timothy John, 22

Berossus, 20

Bible, 64, 96, 142, 258, 284–85, 289

Bible in Spain, The (Borrow), 285

Bibliophile, The (Damophilus of Bithynia),
139

Bibliotheca Alexandrina, 216–17

Bingham, Hiram, 87

Bíró, László, 269

Blades, William, 360

Blair, Eric, *see* Orwell, George

Blaisten, Isidoro, 341

Blom, Philipp, 130

Bloom, Harold, 355

Bloom, Molly, 157

Blume, Anna, 206

Bodleian Library, 43–44, 46

Boeo, 144

Bolaño, Roberto, 341

bookbinding, origins of, 302

Book of the Dead, 336

books, 96, 123, 258–59, 275
affordability of, readership and, 302
burning of, 108–9, 151, 199–201, 207,
216, 289, 333, 334, 373
camouflaged, 55–56, 171
censorship of, 189–90, 191, 193–94, 195,
196, 287–88, 289
comfort provided by, in difficult times,
220–28
computers and, 299–300
copying of, *see* copyists
destruction of, in Spain, 360–61
distribution of, 245, 260–62, 276, 277–80
as extension of memory, 106–7, 108–10,
376–79
fragility of, 55–56, 171, 199
future of, 297–98
in Greek educational model, 178–79
harmful ideas in, 377–79
illustrations in, 336–38
indexes of, 338
literary canon, 352–59
literary classics, 344–51, 353, 354–55,
357–58

books (*continued*)
 miniature, 337
 murderous, 196–99
 "page book," 301–2, 305–7
 printing press and, 375
 sellers of, *see* booksellers; bookstores
 titles of, 338–41
 see also codices
booksellers, 170, 291–92, 306
 in *Austerlitz,* 295, 296
 in *84, Charing Cross Road,* 280–82
 European, 374
 in fifth and fourth centuries BC, 122,
  123, 124
 in first century BC, 276–79
 in *Parnassus on Wheels,* 124–25
 risky job of, 283–88, 290–91, 292–93, 294
 in Spain, 284–85, 292–93
Bookshop in Berlin. A (Frenkel), 287
Bookshop Memories (Orwell), 291
bookstores, 124, 277
 attacks on, 216, 293, 294
 chaos of, 294–95
 influence on cities, 290
 during periods of tyranny, 285–86
 as a refuge under siege, 291–93, 294
 in Rome, around mid-first century BC,
  277–79
 traveling, 121–25
book thieves, 44–45, 48–49, 246, 256
Booth, John Wilkes, 311
Borges, Jorge Luis, 135–36, 201, 346
 on books, 106–7
 on *Citizen Kane,* 354
 dedication of poem to Heraclitus, 119
 "Poem of the Gifts," 142
 "The Library of Babel," 21–22
 A Universal History of Infamy, 339
Borrow, George, 284–85, 290
Bosnian Muslim singers, 76
Boxall, Peter, 138
Bradbury, Ray, 108, 109, 218
Brainard, Joe, 143
Brassens, Georges, 149–50
Brigham Young University, 327
British and Foreign Bible Society, 284
British Museum, 25, 48, 54, 197, 300
Brodsky, Joseph, 220

Brutus, 263, 333
Buchenwald, 221
"Buchmendel" (Zweig), 376
bullying, 225–26
Burgos, Jorge de, 136, 137
Byblos, 95, 96, 258
*By Grand Central Station I Sat Down and
 Wept* (Smart), 340–41
By Night in Chile (Bolaño), 341

Cadmus, 165
Caerellia, 263
Caesar, Julius, 325, 343
 assassination of, 263, 311–12, 333
 Cleopatra and, 202, 204
 as part of Roman canon, 354
 rebellion in Alexandria against, 203
 slavery and, 239
 writing of, 262
Cairo, founding of, 54
Cálamo, 292
Calderón, Pedro, 346–47
Caligula, 333, 334, 353
Callatiae, 169
Callimachus, 34, 131–33, 135, 138, 140,
  195–96, 259
*Call of Cthulhu and Other Weird Stories,
 The* (Lovecraft), 197
Calvino, Italo, 142, 339, 346, 347
Calvus, Licinius, 277
Calypso, 71, 72
Campos de Castilla (Machado), 259
Canetti, Elias, 377
Cannae, Battle of, 238
canon, literary, 352–59
canons (yardsticks), 351–52
Capra, Frank, 137, 251
Capriolo, Ettore, 294
Caracalla, 205, 315, 334, 353, 367, 368–69
Carfania, 366
Carrère, Emmanuel, 101
Carrington, Leonora, 220–21
Carrión, Jorge, 124, 283, 289
Carroll, Lewis, 45, 135
Carthage, 243, 318, 319, 371
Carver, Raymond, 340
Cassian, 270

Cassius Dio, 204, 205, 368
catalogs
  of Athens library, 184
  of collectors/collections, 130, 131
  of Library of Alexandria, 131–33, 138,
    139, 140, 174, 228–29, 339
  of library of Hattusa, 49–50
  of Rome's public libraries, 317
Cato the Elder, 248, 262
Cato the Younger, 330–31
cats, 18, 31, 312
Catullus, 258, 277, 278, 354
Cavafy, Constantine, 6
celebrity, first use of term, 320
censorship, 195, 196, 200–201, 283–84,
    333–34, 335
  of children's classic books, 189–90, 194
  Plato and, 190, 191, 193–94, 195
  in Rome, 332–33
  self-censorship, 334–35
census, Roman, 345, 353
Cercas, Javier, 160–61
Cérémonie, La, 92
Cervantes, Miguel de, 262, 286, 346, 358,
    359
Chabrol, Claude, 92
Champollion, Jean-François, 54–55
Chaplin, Charlie, 175, 176, 251
Charlemagne, 300
Charles III, 328
Cheever, John, 224–25
Chesterton, G. K., 220, 339
childhood, invention of, 115, 353
China, 93, 108–9, 216, 239, 289, 374
chorus in Greek tragedy, 154
Christianity and Christians, 337
  ecclesiastical canon and, 352–53
  as official religion in Roman Empire,
    52–53, 208–9, 334, 374
  preference for codices over scrolls, 306
  religious persecution of, 209–10, 270–71,
    334
  riots between Jews and, 212–13
  Roman baths and, 316–17
Cicero, 109, 127, 261, 262, 306, 336
  on daughter Tullia, 263
  on Leontion, 155–56

  on miniature parchment of *The Iliad,*
    302
  as part of Roman canon, 354
  Petrarch's letter to, 378
  on Piso Caesoninus, 325
  slaves of, 255–56, 258
  On the Supreme Good, 263
cinema, 88, 251, 309–10
Circe, 157–58
Citizen Kane, 164, 354
citizenship
  cultural, concept of, 179
  in Roman Empire, extension of, 367–68,
    370, 377
City of Glass (Auster), 346
City of God (Augustus), 339–40
Civil War, The (Caesar), 203
classics, literary, 344–51, 353, 354–55,
    357–58
Claudius, 365
clay tablets, 49, 56, 100
Clemens, Aurelius Prudentius, *see*
  Prudentius
Clement of Alexandria, 316–17
Cleobulina, 144, 148, 149
Cleobulinas, The, 148
Cleobulus, 148
Cleombrotus of Ambracia, 195–96
Cleomedes of Astypalea, 112
Cleopatra, 5–6, 28, 54, 201–2, 204, 205
Clodia, 366
Closed Due to Melancholy (Blaisten), 341
Code, as a term, 307
codices, 268, 301, 310, 370
  advantages of, 302–6, 307
  pugillares, 302, 305
  scrolls as coexisting with, 307–8
  titles of, 340
Coetzee, J. M., 172, 355
comedy, 172–74, 175–78
comic strips, 337–38
Commodus, 334
Companion cavalry, 13, 25
Complete Works and Other Stories
  (Monterroso), 340
computers, 299–300, 309
Confederacy of Dunces, A (Toole), 340
Confessions (Augustine), 41

Conrad, Joseph, 226
Constantine, 208
Constantius II, 310
Constitutio Antoniniana, 369
Constitution of Athens, The (Aristotle), 183
"Contribution to Statistics, A" (Szymborska), 143
Convent of San Marco, 65–66
copyists
    European, 374, 375
    Greek, 63, 66–67, 123, 139, 170, 183, 228
    as risky job, 283–84
    Romans' use of, 256, 257, 260, 261, 277–78, 283–84, 334, 371
    slaves as, 256, 257, 260, 277, 334, 371
    workshops, 277
Cordus, Aulus Cremutius, 332–33, 334
Cornelia (mother of Gracchi), 263, 366
Corvinus, Marcus Valerius Mesalla, 362
cosmopolitanism, 31, 230, 232
Crates, 156
Crete, 56, 74, 148, 165, 238
Crete, Battle of, 74
crucifixion, 284, 368
cryptography, 54
cultural citizenship, concept of, 179
Cultural Revolution, Chinese, 216, 289
cultural studies, field of, 355
culture
    alternative youth, graffiti and, 272–73
    expansion of, 302–3
    Greeks and religion of, 126–28
    lists as origin of, 139
    oral, *see* oral tradition
    primitive, 174–75
    Roman Empire's imitation of Greek culture, 241–42, 243, 244, 248, 249, 342, 343–44
Curtius Rufus, 16
Cyril, 212–13

Dachau, 221–23, 224
Dacian Wars, 314
Damascius, 212
Damophilus of Bithynia, 139
D'Annunzio, Gabriele, 199
Darius, 10, 169

Darius III, 13
Dea Tacita, 364
Death Will Come and Have Your Eyes (Pavese), 340
Deipnosophists, The, 141
del Castillo, Michel, 224
Demetrius of Phalerum, xvii, 27, 28, 29, 215
Demo, 144
Democritus, 147
Demosthenes, 182, 184, 185, 187, 336, 343
De Niro, Robert, 185
De Profundis (Wilde), 331
De rerum natura (Lucretius), 353
Description of Greece (Pausanias), 112
Diadochi, 27
Diccionario de uso del español (Moliner), 137
Dick, Philip K., 341
Dickens, Charles, 31, 91
Dickinson, Emily, 149, 354
Didymus, 68
Digital Revolution, 273
Diocletian, 205, 334
Diodorus, 20, 31
Dion, 253
Dionysius (slave of Cicero), 255–56
Dionysius I, 253
Dionysius Thrax, 34
Dipylon Amphora, 100–101
"Disappearance of Literature" (Twain), 347
Django Unchained, 32
Do Androids Dream of Electric Sheep? (Dick), 341
Dodecanese Islands, 112
Domitian, 283–84, 285, 287, 342
Domna, Julia, 370
Don Giovanni, 131
Donoso, José, 93
Don Quixote (Cervantes), 199, 224, 286, 354, 359
Doryphoros (Polykleitos), 352
Dowdy, Doc Daniel, 256
Doyle, Arthur Conan, 54
Dressed for a Dance in the Snow (Zgustova), 224
DSPF *(de sua pecunia fecit),* 317

Dua-Khety, 52

Dumas, Alexandre, 198

Duras, Marguerite, xv

Durrell, Lawrence, 6–7

Dylan, Bob, 89

Dynabook, 299

Eastwood, Clint, 32, 160

ebooks, 310, 335, 376

Ecclesiastes, 81

ecclesiastical canon, 352–53

Echenique, Alfredo Bryce, 93

Eco, Umberto, xviii, 136, 139, 172, 173

Edda, The, 84

education

    Greek system of, 110–12, 114–15, 126,
        127, 128, 147–48, 150–51, 178–80, 183

    Plato on, 191, 193–94

    Roman system of, 179–80, 263–67, 269,
        270–72, 343, 357, 364–65, 372

    universities, first, 374

Edwards, Jorge, 93

Egypt

    Alexander the Great's conquest of, 8

    ancient landfills in, recovery of texts
        from, 181

    grain trade dominated by, xvi

    hieroglyphics in, 51, 53–55

    literacy in, 51, 128

    papyrus trade of, 24–25, 58

    Romans' annexation of, 41, 204

    scribes in, 51–52, 95

    during World War II, 7

    writing in, origins of, 93

    see also Alexandria, Egypt

84, Charing Cross Road (Hanff), 280–82

Eisenstein, Sergei, 355

Eleazar, 29

Elements (Euclid), 211

Ende, Michael, 226

Enheduanna, 146, 148

Enlightenment, 328, 353, 378

Ephesus, 117, 120, 318

epic songs, 74, 75, 76

Epicurus, 155, 327

Epigrams (Martial), 359, 378

Epiphanius, 43

Epirota, Quintus Caecilius, 264, 357

Eratosthenes, 34, 231, 377

Erinna, 144

Ernaux, Annie, 101

Ernst, Max, 250

Eros, 346

Erotion, 329

Esmet-Akhom, 53

ethnography, 169

Etruscans, 243

Euclid, 34, 211

Eugenides, Jeffrey, 196, 340, 346

Eumenes, *see* Cleobulina

Eumenes II, 58

Eumetis, 148

Euripides, 30, 73, 141, 159

    Macedonians and, 33

    Medea, 154

    popularity of, 182–83, 184

    Ptolemy III and, xvi

    The Trojan Women, 252, 348–49, 379

Europa, 162–63, 164–66

Europe

    moralizing in, beginning of, 332

    paper in, introduction of, 374–75

    see also specific countries

Eusebius of Caesarea, 352

Expertise Concerning Books (Telephus of
    Pergamum), 139

eyeglasses, 274–75

fables, animal, 357

Fahrenheit 451 (Bradbury), 108, 109, 110,
    218–19

fame, 319–21

fans

    archaeological sites as attracting, 328

    fame and, 319–20, 321

Fårö, 29, 35

fatwa, 216, 294

Faulkner, William, 73, 118, 339

feminism, rise of, 353–54

Fernando VII, 284, 285

Ferrer, Eulalio, 224

film, 88, 309–10

Finch, Atticus, 187

Finnegans Wake (Joyce), 118

First Punic War, 241, 244

Fitzgerald, F. Scott, 247, 340

Fleurs du mal, Les (Baudelaire), 341

Ford, John, 70, 251

forgers, xvii

Foucault, Michel, 126

Frame, Janet, 149

France, 48, 249–50, 251

Franco, Francisco, 251, 286

Frankl, Viktor, 188, 224

fratricide, 235

French Revolution, 48, 308

Frenkel, Françoise, 287, 288, 289, 292

Freud, Sigmund, 115, 188, 351

Fromm, Erich, 339

Fronto, 313

Fuertes, Gloria, 135

Fulvia, 366

Gaius Atilius, 238

Galen, 179, 199

Galileo, 34

Gallienus, 205

Games of the Late Age (Landero), 341

Gangs of New York, 208

Garden of the Finzi-Continis, The (Bassani), 33

Gargantua and Pantagruel (Rabelais), 353

Garner, James Finn, 190

Gatsby, Jay, 247

Gaul, 237, 239, 254, 311, 321

Gaza, 9–10

Gellius, Aulus, 43, 313, 345

Gelman, Juan, 341

General of the Dead Army, The (Kadare), 340

Germanicus, 365

Germany, 289

Gesta Romanorum (Worde), 360

Getty, Jean Paul, 325

Getty Museum, 325

Gide, André, 354

Giné, Víctor Lapuente, 297

Ginzburg, Natalia, 341

globalization, 126, 230–31, 239–40, 248, 249, 318, 320, 370–71

Glück, Louise, 157–58

Goethe, Johann Wolfgang von, 196, 198, 222

Goethe in Dachau (Rost), 221

"Gold-Bug, The" (Poe), 54

"Google effect," 105

Gorgias, 189

Gorodischer, Angélica, 340

Gospels, 87, 118, 352

Goytisolo, Juan, 219

Gracchi, 263, 366

Gracián, Baltasar, 354

graffiti, 272–73, 302

Grant, Cary, 352, 353

Great Harris Papyrus, 25

Great Jewish Revolt, 314

Greco-Persian Wars, 160, 161

Greek alphabet, 77, 96, 99–100, 110–12, 114–15, 243

Greek Anthology (Palladas), 210

Greek language, 20, 2930

Greeks, 57

　adoption of Phoenician writing system, 97, 98, 166

　booksellers in, 122

　copyists, 63, 66–67, 123, 139, 170, 228

　education and, 110–12, 114–15, 126, 127, 128, 147–48, 150–51, 178–80, 183

　libraries of, 314, 318

　marriage and, 152–53, 264

　orators, 185–89

　pederasty and, 110–11

　reaction to Hellenism, 30–31

　religion of art and culture, 126–28, 230–31

　Romans' imitation of, 241–42, 243, 244, 248, 249, 342, 343–44

　as slaves, 252–53, 254–56, 262, 266

　stereotypes about, 247–48

　women, 98, 111, 128, 141, 144, 146–49, 151–56, 264

　see also specific Greeks

Greek theater, 155, 158

Greek tragedies, 154, 155, 158–59

　see also specific Greek tragedies

Greenblatt, Stephen, 371

Gregory VII, 151, 353

Gual, Carlos García, 148

Guernica (Picasso), 65, 250

Guerriero, Leila, 340, 341
Guggenheim, Peggy, 249–50
Guggenheim, Solomon R., 48
Gutenberg, Johann, 375
Gutenberg Bible, 64
Gyllis, play about, 3–5
gymnasiums, 69, 184

Hadrian, 204, 317, 318
Hadrian's Wall, 268
Haneke, Michael, 270
Hanff, Helene, 280–82
Hannibal, 238, 239
Harari, Yuval Noah, 383
Harris, W. V., 266
Hattusa, library of, 49, 338
Havelock, Eric A., 82, 84, 103
Hays Code, 237
Heart Is a Lonely Hunter, The (McCullers), 340
Hebrew, 29, 81, 96, 114
Hecataeus, 31, 51
Hecuba, 349
Hedyle, 144
Heine, Heinrich, 200
Helen of Troy, 163
Hellenic civilization, 31, 180, 231, 239
Hellenism, 30–31, 33–34, 231, 369
Hera, 83, 165
Heracles, 122
Heraclitus, 117, 118–19, 120–21, 346
Heraldo de Aragón, 290
Herculaneum, 324, 325, 326–27, 328
Hermogenes of Tarsus, 283, 284
Hernández, Miguel, 102
Herodas, 115
Herodotus, 162, 231, 343, 346
    background of, 168–69
    on Greek generals before Battle of
        Salamis, 186
    The Histories, 86, 161–64, 167, 169–70,
        171, 379
    on Homer, 68
    on tattooing of slave's scalp, 60
Hero of Alexandria, 34
Herophilos, 34
Herostratus, 119–21

Herostratus syndrome, 120
Hesiod, 101–3, 114, 122, 182, 191, 339
hetaeras, 152, 155–56, 264
hexameters, 81, 101, 102
hieroglyphics, 51, 53–55
Hipparchia of Maroneia, 156
Hippocratic oath, 377
Hirtius, Aulus, 203
Histiaeus, 60, 61
Histories, The (Herodotus), 86, 161–64, 167,
    169–70, 171, 379
history, discipline of, 161–62
History of Reading, A (Manguel), 44–45,
    257
History of Sexuality (Foucault), 126
Hitler, Adolf, 16, 176, 288–89
Hölderlin, Friedrich, 107, 135
Holiday, 352
Homer, 67, 68–73, 78, 343, 346
    Caligula and, 334, 353
    Plato on, 191–92
    popularity of, 30, 69–70, 85, 114, 121,
        129, 182, 183
    see also Iliad, The (Homer); *Odyssey, The*
        (Homer)
homosexuality, 6, 150–51
Horace, 242, 267, 279, 280, 304, 320–21,
    358, 379
Hortensia, 366
Hostia, 366
How to Talk About Books You Haven't Read
    (Bayard), 347
Hrabal, Bohumil, 361–62
Hugo, 309
humanism, European, dawning of, 127
humor, 172–74, 175, 354
Hurt, William, 208
Hypatia, 210, 211–13
Hyperion (Hölderlin), 107

Ibn al-Qiftī, 214, 215
Iccus of Epidaurus, 112
Ides of March, 311, 312
If on a Winter's Night a Traveler (Calvino),
    339
Igarashi, Hitoshi, 294
Ignorant Book-Collector, The, 276

Iliad, The (Homer), 12, 74, 78, 84, 109, 131, 142, 379, 383
    Alexander the Great and, 8, 10, 19, 32, 70–71
    classism in, 83, 103
    homage to, on Nestor's Cup, 101
    inherited wisdom from, 82
    miniature parchment of, 302
    narrator of, 101
    opening hexameter of, 73
    overview of, 70–71
    popularity of, 69, 85, 182, 183, 348
illiteracy
    in Kentucky, 381–82, 383
    orality and, 87
    in *The Reader,* 90–92
    silent exclusion and, 92
    slaves and, 256–57
    in Spain, 92
illumination, art of, 374
illustrations in ancient books, 336–38
Imaginary Lives (Schwob), 120
Imagines (Varro), 337
Inanna, 146
Inca culture, 80
indexes, 338
India, 8, 18, 30, 93, 96
Infinity of Lists (Eco), 139
In Search of Lost Time (Proust), 340
Institutes of Oratory (Quintilian), 271, 343
internet, 22, 105, 106, 333, 335, 355
In the Country of Last Things (Auster), 206–7
Invention of Hugo Cabret, The (Selznick), 309
Invention of Solitude, The (Auster), 230
Io, 162
Iranzo, Pilar, 144–46
Iraq, 216
I Remember (Brainard), 143
Iron Maiden, 17
I Should Have Said I Love You (Gelman), 341
Isis, 201
Isis, Temple of, 53
Isocrates, 179
Israel, 56, 96

Italy, 237
It's a Wonderful Life, 136, 137

Jenkyns, Richard, 117
Jerome, 310, 336
Jesus of Nazareth, 29, 87
Jeusalem, 29
Jews
    in Alexandria, 7, 29, 31, 212–13, 214
    fleeing from Nazi invasion, 250, 295
    Great Jewish Revolt, 314
    reading and, 114
    scrolls and, 24, 57, 306
Jiménez, Juan Ramón, 251
Jobs, Steve, 299
John, Gospel of, 87, 118
Johnson, Samuel, 261
Joke, The (Kundera), 175
Jones, Terry, 200–201
Journey to Italy (Rossellini), 325
Joyce, James, 71, 118, 142, 157, 200, 339, 346
Judgment in Stone, A (Rendell), 92
Julia Drusilla, 366
Julian the Apostate, 179, 180
Jupiter, 364
Justinian I, 53, 307, 373
Juvenal, 248, 264–65, 321, 364

Kadare, Ismail, 340
Kama Sutra (Vatsvayana), 268
Kapital, Das, 286
Kapuściński, Ryszard, 166–68, 169
Kay, Alan, 299
Kennedy, John F., 153
Kentucky, 381–82
Khomeini, Ayatollah, 294
Kindles, 335
Klein, Ernest, 165
knowledge, technology and, 105, 106
Koiné, 30
Koran, 16, 200–201, 215, 306
Korybut, Elena, 223–24
Kristallnacht, 288
Kubrick, Stanley, 175
Kundera, Milan, 175

Kurosawa, Akira, 88
Kurosawa, Heigo, 88

Lacarrière, Jacques, 162
Landero, Luis, 341
Landscapes of War (Goytisolo), 219
Lang, Fritz, 251
language, 80–81, 84–85, 189–90, 229, 272
Lastheneia of Mantinea, 155
Latin alphabet, 96, 243
Latin literature, development of, 243–44
laughter, 172–74, 175
Laws, The (Plato), 192, 193–94
learning, Greeks and, 126, 127–28
lecture, inauguration of genre of, 188
Lee, Harper, 187, 340
Leningrad, 59, 207
Leontion, 155–56
Lesbos, 147, 150
letters, 94
    see also alphabet
Letters from Iwo Jima, 160
"Letter to the Year 2176" (Sarajlić), 300–301
Levinas, Emmanuel, 164
librarians, 228
    creation of position of, 27
    early, 131–33, 135, 184
    equestrian, and outreach in Kentucky, 381–83
    local, 128, 183–84
    stereotype of, 136–37
    women as, 136–37, 381–83
libraries, 134–35
    attacks on, 216, 217–18, 219
    decline of, 371–72
    early growth of, 50
    in Egypt, 51
    Greek, 314, 318
    modern, 137–38
    in Nazi concentration camps, 221, 222
    Near East, 49–50
    public, 137–38, 302, 312–16, 317–18, 324, 371, 374
    Roman, 302, 312–16, 317–18, 324, 371–72, 374
    in Spain, 134
    spread of, 134

Works Progress Administration and, 381–83
    world's earliest, 49–50
    see also specific libraries
Library of Alexandria, 19–20, 34–37, 128, 183, 201, 216–17, 232, 246
    acquisition of books, xii–xiv, xv–xvii, 28–29, 42, 68, 108, 124
    books surviving from, 219
    canon, 356, 358
    catalog of, 131–33, 138, 139, 140, 174, 228–29, 339
    copying of books from, 220
    destruction of, 203–5, 207, 208, 210, 214–15, 219
    famous lists established at, 141–42
    management of, xvii, 27, 28, 231
    Plato and, 195
    Ptolemy I and, 18, 130–31
    restoration of texts' original forms, 67
    size of, 43
    translation of works for, 20, 29, 229–30
"Library of Babel, The" (Borges), 21–22
Librería Antígona, 291
Librería París, 291
Life: A User's Manual (Perec), 340
Life Is a Dream (Calderón), 346–47
Life of Brian, 134
Lincoln, Abraham, 311
list-making, 138–40, 142, 144, 355
    of Greeks, 141–42
    impulse of, 138–40, 142, 144, 355
    internet and, 355
    in literature, 142–43
    of Quintilian, 343
Liszt, Franz, 319–20, 321
Lisztomania, 319–20
literacy, 84–85
    in ancient Greece, 121–22, 144
    in Egypt, 181–82
    in modern era, 266
    Romans and, 266
    spread of, 128, 180
    see also illiteracy
literary canon, 352–59
literature
    birth of, 96
    children's, 82, 353

literature (*continued*)
    classics, 344–51, 353, 354–55, 357–58
    erotic, 307, 329
    Latin, 243–44
    Roman Empire and, 244–45, 246–47,
        260–62, 276
Lithos, 300
Liu, Jenny, 105
Livius, Titus, *see* Livy
Livro (Veloso), 16
Livy, 171, 235, 236, 320, 321, 343, 370
Llosa, Mario Vargas, 93
London, Jack, 226
López, Aurora, 365
Lord, Albert, 76
Louvre Palace, 48
Lovecraft, H. P., 197
Lovrenović, Ivan, 217
Lucian of Samosata, 122
Lucretius, 353
Lucullus, 246–47
lustrum, 345
Lying Bitch (Sanz), 340
"lyric poetry," as a term, 149
Lysistrata, 154, 155

Macedonia, 12–13, 246, 249, 254
Macedonians, 11–15, 17–18, 26, 33, 125–29
    conquerors, culture of, 69, 128–29
    mutiny in the Ganges, 11–12, 13
    polygamy and, 13
    see also Alexander the Great
Machado, Antonio, 259, 322, 364
Machu Picchu, 80, 87
Maecenas, 358
Magna Graecia, 243
Mahfouz, Naguib, 216
Maison du Livre, La, 287, 288
Mallarmé, Stéphane, 138
Manetho, 20
Manguel, Alberto, 44–45, 257
Manlius, Titus, 238
Manrique, Jorge, 119
Man Who Shot Liberty Valance, The, 70
Man Who Was Thursday, The (Chesterton),
    339
Mao Zedong, 289, 291

Marchamalo, Jesús, 220
Marcia (daughter of Cordus), 333
Marcia (wife of Cato the Younger), 331
Marcus Aurelius, 313
Marías, Javier, 340
Mariout, Lake, 7, 23, 38
Márquez, Gabriel García, 93, 340
marriage
    as an economic institution, 152–53
    Greeks and, 152–53, 264
    Juvenal on, 265
    Romans and, 236–37, 264, 330–31,
        364
Martial, 309, 313, 321, 322–23, 354
    on *The Aeneid,* 339
    The Apophoreta, 304–5
    background of, 303–4, 319
    on books, 304, 305–6, 310, 359
    booksellers and, 278–79, 280
    on copying of second book of epigrams,
        277
    desire for young slave girl, 329
    Epigrams, 359, 378
    on profitability of writing, 261
    on public baths, 315
    on vision from reading tablets, 274
Marx, Karl, 251, 286, 346, 351
Matidia, 317
Matrix movie saga, 191, 346
Matute, Ana María, 341
McCullers, Carson, 340
Medea, 140, 154–55, 157–58
media, mass, 297
Medici, Catherine de, 198
Medici de', Cosimo, 65
medicine, 179, 262
Mein Kampf (Hitler), 219, 289
Meirelles, Fernando, 340
Méliès, Georges, 309–10
Melinno, 144
Memento, 61
Memnon, 74
memory
    books as an extension of, 106–7, 108–10,
        376–79
    capacity, experiment measuring, 105
    "Google effect" of, 105
    Herodotus on, 163–64

in preservation of culture, 80–82
transactive, theory of, 106
writing and, 108, 109
Menander, 129, 177, 178, 182, 184
Mesia, 366
Mesopotamia, 200
    curses against book thieves and
        destroyers, 48
    first written symbols in, 93
    slavery and, 239
    tablets in, 49–50, 59, 94
Metamorphoses (Ovid), 305, 346,
    358–59
Metropolitan Museum, 48, 250
Michelozzo, 65
Mifflin, Mr., 124–25
Milan, Nan, 382
Miletus, 60, 61, 128
Mithra, 209
Mnemosyne, 33, 81
Moero, 144
Moix, Ana María, 93
Molière, 85, 148
Moliner, María, 137
monasteries, 63, 374
money, introduction of, 174
Montero, Rosa, 341
Monterroso, Augusto, 340
Moral Letters to Lucilius (Seneca), 350
Morley, Christopher, 124–25
Mortuary Roll of Matilda, The, 308
Moschine, 144
Moses, 24
multiperspectivism, 163–64
Munich Putsch, 289
Murko, Mathias, 76
Musaeum of Alexandria, 33–35, 228, 232,
    374
    contemporaries' opinion of, 67–68
    destruction of, 205, 213
    financial cuts to, 204
    fire in, 203, 204, 207
    founding of, 18, 33–34
    last resident at, 211
    rituals of the Muses enacted at, 128
    Strabo's description of, 38
    see also Library of Alexandria
Muses, 33, 81, 102, 127, 128, 170, 209

Myers, Belle, 256
Myrtis, 144

Nabokov, Vladimir, 251–52, 273–74, 287
Name of the Rose, The (Eco), 136, 137,
    172–73, 178, 198, 275
Napoleon, 13, 23, 53
Naram-Sin, 146
National Library in Sarajevo, 217–18, 219
Nazis, 175, 295, 349, 353, 360, 377
    bombing of London, 219
    burning of books, 200, 216, 334
    concentration camps of, 221–23, 224
    films, 355
    invasion of France, 249–50
    persecution of booksellers, 287–88
    siege of Leningrad, 207
Necronomicon (Lovecraft), 197
Nelson, Admiral, 54
Nero, 272, 274, 315, 365
Nestor's Cup, 101
Niccoli, Niccolò, 65, 66
Nietzsche, Friedrich, 351
1984 (Orwell), 192–93, 335
Nineveh, library of Ashurbanipal in, 19, 50
Nip the Buds, Shoot the Kids (Ōe), 340
Nobel Prize, 89, 313
Nolan, Christopher, 61
No Longer at Ease (Achebe), 97–98
nomadic tribes, oral tradition of, 73
Northup, Solomon, 253–54, 256–57
Nossis, 144
Nuremberg Race Laws, 288
Nygaard, William, 294

Obama, Barack, 153, 200
O'Connor, Flannery, 194–95
Octavia Minor, 366
Odysseus, 69, 71–72, 156, 240
    Circe and, 158
    treatment of Thersites, 83
Odyssey, The (Homer), 69, 70, 73, 74, 78, 84,
    109, 339, 348
    Circe in, 158
    expressions of oppressive ideology in,
        82–83, 146–47

Odyssey, The (Homer) (*continued*)
  festive competitions in, 100
  mention of Pharos in, 9
  narrator of, 101
  Penelope's handling of suitors in,
    156–57
  popularity of, 85, 182
  in *The Reader,* 90, 91
  representation of homesickness in,
    71–72
  translation of, 244–45
Ōe, Kenzaburō, 340
Oedipus, 74, 140, 159, 165, 240, 346
Oedipus Rex, 339
Olmos, Alberto, 360
One Hundred Years of Solitude (Márquez),
  340
Onetti, Juan Carlos, 341
On Libraries (Varro), 312
On Nature (Epicurus), 327
On Nature (Heraclitus), 117
On the Purchase and Selection of Books
  (Philo of Byblos), 139
On the Supreme Good (Cicero), 263
Open Society and Its Enemies, The (Popper),
  193
oral tradition, 77, 108–10
  of adults reading to children, 78–80, 90
  among nomadic tribes, 73
  bards' performances, 74–76, 89
  efforts to endure, 80–81
  shift toward writing, 97
  technological progress and, 87–88
  transformation after contact with the
    alphabet, 104
  written language and, bond between,
    85–86
oratory, Greek, 185–89
Orestes, 212–13
Orlando (Woolf), 346
Orosius, 203
Ortega y Gasset, José, 177
Orwell, George, 192, 291, 335
Osiris, 201
Ovid, 304, 320, 334, 362
  on *The Aeneid,* 339
  The Art of Love, 268, 329–30, 332, 339,
    379

  Augustus and, 328–29, 331, 332, 353
  background of, 328
  banishment of, 331–32
  cosmetic advice for women, 303, 329
  death of, 332
  Metamorphoses, 305, 346, 358–59
  Tristia, 331–32
  on Zeus, 165

pacifism, 350, 379
paganism, 208–10, 373, 374
Pale Fire (Nabokov), 273–74
Palestine, 9
Palladas, 210–11, 213–14
Palo Alto Research Center, 299
paper, introduction of, 374–75
papyrus, 57–58, 77, 340
  disadvantages of, 57, 117, 170–71, 307
  Egypt's monopoly over, 24–25, 58
  finest quality of, 275–76
  invention of scrolls of, 170
  price of, 24, 122, 336
  process of creating scrolls from, 24–25,
    276
  storage and transportation of, 171
  title and author's name on scrolls of, 340
Parallel Lives (Plutarch), 339, 343, 365
parchment, 58–59
  expense of, 336
  monks and nuns learning art of making,
    374
  production process of, 59, 63
  Romans' use of, 301
  rotuli mortuorum, 308
  types of, 63–64
Paris, 163, 250, 273
Parnassus on Wheels (Morley), 124–25
Parry, Milman, 76, 87
Paul the Apostle, 377
Pausanias, 112
Pavese, Cesare, 340
PDF (portable document format), 300
Peacefull, Penelope, 295, 296
Peck, Gregory, 187
pederasty, 110–11, 264
pedophilia, 329
Peloponnesian War, 182

Penelope, 72, 82, 146–47, 156–57, 158, 367
Penguin, 294
Pepi, 52
Perdiccas, General, 26
Perec, Georges, 143, 309, 340
Pérez-Reverte, Arturo, 218
Pergamum, library in, 58, 128, 246, 318
Pericles, xvi, 152, 153, 176
Perilla, 366
Peristephanon (Clemens), 270
Perret, Jacques, 229
Persepolis, 16, 109
Perses, 102
Persia, 8, 30, 48, 215, 254
Persian Empire, 159, 160
Persians, The, 159, 160, 161
Persius, 269
Petrarch, 62, 63, 378
Petronius, 272, 303
Phaedo (Plato), 196
Phaedrus, 357
Phaedrus (Plato), 104–5, 106, 107
Pharos, 9, 35–36, 203
Phidias, 120
Philinna, 144
Philippics, The (Demosthenes), 187
Phillips, David, 196
Philocleon, 186
philologists, 67, 68, 87, 166, 219, 228
Philo of Byblos, 139
philosophy, Greek, birth of, 117
Phoenicia, 9, 258
Phoenicians, 95–96, 97, 99, 166, 243
Picasso, Pablo, 65, 250
Pilia, 366
Pillow Book, The (Sei Shōnagon), 142
Pínakes, The, 132–33, 195, 339
Pindar, 86, 169, 346
Pinker, Steven, 344
pirates, 252
Piso Caesoninus, Lucius Calpurnius, 325, 326–27
Pizarnik, Alejandra, 339
Plato, 30, 86, 119, 122, 129, 182, 198, 343, 373
   Academy of, 33, 123, 155, 190–91, 193
   on Aspasia, 153, 155
   censorship and, 190, 191, 193–94, 195

   on Crete, 148
   on education, 191, 193–94
   on Homer, 69
   The Laws, 192, 193–94
   myth of the cave, 191
   Phaedo, 196
   Phaedrus, 104–5, 106
   on reading aloud, 258
   The Republic, 110, 155, 191–92
   as a slave, 252–53
   as a teacher, 190–91, 193
   on theater, 192
   threats against poets, 353
   true name of, 132
   ultraconservatism of, 190, 191, 193
   on women, 155, 192, 377–78
Plautus, 171, 248–49, 252, 370
plays, titles of, 339
Pleasure (D'Annunzio), 199
Pliny the Elder, 171, 258, 275, 337
Pliny the Younger, 260, 317, 320, 321
Plutarch, 222
   on Alexander the Great, 8, 16, 230
   on Aspasia, 152, 153
   on Cleopatra, 5, 202
   on Demosthenes, 185
   on influence of Greek culture, 30
   on Library of Alexandria fire, 203, 204
   on Lucullus, 246
   Parallel Lives, 339, 343, 365
   on Syracusans' pardoning of prisoners, 182
Poe, Edgar Allan, 54
"Poem of the Gifts" (Borges), 142
poems
   in Archilochus's poems, 115–17
   oral, 73–76, 77, 81–82
   of Sappho, 149–50, 151
   see also specific poems
poetry
   future of, 300–301
   of Greek slaves or freedmen, 262
   oral cultures' use of, 80–81
   Plato on censorship of, 192
   Romans' view of, 262
   social, first generation of, 103
Poetry and Truth (Goethe), 196

Politically Correct Bedtime Stories (Garner), 190

Pollio, Asinius, 312, 313

Pollock, Jackson, 250

Polybius, 237

Polykleitos, 120, 352

Pompeii, 266, 302, 317, 324–25, 328, 357, 358

Pompey, 263, 311

Popper, Karl, 193

Portadores de Sueños, Los, 291, 292

Pórtico Librerías, 293

PostScript, 300

póthos, 11

Pratolini, Vasco, 59

Praxagora, 154, 155

Praxilla, 144

Précieuses ridicules, Les (Molière), 148

printing press, 375

Prometheus Bound, 339

Propertius, 321

property lists, 93–94

prose
    birth of, 103
    titles and, 339

prostitutes, 152, 155–56, 252, 253, 364

Proust, Marcel, 118, 242, 340, 354

Prudentius, 269–71

Psyche, 346

Psycho, 198

Ptolemy I, 18, 41, 50, 69
    Alexander the Great and, 12, 13, 14, 15, 18, 25, 26, 41
    in building of Alexandria, 23–24, 36
    Library of Alexandria and, 18, 29, 33–34, 35, 130–31
    marriage of, 14
    memoir of, 14
    Musaeum of Alexandria and, 18, 33–34

Ptolemy II, xvi–xvii, 41

Ptolemy III, xvi, 41–42, 231

Ptolemy IV, 42

Ptolemy V, 53, 58

Ptolemy X, 42

Ptolemy XIII, 201–2, 203

public readings, 40

Publilia, 366

Puche, Paco, 290

pugillares codices, 302, 305

punctuation, system of, 336

Punic Wars, 239, 241, 244

Quignard, Pascal, 330

Quintilian, 271, 274, 342–43

Rabelais, François, 353

Ramayana, The, 84

rape
    in Greek mythology, 164, 269
    mass, in Rome, 235–37

Rashomon, 157, 164

Reader, The (Schlink), 90–92

reading, 37, 112–14, 279–80, 302–3
    act of, 39–41, 257–58
    to children, adults and, 78–80, 90
    in daily actions of life, 92–93
    in Egypt, 181–82
    Greeks and, 121–22, 144, 183
    Romans and, 265, 266, 267, 277, 302, 364, 371, 372–73
    simplification of, progress towards, 336
    slaves in the United States and, 256–57
    women and, 121, 144, 265, 364

Regulus, 206

Reine Margot, La (Dumas), 198

religion, 126–28, 270–71
    see also Christianity and Christians

Remus, 235

Rendell, Ruth, 38

Republic, The (Plato), 110, 155, 191–92

Requiem (Akhmatova), 59–60, 109

Resurrection (Tolstoy), 224

Rhodes, library at, 184

Rhys, Jean, 339

rhythm of language, 80–81

Riccardiana Library, 62

Ricoeur, Paul, 224

Ridiculous Idea of Never Seeing You Again, The (Montero), 341

Riefenstahl, Leni, 355

Robinson Crusoe, 383

Roman alphabet, 243, 272–73

Roman Empire
    annexation of Egypt, 41, 204

Christianity as state religion of, 52–53, 208–9, 374

citizenship in, extension of, 367–68, 370, 377

collapse of, 371–74

collecting frenzy of, 246–47, 249

economic crisis in, 205

expansion of, 237–38

globalization and, 239–40, 248, 249, 318, 320, 370–71

honestiores and *humiliores,* distinction between, 368

imitation of Greek culture, 241–42, 243, 244, 248, 249, 342, 343–44

making of, 237

reading as flourishing in, 302–3, 371

slavery and, 238, 239, 240, 244, 251, 254–56

war machine of, 237–38, 241

wealth of, 238–39

"Roman Oration" (Aristides), 369

Romans, 258

bookbinding and, 302

census, 345, 353

collection of books, 276

conquering of Greece, 86

contradictions in identity of, 247–48

distribution of books, 260–62, 276

educational system of, 179–80, 263–67, 269, 270–72, 343, 357, 364–65, 372

first literary work in Latin, 244–45

intellectual entertainment as one most beloved privileges of, 325–26

learning to write, 247

libraries of, 302, 312–16, 317–18, 324, 371–72, 374

marriage and, 236–37, 264, 330–31, 364

nobles' commissioning copies of books, 245–46

printing method for use in book trade, 337

public baths of, 315–17

reading and, 267, 276, 302–3, 372–73

religious persecution against Christians, 270–71

slavery and, 252–53, 256, 257, 260, 262, 277, 334, 371, 372

stereotypes about, 247–48

women, 263–64, 330–31, 362–66; *see also specific Roman women*

writing, 57, 267–69

Rome

bad reputation of, 235–37

bookshops in, 277

book titles in, 339

burning of books in, 333

censorship/repression in, 332–33

as center of Mediterranean empire, 5, 32

famous writers in, fans stalking of, 321

first great private library in, 246

foreign policy in, 235

founding of, 235, 368–69

immigrants in, 303

libraries in, 312–15, 324

literature's arrival in, 244–45

marriage and, 236–37

mass rape in, 235–37

slavery in, 252, 254–55, 256

theater in, 248–49

Romulus, 235–36, 241, 343, 368

Romulus Augustulus, 372

Roncagliolo, Santiago, 195

Rosetta Project, 55

Rosetta Stone, 53–54, 56

Rossellini, Roberto, 325

Rost, Nico, 221–23, 224

Roto, El, 216

rotuli mortuorum, 308

Roxana (wife of Alexander the Great), 17

Rushdie, Salman, 216, 293–94

Safonova, Galya, 223, 224

Saladin, 214

Salamis, Battle of, 148, 159, 160–61, 186

Sallust, 343

Samnites, 241

Sánchez, Gervasio, 217

Sanmartín, Fernando, 378

San Pedro de las Puellas monastery, 44

Sanz, Marta, 340

Sappho, 121, 268, 346, 379

Gregory VII and, 353

as only female presence in Greek literary canon, 144

overview of, 149–51

Sarajevo, 217–18, 219, 349

Sarajlić, Izet, 300–301

Sargon, 146, 321

Sartre, Jean-Paul, 120

Satanic Verses, The (Rushdie), 293–94

Satirae (Juvenal), 264

Satyricon (Petronius), 272, 303

Scharoun, Hans, 39

Scheherazade, 91, 138, 198, 224

Schindler's List, 349

Schlink, Bernhard, 90

Schopenhauer, Arthur, 347

Schwob, Marcel, 120

Scipio Aemilianus, 246, 247

Scipio Africanus, 248

Scorsese, Martin, 208, 309

scribes, 51–52, 66–67, 95, 228, 260, 334

scrolls, 310

    Christians' preference for codices over, 306

    coexistence with codices, 307–8

    cost of, 122, 336

    current use of, 308

    disadvantages of, 57, 117, 170–71, 307

    as expensive luxury products, 301, 306

    from Herculaneum, 326–27

    invention of, 170

    placement of title and author's name on, 340

    process of creating, 24–25, 276

    reading, 37

    recovery of, written by regular people in Egypt, 181

    as representing progress in history of the book, 57

    Romans' use of, 301

    rotuli mortuorum, 308

    storage and transportation of, 171

Scuccimarra, Luca, 231

Searchers, The, 341

Sebald, W. G., 295–96

Second Intifada, 209

Second Punic War, 239

Secundus, 278–79

Seeger, Pete, 81

Sei Shōnagon, 142

Seleucus, 17, 18

self-censorship, 334–35

Selznick, Brian, 309

Sender, Ramón, 251

Seneca, 346

    bank of, 350

    on Library of Alexandria fire, 203

    on Marcia, 333

    on pacifism, 379

    on Roman baths, 315–16

    on Sappho, 151

September 11 terrorist attacks, 200

Septuagint, 20, 29

Serapeum, 42, 209, 210, 211, 228

Serapis, 42, 209, 210

Servilia, 263, 366

Servius Tullius, 345

Seven Brides for Seven Brothers, 236–37

Severus, Septimus, 370

Shakespeare, William, 73, 159, 193, 262, 346, 353, 360

Sharon, Ariel, 209

Shelley, Mary, 346

Shihuangdi, 108–9, 360

Sicily, as part of Roman Empire, 237

silence as a protective barrier, 225–26

Simplician, 109–10

Sirk, Douglas, 251

skin, human, as living parchment, 59–61

slavery and slaves, 257–58

    Alexander the Great and, 10

    Aristotle on, 378

    in copying, 256, 257, 260, 277, 334, 371

    global wealth and, 239, 240

    Greeks and, 252–53, 254–56, 262, 266

    Lighthouse of Alexandria and, 36

    Roman Empire and, 238, 239, 240, 244, 251, 252–53, 254–56, 372

    United States and, 253–54, 256–57

Smart, Elizabeth, 340–41

Smoke, 208

social networks, 297–98, 333, 355

Socrates, 86, 176

    Aspasia and, 153

    execution of, 193, 196

    in Plato's dialogues, 104–5, 106, 107, 122

    as a teacher, 151

Soldiers of Salamis (Cercas), 160–61

songs
  of Bosnian Muslim singers, 76
  epic, 74, 75
  traditional, 74
Sontag, Susan, 219
Sophists, 188
Sophocles, 30, 141, 159, 171
  loss of plays by, 132–33
  Ptolemy III and, xvi
  titles in Athens library, 184
Sorrows of Young Werther, The (Goethe),
  196
Sound of Things Falling, The (Vázquez),
  341
Soviet gulag, 223–24
Spain
  Barcelona Olympics and the World
    Expo in Seville in, 217
  booksellers in, 284–85, 292–93
  destruction of books, 360–61
  illiteracy in, 92
  preservation of films with sound, 309
  public libraries in, 134
  Transition in, 292–93
Sparrow, Betsy, 105
Sparta, 111, 116, 177, 182
spectacles, eye, 274–75
"Specters" (Palladas), 211
Staatsbibliothek, 39
Stabiae, 328
Staël, Madame de, 263
Star Wars, 346
Steiner, George, 231
Stevenson, Robert Louis, 226
Stewart, James, 136
Stone, Oliver, 14
Stone, Sumner, 300
Strabo, 34, 37–38, 123, 203
Streetcar Named Desire, A (Williams), 341
Stylites, Simeon, 316
Suetonius, 203, 284, 303, 311, 334
Suez Crisis, 7
suicide, 196
Suicides at the End of the World, The
  (Guerriero), 340
Sulla, 246, 247, 255
Sulpicia, 362–64, 365, 366
Sumerian literature, 146

Sumerian tablets, 49, 94, 272
Sur, 354
symbols, written
  first appearance of, 93
  transition to letters, 94
Syracuse, 182
Syria, 9
Szymborska, Wisława, 143

tablets, 49–50
  clay, 49, 56, 100
  codices, *see* codices
  current, 310
  in Europe, 56–57
  in library of Ashurbanipal, 50
  in library of Hattusa, 50
  in Middle East, 170
  rectangular, 57
  Roman, 267–69, 274
  royal accounting records on, 100
  secondary status to papyrus scrolls,
    57
  Sumerian, 49, 94, 272
  wax, 267, 268, 274
Tacitus, 262, 266, 379
  on censorship, 333, 334
  competition between Pliny the Younger
    and, 321
  on repression under Tiberius's rule,
    332
Tarantino, Quentin, 32, 270
Taranto, 244
tattoos, 60, 61
Taxi Driver, 185
teaching in ancient world, 266–67, 270–72,
  363
Telemachus, 82–83, 146–47, 158
Telephus of Pergamum, 139
Telesilla, 144
Temple Mount, 209
Temple of Amon, 51
Temple of Artemis, 117, 120
Temple of Athena Polias, 300
Temple of Isis, 53
Temple of Minerva, 244
Temple of Peace, 314
Tender Is the Night (Fitzgerald), 340

Tenorio, Don Juan, 131

Teos, 128, 180

Terence, 246, 248

Terentia, 366

Thamus, 104–5

theater

    Plato on, 192

    in Rome, 248–49

Thebes, 74, 165

Themistius, 310

Theodore of Sykeon, 316

Theodosius I, 52, 208, 209

Theodotus, 205

Theon, 211

Theophilus, 209, 212

Theosebeia, 144

Thersites, 83, 84, 86, 103

Theseus, 343

Theuth, 104–5

thieves, book, 44–45, 48–49, 246, 256

Thomas's Guide to Practical Shipbuilding (Chesterton), 220

Thousand and One Nights, The, 84, 197, 198, 215

Through a Glass Darkly, 35

Thucydides, 111, 129, 182, 222, 343

Tiberius, 68, 314, 332

Tibullus, 362, 365

Tiro, 255

titles, book, 338–41

Titus, 324

Tocar los libros (Marchamalo), 220

To Kill a Mockingbird, 187, 340

Tolkien, J. R. R., 15, 17

Tolstoy, Leo, 224, 341

Tomorrow in the Battle Think on Me (Marías), 340

Toole, John Kennedy, 340

Too Loud a Solitude (Hrabal), 361–62

Torah, 20, 29, 84, 275–76

tourism, beginnings of, 328

Trajan, 300, 314, 315

transactive memory, theory of, 106

translation

    art of, 229–30

    of tragedies and comedies in Rome, first, 244–45

Travels with Herodotus (Kapuściński,), 167–68

Trebulla, Caecilia, 144

trees, writing and, 258–60, 268

Trilce (Vallejo), 283

Tristia (Ovid), 331–32

Trojan War, 70, 74, 82, 159, 163, 349

Trojan Women, The (Euripides), 252, 339, 348–49, 379

Tullia, 263, 366

Turkey, 7, 9

Twain, Mark, 189–90, 194, 347, 383

12 Years a Slave, 253–54, 256–57

Twitter, 89

2001: A Space Odyssey, 175

Two Towers, The (Tolkien), 15

Tyre, 9, 163, 164, 165

Tzetzes, 42, 43

Ulysses (Joyce), 142, 157, 200, 339

Umar I, 214

Unforgiven, 32

Uninhabited Paradise (Matute), 341

United Nations Commission of Experts, 219

United States

    art in, 250–51

    book ownership in, 124–25

    cinema in, 251

    European immigrants in, 250–51

    fascination with the western, 70

    immigration forms of, 44

    Metropolitan Museum of, 48, 250

    slavery and, 239, 253–54, 256–57

Universal History of Infamy, A (Borges), 339

universities, first, 374

University of Oxford, 43–44, 45–46, 47, 319, 374

"Unpacking My Library" (Benjamin), 19

Valcárcel, Amelia, 228

Valerianus, Quintus Pollius, 278

Valle-Inclán, Ramón del, 354

Vallejo, César, 283

Vallejo, Irene, 90, 269, 335, 367
  bullying endured during childhood,
    225–28
  first library of, 134–35
  in Florence, 62–63, 64–65
  learning to read, 112–13
  mother's reading of books to, 78–80, 90,
    113, 366
  at Oxford, 43–44, 45–47
  reading first newspapers, 217
  as a teacher, 145
  visits to bookstores, 287, 290, 293
Varro, Marcus Terentius, 127, 312, 313,
  337
Vatsvayana, 268
Vázquez, Juan Gabriel, 341
vellum, 64
Veloso, Caetano, 16
Vespasian, 314, 342
Vesuvius, 49, 266, 324–25, 326, 357
Vidal, Agustín Sánchez, 309
vignette, origin of term, 337
Villa of the Papyri, 325, 326–27
violence among children and teenagers,
  225–26
Virgil, 109, 259–60, 321, 325, 343,
  357–58
Virgin Suicides, The (Eugenides), 196,
  340
vision, after spread of reading, 274
Vision from the Bottom of the Sea
    (Argullol), 232
Vitruvius, 130

War and Peace (Tolstoy), 341
Watson, Peter, 64
wax tablets, 267, 268, 274
Wegner, D. M., 105, 106
Wells, Julia, 136–37
Wenders, Wim, 39
"Werther effect, the," 196
Wharton, Edith, 341
When It Matters No More (Onetti), 341
Whitehead, A. N., 193
White Ribbon, The, 270
Wide Sargasso Sea (Rhys), 339
Wilde, Oscar, 26, 331

Wilder, Billy, 251
William of Baskerville, 172, 198,
  275
Williams, Tennessee, 341
William the Conqueror, 308
Will You Be Quiet, Please? (Carver),
  340
Winckelmann, Johann Joachim, 328
Wings of Desire, 39
Wisniewski, Edgar, 39
women
  education of, 128, 147–48, 180, 263–64,
    364–65
  European nuns, 374
  Greek, 98, 111, 121, 128, 141, 144–49,
    151–56, 264
  librarians, 136–37, 381–83
  marriage and, 13
  in *The Odyssey,* silencing of, 82–83,
    146–47
  Plato on, 155, 192, 377–78
  prostitution and, 152, 155–56, 252, 253,
    364
  reading and, 121, 144, 265, 364
  Roman, 263–64, 330–31, 362–66
  sold into slavery, 10
  songs composed by, 149
  as weavers of stories, 144–58, 366–67
  writers, 144, 146–47, 148, 151, 153,
    362–66
Woolf, Virginia, 346, 365
Worde, Wynkyn de, 360
Works and Days (Hesiod), 102–3, 339
Works and Nights (Pizarnik), 339
Works Progress Administration (WPA),
  381–82, 383
World Heritage Sites, 140
World War I, 176, 238
World War II, 7, 16, 91, 349, 383
writers
  of ancient literature, 260–62
  origin of, 103–4
  women, 144, 146–47, 148, 151, 153,
    362–66
writing, 115–17, 336
  art of, origins of, 93–94, 142
  bond between orality and, 85–86
  Egyptians and, 181

writing (*continued*)
  Greeks and, 77, 183
  memory and, 108, 109
  primitive systems of, 94–95
  Romans and, 262, 266, 267–69,
    270–71
  Sumerian system of, 49
  trees and, 258–60, 268
  in the twentieth century, 272–73
  widespread use of, slow progression to,
    93, 103

Xanthippe, 86
Xenophon, 123
Xerox, 299
Xerxes, 160

Yes, Minister, 147
Young, Thomas, 54
Yugoslavia, 217–18, 219

Zambrano, María, 373
Zamira, *see* Demetrius of Phalerum
Zayas, María de, 353
Zenobia, 205
Zeus, 83, 164–65
Zeus Serapis, temple to, 209
Zgustova, Monika, 223–24
Zimmer, Ernst, 107
Zoilus, 69
Zoroaster, 16, 20
Zoroastrianism, 109
Zweig, Stefan, 376, 378

A Note About the Author

Irene Vallejo earned her doctorate from the Universities of Zaragoza and Florence. *Papyrus* was awarded the National Essay Prize and the Critical Eye Prize for Narrative in Spain, and it will be published in over thirty countries. Vallejo is a regular columnist for *El país* and *Milenio,* and she is the author of two previous novels, four collections of essays, articles, and short fiction, and two children's books.

A Note About the Translator

Charlotte Whittle is an editor, writer, and translator whose recent translations include novels by Norah Lange, Jorge Comensal, and Elisa Victoria. She has received two PEN Translates awards and her translation of Lange's *People in the Room* was nominated for several prizes. She divides her time between England and the United States.